"This book provides a detailed, nuanced, and novel perspective on the role of emotions in intergroup conflict and conflict resolution. Drawing on Halperin's own extensive work in this area and integrating it with other relevant research, this book has the potential to quickly become a classic in the field."

—Johanna Ray Vollhardt,
Clark University, USA

"Although many books have been written about violent conflicts, relatively few focus on the important factor that is also responsible for their eruption, escalation and resolution—namely human emotions. This book is a pivotal contribution in closing this lacuna. He originally, eloquently, and comprehensively tackles the issue of emotions in conflict by providing a holistic analysis that not only elaborates on the role of specific emotions, but also and especially provides a holistic conceptual framework of emotions' functioning in the challenging context of intergroup violence."

—Daniel Bar-Tal, Tel Aviv
University, Israel

EMOTIONS IN CONFLICT

Social and political psychologists have attempted to reveal the reasons why individuals and societies that acknowledge that peace would improve their personal and collective well-being, and are aware of the required actions needed to promote it, are simply incapable of making this step forward. Some social psychologists have advocated the idea that certain societal beliefs and collective memories about the nature of the opponent, the in-group, the history, and the current state of the conflict distort the perceptions of society members and prevent them from identifying opportunities for peace. But these cognitive barriers capture only part of the picture.

Could identifying the role of discrete emotions in conflicts and conflict resolution potentially provide a wide platform for developing pinpoint conflict resolution interventions?

Using a vast array of primary sources, critical literature analysis, and firsthand personal experiences in various conflict zones (Middle East, Cyprus, Bosnia, and Northern Ireland), Eran Halperin introduces a new perspective on psychological barriers to peace. Halperin focuses on various emotional mechanisms that hamper peace processes, even when parties face real opportunities for conflict resolution. More specifically, he explores how hatred, anger, fear, angst, hope, despair, empathy, guilt, and shame, combined with various emotion regulation strategies, provide emotions-based explanations for people's attitudinal and behavioral reactions to peace-related events during the ongoing process of conflict resolution.

Written in a clear and accessible style, *Emotions in Conflict* offers a thought-provoking and pioneering insight into the role discrete intergroup emotions play in impeding, as well as facilitating, peace processes in intractable conflicts. This book is essential reading for those who study intractable conflicts and their resolutions, and those who are interested in the 'real-world' implication of recent theories and findings on emotion and emotion regulation.

Eran Halperin is currently an associate professor and the active dean of the School of Psychology at the Interdisciplinary Center, Herzliya, Israel. His research uses psychological and political theories and methods to investigate different aspects of intergroup conflicts. More specifically, he is interested in widening our understanding on the emotional roots of some of the most destructive political ramifications of intergroup relations.

Routledge Studies in Political Psychology

Edited by Howard Lavine, University of Minnesota

Advisory Board: Ted Brader, University of Michigan; Eugene Borgida, University of Minnesota; Marc Ross, Bryn Mawr College; and Linda Skitka, University of Illinois, Chicago

Routledge Studies in Political Psychology was developed to publish books representing the widest range of theoretical, methodological and epistemological approaches in political psychology. The series is intended to expand awareness of the creative application of psychological theory within the domain of politics and foster deeper appreciation of the psychological roots of political behavior.

1   **The Many Faces of Tolerance**
    Attitudes Towards Diversity in Poland
    Ewa A. Golebiowska

2   **Emotions in Conflict**
    Inhibitors and Facilitators of Peace Making
    Eran Halperin

EMOTIONS IN CONFLICT

Inhibitors and Facilitators of Peace Making

Eran Halperin

Routledge
Taylor & Francis Group

NEW YORK AND LONDON

First published 2016
by Routledge
711 Third Avenue, New York, NY 10017

and by Routledge
2 Park Square, Milton Park, Abingdon, Oxon, OX14 4RN

Routledge is an imprint of the Taylor & Francis Group, an informa business

Library of Congress Cataloging-in-Publication Data
Names: Halperin, Eran, author.
Title: Emotions in conflict : inhibitors and facilitators of peace making /
    Eran Halperin.
Description: New York, NY : Routledge, 2016. | Series: Routledge studies in
    political psychology ; 2 | Includes bibliographical references and index.
Identifiers: LCCN 2015030093 | ISBN 9780415729734 (hbk) |
    ISBN 9781138123427 (pbk) | ISBN 9781315850863 (ebk)
Subjects: LCSH: Peace-building. | Conflict management. | Emotions—
    Political aspects.
Classification: LCC JZ5538 .H35 2016 | DDC 303.6/6019—dc23
    LC record available at http://lccn.loc.gov/2015030093

ISBN: 978-0-415-72973-4 (hbk)
ISBN: 978-1-138-12342-7 (pbk)
ISBN: 978-1-315-85086-3 (ebk)

Typeset in Bembo
by Apex CoVantage, LLC

Printed and bound in the United States of America by Publishers Graphics,
LLC on sustainably sourced paper.

To Tal, my beloved wife, the source of my emotions and the resolution to my conflicts

CONTENTS

Acknowledgments   *xi*

1 Introduction   1

2 The Emotion-Based Approach to Conflict
   Resolution—Some Basic Concepts   16

3 Intergroup Hatred in Intractable Conflicts—
   The Ultimate Barrier to Peace   34

4 Intergroup Anger in Intractable Conflicts—
   Not Exactly What You Had in Mind . . .   50

5 Societies Under Threat—Collective Fear and Angst
   As Barriers and (at Times) Catalysts of Peace   67

6 Is Peace Really an Option? Hope, Despair, and
   the Peace Process   84

7 Moral Emotions in Intractable Conflicts: Group-Based
   Guilt, Conflict Resolution, and Reconciliation   101

8 Empathy As a Peace Catalyst in Intractable
   Conflict: Is It Feasible? Is It Enough?   120

9 The Catch-22 of Intractable Conflicts: The Role of
Pride and Humiliation in Conflicts and Peace Processes 139

10 Changing Feelings to Promote Peace: Emotion
Regulation as a New Path to Conflict Resolution 155

References *183*
Index *225*

ACKNOWLEDGMENTS

As someone who lived his entire life in the context of violent conflict, this book is an encapsulation of what I see as the hidden story of the people living in such contexts. Thinking back on my own life experiences and the ones of my friends and family members, they can very easily be described as a roller coaster of intense conflict-related emotions. Feelings of intense fear, repeated anger, and, at times, even guilt and shame are blended with acute experiences of sadness, sorrow, and empathy. Long-term despair about the possibility of resolving the conflict is jolted from time to time with transient waves of hope for a better future, which quickly disappears after another failed attempt to reach an agreement. I call this story a hidden story because of its (often too) limited presence on public discourse as well as on the agenda of researchers in the field. People rarely talk about their political or conflict-related emotions, and researchers (or at least empirical scholars) of conflicts do not study them in a way that does justice to their actual role within conflict dynamics. My goal in this book, and more broadly in my research in the recent decade or so, is to bring conflict-related emotions to the center of public and academic discourse of intractable conflict. Even more importantly, I aim to demonstrate how such change in perspectives can contribute to promoting conflict resolution, even when dealing with some of the most violent and destructive conflicts worldwide.

Many people, all of whom share the same goals and values mentioned above, took part in that endeavor. Although I am formally the single author of this book, it is in fact a summary of amazing teamwork, which I was fortunate to lead in the last decade or so. I see my collaborative work with my students, friends, and colleagues as the biggest privilege of our profession, and this book, which is composed of studies conducted with more than 40 collaborators, reflects this approach. These successful collaborations enabled me to perform a relatively intense research program, which occurred in various places around the world and in a relatively short period of time. But more importantly, it dramatically enriched my thinking on these important issues and provided me with the opportunity to get to know some true friends who have accompanied me for many years. Unfortunately, the scope here is too limited to thank them all, but I would like to first thank my first four students, with whom I practically created my first research lab at the Interdisciplinary Center (IDC) Herzliya: Smadar Cohen-Chen, Roni Porat, Ruthie Pliskin, and Amit Goldenberg. Most of the ideas appearing in this book grew in that small room in which we held our lab meetings in the first year. I thank each and every one of them for the opportunities I had to share time and thoughts with them, and for being beside me in the best years of my career. I would also like to express my deep gratitude and admiration to my two mentors: Daniel Bar-Tal and James Gross. I learned so many things from both of them, and the biggest challenge of my work is to bring together the two very different approaches of these two academic giants into one coherent line of thought. I hope this book will rise to their very high standards. Special thanks are extended to my two closest friends and collaborators, Maya Tamir and Tamar Saguy, who taught me most of what I know about emotions (Maya) and intergroup relations (Tamar), but mostly have taught me about real friendship and camaraderie. As I mentioned, I was fortunate to work with a relatively large group of brilliant friends and students on studies referred to in this book, and I would like to express my deep gratitude to some of them (and send apologies to the others I could not mention) here: Siwar Aslih, Daphna Canetti, Richard Crisp, Sabina Čehajić, Carol Dweck, Julia Elad-Strenger, Chris Federico, Tamar Gur, Boaz Hameiri, Yossi Hasson, Sivan Hirsch-Hoefler, John Jost, Saulo Fernández, Aharon Levy, Melissa McDonald, Liat Netzer, Michal Reifen Tagar, Lee Ross, Noa Schori-Eyal, Nevin Solak, Keren Sharvit, Gal Sheppes, Linda Skitka, Martijn Van-Zomeren, Johanna Ray Vollhardt, Michael Wohl, and Nechumi Yaffe. Finally, special thanks go to Shira Kudish for assisting me with everything that was needed to transform the first drafts created on my computer into reasonable book materials.

Above all, I want to thank my wife, Tal, and my kids, Mika, Neta, and Omer. The support I got from you enabled me to write this book, and the love and warmth filling our home provided the book with what I hope is its unique flavor. Thank you for being there for me. I promise to do anything possible to make sure you will have a peaceful future in our region.

1

INTRODUCTION

Intractable conflicts are one of the most difficult problems of contemporary human society. They involve mass violence and fundamentally harm the well-being of the involved citizens as well as hindering the potential development of the involved societies in their entirety. Even beyond the immediate costs of sacrificing human lives, in these conflicts individuals feel obligated to sacrifice their personal interests for the sake of the conflict, and societies pay a high price in terms of economy, education, and other social aspects to survive the conflict. Although it is important to remember that conflicts are sometimes necessary to bring about social change, especially when discrimination and injustice are present, most people probably would prefer to rectify these social and moral wrongdoings in peaceful rather than in violent ways. In other words, all other factors held constant, we can assume that most people would prefer living in peace and security over the destructive alternative of being actively involved in long-term, violent conflict. And indeed, research has shown that even societies that have been involved in violent conflicts for decades highly value the concept of peace (albeit in an abstract way) and at least declare that they would do "everything that is needed" to promote it (e.g., Bar-Tal, 2013).

But recent data shows that out of the 352 violent conflicts that have erupted since World War II, only 144 have concluded in peace agreements (Harbom, Hogbladh, & Wallensteen, 2006). This means that the involved societies in most conflict situations worldwide have failed to mobilize their citizens for peace to make the abovementioned transition. For an outsider, this must be seen as very strange. If most people really prefer peace over war and violence, we would expect societies in conflict to spend most of their time, resources, and energy on attempts to promote peace rather than on maintaining or improving their status vis-à-vis their adversary. But we know that this is not necessarily the situation, and therefore, any objective observer probably would search for that dramatic engine that overrides the wish for peace and maintains long-term conflicts even when the price they extract is so terrible. In a way, this is the million-dollar question put forward by conflict resolution scholars and practitioners—why can't societies that are involved in long-term conflicts find a balanced and fair solution that will dramatically improve the well-being of their citizens and enable rapid development of various socioeconomic and political objectives?

For many years conflict resolution scholars and practitioners believed that the answer to this question was rather simple. We tend to think that intractable conflicts are over real disagreements, and as such, fundamental ideologies and conflicting goals and interests are the driving forces behind these conflicts. According to that approach, intractable conflicts are so hard to resolve because the real or tangible disagreements at the root of these conflicts cannot be bridged. These disagreements are usually driven and fueled by conflicting ideologies that, at the beginning, help to define the fundamental interests of each side and then also guide the kind of (often aggressive) behavior that is meant to serve these goals and interests. Bar-Tal (2013) has defined this "ideology of conflict" as an ethos, and Ginges, Atran, Medin, and Shikaki (2007) have taken it one step forward by suggesting that, in the context of long-term conflicts, people tend to believe that certain issues or values are sacred, namely, that they cannot be compromised in any situation or for any exchange.

And to some extent this is true. Let us take the Israeli-Palestinian conflict as a prototypical example of an intractable conflict that has lasted for more than two generations. This conflict is by all means based on real disagreements over real issues, such as the questions of the territory, settlements, the future of Jerusalem, and the future of the Palestinian refugees. The conflict over these real disagreements is driven by conflicting ideologies held by two national movements—the Jewish Zionist and the Palestinian national movements. Accordingly, those who strongly adhere to the Zionist or Palestinian ethos of the conflict see the above-mentioned issues as sacred and will probably immediately reject any offer for a peace agreement that inherently includes compromise on what they perceive as sacred values.

But, surprisingly, when one looks more deeply into the current state of affairs within that conflict (and many other long-term conflicts), it is quite clear that although core disagreements and conflicting ideologies still exist, they do not constitute the main obstacles for peace. Public opinion polls from the last decade show vast support among both Israelis and Palestinians for compromises based on previous US-mediated negotiations and peace proposals (e.g., "the Clinton parameters"). For example, in recent poll we have conducted, 65 percent of Palestinians and a similar proportion of Israelis expressed support for peace based on such well-known compromises. These numbers are consistent with the ones revealed in many other polls conducted in the region in the last two decades. As in many other conflicts, such support is conditioned by the premise that an agreement based on these compromises will bring about an end to the historical conflict and a minimization of violence. In other words, at least in the case of that prolonged conflict (and many others), both parties are aware of the costs of ending the conflict, and the large majority among both populations is willing to pay the required price to achieve peace. Accordingly, even if disagreements over real issues still exist, they can no longer be attributed as the core reason for the continuation and at times even for the escalation of the conflict.

Again taking the perspective of a naïve, objective observer, the immediate question raised is why these people can't make this move or walk this dramatic extra mile, which immediately would improve their lives? If these people and their leaders are aware of the kind of concessions that can bring about peace, and if they are actually willing to make these required concessions to promote peace, why do they keep on fighting and killing each other for such long time?

According to the approach to be promoted in the current book, the answer to that crucial question is rooted in the boundary conditions that were described previously. People in many conflicts, even in the most violent and destructive ones, are willing to make ideological concessions over the real issues, but they lack the faith that such concessions would actually lead to the end of the conflict and the minimization of the violence. They do not have such faith because they do not trust their adversary, because they do not believe the adversary can change its immoral and aggressive behavior, because they are afraid that such concessions will put them in a position of high risk and threat, and also because they do not want their concessions to be perceived as an ultimate confession of responsibility for all past (immoral) events of the conflict.

These processes, which I see as the ultimate barriers to peace making and conflict resolution, are best described as emotional phenomena or emotional processes (Frijda, 1986). I see them as emotional phenomena because they encapsulate the core beliefs and appraisals of societies in conflict together with the core political motivations that are implied by these appraisals. When these appraisals and motivations are accompanied by strong affective experiences, which are typical to violent conflicts, they create extremely negative emotions that have a destructive influence on the probability to promote peace.

In more detail, according to *Appraisal Theories of Emotions* (e.g., Lazarus, 1982; Roseman, 1984; Scherer, 1984) each belief mentioned above reflects a core appraisal theme of a dominant negative emotion. For example, when people believe that the outgroup poses a fundamental threat to their existence and that a peace agreement will not enable them to defend their group vis-à-vis that threat, they actually feel fear (Bar-Tal, 2001; Jarymowicz & Bar-Tal, 2006; Halperin, Bar-Tal, Nets-Zehngut, & Drori, 2008). Hatred toward the outgroup is associated with the belief that the outgroup is evil by nature and will never change its immoral or violent behavior (Halperin, 2008; Sternberg, 2003). Anger, on the other hand, is driven by an appraisal of the outgroup's actions as unfair and unjust (Lerner & Keltner, 2001; Mackie & Smith, 2000).

But even more importantly, each of these emotions leads to a concrete motivation that constitutes a building block of the general narrative that structures the opposition to peace. To use the same examples described in the appraisals part, when people feel fear they are motivated to avoid political (and other) risks, making them averse to new ideas or initiatives for peace, which inherently include some flavor of risk. For those who are dominated by hatred, there is no real good reason to support negotiations, gestures, or compromises because they do not really believe that such political moves can bring about a meaningful change in the outgroup's destructive behavior or its intentions. Finally, anger sometimes can motivate people to respond aggressively even to seemingly constructive cues coming from the outgroup.

Having said that, we must not forget that many times, negative emotions constitute an accurate and correctly adjusted reaction to the outgroup's immoral actions, provocative statements, and aggressive tendencies. In these cases negative emotions, such as fear, anger, and in extreme cases even hatred, are functional because they prepare group members to cope with difficult, conflict-related events. For example, fear is known as a highly functional emotion that helps individuals and groups to take the necessary measures to defend themselves in the face of external threat. Societies dominated by a high sense of security, also termed *optimistic overconfidence* (Neale & Bazerman, 1991; Kahneman & Tversky, 1996), like the American society prior to the 9/11 terror attack or the Israeli society prior to the Yom Kippur war, may underestimate potential threats and be caught unprepared. So emotions can be functional sometimes . . .

On the other hand, oftentimes, emotions are not functional and are even counterproductive. As such, they have the potential of playing a central role as psychological barriers to conflict resolution. Outside the context of intractable conflicts, several decades of research point to discrete negative emotions as having a destructive influence in interpersonal conflict resolution and negotiation (for a review see Van Kleef, De Dreu, & Manstead, 2010). In the recent two decades, side by side with the study of other psychological barriers to conflict resolution (e.g., Bar-Tal & Halperin, 2011; Maoz, Ward, Katz, & Ross, 2002; Mnookin & Ross 1995; Ross & Ward, 1995), scholars have begun to investigate the impact of emotions on public opinion and public behavior in intractable conflicts. Their findings suggest that emotions play a causal role by forming attitudes, biasing attention and action, and shaping reactions to conflict-related events. Some of these studies even show that the effects of emotions on aggressive and conciliatory political attitudes are evident above and beyond other prominent factors, such as ideology and socioeconomic conditions (e.g., Halperin, Russell, Dweck, & Gross, 2011; Spanovic, Lickel, Denson, & Petrovic, 2010).

But what exactly are the destructive effects of negative emotions on conflict resolution and peace making? Research suggests that negative emotions lead to the rejection of positive information about the opponent (Cohen-Chen, Halperin, Porat, & Bar-Tal, 2014) and lead individuals to oppose renewal of negotiations, compromise, and reconciliation (e.g., Halperin, 2011b; Sabucedo, Durán, Alzate, & Rodríguez, 2011). Other studies have suggested that emotions like fear and collective angst may result in higher sensitivity to outgroup threats, more right-wing inclinations (Hirschberger & Pyszczynski, 2010), as well as strengthening ingroup ties (Wohl, Branscombe, & Reysen, 2010) and promoting risk-aversive political tendencies (Sabucedo et al., 2011). Research also has shown that negative emotions, mainly anger and hatred, increase support for extreme aggression and military actions aimed at harming or even at eliminating the opponent (Halperin, 2008, 2011b). Furthermore, although recent studies show that anger can sometimes promote conflict resolution (e.g., Halperin, 2011b; Halperin, Russell, Dweck, & Gross, 2011; Reifen Tagar, Frederico, & Halperin, 2011), in most cases anger leads to the appraisal of future military attacks as less risky and more likely to have positive consequences (Lerner & Keltner, 2001).

Even more recently, scholars have begun to examine the role positive emotions play in conflicts. Hope, for example, has been found to play a constructive role in reducing hostility, increasing problem solving in negotiations, and promoting support for conciliatory policies (Carnevale & Isen, 1986; Cohen-Chen, Crisp, & Halperin, 2015a; Cohen-Chen, Halperin, Crisp, & Gross, 2014). Furthermore, several studies conducted in the post-conflict settings of Northern Ireland (Moeschberger, Dixon, Niens, & Cairns, 2005) and Bosnia (Čehajić, Brown, & Castano, 2008) reveal a positive relationship between empathy and willingness to forgive opponents for past wrongdoings.

Why Have We Only Recently Started Studying Emotions in Conflicts?

But if emotions are such powerful engines of human behavior and of conflict behavior more specifically, why have we only recently started studying emotions in the context of intractable conflicts? Interestingly enough, although the central role played by emotions in conflict has long been recognized by many of the scholars who study ethnic conflicts and conflict resolution (e.g., Bar-Tal, Halperin, & De Rivera, 2007; Horowitz, 1985; Lindner, 2006a; Petersen, 2002; Staub, 2005; Volkan, 1997), empirical investigations into the nature, role, and implications of emotions in long-term conflicts were quite rare until the last two decades. How can this dissonance between consensual acknowledgment and scarcity of empirical research be explained?

I would argue that the answer to this question is rooted in the fundamental nature of human beings, in the nature and development of some academic disciplines, and in the problematic relationships (or lack of them) between different disciplines. Starting with the nature of human beings, it would be fair to assume that most people (lay citizens, leaders, and scholars alike) do not want to believe that emotions are driving them to hurt themselves and others. Just think of a leader who sends people to war knowing that many of them will not return to their families and loved ones. Such a leader must be totally convinced that she had no other alternative but making that difficult decision, that the decision was driven by ideological and maybe even existential considerations, and that the decision-making process was clean, normative, and unbiased. These parameters can help the leader to optimally rationalize and justify the dramatic decision of going to war. Yet the fundamental idea that emotions play some role in driving such decisions challenges all these parameters. Accordingly, people prefer to avoid the emotional aspects while focusing on the more rational or ideological considerations because it helps them preserve their positive self-image even when engaging in one of the most difficult actions—violent conflict.

That idea speaks nicely to the concept of naïve realism (Ross & Ward, 1996). This bias denotes a human tendency to believe that: (a) the individual sees events in objective reality and holds social attitudes, beliefs, preferences, and priorities that stem from a relatively dispassionate, unbiased, and essentially 'unmediated' apprehension of the information or evidence at hand; (b) other rational social perceivers will generally share her reactions, behaviors, and opinions—provided that they have had access to the same information and that they too have processed that information in a reasonably thoughtful and open-minded fashion; and (c) the failure of a given individual or group in question to share her views arises not from rationally held information and beliefs but rather from other reasons (Ross & Ward, 1996). Although in their empirical work, Lee Ross, Emily Pronin, and others focused mainly on people's tendency to believe that cognitive biases do not distort their own decision-making processes (e.g., Pronin, Lin, & Ross, 2002), I think that the same principle can be applied to emotions as well. Accordingly, if most people believe that emotional processes do not intervene in the way they think and act regarding conflicts, it makes sense to focus on other factors when trying to study conflict resolution processes.

The second reason why emotions have only recently been incorporated into the study of intergroup conflicts and their resolution is that developments in the field of conflict resolution have slowly followed the more rapid developments in psychology that have experienced a spectacular growth in the study of emotion (Lewis, Haviland-Jones, & Barrett, 2008). As parts of that so-called emotional revolution, emotional theories have been expanded, a wider set of emotions has been studied, and more accurate and validated measurements have been created (Mauss & Robinson, 2009). In addition to all other obvious advantages of that revolution, it also made the study of emotions more accessible to other disciplines, and today emotions are becoming more and more common in research disciplines like political science (e.g., Marcus, Neuman, & MacKuen, 2000), sociology (Scheff, 2003), law (Maroney & Gross, 2014), and philosophy (Griffiths, 2013). But the interdisciplinary boundaries still have remained difficult to cross, and one pivotal challenge on the way toward achieving this goal is to knit together several communities of scholars. I'll elaborate on this point further in the last chapter of the book.

Finally, another reason why conflict resolution scholars feel reluctant to study the effects of feelings and emotions on the dynamics of political conflicts is because most of them express a rather deterministic view regarding the existence and implications of intense or negative emotions in long-term conflicts. According to this view, intense or negative emotions, such as fear, anger, and contempt, are an inherent part of political conflicts. As such, studying them can promote the understanding of political conflicts, but it can do little to promote their resolution. Given that the conflict resolution field is oriented toward an applied approach aiming at promoting the resolution rather than just the understanding of conflicts, studying emotions can be seen oftentimes as a waste of time.

Some Basic Assumptions of This Book

Together with the increasing acknowledgment of the centrality of emotional processes in conflicts and their resolution, various approaches to the study of emotions generally and, more specifically, to the study of emotions in conflicts have emerged. The scope of this book is too limited to present a comprehensive overview and a critical examination of all those different approaches, so in the following paragraphs, I will briefly try to introduce the main assumptions that constitute the building blocks of the way I have been studying emotions in conflicts in recent years.

> *First Assumption: Emotions do not operate in a vacuum, and hence, studying emotional processes in intractable conflicts should be different than studying emotions in other domains in life.*

Kurt Lewin (1951) has suggested that human behavior is a function of an environment in which a person operates and that any behavioral analysis must begin with the description of the situation as a whole. This is due to the fact that people's conception of the context to a large extent determines their behavioral options and eventually their chosen routes of action. In line with this classic notion, I argue that emotions in general, and collective emotions more specifically, do not operate in a vacuum. As such, their generation, nature, and implications are influenced by the specific context in which they appear. This notion is in line with Barrett's and Mesquita's work suggesting that a more satisfactory definition of emotion should incorporate the basic fact that emotions are contextually constituted (Barrett,

2006; Barrett, Mesquita, Ochsner, & Gross, 2007; Mesquita, 2003; Mesquita et al., 2006; Mesquita & Leu, 2007). Rather than defining emotions as features of the mind or—in Klaus Scherer's terms—"synchronized changes in the states of . . . organismic subsystems" (p. 697), these authors suggest that emotions should be placed at the interface between mind and context.

The collective context's significance lies in the fact that it dictates society members' needs and goals as well as the challenges they encounter to satisfy them. Therefore, as Halperin and Pliskin (2015) have argued recently, when analyzing the role of collective emotions in intractable conflicts, special attention should be given to the conflict's unique context and, more specifically, to its psychological implications. The psychological context should be considered in all stages of the emotion generation process and also when studying emotion regulation processes (Halperin & Pliskin, 2015).

The psychological context of intractable conflicts usually is defined by the following characteristics (Bar-Tal, 2007): (a) the conflicts are perceived as being about essential and even existential goals, needs, and/or values; (b) they are perceived as irresolvable; (c) they include an enduring and destructive element of mutual violence; (d) they are perceived as being of a zero sum nature; (e) they occupy a central place in the lives of individual society members and of society as a whole; (f) they demand extensive material (i.e., military, technological, and economic), educational, and psychological investment; and (g) they persist for a long period of time, that is, for at least one generation.

The collective setting of intractable conflict should be seen as one lasting for decades as durability is one of its most important characteristics. Throughout these years, members of societies live under high levels of perceived threat and uncertainty, and many of them even face violence, suffering, and victimization in the most direct and personal ways. Thus, the nature of the *lasting context of conflict* has relevance to the well-being of society members—it engages them personally as well as occupying a central position in public discourse. It supplies information and experiences that compel society members to construct an adaptable worldview.

Consequently, individuals living in such an environment often are characterized by more competitive worldviews, less cognitive flexibility, more 'black-and-white' thinking, and higher sensitivity to various threat cues. These characteristics have wide influence on the kinds of emotions experienced by people, on the magnitude of these emotions, as well as on regulatory processes they utilize to alter or manage these emotional experiences. For example, extreme negative emotions, like hatred, extreme anger, and fear, are more commonly experienced and also seen as more acceptable or legitimate in societies involved in long-term conflicts. Such emotions are perceived as more justified given the horrible events of the conflict, and therefore people feel freer to express them and invest less effort to downregulate them. Oftentimes, the expression of these extreme negative emotions helps society members to cope with the psychological challenges of the conflict, whereas in other times they help leaders to mobilize public support for war and other aggressive policies (Staub, 2005).

But how exactly does the physical, violent context of intractable conflict affect the type and magnitude of the emotional experience? I believe that it does so through the mediation of the psychological context that is so unique to these types of conflicts (see Bar-Tal & Halperin, 2013). According to that view, to fulfill the dramatic social needs of intractable conflicts, the involved societies develop a functional psychological infrastructure composed of biased, one-sided, and over-simplified collective memories of the conflict, accompanied by a tailored ethos of conflict (Bar-Tal, 2013) and long-term emotional sentiments targeted at the outgroup (Halperin & Gross, 2011). This mechanism fulfills basic psychological needs of forming a meaningful worldview that provides a coherent and orga-nized picture in times of stress, threat, and deprivation (e.g., Greenberg, Solomon, Pyszczynski, 1997; Janoff-Bulman, 1992).

Emotional experiences and their behavioral and political consequences should be understood and analyzed as by-products of that unique context. In other words, when a new conflict-related, meaningful event occurs, it will be appraised and emotionally responded to when all prior cognitive and emotional dispositions of the society's members are taken into account. Accordingly, a mildly threatening cue can be interpreted and experienced as a major threat when one takes into account the ingroup's past collective victimization, current long-term fears, and the satanic view of the outgroup. A seemingly promising message conveyed by an outgroup leader will be responded to by heightened despair if one takes into account repeated memories of past failed attempts and lack of belief in the mal-leability of the outgroup (Halperin et al., 2011). Therefore, the physical as well as the psychological context of intractable conflicts must be taken into account if one wishes to seriously study emotions in conflicts.

Second Assumption: Emotions are powerful engines of human behavior, and they are even more powerful in social contexts and may be most powerful in a conflictual social context.

Most people agree that emotions exert a vast influence on people's attitudes, moti-vations, and behaviors in almost every domain of life. Some would even argue that emotions are the most powerful engines of human behavior (e.g., Arnold, 1960; Frijda, 1984). Yet in some domains, emotions operate merely peripherally and at times even as negligible psychological forces. In other domains, however, and under specific circumstances, emotions play a pivotal role in producing the screen-play of events and orchestrating the behavior of all involved individuals and groups.

The second assumption of the current book is that this is the case in intrac-table conflicts. Anyone who has ever experienced, either directly or indirectly, a conflict such as those ongoing in the Middle East, Kashmir, Sri Lanka, Chechnya, or Rwanda knows that these conflicts are fueled by high-magnitude, negative emotions like fear, hatred, despair, and contempt. This has led Donald Horowitz (1985), one of the most prominent researchers of violent conflicts, to claim that "[t]he sheer passion expended in pursuing ethnic conflict calls out for an explanation that does justice to the realm of feelings. . . . A bloody phenomenon cannot be explained by a bloodless theory" (p. 140).

But what makes intractable conflicts such fertile ground for the development and dominancy of emotions? I believe that the answer to this question is rooted in two complementary processes that characterize long-term, intractable conflicts. First, the social nature of these conflicts, and even more importantly the extremely high identification people in these contexts feel to their groups, makes the development of group-based emotions highly probable (Mackie, Devos, & Smith, 2000; Yzerbyt, Dumont, Wigboldus, & Gordin, 2003). According to *intergroup emotions theory* (Smith, 1993), the more people identify with a certain group, the more they tend to experience emotions in the name of the group or its members. As such, it is enough for a single group member to be mistreated by an outgroup member for the entire group to simultaneously experience group-based anger. Furthermore, when such anger is experienced simultaneously, its magnitude amplifies, and the individuals' ability to downregulate it diminishes (Porat, Halperin, Mannheim, & Tamir, in press; Rimé, 2009; von Scheve & Ismer, 2013). Accordingly, extreme negative emotions can be felt when personally interacting with individuals involved in these violent conflicts, but they are also very dominant in the general atmosphere of these societies and hence can be found in public discourse, mass media, cultural products (e.g., arts and literature), national ceremonies, and so on (e.g., Bar-Tal, Halperin, & De Rivera, 2007).

But intractable conflict is not just an ordinary intergroup setting with very high identification of the involved societies. It is also an enduring context, characterized by high levels of perceived threat and uncertainty, in which many of the involved human beings also face violence, suffering, and victimization in the most direct and personal ways (e.g., Canetti, Hall, Rapaport, & Wayne, 2013; Hobfoll, Canetti-Nisim, & Johnson, 2006). That personal involvement has immediate psychological ramifications. For example, in one recent study (Chipman, Palmieri, Canetti, Johnson, & Hobfoll, 2011) almost 30 percent of a sample of 1,001 Israeli citizens reported some form of impairment caused by posttraumatic stress, and 18 percent of these respondents met the full criteria for diagnosis with posttraumatic stress disorder (PTSD). A second study (Canetti et al., 2010) discovered that the prevalence of PTSD and depression for Palestinian men living in the West Bank, Gaza, and East Jerusalem was also extremely high, 25.4 percent PTSD/29.9 percent depression, 22.6 percent/27.6 percent, and 16.1 percent/16.1 percent, respectively. For women, the prevalence of PTSD and depression was 23.8 percent/29.0 percent, 23.9 percent/28.9 percent, and

19.7 percent/27.6 percent in each of the respective areas. Altogether, that unique physical and psychological context, saturated by violence and psychological distress, prompts the emotional aspect of human psychology to play a more central role than in other domains in life.

Third Assumption: We can study decision makers' and leaders' emotions and decision-making processes, but it is equally as important to study bottom-up processes, namely, the way the emotions of the masses shape and operate to form leaders' decision-making processes.

There are different ways to think about conflicts and conflict resolution, and therefore there are also different ways to study emotions in conflicts and conflict resolution processes. Those who believe that intractable conflicts are first and foremost top-down processes focus their research in the way leaders and other policy makers make key decisions about war and peace (e.g., Jervis, 1976; Levy, 1988; Mintz, 2004). In recent years, researchers have started to investigate empirically the role emotions play in what previously was seen as a rational and well-structured decision-making process—leadership decision making (e.g., Renshon & Lerner, 2012).

This literature on emotions and foreign policy decision making has been inspired heavily by a broader line of research on the role of emotions in interpersonal negotiation and conflict resolution (for a review, see Van Kleef, De Dreu, & Manstead, 2010). The dominant research paradigm of most researchers in that field has been characterized by a focus on the decision maker's own positive or negative mood as a predictor of her negotiation decisions and behaviors (e.g., Baron, Fortin, Frei, Hauver, & Shack, 1990; Carnevale & Isen, 1986). More advanced views offer a complementary focus on interpersonal effects (i.e., the effects of one individual's emotions on the other's behavior), like, for example, the *emotions as social information* (EASI) model (Sinaceur & Tiedens, 2006; Van Kleef & De Dreu, 2010; Van Kleef, De Dreu, & Manstead, 2004b).

In the current book, I take an approach that is different from the ones described in at least two main aspects. Most importantly, in line with the writing and research of some of the most important scholars who study psychological aspects of intractable conflicts (e.g., Bar-Tal, 2013; Kriesberg, 1993; Staub, 2011), I see intractable conflicts mostly as bottom-up rather than top-down processes. As such, emotions influence the continuation of these conflicts and their (lack of) resolution either by creating an extremely negative emotional climate (e.g., De Rivera & Páez, 2007) and collective emotional orientation (Bar-Tal et al., 2007) or by shaping people's concrete attitudes and behaviors in response to conflict related events (e.g., Halperin, Russell, Dweck, & Gross, 2011; Maoz & McCauley, 2005; Spanovic, Lickel, Denson, & Petrovic, 2010). According to the bottom-up approach, both the social emotional climate and the aggregated positions of individuals living in these conflict zones then shape leaders' decision-making processes and consequently change the course of the conflict.

Interestingly enough, in both these cases emotions shape people's political attitudes and behaviors, although these people do not directly communicate with adversary group members. When emotions influence leaders' decision making inside the negotiation room, it is a dynamic, interactive process in which ones actions or emotional expressions lead to another's emotional reactions, which in turn, bring about another emotional chain reaction. On the other hand, the current approach, which focuses on citizens' emotional reactions to conflict-related events or messages, sees emotions as an internal rather than an interactive process. In this process, people are exposed to a meaningful conflict-related event or information mainly through the mediation of the mass media or their leaders. When this information is absorbed and appraised, it stimulates a certain emotion that in turn elicits a certain position regarding the desired policy in response to the stimulating information. Although when shared with other society members, these emotions can be amplified; this entire process is inherently internal and does not require interactive communication or face-to-face encounters with outgroup members.

> *Fourth Assumption: Each discrete intergroup emotion has a unique nature, appraisals, emotional goals, and action tendencies, and as such, each discrete intergroup emotion leads to concrete political implications regarding conflict and conflict resolution dynamics.*

For many years the dominant approach to studying emotions in general, and emotions in conflicts more specifically, focused on separating emotions by valence, trying to identify the different roles played by positive and negative emotions in explaining human behavior. This approach is still dominant in the conflict resolution field in which most intervention programs still see one of their main goals as reducing negative intergroup emotions like fear and anger and encouraging positive emotional experiences like hope and empathy. The dominant theory on emotions in politics in the political science and political psychology fields, the *Affective Intelligence Theory* (Marcus & MacKuen, 1993), focuses on two main emotional systems (recently expanded to three) but still does not value the need for studying the nature and the political implications of each and every emotion separately.

Contrary to the abovementioned approach, I argue that this emphasis on positive versus negative valence or on diffuse mood states blurs our understanding of the multifaceted role of emotion in shaping people's attitudes and behaviors in conflict situations. According to the discrete emotions approach, each discrete emotion has its own antecedents, appraisal components, relational themes, and action tendencies (Frijda, Kuipers, & ter Schure, 1989; Lazarus, 1991; Manstead & Tetlock, 1989; Roseman, Wiest, & Swartz, 1994; Smith, Haynes, Lazarus, & Pope, 1993). Emotions therefore provide more differentiated information and carry more clear-cut behavioral implications than moods (Weiner, 1986). As James Averill (1984) has maintained, each emotional experience represents a unique story that guides and then justifies people's reactions to specific events.

Numerous studies conducted in recent years in various contexts of political, intergroup conflicts suggest that the discrete emotions approach should be used as the basic framework for studying emotions in conflicts as well (e.g., Halperin, 2011b; Halperin, Russell, Dweck, & Gross, 2011; Huddy, Feldman, & Cassese, 2007; Lerner & Keltner, 2001; Maoz & McCauley, 2008; Sabucedo et al., 2011; Skitka, Bauman, Aramovich, & Morgan, 2006; Small, Lerner, & Fischhoff, 2006; Spanovic, Lickel, Denson, & Petrovic, 2010). These studies demonstrate how emotions of the same valence (e.g., fear and anger, guilt and shame, and hope and empathy) can have totally different and at times even contradictory implications on people's attitudes and behaviors in conflict. For example, scholars who have studied Americans' reactions to the 9\11 terror attacks point toward intergroup anger as one of the major engines leading people to support militant actions in response to the outgroups' aggressive actions while identifying fear as increasing risk estimates, pessimistic predictions, and support for defensive rather than offensive measures (Cheung-Blunden & Blunden, 2008; Huddy et al., 2007; Lerner & Keltner, 2001; Lerner, Gonzalez, Small, & Fischhoff, 2003; Skitka, Bauman, Aramovich, & Morgan, 2006).

These studies highlight the importance of distinguishing among emotions from the same valence because their political implications may differ substantially. Such distinction is even more important because recent studies show that seemingly negative emotions can be positive or constructive in terms of conflict resolution and vice versa (e.g., Gayer, Landman, Halperin, & Bar-Tal, 2009; Halperin, Russell, Dweck, et al., 2011; Reifen Tagar, Federico, & Halperin, 2011; Spanovic et al., 2010). For example, Halperin, Russell, Dweck, et al. (2011) have demonstrated that anger can lead to higher support for compromises in the absence of hatred within the context of an upcoming opportunity for peace. This is mainly due to the fact that anger can induce risk-seeking behavior, optimistic forecasting, and a belief in one's own capability or that of the ingroup to correct the negative situation (Halperin, 2011b; Halperin, Russell, Dweck, et al., 2011; Reifen Tagar et al., 2011). Additionally, similar patterns were found regarding fear and collective angst. Spanovic et al. (2010) have shown that fear of the outgroup was related to increased motivation for aggression within an ongoing conflict but was related negatively to aggression in a conflict that had already been resolved. Halperin, Porat, and Wohl (2013) have pointed to the positive effect of collective angst as leading to more willingness to compromise in intractable conflict. Altogether, these findings highlight the need to go beyond the valence-based approach and to study the unique role played by discrete emotions in intractable conflicts.

Fifth Assumption: Emotions can be changed and, in this way, they can also change political processes.

As mentioned, even when conflict resolution scholars started taking emotions more seriously in their studies, their dominant assumption regarding emotions was rather deterministic. As such, studying them can promote the understanding of political conflicts, but it can do little to promote their resolution. In this book (see Chapter 10), and in our research in recent years (e.g., Cohen-Chen, Halperin, Crisp, et al., 2014; Halperin, Pliskin, Saguy, Liberman, & Gross, 2014; Halperin & Pliskin, 2015; Halperin, Porat, Tamir, & Gross, 2013), we introduce a different approach, suggesting that strategies of emotion regulation, previously used in basic psychology, and mainly in intra- and interpersonal domains, can be used in the context of intergroup conflicts and potentially can constitute a tool to promote resolution of conflicts (Goldenberg, Halperin, Van-Zomeren, & Gross, in press).

This new approach is predicated on the idea that even powerful emotions can be modified. This insight is at the heart of a relatively new field of research in affective science that is concerned with emotion regulation, defined as the processes that influence which emotions we have, when we have them, and how we experience and express these emotions (Gross, 1998, 2014). Because emotions are multi-componential processes that unfold over time, emotion regulation involves changes in the latency, rise time, magnitude, duration, and offset of responses in behavioral, experiential, or physiological domains (Gross & Thompson, 2007). Emotion regulation may increase or decrease the intensity and/or duration of either negative or positive emotions.

Most of the research on emotion regulation to date has focused on individuals or dyads. However, I argue that many of the insights from such research are applicable to the context of intergroup conflicts. Given that effective strategies of emotion regulation (e.g., reappraisal) allow people to appreciate the broader meaning of events (Ray, Wilhelm, & Gross, 2008), leading to a more balanced perspective (Gross, 2002), these techniques have the potential to increase support for conciliatory attitudes by decreasing the negative intergroup emotions associated with conflict-related events and broadening the constricted perspective through which people view the conflict.

All five assumptions are integrated in Chapter 2 of the book, which offers a basic framework to the study of emotional processes in intractable conflicts. The general theoretical framework presented in the second chapter is followed by seven chapters in which the role of discrete intergroup emotions (e.g., hatred, anger, fear, hope, empathy, and pride) or groups of intergroup emotions (e.g., moral emotions) during peace processes are discussed. In each of these chapters, the fundamental nature of the emotional phenomenon is briefly reviewed, followed by an elaborated description of the emotion's nature and implications in the intergroup context and more specifically in the context of intractable conflicts. Following this, an extended chapter (Chapter 10) is devoted to various regulation strategies for these emotions, which can potentially contribute to conflict resolution processes. In that sense, the book in its entirety offers a new way of thinking and to some extent also studying emotional processes in intractable conflicts. It identifies the unique role of each intergroup emotion in inhibiting or facilitating public support for peace but also offers ways to change or regulate emotions to promote peace.

2

THE EMOTION-BASED APPROACH TO CONFLICT RESOLUTION— SOME BASIC CONCEPTS

We all understand intuitively that emotions play a central role in guiding human behavior. But do we really know what emotions are? And even if we think we know how to define the concept or idea of emotions, are we sure that all people around us understand it in the same or even in a similar way? Some people argue that emotions are like pornography in the sense that one knows that it is a certain emotion when she experiences it. Or in the words of some of the most classical scholars in the field, emotions are what people say they are (e.g., Averill, 1980; Frijda, Markam, Sato, & Wiers, 1995). In other words, according to this approach, there is no need to define emotions in general, or discrete emotions more specifically, because people just automatically identify them when they experience them.

It gets even more complicated when we deal with emotions that are experienced in the social spectrum rather than within the inner self. Can people really experience emotions in the name of their group, or even more interestingly, can groups act as unified entities and experience certain emotions simultaneously? And finally, how do these individual or collective emotions influence people's attitudes and behaviors in political conflicts? To put the matter differently, even if we do have some intuitive ideas about the centrality of emotions in conflict processes, do we really understand the mechanism that bridges between the emotional experience on the one hand and the political outcome on the other?

The goal of the second chapter will be to provide the theoretical platform for the chapters to come, namely, to address the abovementioned questions, define the main concepts, and introduce the general emotion-based conceptual framework to intergroup conflicts. As such, it will begin with an in-depth discussion of the nature of emotions, their characteristics and expressions, and a distinction between emotions and other affective phenomena like mood, sentiments, and general affect. Then, I'll turn the spotlight on various social aspects of emotions, like group-based emotions, collective emotions, and collective emotional climate, with special attention to the relationships between the collective experiences of emotions and the individual ones. Finally, a comprehensive framework for the role played by emotions in determining people's political attitudes and behaviors in conflict situations will be presented, followed by examples of the way this framework applies to different conflict-related events.

The Nature of Emotions

As early as 1897, Wilhelm Wundt wrote that people are "never in a state entirely free from feeling" (1897/1998, p. 92), such that all mental states, including thoughts and perceptions, are infused with affect (for similar ideas, see Spencer, 1895; Sully, 1892). The implication is that affective and emotional experiences are some of the most pivotal and common psychological experiences. At the same time, when we ask laypeople what emotions are, they mostly provide examples (e.g., "emotions are anger or fear") rather than giving a more nuanced description of their psychological experiences. The situation is not dramatically different among students of emotions. Despite spectacular growth in the field of emotion, a consensual definition of the concept is still elusive (Lewis, Haviland-Jones, & Barrett, 2008). The number of scientific definitions proposed has grown to the point where counting seems quite hopeless (Kleinginna and Kleinginna already reviewed more than 100 in 1981). Part of the difficulty here is that there are fundamental disagreements regarding the theoretical boundaries of the field. Because the term *emotion* is drawn from common usage, there remains disagreement about the phenomena that require explanation (e.g., emotional words, emotional experience, emotional expressions, or emotional behavior; see Frijda, 2004; Niedenthal, Krauth-Gruber, & Ric, 2006).

Yet, quite surprisingly, although laypeople and scholars alike find it hard to define the abstract concept of emotions, they have rather accurate lay theories regarding the nature of specific or discrete emotional experiences (e.g., Fitness & Fletcher, 1993). In a nice exercise I have been doing with my students in our first meeting at the beginning of the semester every year, I ask them to think of an event in which they felt anger (or any other common emotion). Now, I ask them, "Please tell me about the event that elicited your experience of anger, but more importantly, try to explain **how exactly you knew that what you felt was anger**". In all instances, in the past 10 years or so, the result of that brief simulation is astonishingly identical. Students tell very similar anger stories, but more importantly, they accurately identify the story behind anger in terms of its cognitive appraisals (e.g., unfair behavior or high control), certain physiological experiences, high motivation to correct the wrongdoing, and an action tendency to confront, hit, or maybe just scream at the other person or group. Also interestingly, the students are always surprised by the wide overlap between what they mistakably perceive as their unique story of anger and the stories told by other students in the class. Given their intuitive belief that emotions are subjective, rather fluid, inner states, the similarities with the other students' anger stories catch them by surprise.

But what do we learn from that? As I see it, we learn that there is a prototypical anger (or any other emotion) story composed of certain appraisals, certain affective or physiological experiences, and a convergent emotional goal and action tendency. This fits nicely with Averil's (1984) notion of emotions as stories that guide and then justify people's reactions to specific events. The main role of that emotional story, according to the seminal writing of William James (1884), is to direct and prepare people to respond adaptively to the emotion-eliciting stimulus. As such, emotions are defined as functional states (Cosmides & Tooby, 2000; Frijda, 1986; Mesquita & Albert, 2007; Oatley, 1992) or as flexible response sequences (Frijda, 1986; Scherer, 1984) that are called forth whenever an individual evaluates a situation as offering important challenges or opportunities (Tooby & Cosmides, 1990). In other words, emotions transform a substantive event into a motivation to respond to it in a particular manner (Zajonc, 1998). But how exactly do emotions serve such an important function?

In my view, they do that by encapsulating various psychological, perceptual, sensory, physiological, and motivational dynamics and directing them toward the important mission of developing a proper response to a status quo-breaking event. In most cases, when the emotion eliciting event is absorbed and appraised by the sensory and perceptual systems, it is compared to the well-established emotional stories or schemes and rather quickly produces adjusted emotional goals and action tendencies. A very similar process is well captured in the *Component Process Model*, which defines an emotion as an episode of interrelated, synchronized changes in the states of all or most of the five organismic subsystems in response to the evaluation of an external or internal stimulus event as relevant to major concerns of the organism (Scherer, 1987, 2001). Accordingly, emotions consist of five key components: recognition of the existence of the stimulus (change), an appraisal of its potential effect, subjective feelings we have in regard to the stimulus, motor expression component (facial and vocal expression), and motivational component that includes emotional goals and action tendencies in response to the meaningful event. These components help to distinguish emotions from other phenomena, such as attitudes or beliefs (Cacioppo & Gardner, 1999).

However, given that the approach of this book highlights the role of emotions in the public, rather than in the private sphere, I focus mainly on two of the above-mentioned components—cognitive appraisals and response tendencies—which I see as central to the understanding of the role of emotions in intergroup conflicts. By that, I do not mean to claim in any way that other aspects of the emotional experience, such as facial expressions, neural processes, or emotional communication, are less important than the appraisal and the motivational aspects.

Instead, I would like to suggest that these last two components are the ones that are probably most relevant to our understanding, and then, perhaps also to our ability to change people's political, attitudinal, and behavioral reactions to meaningful conflict-related events.

The most basic assumption of most *Appraisal Theories of Emotions* (see Roseman, 1984; Lazarus, 1991; Scherer, 2004; Smith & Ellsworth 1985) is that people do not respond emotionally to specific events but rather to the way they subjectively appraise these events. This rather simple idea contradicts the dominant age-old conviction that viewed cognition and emotions as two separate and sometimes even conflictual psychological mechanisms. Although we still cannot firmly argue whether appraisals precede the affective response or, alternatively, appear as a retrospective explanation of it (see Zajonc, 1980), after more than three decades of research along the lines of the appraisal theories of emotions, it is now well established that in most situations, emotions include a comprehensive evaluation of the emotion-eliciting stimulus, which may be conscious or unconscious (for a comprehensive review of the state of the art in appraisal theories of emotions, see the 2013 special issue of *Emotion Review*). Despite differences in terminology, it is possible to identify several appraisal dimensions that are common in the writings of most scholars. These include pleasantness, anticipated effort, attentional activity, certainty, perceived obstacles, responsibility attribution (to the self, other, or situation), and relative strength (controllability).

Accordingly, when one experiences an event that is appraised as unpleasant, uncertain, and one in which levels of control or efficacy are low, the experience of fear is most likely to be felt as the dominant emotional experience. On the other hand, if the same unpleasant event is attributed to another person or group, if it is appraised as unjust and if it is perceived as controllable, anger reactions are most likely to appear. Finally, if the same unjust and unpleasant action is attributed to the self (or the ingroup) and the result yields negative implications to another person or outgroup, guilt feelings are expected to take the emotional lead. Importantly, these evaluations or appraisals are driven not only by the event itself but also by each individual's interests, norms, ideologies, prior experiences, prior knowledge, and even personality characteristics.

As stated, while cognitive appraisals play a pivotal role in emotional processes in all domains in life, they play an even more important role when it comes to emotions experienced in the public sphere. This mainly results from the way emotions develop within the public sphere and, more specifically, because of the role played by political leaders and the mass media in framing conflict-related events in certain ways (Gross 2004; Halperin, 2011b). In most of these cases, citizens are not directly exposed to conflict-related events, and hence part of the appraisal process takes place in the public sphere and outside people's 'black box', namely, in the way their leaders or media channels construe the events for them. This does not suggest in any way that different people cannot differently appraise the same event to which they were exposed in an identical way (see the classic examples of the 9/11 events: Lerner, Gonzalez, Small, & Fischhoff, 2003; Skitka, Bauman, Aramovich, & Morgan, 2006), but we can assume that the more variance in the way events are appraised is minimized, the more the message conveyed by leaders and the media is consensual.

But the appraisal aspect of emotions is highly important for our purposes, not only because it enables us to better understand emotion generation processes in the public sphere but also because it opens the gate for a new avenue of emotional change in political conflicts (see Gross, Halperin, & Porat, 2013; Halperin, Cohen-Chen, & Goldberg, 2014). In recent years, more and more studies show that it is possible to moderate negative emotional responses to conflict-related events by helping people change the way they think of these events. I'll elaborate about these processes in the chapters dealing with emotion regulation processes (mainly Chapter 10), but in a nutshell, this can be done either by providing people with effective strategies to reappraise negative events (e.g., Halperin et al., 2013; Halperin, Pliskin, et al., 2014) or by conveying (through the media or education processes) focused messages aimed at altering specific cognitive appraisals, thus leading to emotional change (e.g., Čehajić, Effron, Halperin, Liberman, & Ross, 2011; Cohen-Chen, Halperin, Crisp, et al., 2014; Halperin, Crisp, et al., 2012).

While the appraisal component provides the interpretive aspect of the emotional experience, the motivational component of the emotional process is the one that actually determines the reaction to the meaningful stimulus. For some scholars of emotions, the motivational part of the affective process is actually the most purified expression of the emotion itself. For example, we know that we feel anger because we want to hit the wrongdoer, and we know that we experience fear when our body tells us that it is ready to run away (flight) or hit back (fight). Along the same lines, to say that we are 'in love' actually means that we want to spend as much time as possible with the target of that love, and to say that we hate someone implies that we would like that person or group to be excluded from our social environment and to suffer as much as possible (Sterenberg, 2003).

In more scientific terms, Arnold (1960) has suggested that each emotion is related to a specific action tendency. In the mid-1980s, Frijda (1986) identified specific types of action readiness that characterize 17 discrete emotions. Contemporaneously, Roseman (1984, 1994) has distinguished between actions, action tendencies, and emotional goals. While general motives or goals are inherent components of each emotion, and thus can be predicted by specific emotions, the transformation of these general motives into context-specific response tendencies and actual behavior depends on numerous external factors and is therefore quite flexible (Frijda, Kuipers & ter Schure, 1989; Roseman, 2002). The classic example of this pluripotentiality can be seen with fear, which is related to the general motive of creating a safer environment, but can take the form of either fight or flight response tendencies, depending on the situation.

Importantly, both the emotional goal and its respective action tendencies are direct by-products of the appraisal component described. When a person feels guilty for her own action, which she appraises as wrong, immoral, and controllable (which means that she could have behaved differently), it only makes sense to assume that the main emotional goal will be to act to correct the wrongdoing for which she feels responsible. Or in another situation in which a person appraises another person's behavior as threatening and does not feel that she has the defensive resources to withhold that threat, the emotional goal of threat reduction appears to be the only reasonable or relevant motivation. In the latter case, the transformation of the general emotional goal (i.e., threat reduction) into concrete action tendencies also depends on specific appraisals. If the flight option is appraised as feasible and potentially effective, it will be selected in most cases, but if it is not, most people will be ready to fight.

According to the framework to be presented in the second part of the current chapter, the emotional goals and action tendencies also determine the political implications of discrete emotions in the public sphere. In other words, the motivational aspect of the emotion highly contributes to the formation of political attitudes and political behaviors in response to specific social or political events. That political response (either attitudinal or behavioral) is a direct translation of a general emotional motivation into a concrete political context or dilemma.

For example, to again use the classic case study of the 9/11 terror attacks on the US, individuals who were dominated by anger tended to appraise future military attacks as less risky (Lerner & Keltner, 2001) and to forecast more positive consequences of such attacks (Huddy et al., 2007). Accordingly, quite naturally, they also tended to support an American military response in Iraq and elsewhere (Cheung-Blunden & Blunden, 2008; Huddy et al., 2007; Lerner et al., 2003; Skitka et al., 2006). On the other hand, those who were dominated by fear opposed such a possible attack exactly because of their opposite appraisals of the events. But more importantly, those who were dominated by fear opposed possible attack because they were driven mainly by the goal of reducing future threat (rather than teaching the terrorists a lesson), and they probably did not feel that this was the best avenue to take to serve that goal. On the other hand, the main emotional goal of citizens who were dominated by anger was to correct the wrongdoing and to teach the terrorists a lesson, and to that end, a determined attack seemed like the ultimate tactic.

Emotions, Mood, and Sentiments—Further Clarifications

Although emotions constitute the main focus of the book, they represent just one of several types of affective responses (Gross, 2007). Generally, affective experiences have been treated for years as involving at least two main properties (see

Wundt, 1912/1924): valence (ranging from feeling pleasant to unpleasant) and arousal (ranging from feeling quiet to active). Different scholars slightly differ in the way they see these affective properties, offering different views regarding the number of dimensions and their exact labeling (e.g., Barrett & Russell 1999; Fontaine, Scherer, Roesch, & Ellsworth, 2007; Lang, 1995; Larsen & Diener, 1992).

Yet, as could have already been understood, I see emotions, and particularly emotions in the public sphere, as multi-componential and more complex phenomena that cannot be reduced to a valence/arousal perspective. According to a discrete emotions perspective, two emotional phenomena can have the same valence and even induce an identical level of arousal, but they will be experienced in totally different ways because they encapsulate different stories. More importantly, for the purposes of the current book, these two seemingly identical affective responses could potentially lead to totally different and sometimes even contradictory motivational and, then, political implications. The abovementioned example of anger and fear experienced in response to a major terror attack nicely demonstrates this process.

This distinction between discrete emotions and other approaches to affective processes further highlights the importance of conceptually distinguishing among different types of affective phenomena. For our purposes in this book, it is mostly important to distinguish among emotions, moods, and emotional sentiments. Emotions are different from moods in that they are *intentional*, that is, directed toward a specific stimulus—be it a person, object, or event (Frijda, 1994). In other words, emotions are *about* something, whereas moods are not (or not necessarily). A person in a cheerful mood is not necessarily happy about anything in particular; she is just in a good mood for no apparent reason. Furthermore, emotions are characterized by distinct, subjective experiences, physiological reactions, expressions, and action tendencies (Ekman, 1993; Levenson, Ekman, & Friesen, 1990; Parkinson, Fischer, & Manstead, 2005; Roseman, Wiest, & Swartz, 1994). For these reasons, discrete emotions are inherently more complex but also more informative than diffuse moods. The fact that emotions are targeted at a specific object also makes them more dominant than moods in terms of the motivation they produce. Emotion-based motivation is more focused but also more powerful than motivation initiated by general moods.

But even more important when considering the role of emotions in long-term conflicts is the distinction between emotional reactions and emotional sentiments, both major players in the game of attitudes and behavior formation among people in conflicts. Emotion theorists have long suggested that one important antecedent to an emotional response is the individual's enduring affective traits or sentiments (Frijda, 1986). Importantly, these long-term predispositions to respond with particular emotions are thought to be emotion specific and not the result of a general predisposition to respond with negative affective responses. Thus, Rosenberg (1998) has suggested that

> there is specificity in the threshold-setting function of affective traits, which implies that a particular trait would predispose someone to emotions that are congruent with that trait and not to trait-incongruent emotions. . . . Hostile people are not necessarily primed for negative emotions generally, rather there is some specificity with respect to the threshold for anger.
>
> *(p. 248)*

But while affective traits represent a general tendency to respond with certain affective properties to events of almost any kind, emotional sentiments are more similar to emotions in the sense that they are tied or connected to a specific person, object, event, or group. Hence, while *emotions* are short-term, multi-componential responses to specific events, *emotional sentiments* represent enduring configurations of these very same emotions (Arnold, 1960; Ekman, 1992; Frijda, 1986, 1994). In this view, an emotional sentiment is a temporally stable, general emotional disposition toward a person, group, or symbol that is unrelated to any specific action or statement by this object (Halperin, 2011b; Halperin, Sharvit, et al., 2011).

According to Ben-Zeev (1992), apart from the sensory component, the sentimental chronic emotion has the same structure, as does the immediate one. As such, long-term sentiments can take the form of any discrete emotion. We can think of people experiencing long-term feelings of fear of a specific group or event, of people feeling long-term despair regarding the feasibility of change of a specific negative situation (e.g., conflict or poverty), or people experiencing long-term guilt for their unfair behavior that has not been forgiven for many years. Yet it would be reasonable to assume that certain emotions such as hatred or love, targeted at general objects, are more susceptible to transformation into sentiments, compared to event-targeted emotions (e.g., anger or humiliation). The emotions that more easily transform into sentiments are usually more cognitively based and, as such, are often termed as *secondary* (rather than *primary*) emotions.

We have recently suggested (Halperin et al., 2011) and then empirically demonstrated (Halperin, 2011b; Halperin & Gross, 2011) that long-term emotional sentiments toward the outgroup influence emotional reactions to specific events via their impact on cognitive appraisals. In other words, this framework suggests that discrete emotional sentiments should determine emotional reactions to a specific outgroup-relevant event by influencing appraisals of that event. This framework is based on an integration of classical *appraisal* theories of emotions (e.g., Lazarus, 1991; Roseman, 1984; Scherer, Schorr, & Johnstone, 2001), with the more recent *appraisal tendency framework* introduced by Lerner and Keltner in 2000.

For example, in a recent study we used a unique, two-wave, nationwide representative panel design (N = 501) conducted in Israel during the first war in Gaza to test the effects of long-term sentiments of anger experienced by Jewish Israelis toward Palestinians on their anger reaction to Palestinian violence during the war (Halperin & Gross, 2011). Results showed that the long-term sentiment of anger toward Palestinians (and not general negative affect), measured 13 months prior to the Gaza war, predicted participants' anger responses toward the Palestinians during the war. Furthermore, we found that the effects of long-term anger sentiments were mediated by the participants' current appraisals of the unfairness of Palestinian behavior. Interestingly, the effects of these long-term sentiments of anger on anger reactions remained significant even when taking into account people's political ideologies and, even more interestingly, when taking into account their direct and indirect experiences during the war.

The Collective Aspect of Emotions

To understand the role played by emotions in political conflicts, emotions must be understood beyond the intra- or even the interpersonal context. Intuitively, most people see emotion as a highly personal phenomenon, which is experienced within the minds and hearts of people. Yet, in the past two decades, scholars have begun studying emotions beyond the individual level, and it is well established today that emotions are an important part of most societal dynamics. Scholars of emotions have acknowledged that emotions must be studied within their social context, while those who study intergroup relations now accept the notion that these relations cannot be fully understood without paying proper attention to emotional processes. There is wide consensus today that emotions are driven by intra- and intergroup dynamics, that they are frequently expressed within social contexts, and that they influence the nature of intra- and intergroup relations. When emotions are experienced within the destructive context of intractable conflicts, their implications are further amplified.

Social and group processes interlock with emotional phenomena in several different ways. The simplest and probably most common form consists of the 'traditional' individual emotions that are elicited, experienced, and expressed in social contexts. Take for example a Palestinian woman who lives in the context of prolonged conflict between Israelis and Palestinians. That Palestinian has to go through Israeli military roadblocks every day on her way to work and must be feeling both fear and, at times, humiliation while going through these roadblocks and encountering the young soldiers pointing their looks and weapons toward her. These experienced emotions of fear and humiliation are felt on the individual level and are driven by actual events that are experienced directly and personally by that Palestinian woman. As such, these intense feelings of fear and humiliation meet all well-known criteria of individual-level emotions.

At the same time, to fully understand these feelings of fear and humiliation, they must be contextualized (i.e., considered within the context of the Israeli-Palestinian conflict) in a number of ways. First, the direct cause of the emotion-eliciting event (or object in the case of a military roadblock) is rooted within the dynamics of a hostile intergroup conflict. Second, the Palestinian woman's cognitive appraisals probably are driven by her group's values, ideologies, and even by its collective historical narrative regarding the Israeli-Palestinian conflict (Bar-Tal et al., 2007). Third, the Palestinians as a group have already provided their own social appraisals (Kuppens, Yzerbyt, Dandache, Fischer, & Van Der Schalk, 2013; Manstead & Fischer, 2001) of these events, and these appraisals feed into the individual ones, altogether creating discrete emotional reactions. Finally, a Palestinian's emotional reactions to the Israeli military roadblocks play an important role in the public discourse (local and international) regarding the future of the territories and potential solutions to the Israeli-Palestinian conflict.

So, we now know that individual emotions often are experienced within a social context. But recent research in social psychology takes the social approach to emotion one step forward by showing that people actually can experience emotions in the name of their group members, even if they have not directly experienced the emotion-eliciting event. Developed by Mackie and Smith, *intergroup emotions theory* (IET) suggests that people are capable of experiencing emotions such as (but not only) fear, anger, and guilt 'in the name' of their group or other members of it (Mackie, Devos, & Smith, 2000; Smith, 1993). This approach, which integrates social identity theories (Tajfel & Turner, 1986) with appraisal theories of emotions (e.g., Roseman. 1984; Scherer, 2004), offers a new perspective on people's emotional reactions to events they might experience indirectly through the involvement of another group member (Cialdini et al., 1976; Doosje, Branscombe, Spears, & Manstead, 1998). In fact, group-based emotions can be elicited if the emotion-eliciting event has involved the nation as a whole, its representative, and even ordinary members of the group (Branscombe, Slugoski, & Kappen, 2004; Lickel, Schmader, & Barquisau, 2004).

Group-based emotions are influenced by a combination of two factors: level of identification with the group and unique appraisals of the event—which are determined both by the group members' personalities, values, and interests as well as by the type of the event (Mackie, Devos, & Smith, 2000; Smith, 1993). People experience group-based emotions only to the extent that they categorize themselves as part of the relevant group. Whereas self-categorization relates to whether individuals perceive themselves as a member of a group (Turner, Hogg, Oakes, Reicher, & Wetherell, 1987), *group identification* is the cognitive and emotional valuation of the individual's relation to the group (Tajfel, 1978). Therefore, group identification serves as an amplifier (or attenuator) of group-based emotions. The more the individual identifies with the group, the stronger the experience of group-based emotion (e.g., Doosje et al., 1998; Gordijn, Yzerbyt, Wigboldus, &

Dumont, 2006; Smith, Seger, & Mackie, 2007; Van-Zomeren et al., 2008; Wohl & Branscombe, 2008). Thus, self-categorization reflects a psychological basis for group-based emotions, whereas group identification amplifies their experience.

Thinking back to the previous example regarding the emotional experience of Palestinians going through Israeli roadblocks in the occupied territories, IET suggests that Palestinians can feel group-based fear and humiliation (and probably also group-based anger) even if they have not directly encountered an Israeli roadblock in their entire lives. This will happen when they are exposed to a story or even footage of a Palestinian woman being searched and undressed at an Israeli roadblock. The natural Palestinian identification with that woman, coupled with humiliation and fear associated appraisals, will probably lead to the experience of group-based humiliation and fear.

To make the story more complicated, this very same event can potentially elicit group-based emotions among members of the other involved group (i.e., Israeli Jews) who also did not directly take part in it. Most probably, in that case, the dominant group-based emotional reaction would be guilt. Group-based guilt has been found to be associated with acceptance of responsibility for wrong-doings committed by individuals one identifies as part of one's social group (e.g., Branscombe & Doosje, 2004; Brown & Čehajić, 2008). As such, group-based guilt holds the potential of playing a highly constructive role in conflict resolution processes, yet it is considered a rare emotion, especially in long-term conflicts, and groups often tend to avoid it as well as to prevent group members from experiencing it (Wohl, Branscombe, & Klar, 2006; Wohl & Branscombe, 2008).

Both individual and group-based emotions capture situations in which the social context coupled with group identification influence individual experiences of emotions. Yet emotions theorists and researchers in recent years have suggested that emotions can be experienced beyond the individual level and that groups or societies have their own feelings, emotions, and other affective tendencies. For example, an accumulation of many group-based emotional responses to a societal event easily can turn into what is now defined as a collective emotion, namely, emotions that are shared by large numbers of individuals in a certain society (Stephan & Stephan, 2000; von Scheve & Ismer, 2013). Note too that we may distinguish social groups formed by social relationships from groups that are simply based on a common attribute (such as businesspeople). Barbalet (1998) has pointed out that in the former, a collective emotion may lead to common action with a group goal even though individual members of the group may experience different personal emotions because they occupy different roles in the group. By contrast, collective emotions in the second sort of group lead to the *common action* of individuals who are subject to the same conditions as when businesspeople feel confident that there is a good business climate.

Initial work by de Rivera (1992) has focused on the context in which collective emotions are evoked. He suggested that it is important to differentiate emotional atmosphere from emotional culture and emotional climate. *Atmosphere* refers to emotions that arise when members of a group focus their attention on a specific short-term event that affects them as a group. *Emotional culture* refers to the emotional relations that are socialized in any particular culture. *Emotional climate*, on the other hand, refers to the collective emotions experienced as a result of a society's response to its sociopolitical conditions. More recently, Bar-Tal (2001) has suggested the concept of a *collective emotional orientation*, a concept that refers to the characterizing tendency of a society to express a particular emotion. He has provided some criteria to identify such a characterizing orientation—for example, he noted that the emotion and the beliefs that evoke a particular emotion are shared widely by society members and appear frequently in the society's public discourse, cultural products, and educational materials. These orientations may even characterize entire 'civilizations' as when Moisi (2007) has referred to "cultures" of fear, humiliation, and hope in the Western, Islamic, and Eastern worlds. Referring back to the example of the Palestinian woman and the Israeli roadblock, it can be assumed that the woman's individual emotional reactions are amplified by a widely shared Palestinian emotional climate of fear and humiliation.

It is thus not surprising that, like individuals, societies can become characterized by a particular emotional orientation. For example, an Inuit group called Utku, who live in the Arctic Circle, disapprove of anger and suppress it (Briggs, 1970). The Japanese have a specific emotion *amae* in their emotional repertoire, which expresses a passive object of love, a kind of helplessness and the desire to be loved (Morsbach & Tyler, 1986). Páez and Vergara (1995) have found differences in feelings of fear among Mexicans, Chileans, Belgians, and Basque Spaniards. The Chileans were found to be characterized by the highest level of fear, while the Mexicans had the lowest. Bellah (1967) has proposed that hope characterizes American society: it is a central ingredient in what he called the "civil religion" of the United States. It is this sort of emotional orientation that de Rivera (1992) has termed *emotional culture*.

I always find it easier to better capture the idea of emotional climate or collective emotional orientation by thinking of real-world situations in which people were able to distinguish between their individual feelings and the way they perceive the dominant collective feeling at a certain time. For example, after the Second Lebanon War (in 2006), morale among Jews in Israel was not at its peak. When politicians and other influentials were interviewed in different media channels and were asked at the beginning of the interview how they felt, oftentimes they said, "On an individual level I feel great, but on the national level I'm deeply disappointed". In other words, people have two different emotional assessment tools—one for their own feelings and the other for the way they think most society members feel. Relevant empirical evidence for the same process can be found in a paper by Conejero and Etxebarria (2007) dealing with emotional reactions to the March 11, 2004, terrorist attack in Madrid that resulted in 191 deaths and more than 1,500 injuries. In this paper the authors distinguish between the personal and the collective emotions that were evoked and show how measures of emotional climate contribute to our ability to predict the behavior that resulted.

Yet, looking at previous studies describing the relationship between collective emotions (or associated terms) and group-based emotions, one can deduce that it is extremely simple: when a certain collective emotion (e.g., fear or anger) is strong, or when the emotional climate and orientation lead a group to share a certain emotion, individuals who see themselves as part of that group will be more likely personally to experience that emotion. Stated differently, when a collective feels a certain emotion, a group member will be driven to feel the same way. A good example of that approach can be found in a study by Fischer and colleagues (Fischer, Rotteveel, Evers, & Manstead, 2004) showing that individuals who were exposed to the same emotional event tended to assimilate emotionally to each other; that is, they tended to experience and express similar emotions, especially when an interdependent self was made salient.

Yet a recent paper by Goldenberg, Saguy, and Halperin (2014) have demonstrated that this is not always the case. As will be elaborated in Chapter 10, in cases in which the event is perceived by the group member as one in which the collective should feel a certain emotion, but the collective is perceived as not sharing this emotion, the authors showed that individuals experienced *emotional burden*. This situation results in a stronger group-based emotion when perceiving the collective as not sharing these emotions, compared to when the collective is perceived to share the same emotion. For example, according to this approach, Palestinians who think that the Palestinian emotional reaction to the Israeli roadblocks is not as intense as it should be will amplify (or upregulate), rather than downregulate, their group-based feelings of fear and humiliation. However, when the individual does not have a strong feeling that the collective should experience a certain emotion, she will choose to conform to her perception of the collective emotion.

Emotions and Public Opinion in Intergroup Conflicts—An Appraisal-Based Framework

In the previous parts of this chapter, I have conceptualized and defined various emotional phenomena (e.g., emotions, sentiments, and group-based emotions) and provided some preliminary indications regarding the way these emotional phenomena can shape people's political reactions to conflict-related events. In the remaining part of the chapter, I will try to integrate these emotional processes together with contextual and other cognitive processes into a comprehensive model, with the aim of explaining what specific role is played by emotions in shaping public opinion and potentially also public behavior during intractable conflicts.

Interestingly, despite increased interest in the role of emotion in conflicts, until recently, there was no comprehensive framework for understanding how emotions influence individual and collective beliefs, attitudes, and behaviors regarding war and peace. We (see Halperin, Sharvit, & Gross, 2011) have recently offered and then tested (Halperin, 2011b) such an appraisal-based theoretical framework that captures key aspects of this process and may therefore be useful as a theoretical platform for further empirical work in the field. The appraisal-based framework describes the sequence of processes by which emotional sentiments and group-based emotions contribute to the formation of specific attitudinal and behavioral responses to conflict-related events. It focuses on the entire psychological process that takes place after an individual has been exposed to a meaningful conflict-related event and before that very same individual has decided how she wishes to personally and politically respond to that event. In other words, my main focus is on the way emotional processes determine how individuals politically respond to conflict-related events (see Figure 2.1 for an illustration of the entire process).

More specifically, the process begins with the occurrence of a new event and/ or the appearance of new information related to the conflict and/or recollection of a past conflict-related event. The event or information can be negative (e.g., war eruption, terror attack, or rejection of a peace offer) or positive (e.g., a peace gesture or an indication of willingness to compromise), but it must be appraised

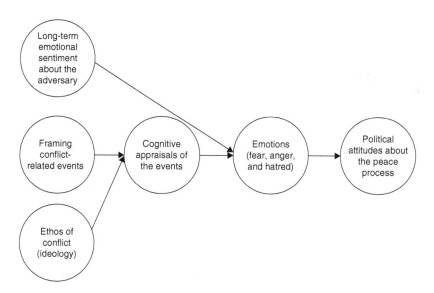

FIGURE 2.1 A general theoretical model: framing, emotions, ideology, and public opinion about the peace process

as meaningful, or otherwise it will not stimulate any emotional process. Although events can be experienced personally, in most cases they are experienced directly by a few group members and transmitted to other group members through the mediation of leaders, the mass media, or other individuals. For example, a new Palestinian proposal for renewal of peace negotiations is presented directly only to a handful of Israeli representative or decision makers, but the information regarding such new proposal is then conveyed to the Israeli public through various channels of communication. In these cases, if individuals identify with the same group, in this case, Israeli Jews, as the directly exposed individuals, they will experience group-based emotions (Smith, 1993; Mackie, Devos, & Smith, 2000).

As suggested by appraisal theories of emotions (e.g., Roseman, 1984; Scherer, 1984), such short-term events will elicit individual and group-based emotions and the ensuing political response tendencies, depending on the manner in which they are appraised. For example, a violent act committed by outgroup members toward the ingroup that is appraised as unjust and is accompanied by the evaluation of the ingroup as severe would induce anger (Huddy, Feldman, & Cassese, 2007; Halperin, 2008), whereas the very same event that is evaluated as justified, yet still painful, would probably induce sadness and despair. Hence, the subjective appraisal of an event is a crucial factor in determining the kind of emotion that will result from the event.

But the appraisal of the event does not appear in a vacuum. Generally, cognitive appraisals are driven by people's goals, interests, prior dispositions, personality characteristics, and even prior emotional experiences. In the context of long-term conflicts, the proposed framework emphasizes four main factors that potentially can shape the concrete appraisals of the events. First, the event may be framed by leaders and the media in a certain way, and this framing influences individuals' appraisal of the event (Halperin, 2011b). Different frames for the same event may lead to different cognitive appraisals, which in turn, will lead to different emotional responses (Gross, 2008). For example, if a military action by the opponent is framed as a defensive response to previous militant actions by one's own side, it may elicit fear or possibly sadness. But if framed as an aggressive action with no justified causes, it may lead to extreme anger or even hatred.

Second, the appraisal of the event will be influenced by a relatively wide range of non-affective factors, many of which are directly related to the psychological infrastructure developed by societies involved in intractable conflicts (Bar-Tal, 2013). An extensive review of these factors is beyond the scope of the current chapter, but a non-exhaustive list of them would include personality factors (e.g., authoritarianism, need for structure, and implicit theories), adherence to moral values, socioeconomic status, and long-term ideology about the conflict and the opponent (see Halperin, 2011b; Pliskin, Halperin, Sheppes, & Bar-Tal, 2014). For example, if a certain society is dominated by the societal belief of collective victimhood (Bar-Tal, Chernyak-Hai, Schori, & Gundar, 2009; Noor, Shnabel, Halabi, &

Nadler, 2012; Vollhardt, 2012a, 2012b), almost any action of the outgroup will be appraised as threatening and, as such, very easily can lead to group-based fear.

Third, as already suggested, our appraisal-based framework assumes that long-term emotional sentiments will bias the cognitive appraisals of specific events. This premise is based upon the *appraisal tendency framework* (Lerner & Keltner, 2000), according to which each emotion activates a cognitive predisposition to interpret events in line with the central appraisal dimensions that triggered the emotion. For example, a long-term external threat to the group will make society members more attuned to threatening cues and will lead to higher appraised danger that will, in turn, elicit more frequent fear responses (Bar-Tal et al., 2007).

Finally, it can be assumed that both positive and negative conflict-related prior experiences can bias the way individuals appraise current events. For example, people who have experienced solitary or repeated occurrences of positive contact with outgroup members (Al Ramiah & Hewstone, 2013; Pettigrew & Tropp, 2006), either through long-term friendships or through structured dialogue groups, will probably appraise even outgroup provocations in a less harsh way compared to those who have not experienced such contact. On the other hand, people who have suffered either directly or indirectly from outgroup violence tend to be more sensitive to potential threats and to appraise even a nonthreatening stimulus accordingly (Canetti, Halperin, Sharvit, et al., 2009).

I suggest that the occurrence of a new event, integrated with these four groups of factors, will shape the cognitive appraisal of the event, which will provide the basis for the development of corresponding discrete emotions. In turn, these discrete emotions, and particularly the emotional goals and response tendencies embedded within them, will dictate the behavioral and political responses to the event (see Halperin, 2011b).

But how exactly do discrete emotions influence people's political reactions to specific events? As already suggested, they do that by simple translation of the core emotional goals and action tendencies of the emotion into support (or opposition) for practical policies that are considered as relevant reactions to the emotion-eliciting event. Accordingly, the same event will lead to support for different policies among different individuals who experienced different emotions in response to that event. Just to mention few examples, if the dominant feeling is group-based guilt, one will support policies aiming to correct the ingroup's wrongdoings and to compensate the outgroup (Čehajić et al., 2011). If one is dominated by hope, she will be motivated to search for new avenues to change the future, probably by seriously considering new political information and creative political solutions (Cohen-Chen, Halperin, Crisp, et al., 2014). And if one is dominated by fear, most efforts will be devoted to the support of policies that will increase the feeling of security (Spanovic et al., 2010).

An empirical demonstration of that process can be found in a study I have recently conducted among a representative sample of Jews in Israel (Halperin,

2011b). During the study three discrete negative emotions—fear, anger, and hatred—were induced by offering different frames or explanations for the current Palestinian policy during negotiations with Israel. Interestingly, as can be seen in Figure 2.2, each of these group-based emotions led to support for very unique policies with regard to the ongoing negotiation.

According to the results, fear was found to be the only emotional antecedent fostering an opposition to taking risks during negotiations. This could be a crucial obstacle to any progress toward peace, which inherently requires mutual risk taking. In addition, fear reduced the support for making territorial compromises that might lead to security problems. It should be noted, though, that while 'fearful' individuals did oppose compromises that might increase future risks, they did not oppose other types of compromise (e.g., symbolic ones).

Hatred, on the other hand, was found to be a major emotional barrier to peace. It is the only emotion that reduces support for symbolic compromise and reconciliation and even remains an obstacle to every attempt to acquire positive knowledge about the Palestinians. These results accurately correspond with the fundamental characteristics of hatred that attribute a stable negative character to the outgroup and negate any possible change or improvement in their behavior (Sterenberg, 2003; Halperin, 2008).

Finally, according to the study results, anger is the most complicated and ambiguous emotion. On the one hand, anger is the only emotion that leads to the belief that the Palestinians are entirely responsible for failed talks. On the other

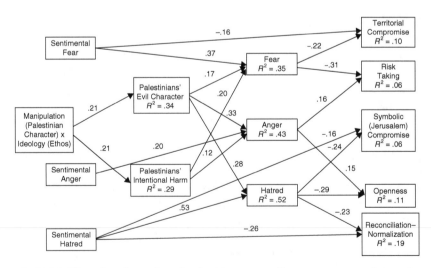

FIGURE 2.2 The role of emotions in shaping support for peace: structural equation model (standardized significant p < .01 coefficients are reported) for predicting catalysts of peace (N=261).

hand, anger is also the only negative emotion that induces support for taking risks in negotiations and openness to positive knowledge about the opponent. This nicely corresponds with anger core appraisals of high control and, even more importantly, with its emotional goal, which motivates individuals to try and correct the perceived wrongdoing. Thus, individuals experiencing anger maintain two very different, but not mutually exclusive, positions. On the one hand, they blame the opponent. On the other hand, they concomitantly are willing to offer the opponent a means to change their ways. Individuals who are dominated by anger feel that they are strong enough to bring about correction and change, even if it means taking some risks (Mackie et al., 2000). Under certain circumstances, such motivation will turn anger into a substantial barrier for peace, but in other situations, anger has the potential to become a peace facilitator.

3

INTERGROUP HATRED IN INTRACTABLE CONFLICTS—THE ULTIMATE BARRIER TO PEACE

Look, how constantly capable and how well maintained in our century: hatred. How lightly she regards high impediments. How easily she leaps and overtakes.

She's not like other feelings. She's both older and younger than they. She herself gives birth to causes that awaken her to life. If she ever dozes, it's not an eternal sleep. Insomnia does not sap her strength but adds to it.

Religion or no religion, as long as one kneels at the starting block. Fatherland or no fatherland, as long as one tears off at the start. She begins as fairness and equity. Then she propels herself. Hatred. Hatred. She veils her face with a mien of romantic ecstasy.

Oh, the other feelings—decrepit and sluggish. Since when could that brotherhood count on crowds? Did ever empathy urge on toward the goal? How many clients did doubt abduct? Only she abducts who knows her own.

Wislawa Szymborska (translated by Walter Whipple)

In everyday life when we say that we hate something (let's say a certain food or drink), what we actually try to express is the most extreme evaluation we can provide for a certain object. Many people say they 'hate' eggplant. They are trying to say that they *really* don't like this vegetable. They also want to tell the people who surround them that they do not want to see eggplant served on their table ever in their lives. In a similar way, when one hates another person or group, she expresses the most extreme possible evaluation of that object but also implies that she will do everything possible not to encounter that person or group in her environment. Unfortunately, when such evaluations and motivations are coupled with the violent atmosphere of intergroup conflicts, they can potentially lead to dramatic outcomes.

Since the current chapter deals with one of the most destructive and difficult emotional phenomena, hatred, I would like to open it with an optimistic note. My optimism is based on the fact that according to extensive public opinion research we have done in recent years in some of the most violent conflicts worldwide, and perhaps counter to what most of us tend to think, hatred is not the most dominant emotion people experience in these kinds of conflicts. Although when experienced, hatred has a dramatic effect on peoples' attitudes and behaviors in conflicts, most people are driven by their fears, by their anger, and sometimes by their hopes but not necessarily by hatred. This is also one of the reasons why most intergroup conflicts and even most violent ones do not involve mass murder and massacre. In most conflicts, people strive for security (driven by fear), sometimes they seek for revenge or correction (driven by anger and humiliation), but most of them do not necessarily want to see the outgroup disappear or be annihilated. At the same time, though, hate does exist in some cases, and its impact on conflicts and their (lack of) resolution extends way beyond its actual dominancy among the mass population. In other words, a meaningful minority of 'haters' can have more influence on the life span of intergroup conflicts than a majority of non-haters.

For that reason, among other things, it is crucial to study the nature and the implications of intergroup hatred. Many decades ago, Aristotle defined hatred as one of the most momentous emotions because of the way it undermines people's sense of judgment. In a comprehensive review of classic as well as more contemporary conceptualizations of hatred, Royzman and colleagues (Royzman, McCauley, & Rosin, 2005) defined hatred as the most destructive affective phenomenon in the history of human nature. These destructive implications of hatred on human life have been documented widely in several recent contributions (e.g., Sternberg 2005; Opotow & McClelland, 2007).

Although destructive in most domains of life, hatred is particularly destructive in the violent effect it exerts on intergroup relations. Recent studies have shown that in the context of long-term intergroup conflict (e.g., the Israeli-Palestinian conflict), above and beyond the effects of other negative emotions, hatred reduces people's support for making compromises to resolve the conflict (e.g., Halperin, 2011b; Halperin, Russell, Dweck, et al., 2011; Maoz & McCauley, 2005) and induces their support for initiating aggressive actions targeted at the outgroup (Maoz & McCauley, 2008). Furthermore, hatred also has the potential to impel people to engage in massacres (Staub, 2005). Hence, hate makes a huge contribution to the escalation and maintenance of long-term conflicts, and it stands as a powerful barrier to conflict resolution. Yet such extreme violent expressions of hatred are only the tip of the iceberg. Hatred toward other groups is a widespread human phenomenon that is rooted in everyday intergroup and political relations.

But do we really know why intergroup hatred plays such a central role in intergroup conflicts? To seriously address this question, we first have to understand what hatred is and how it differs from other, mainly negative, affective phenomena. Interestingly, despite extensive acknowledgment of its potentially destructive impact, there are few contemporary definitions of hatred (For a recent review, see Royzman, McCauley, & Rosin, 2005, and see also Gaylin, 2003; Sternberg, 2005; Yanay, 2002). Some of these definitions have been very general and all-inclusive, while others have concentrated on very specific features of hatred. During our work in which we tried to reveal the nature and implications of hatred in conflicts (e.g., Halperin, 2008, 2011b; Halperin, Canetti-Nisim, & Hirsch-Hoefler, 2009, Halperin, Russell, Dweck, et al., 2011), we have defined intergroup hatred as a secondary, extreme, and continuous emotion that is directed at a particular group and fundamentally and all-inclusively denounces the group and its members. I'll get back to the definition and nature of hatred later in the chapter.

Even more surprisingly, only a few social scientists have undertaken in-depth empirical research on hatred both as an individual and as a collective emotion and on the role it plays in intergroup conflicts. Thus, a huge gap exists between the prevalence and influence of hatred in the social and political realms and the paucity of research in the field. There are two main reasons for the creation of that gap. First, scholars of emotions oftentimes do not see hatred as a standard emotion. It is treated in most cases as an extreme attitude, an emotional attitude, or at best an emotional sentiment. As such, hatred did not gain from the rising popularity of the study of emotions in recent years. For example, in most empirical investigations based on appraisal theories (e.g., Roseman, 1984; Scherer, 2004), one can find emotions like dislike or anger but cannot find evidence regarding the appraisal basis of hatred (but see Fitness & Fletcher, 1993; Halperin, 2008).

But even more importantly, the shortage in research and definitions of hatred is due to the fact that hatred is commonly viewed as an illegitimate social emotion by laypeople and scholars alike. In other words, people hate to admit that they hate, societies do not want to see themselves as dominated by hate, and even social scientists hate to think that hatred is dominant enough among human beings to justify its research. In the first empirical study I conducted when I started studying hatred (Halperin, 2008, Study 1), I tried to discover people's lay theories of hatred. To that end, I asked 30 Israelis to think of one event in their lives in which they felt hatred. All 30 interviewees (100 percent) said immediately that they had never experienced hatred. They said that they had felt extreme anger, that they knew some other people who had experienced hatred, and that they were aware of the dominancy of hatred in conflict situations. But to feel hatred toward other people? Not them. They were not the kind of people who experience hatred. . . . Ironically, some of the interviewees who said that they had never hated then described specific situations in the history of the conflict in which they had wanted to bomb a large Palestinian city or situations in which they had wanted to do everything they could to annihilate or destroy the outgroup.

What is it about hatred that, on the one hand, makes it almost illegitimate and at the same time so popular? It is considered illegitimate because it reflects on the hater at least as much as it reflects on the object of hate. People who hate (or haters) are seen as people who make clear-cut evaluations, who see the world in black and white, and who are emotionally invested in the target of hate. You do not hate a person or a group unless you feel strongly dependent or connected to that person or group. But most importantly, people do not want to think of themselves as haters because they do not want to believe that they are capable of carrying out the actions that are commonly seen as associated with hatred. If hatred is about excluding or even annihilating people or groups, and you cannot see yourself as executing such actions, what is the purpose of hating?

Yet although it is not considered legitimate, many society members do feel hatred, and especially in the social sphere, hatred is considered to be one of the most influential intergroup emotions. The main goal of the current chapter is thus to reveal the reasons for the pivotal role played by hatred in that context and then to identify its main implications on attitudes and behavior in conflicts. In a nutshell, it is suggested that the following reasons make hatred so powerful in conflict situations: (a) it is the most extreme and the most unambiguous emotion; (b) it involves deep moral judgments; (c) it is easily transformed into long-term sentiment embedded within the culture of societies; (d) it is transformed easily into a collective emotion, and it is amplified when shared by other group members; (e) it is an effective mobilization tool, and as such, leaders and other influentials try to use it rather than to suppress it.

In what follows I will first describe the nature of intergroup hatred with special emphasis on its associated cognitive appraisals and emotional goals. I will then briefly introduce two unique aspects of hatred, namely, first its dual formation as a short-term emotion and as a chronic emotional sentiment and second its smooth transformation from an individual into a collective emotion. Finally, some studies examining the role played by hatred in conflict resolution processes will be presented, followed by preliminary ideas about the things that need to be done to downregulate intergroup hatred.

What Is Hatred? Nature, Appraisals, and Emotional Goals

To fully understand what role is played by intergroup hatred in conflicts and their resolution, it is necessary first to understand what hatred is and in what way it is different from other negative emotions that are dominant in these contexts. Only the deep understanding of the nature and components of hatred can enable us to understand in what way it uniquely influences people's attitudes and behavior in conflict situations. With that goal in mind, in 2008 I conducted a study based on in-depth interviews with 30 Israeli citizens in which I tried to reveal their lay theories about hatred. I was curious about the way people naively theorize the feeling of hatred, namely, what kind of events, thoughts, feelings, and action tendencies would be classified as those that reflect intergroup hatred experiences.

To that end, interviewees were asked to describe a situation in their lives in which they experienced intergroup hatred and then to explain why they consider the event they described as a *hatred event*. As mentioned, while at first all participants had some difficulty in identifying such feelings in their own private emotional history, after some encouragement and guidance, all participants managed to do so. Not surprisingly, when conducting such a study in the context of an ongoing intractable conflict, most participants described events that were related to the Israeli-Palestinian conflict, and for most of them, the felt hatred was targeted at the Palestinian people, although others described hatred toward different social groups like sports teams, religious groups, and others.

As for the actual experience of hatred, the interviews demonstrated that participants perceived hatred as an extreme (60 percent), long-term (66.6 percent), and highly emotional phenomenon (63.3 percent). Interestingly, although all participants admitted feeling hatred at least once or twice in their lives, most of them treated it as an immoral or illegitimate emotion (93.3 percent), and some even said that, in retrospect, they regret that feeling; they were not very proud of themselves for feeling it, and they would rather not repeat the experience in the future. In addition, most participants (56.6 percent) argued that it was possible to clearly distinguish between acute and immediate hatred and chronic hatred. I will elaborate about that point in a later part of the current chapter.

As for hatred antecedents, with one exception, all other hatred experiences (96.6 percent) were driven by events in which the outgroup seriously and in some cases repeatedly harmed the hater, her close ones, or other members of her group. Many of these events included situations of direct or indirect exposure to political violence, mostly when such violence was targeted at innocent civilians or when it was done in an extremely brutal way. Other types of harm that were mentioned frequently were discriminatory actions, acts of public humiliation, and repeated threatening acts or messages.

Another dominant contextual factor was learning. A huge majority of the interviewees (86.6 percent) mentioned that their hatred either originated or was amplified by learning processes, driven mainly by their parents, friends, and schoolteachers. Interestingly, more than half of the participants admitted that they had never personally met the target of their hatred, and therefore their knowledge and assessments of that group were based on things they had heard secondhand in the media, from leaders, or in their close environment.

But these extreme events of threat, discrimination, and harm or extensive learning processes do not always lead to hatred and hence can be thought of as necessary but not sufficient preconditions for hatred to evolve. We know that because many people around the world suffer from discriminatory actions, abuse, and even from direct violence, but not all of them develop extreme feelings like hatred toward these outgroups. When it comes to people who were exposed to extreme political violence, a study by Canetti, Muldoon, Hirsch-Hoefler, & Rapaport (2009) has shown that personal exposure to terrorism would result in extreme intergroup emotions and attitudes to the extent that it would stimulate PTSD symptoms and to the extent that it would increase the perceived threat posed by the outgroup. Accordingly, it is not the harmful events themselves that lead to hatred but their psychological symptoms and implications.

Even more interestingly, on the extreme end of the spectrum, we can find people for whom personal loss and suffering served as a catalyst for psychological change toward more positive rather than negative emotions toward outgroups and, as such, also led them to take part in actions meant to promote peace rather than further violence. In the Israeli-Palestinian context, these people have formed two fascinating groups, Combatants for Peace and the Parents Circle—Families Forum. These groups bring together Israelis and Palestinians who have experienced dramatic losses and who have chosen to channel their sorrow into constructive rather than destructive political actions.

What follows is that the event itself does not necessarily lead to hatred but only the subjective appraisals of it. So the question is: what are the subjective appraisals of the situation that mediate between the actual experience of loss, insult, or victimization (or the learning about such experiences), on the one hand, and the experience of hatred, on the other. In other words, how do people have to evaluate or appraise the outgroup's behavior for them to experience hatred toward that outgroup?

According to our work in recent years, these hatred-associated appraisals can be divided into two different groups. The first group includes those appraisals that are not unique to hatred and that characterize other negative emotions that often accompany the experience of hatred, for example, appraising the event as contradicting one's group's goals and interests (relevant to all negative emotions) or perceiving the outgroup's behavior as unjustified and unfair (relevant mostly to anger). In addition, at times hatred is driven by or associated with appraisals of high threat, frequently mentioned as the core appraisal themes of fear. According to the narratives provided by our interviewees, while fear is more dominant as an antecedent of hatred, anger plays a central role in the hatred experience itself.

But hatred is much more than just an extreme form of anger (see White, 1984 for that argument) or a mixture of anger and fear. Instead, it has some unique characteristics that turn it into such a destructive emotion in life generally and in intergroup conflicts more specifically. The core of that unique aspect of hatred is embedded within its unique appraisals, which in turn also reflect on its motivational and behavioral implications. In short, all hatred's unique appraisals imply stability and incapability of change of the extremely negative characteristics attributed to the outgroup (Allport, 1954; Royzman, McCauley, & Rosin, 2005; Sternberg, 2003). In more detail, one of the most unique characteristics of hatred is that its appraisals are targeted at the hate object itself rather than at specific actions carried out by that object (Ortony, Clore, & Collins, 1988). While we can feel anger because a certain action taken by a certain outgroup is appraised as immoral, unfair, or unjust, if that very same group changes its behavior, levels of anger would be reduced dramatically. On the other hand, the entire configuration of hatred appraisals is targeted at the innate nature, motives, and characteristics of the object itself (i.e., person or group), and as such, a momentary change in certain behavioral patterns will not necessarily diminish levels of hatred.

It follows that for intergroup hatred to develop, one has to first create a clear distinction between the ingroup and the outgroup and then also to perceive the outgroup as a rather homogeneous entity. Perception of outgroup homogeneity is essential for people to be able to generalize from a negative behavior of a single outgroup member into appraisals targeted at the entire outgroup. For example, a Palestinian woman who has suffered from the abusive behavior of an Israeli soldier at a military checkpoint will develop hatred toward all Jews only to the extent that she believes that all Jews are the same and that the behavior of that one soldier actually represents the innate characteristics of the entire Jewish people. In line with that idea, evidence for the negative association between levels of perceived outgroup variability and extreme negative attitudes and emotions toward outgroup members have been documented repeatedly in different contexts and intergroup conflicts (e.g., Er-rafiy & Brauer, 2013).

Although it is a necessary precondition for experiencing intergroup hatred, the fundamental idea of seeing the outgroup as a homogeneous entity is not unique to hatred. As a matter of fact, as suggested by Allport (1954) in the early 1950s, this process constitutes the psychological basis for all cases of stereotyping and those of extreme prejudice. So what makes intergroup hatred different from these previously mentioned phenomena?

First, not just is the outgroup viewed as a cohesive entity, but that entity also is perceived as completely different from the ingroup, especially in terms of moral value and moral behavior. For example, in the qualitative study previously described, most participants (70 percent) mentioned the perception of acute conflict between their ingroup and the hated group in regard to their basic goals as well as in the perception of a disparity in the values and ideology of the groups. Many times (76.6 percent), this disparity placed the outgroup outside the accepted norms of the so-called civilized groups, which in psychological terms means that the outgroup has been delegitimized, and hence social norms that apply to 'civilized groups' do not necessarily apply to it (Bar-Tal & Hammack, 2012). According to *moral exclusion theory*, our scope of justice is the psychological boundary within which concerns about fairness govern our conduct (Deutsch, 1985), and those who are outside that boundary are eligible for deprivation, exploitation, and other harms that ignore our moral values (Opotow, 1990). For most of our participants (90 percent), moral exclusion and delegitimization of the outgroup also helped ascertain the superiority of members of the ingroup and thus amplified the good old process of outgroup hate strengthening ingroup love (Brewer, 1999; Sumner, 1906).

So what we have by now is a negative event committed by members of an outgroup that is appraised as homogenous and as morally inferior to the ingroup. The outgroup's actions are appraised as unjust and as potentially threatening, and this appraisal is attributed to the outgroup as an entirety rather than to specific representatives of that group. But that still does not fulfil all necessary criteria of hatred because two of its most crucial and unique aspects are still missing. According to our interviews, hatred also was accompanied by the appraisal that the offense committed by the outgroup was intentional or was lacking any functional goals or motivations, except for the pure aspiration to hurt and damage the ingroup (66.6 percent). Even more importantly, members of the outgroup were perceived as evil and dispositionally bad, and therefore, their actions were not perceived as a coincidental or one-time occurrence (73.3 percent). This is in line with Ben-Zeev's (1992) view of hatred as an emotion directed at a defined object or group and denouncing that object or group fundamentally and all-inclusively.

The combination of these last two appraisals cannot be found in any other negative emotion, although the idea of stable, negative characteristics oftentimes also is attributed to contempt (Fischer & Roseman, 2007). Together, these two appraisals represent an extreme and deterministic view of the outgroup, its motivations, and roots of behavior. For example, when describing her hatred toward Palestinians, one of our participants said, "They will never change. They were born unfaithful, and they will die this way. Even after 40 years in the grave, you shouldn't trust an Arab". Along the same lines, another participant highlighted the fact that the Palestinians' aspirations to annihilate Israel cannot be stopped by any Israeli conciliatory action, compromise, or gesture. "They will always want to destroy us. Even if we give them everything they want, they will still try to throw us into the sea".

The dominancy of these last two appraisals was further supported in an experimental study (Halperin, 2008, Study 2) in which participants ($N = 240$) were provided with a questionnaire that included a detailed description of four emotionally conflicting scenarios (e.g., a terror attack and an intergroup violent event in a nightclub) followed by a manipulation of the cognitive appraisals of the protagonist in the story regarding five dichotomous appraisal dimensions: (1) just/unjust event, (2) outgroup/circumstances were responsible, (3) intentional/unintentional harm, (4) outgroup is evil/not evil, and (5) low/high coping potential. After reading the scenario and the protagonist's appraisals, participants were asked to rank the extent to which the protagonist experienced hatred, fear, and anger (separately) in response to that event.

The results of that study showed that only two of the five appraisals are unique to the hatred experience—the appraisal that outgroup harm is intentional and does not intend to achieve any functional goals and the appraisal that this harm is a result of the stable, evil character of outgroup members. On the other hand, the attribution of responsibility to the outgroup and the unjust appraisals were shared both by hatred and anger, and the appraisal of the individual or group as not being able to cope with the situation drove both fear and hatred.

The perception of the outgroup as evil by nature is worth another thought because it is a prism that enables people to judge any outgroup behavior in the most severe way. As such, it does not only shape the general view of the outgroup but also determines the way one should respond emotionally and behaviorally to the outgroup's negative actions. Staub (1989) has suggested that designating something as evil is sometimes used to suggest that the actions are not comprehensible in an ordinary human framework: they are outside the bounds of morality or even of human agency. He also suggested that another defining element of evil is the tendency of outgroups to engage in extremely harmful acts that are not commensurate with any instigation or provocation (Darley, 1992). But most importantly, perception of evil is driven in most cases by the persistence of these brutal and nonfunctional actions committed by the outgroup. As such, according to Staub (1989, 2005), a series of actions also can be evil when any one act causes limited harm, but with repetition these acts cause great harm. In these cases the extreme harm can no more be attributed to the specific circumstances, and hence it is attributed to the innate evil character of the outgroup. As I see it, these are exactly the cases in which the feeling of hatred is not just legitimized but at times even perceived as required.

What Would Haters Like to Do? Motivational and Behavioral Tendencies of Hatred

Interestingly, when reviewing classic definitions of hatred, it turns out that most scholars of hatred have defined it by its motivational and behavioral tendencies. To mention only a few examples, Allport (1954) has suggested that hatred is an "enduring organization of aggressive impulses towards a person or a class of persons"' (p. 363). According to White (1996), hatred reflects the desire to harm, humiliate, or even kill its object—not always instrumentally but rather to cause harm as a vengeful objective in itself. More recently, Bar-Tal (2007) has suggested that hatred is a hostile feeling directed toward another person or group that consists of malice, repugnance, and willingness to harm and even annihilate the object of hatred.

These definitions nicely fit the narrative provided by our study's interviewees (Halperin, 2008, Study 1). The large majority of them (83.3 percent) stated that they would want something very bad to happen to the hated group and its members. This was accompanied by a need to engage in a violent action with the hated people (83.3 percent) to a point where respondents supported the killing of members of the outgroup (50 percent). Still, only a few (16.6 percent) reported the actual execution of a violent action. The three most common actions reported by the participants were complete detachment from the object of the hatred (83.3 percent), delight at the expense or failure of the hated other (36.6 percent), and political action taken against the other (56.6 percent).

Although I am not sure that these motivational and behavioral tendencies are sufficient to reveal the nature of hatred, in my view they well demonstrate the way people identify and express intergroup hatred in their daily lives. For example, when we hear a certain person saying that she would like all Arabs or Jews (or any other outgroup) to be killed, we assume that she feels hatred toward that outgroup. At the same time, I do not think that it is sufficient to define hatred that way simply because the same motivations can be driven by other emotional processes as well. For example, one can be motivated to hurt the outgroup because of perceived self-defense, driven by fear, and not because of generalized hatred toward that group. What is unique about hatred, though, is that it is the only emotion that unambiguously motivates such aggressive action. In other words, while fear can sometimes lead to flight tendencies rather than fight, and anger can lead to constructive rather than destructive corrections (see Fischer & Roseman, 2007; Halperin, 2011b; Halperin, Russell, Dweck, et al., 2011; Riefen Tagar et al., 2011), hatred always will motivate people to such destructive action tendencies.

This can be explained by the understanding that hatred-associated emotional goals are a direct implication of its initial cognitive appraisals. The hatred story, as expressed by the integration of the belief that the outgroup has unjustly hurt the ingroup, together with the core assumption that the outgroup's motivations, immorality, and behavior are stable and will never change, leads only to one reasonable goal—to damage, hurt, and even annihilate that outgroup. As I see it, the core theme here is the idea of stability coupled with extremely negative assessment of the outgroup's moral character. These appraisals also make the emotional goal so different from the goals implied by other emotions. The belief in stable, extremely negative characteristics implies that there is no merit in trying to correct or improve the outgroup's behavior, and as such, only more extreme reactions seem relevant.

To test these assumptions empirically within the context of an intergroup conflict, we asked Jewish Israelis (N = 313) for their emotional reactions to certain Palestinian actions and then tested the emotional goals these emotional reactions yielded as well as their subsequent action tendencies (Halperin, 2008, Study 3). The results showed that group-based hatred is related to a very specific emotional goal—to do evil to, remove, and even eliminate the outgroup. On the other hand, its related action tendencies are not so absolute. The problematic nature of the emotional goals seems to make the more practical tendencies more diverse. In some situations, haters will desire to move away from the outgroup; in others, they will aspire to hurt the outgroup members, and in more extreme events, they might even support or take part in a destruction process.

Is Hatred an Emotion? Hatred Sentiment Versus Hatred Emotion

We have now gained better understanding regarding the nature of hatred, but scholars of hatred have continually debated the question of whether hatred is an emotion or an emotional attitude (Royzman, McCauley, & Rosin, 2005). That debate is driven by the fact that one of hatred's core characteristics is that it generally lasts long after the event that initially evoked it. An interesting illustration of this was recently introduced by Jasini and Fischer (2015) who presented the story of a 20-year old Kosovar Albanian woman who was asked to describe an experience of hatred in the context of their research:

> *I was 10 years old when Serbian paramilitary men broke into my house with violence. They had guns in their hands and they approached my dad and my brothers and asked them for all the money we had in the house. They threatened to kill them all if the family did not leave the house immediately. A few hours after this horror moment, my family and I left the village to seek refuge in the Albanian territory. Even now, ten years after the Kosovo war, I still hate the Serbians and can't forget their hatred for us, nor their maltreatment of my family, relatives and neighbors. I often talked about this event with my family members and friends, but never with Serbian people.* (Italics added.)

The enduring nature of hatred should not come as a surprise for those who deeply understand the nature of hatred and particularly for those who are familiar with its core appraisal themes. As mentioned, hatred appraisals are targeted at the fundamental nature of the hated group. Given that haters see the outgroup as innately evil, hatred reactions are not limited to a short period of time but rather constitute a standing evaluation targeted at the outgroup as long as it exists. If that is the case, though, can we really see hatred as an emotion rather than as an emotional attitude or a sentiment?

In the last two decades, scholars (e.g., Halperin, 2008; Sternberg, 2003) have resolved the dispute by suggesting that hatred can occur in both configurations—immediate and chronic. The long-term configuration of hatred includes all hatred components (i.e., appraisals and emotional goals), except for the affective component, which remains hidden as long as the hated object is not present. In-depth interviews that I have conducted in recent years with people who were asked to describe their own subjective experience of hatred suggest that more than half of the participants, when requested to describe a hatred experience, chose to relate to an ongoing emotional experience, while the remainder focused on a more acute event (Halperin, 2008).

Hence, it is suggested that there are two types of hatred (see Halperin, Canetti-Nisim, & Kimhi, 2012). The first is a sentimental, stable, and familiar hating emotional attitude (*chronic hatred*). This chronic hatred serves as a glue that organizes people's social world and helps strengthens the connection to the ingroup (*ingroup love*) at the expense of distancing various outgroups (*outgroup hate*). It involves a restricted amount of negative feeling as well as a stable cognitive perception that members of the hated group cause offense to the ingroup and its members in a severe, recurrent, unjust, and intentional way. This results from the basic evil that is rooted in the character of hated group members. To prevent future painful offenses, haters desire an absolute separation from members of the other group.

The second is an emotional, powerful, and 'burning' hate (*immediate hatred*) that occurs in response to significant events that are appraised as so dramatic that they lead to the kind of appraisals (e.g., "the outgroup is evil by nature") and motivations (e.g., "I would like it to be destroyed") usually associated with hatred. This severe feeling is often accompanied by unpleasant physical symptoms and a sense of helplessness. It evokes a strong desire for revenge, a wish to inflict suffering, and at times, the desired annihilation of the outgroup.

These two forms of hatred are related yet distinct, and one fuels the appearance and magnitude of the other. Frequent incidents of immediate hatred may make the development of chronic emotion more probable. At the same time, chronic hatred constitutes a fertile ground for the eruption of immediate hatred. Chronic haters encountering outgroup members or the consequences of their actions are apt to react with immediate hatred. These people evaluate almost any negative behavior of the outgroup through the prism of their long-term view of it as evil. As such, they are more susceptible than others to systematic biases like the one captured by the *fundamental attribution error* (Ross, 1977). In practice, people's general tendency to overweight internal or dispositional attributions, especially when they evaluate the negative behavior of outgroup members, is amplified in the presence of chronic hatred. What follows is that the mere presence, mention, or even internal memory of the hated group can transform the chronic hatred into a burning one.

At the same time, the causal mechanism can work the other way as well. Repeated events of hot, immediate, and burning hatred, very easily can turn the feeling of hatred into an enduring sentiment. Our studies unequivocally show that people are capable of short-term hate (Halperin, Canetti-Nisim, et al., 2012), namely, following an unusual, mostly destructive and violent event; they attribute negative behavior of the outgroup to its innate evil character only for a very short period of time, but then when they calm down, they reappraise the situation, and the hatred turns into more moderate feelings like anger or frustration. Yet it is only natural that after repeated events of that kind, it becomes very difficult for people to let go of hatred, and it sticks with them for longer periods of time. In a way, hatred is an emotion that requires more time to evolve, but once it does, it takes much longer to let go.

Hatred in an Intergroup Context: Why Is It So Easily Transformed to a Collective Emotion?

As already mentioned in Chapter 2 of this book, in recent decades, scholars of emotions have acknowledged that emotions can be experienced on a group and not only on an individual level. Yet not all emotions have the same potential to transcend from the individual to the group or collective level. Hatred easily can go through that transformation, and some will even claim that it is the most group-based emotion. Aristotle states succinctly that whereas anger is customarily felt toward individuals, hatred often is felt toward groups. In contrast to fear and anger, rather than at specific individual actions, hatred is targeted at the fundamental characteristics of the individual or the group (Ben-Zeev, 1992). Actions usually are conducted by individuals or by representatives of groups rather than by groups. The generalized attribution of the action to the basic traits and features of members of the outgroup enables a parsimonious explanation of the action. This facile transition of hatred from the interpersonal level to the collective level makes it a pivotal agent in group-based political dynamics in general and in intergroup conflicts in particular.

In addition, the development of hatred requires an accumulative process that can oftentimes take place among groups and collectives that share the same collective narratives and group identification components. Especially in situations of intractable conflicts when groups' collective narratives are dominated by the memory of their past victimization and repeated damage caused by specific outgroups (Bar-Tal, Chernyak-Hai, Schori, & Gundar, 2009; Noor, Shnabel, Halabi, & Nadler, 2012; Vollhardt, 2012a, 2014), the probability for the evolvement of intergroup hatred is even higher. That aggregated group knowledge regarding the immoral and violent behavior of the outgroup that goes beyond time and even generations makes the conclusion of seeing the outgroup as a homogeneous evil entity almost automatic. In the eyes of those who see themselves as part of a trans-generational victimized group, although they personally have suffered from the outgroup behavior only for a relatively short time, the fact that the outgroup's behavior is consistent across generations reflects its innate negative characteristics.

Another interesting aspect of hatred that makes it more susceptible to becoming an intergroup emotion is the fact that it does not require personal interaction or acquaintance between the hater and the hated group. According to Jasini and Fischer (2015), the absence of interactions with the targets of one's hate may further increase one's hate because it diminishes chances of perspective taking by the victim. Allport (1954) has mentioned the lack of direct interaction as one of the most powerful engines bolstering hate and prejudice. According to his approach, further supported by studies in the framework of contact theory (e.g., Pettigrew & Tropp, 2006), lack of direct interaction amplifies hatred because the negative appraisal of the malicious character of the group will never be reappraised. For example, in the Israeli-Palestinian context, since Israel completed the construction of the separation wall, Jewish Israelis do not have to seriously suppress their hate toward the Palestinians because they do not really have the opportunity to directly encounter individual Palestinians who do not necessarily meet the stereotypical Israeli view of Palestinians. Thus, the malicious image of the Palestinians remains intact without contact.

Finally, a recent empirical study conducted by Jasini and Fischer (2015) in Kosovo with ethnic Albanians as participants has shown that hate increases when there are opportunities to share the emotion with ingroup members. Rimé (2009) has demonstrated in several intergroup conflicts that in contexts of collective trauma, people tend to share their emotional experiences with other group members. Social sharing of past events activates the memory of the event and makes the group-based appraisals and their subsequent collective emotions salient (Kuppens et al., 2013; Yzerbyt & Kuppens, 2013). These group-based appraisals fuel the processes of negative generalizations that are necessary for hate to persist and even escalate.

The Implications of Hatred on Conflicts and Their Resolution

Although various negative emotions play roles in mobilizing people to support war and violence and to oppose compromises for peace, intergroup hatred is by all means the most powerful one. There are two main reasons for that. First, since hatred is associated with very low expectations for positive change and with high levels of despair, its associated political action tendencies are by definition destructive rather than constructive. If one does not believe that positive change in the outgroup's violent or immoral behavior is possible, then constructive political reactions, like negotiations, compromises, gestures, or even apologies that are usually meant to establish more friendly relations just seem irrelevant. In addition, the emotional goal associated with hatred, namely, to do evil to, remove, and even eliminate the outgroup, also leads to one-sided political action tendencies that do not really leave any room for positive change. In that regard, as will be elaborated in the chapters to come, hatred's emotional goals are fundamentally different from the ones of other negative emotions like anger and fear, which do leave such room for improvement and positive change.

The evaluation of short-term conflict-related events through the lens of hatred automatically increases support for initiating violent actions and for further escalating the conflict. That is also the reason Ervin Staub (2005) and others (e.g.,

Petersen, 2002; Volkan, 1997) have pointed at hatred as the most dominant emotion in historical and recent mass murders and massacres. If one is convinced of the destructive intentions of the outgroup and feels total despair regarding the likelihood of the outgroup changing its ways, the violent alternative may seem the only reasonable one. Along these lines, a recent study conducted in Israel found that above and beyond any other emotion, hatred increased the tendency of Israelis to support extreme military action toward Palestinians (Halperin, 2011b).

But the influence of hatred on intergroup conflicts goes way beyond its role in such extreme events of mass murder. For example, recently we (Halperin, Canetti-Nisim, & Hirsch-Hoefler, 2009) tested the emotional processes that fuel political intolerance. Political intolerance—the support or willingness to denounce the basic political rights of individuals who belong to a defined outgroup in a particular society (Gibson, 2006; Stouffer, 1955; Sullivan, Walsh, Shamir, Barnum, & Gibson, 1993)—is considered one of the most problematic phenomena in democratic societies because it contradicts basic democratic values of equal rights and political opportunity. To reveal the emotional processes that drive intolerance, we conducted four large-scale, nationwide surveys among Jews in Israel. The surveys made use of various intolerance measurement methods in various contexts (wartime vs. no-war/routine periods). Not surprisingly, the results showed that intergroup hatred is the most important antecedent of political intolerance and that other group-based negative emotions like anger or fear influence political intolerance wholly through the mediation of hatred. Finally, the results also indicated that the role of intergroup hatred in inducing political intolerance is more substantial in the face of heightened existential threat and among unsophisticated individuals than among sophisticated ones.

Furthermore, the deterministic nature of hatred turns it into a destructive emotion even in the midst of peace negotiations. For example, two recent studies found that individuals who experienced short-term episodes of hatred in times of negotiations in the Middle East expressed an emotional goal of harming and even eliminating the opponent (Halperin, 2008). They likewise tended to reject any positive information regarding the opponent (i.e., lack of openness) and opposed the continuation of negotiations, compromise, and reconciliation efforts (Halperin, 2011b). Importantly, given that hatred is associated with a fundamental negation of the outgroup as a whole, and not of the group's concrete actions or behavior, those who feel hatred toward the outgroup oppose even the smallest gestures and symbolic compromises, thus refusing even to entertain new ideas that may lead to peace. In this regard again, haters are fundamentally different from those who experience anger or fear, who are usually open to various kinds of conciliatory actions, as long as these actions serve the emotional goals embedded within the emotion.

Finally, hatred as an emotional sentiment plays a significant role in turning more ambiguous negative emotions into peace barriers rather than peace catalysts.

For example, in two experimental studies we conducted in 2011, on the eve of an important peace summit between Israelis and Palestinians, we found that inducing anger toward Palestinians increased support for making compromises in upcoming negotiations among those with low levels of hatred but decreased support for compromise among those with high levels of hatred (Halperin, Russell, Dweck, & Gross, 2011). It seems that in these cases, hatred sentiment provides the orientation for action (either destructive or constructive), while anger, as an approach emotion, constitutes the fuel and motivates to act in any way.

To sum up, hatred plays a pivotal role in shaping people's attitudes and actual political behaviors in all stages of the cycle of conflicts and their resolution. The political reactions that are driven by hatred are a direct reflection of its emotional goals, which in turn are driven by its one-sided and to some extent even deterministic core appraisal themes. The beliefs that the outgroup is evil by nature and that it is not capable of going through positive change drastically limit the possibilities in terms of adaptive political reactions. Avenues involving gestures, apologies, or even simple negotiation do not make sense when such an emotional sentiment is at its peak.

Yet, as will be demonstrated in more detail in Chapter 10, intergroup hatred can be reduced and its reduction holds wide potential in terms of conflict resolution processes. Most importantly, any attempt to reduce levels of hatred should concentrate on undermining its unique characteristics and specifically those characteristics that distinguish it from other (less-destructive) negative emotions. Accordingly, these attempts should emphasize the humanness and heterogeneity of the outgroup as well as the ability of individuals and groups to change their characteristics, moral values, positions, and behaviors (Halperin, Russell, Trzesniewski, et al., 2011). In addition, strategies of *perspective taking* can be used to increase understanding regarding the motives and goals of the adversary. I propose that such long-term processes, disseminated through education channels, cultural products, and other societal mechanisms, will alter the behavioral manifestations of reactive negative emotions, which are themselves natural and legitimate responses to offensive acts or provocations.

4

INTERGROUP ANGER IN INTRACTABLE CONFLICTS— NOT EXACTLY WHAT YOU HAD IN MIND . . .

The previous chapter demonstrated the destructive nature of intergroup hatred but at the same time also suggested that luckily, hatred is not the most dominant emotion even in the most violent types of intergroup conflicts. In many ways, my view of intergroup anger is exactly the mirror image of that; namely, I would like to suggest that intergroup anger is the most dominant emotional reaction in conflict situations (or at least one of the two most dominant ones, together with fear) but also to challenge the common view of anger as a purely destructive emotion. In other words, I would like to put forward the counterintuitive argument that although anger is felt very frequently and at high intensity among the majority of the citizens who are living in violent conflict zones, and although it may lead some of them to support or even take active part in aggressive actions, anger does not always yield such destructive consequences and under certain circumstances may even serve as a catalyst rather than as a barrier to peace.

The first part of that argument, according to which anger is a dominant emotion in conflict situations, is probably more intuitive and easier to support. Think for example of the emotional experiences of US citizens who watched the 9/11 terrorist attacks on the World Trade Center on television almost as they were happening. Surely rage (among other emotions) was central to their experience. Similarly, it is not hard to imagine the rapid heartbeats, the sweaty palms and faces, and the extreme anger felt by Jewish Israelis who sat down to a Passover dinner on March 27, 2002, and suddenly heard about the destructive suicide bombing at the Park Hotel in Netanya, which resulted in the deaths of 30 citizens dressed in festive holiday clothing.

Although they may seem extreme, these events are typical to intractable conflicts. Such conflicts often are marked by belligerent actions, provocative statements, and mutual insults. Notable examples, in addition to the ones mentioned before, are the killing of innocent civilians, the kidnapping of citizens or soldiers, offensive maneuvers of military forces, and extremely threatening speeches by political and religious leaders. In most such cases, members of conflicting societies or groups view the conflict through a unidimensional, biased lens and therefore perceive the other group's actions as unjust, unfair, and incompatible with acceptable norms (White, 1968). Often these perceptions are amplified by blindness to the previous wrongdoings of one's own group, which are considered by the opponents to be the reasons for their current actions or statements (Halperin & Bar-Tal, 2007).

These biased evaluations of the events are exactly the core appraisal themes usually associated with anger, and hence it is not surprising that intergroup anger is a pivotal emotion in every conflict. To many people who are personally involved in such occurrences, anger seems like the ideal and most adaptive emotional reaction to outgroup provocations. It reflects a kind of reaction that provides people with the energy to fight back, but at the same time does not close the door to potential improvements and positive changes (in the way that hatred and contempt do).

Accordingly, in the vicious cycle of perceived provocation that leads to violence, and that in turn leads to additional provocation, anger can be viewed as the emotional fuel that keeps the engine of that cycle working at full capacity. According to this view, people who feel angry blame the outgroup for unjust or immoral behavior, believe that urgent action is needed to correct the perceived wrongdoing, and may believe that their group is capable of initiating such corrective action (Mackie, Devos, & Smith, 2000). This often leads to a confrontational tendency (Berkowitz, 1993; Mackie et al., 2000) to hit, kill, or attack the anger-evoking target (Roseman, Wiest, & Swartz, 1994).

All of the above nicely correspond with the age-old conviction in social psychology that anger is the most powerful emotional determinant of aggressive behavior (e.g., Berkowitz, 1993). Accordingly, there is evidence that flare-ups of public anger automatically lead to widespread support for vengeful aggression (Huddy, Feldman, & Cassese, 2007; Skitka, Bauman, Aramovich, & Morgan, 2006). In reality, however, despite the prevalence of ingroup anger following an outgroup provocation, public opinion often is divided about the best response (Maoz & McCauley, 2008). Some people clearly advocate an aggressive response, but others counsel self-restraint, and a third group sometimes translates its anger even into support for conciliatory actions. These differences in opinion lead us to the second argument of the current chapter, according to which under certain conditions, and when accompanied by certain psychological mechanisms, anger functions as a peace catalyst instead of a barrier (Halperin, 2008; Halperin, Russell, Dweck, & Gross, 2011; Reifen Tagar, Halperin, & Federico, 2011).

The suggested provocative approach emphasizes the need to take risks and initiate meaningful actions to promote peace. In that regard it sees anger as the opposite of apathy rather than the opposite of empathy (which probably could be attributed to hatred). In the current chapter, this relatively new approach will be supported by empirical findings, demonstrating that under certain circumstances, anger increases support for constructive actions such as long-term reconciliation (Fischer & Roseman, 2007), support for risk taking in peace negotiations (e.g., compromises) (Halperin, 2011b; Reifen Tagar, Halperin, & Federico, 2011), and willingness to take part in normative (but not nonnormative) collective action aimed at status-quo change (Tausch et al., 2011; Van-Zomeren, Spears, Fischer, & Leach, 2004).

One possible explanation for these surprising results, extensively discussed in the chapter, is that contrary to hatred or even contempt targeted at a complete object, anger is targeted at a specific *action*. As such, anger leads to the aspiration to correct the perceived unjust action but not necessarily to harm the acting group. In the context of an intractable conflict, such an emotional goal, when accompanied by feelings of relative strength (which also characterize anger), potentially can lead to more risk-seeking behavior, support for collective action, and support for close communication with the outgroup. The chapter will focus on the specific psychological and contextual mechanisms that potentially can boost that process and turn intergroup anger from a barrier to peace into a peace catalyst. These mechanisms also provide some preliminary indications for the way anger can be channeled toward constructive goals during conflicts.

Hence, in the following chapter first I will provide definitions and basic concepts concerning anger followed by a brief overview of its implications on conflicts and negotiations on an interpersonal level. Then the concept of intergroup anger will be introduced, and its close connection with various forms of aggression or support for such aggression in an intergroup context will be discussed. In the third part of the current chapter, a rationalization for the potentially constructive role of anger in intractable conflicts will be presented followed by supporting empirical evidence both from the literature of collective action as well as from the findings on emotions in conflict resolution. Finally, some preliminary thoughts about anger regulation in intractable conflicts will be presented.

The Nature of Anger—The Anger Story

The arguments regarding the pivotal and ambiguous role of anger in conflicts and conflict resolution processes rely on a fundamental understanding regarding the unique nature and components of anger. In general terms, anger is seen as a negative feeling evoked in response to a perceived negative event that frustrates a desired goal and is intensified when the event is caused by a specific agent and viewed as unjust or illegitimate (Lazarus, 1991). For many years anger has been thought of as one of the most powerful engines of human behavior. On the one hand, it is perceived as the main motivator of aggressive behavior (Berkowitz, 1993), but at the same time, it is seen as the energetic force behind many other, more constructive behaviors. As such, it is not surprising to find some quotes that glorify anger and its consequences (e.g., Martin Luther King: "When I am angry I can pray well and preach well"), while others see it as one of the biggest enemies of rational thinking and humanistic behavior (e.g., Mahatma Gandy: "Anger and intolerance are the enemies of correct understanding").

But why does anger constitute such a powerful motivator for action? First and foremost, anger is a powerful motivator because it is experienced as a reaction to events that do not leave people apathetic, the kind of events that make you want to do something; otherwise you will feel weak, humiliated, or frustrated. On a very simple level, people feel angry when they feel that someone has done something wrong to them. In other words, anger appears mostly as a reaction to events in which the actions of others are perceived to be unjust, unfair, or contrary to acceptable societal norms (Averill, 1982). This is very well demonstrated in appraisal theories of emotion (Roseman, 1984; Scherer, Schorr, & Johnstone, 2001). Anger is oftentimes viewed as a moral emotion, which is associated not just with attributions of harm but also with the concepts of blame and responsibility (Alicke, 2000; Goldberg, Lerner, & Tetlock, 1999; Tetlock et al., 2007). The responsibility attribution can further intensify anger experiences when the perceived unjust action is seen as intentional or even if it is seen as avoidable (Schlenker, 1997; Weiner, 1995). Finally, anger oftentimes is accompanied by a sense of high control over the situation and even with appraisals of self-efficacy. In essence, it involves appraisals of relative strength and high coping ability (Mackie et al., 2000).

The link between anger core appraisal themes (i.e., perceived unjust behavior, high power, and high control) and its resulting emotional goals and action tendencies is almost natural. When people feel that they have been mistreated and believe they have the power to change the situation, they naturally want to take action to do so. Accordingly, the emotional goal of anger has been defined as a desire to correct perceived wrongdoing, injustice, or unfairness (Fischer & Roseman, 2007; Halperin, 2008). Along the same lines, anger also has been shown to be an approach-related emotion, making people eager to act (Carver & Harmon-Jones, 2009; Davidson, Jackson, & Kalin, 2000; Harmon-Jones & Sigelman, 2001; Mackie et al., 2000). Consequently, anger results in higher energy expenditure, evidenced by greater autonomic arousal and behavioral activation (Levenson, Ekman, & Friesen, 1990). Moreover, driven by the appraisal of relative high strength, anger is linked to indiscriminate optimism about success (Fischhoff, Gonzalez, Lerner, & Small, 2005) and an increased willingness to engage in risky behavior (Lerner & Keltner, 2001; Rydell et al., 2008). Together, these characteristics usually lead to a tendency to attack the anger-evoking target (Frijda, 1986; Roseman, Wiest, & Swartz, 1994). Finally, anger may even lead at times, and under specific circumstances, to an increase in the willingness to incur costs to punish betrayal (de Quervain et al., 2004; O'Gorman, Wilson, & Miller, 2005).

But anger does not necessarily lead to aggression and, as suggested earlier, at times it can even promote constructive actions. I will explain this argument in detail later in the chapter, but for now I will provide some preliminary indications for it using the anger–hatred comparison as a backdrop. Most importantly, as extreme as it may be, anger is targeted at a very specific action committed by another person or group rather than to that person or group more generally. People who feel angry do not necessarily generalize from the one negative (and unjust and unfair) behavior of the anger-evoking person or group to this person's or group's innate characteristics. That is why we are angry at a certain behavior or at a certain person because of a certain behavior but we are not angry at a person as a whole or because of who she is.

To demonstrate this, in the study dealing with anger and hatred cognitive appraisals that has been described in Chapter 3, both anger and hatred were associated with blaming the outgroup for the conflict-related event and with appraising the outgroup's behavior as unpleasant, hurtful, and contrary to the in-group's interests and goals. Nevertheless, there was also a clear distinction between the appraisals associated with each of these emotional phenomena. The negative appraisals associated with anger focused solely on the unfairness of the outgroup's specific action, whereas the appraisals associated with hatred focused on the nature of the outgroup itself, suggesting that its actions were not aimed at achieving instrumental goals but stemmed from a malevolent disposition to hurt the ingroup. So we hate a person or group because of who they are, but we are angry at that person or group because of a specific action taken. Paradoxically, the mere fact that we are angry at a specific action means that we care about the anger target, or at the very least, we are highly engaged in a relationship with them. This is why, for example, many people find themselves angry at their kids, but not very often do parents feel hatred toward their kids (hopefully . . .). This is also why anger, very different from hatred, leaves hope for positive change. If someone who I care about (or am dependent upon) has done something wrong to me, but I do not think that it was driven by this person's innate negative characteristics, my actions potentially can lead that person to improve her behavior in the future.

This also directly implies that anger-associated emotional goals are again fundamentally different from those of hatred. Although anger, similar to hatred, oftentimes leads to aggression, the goals that drive that aggression are radically different in anger compared to hatred. While people dominated by hatred aggress to hurt, exclude, and sometimes even annihilate the hate target, aggression driven by anger is meant to improve the behavior of that target or correct the perceived wrongdoing. Empirical support for these differences were found in the study mentioned in Chapter 3 (Halperin, 2008, Study 3), in which I found that hatred was the only emotion associated with the goals of exclusion (removal of outgroup members from one's life) and annihilation of the outgroup. On the other hand, anger was associated with the goal of correction (improving the behavior of outgroup members). Thus, whereas anger causes people to take action to right a specific wrong, hatred reflects avoidance of any dealings with the outgroup based on having given up on the outgroup's capacity for change.

The findings regarding the response tendencies associated with hatred and anger were even more complex. Naturally, participants who reported relatively high levels of hatred were more likely to support "denying Palestinians' basic political and social rights" as well as "physical and violent actions toward the Palestinians". Interestingly, although anger also was associated with support for "physical and violent actions toward the Palestinians", it was associated as well with "support for educational channels to create perceptual change among Palestinians". This latter response was obviously a more constructive approach to changing the Palestinians' (perceived) unjust behavior.

It seems, based on my research and previous studies by other researchers, that people who feel angry have one key emotional goal—that is, they wish to correct and redirect behavior that they perceive to have been unfair and unjustified. As mentioned, researchers have documented that when people feel angry, they believe they have (or at least deserve to have) high control over the situation, are more willing to take risks, and believe they have the ability to create beneficial changes (Lerner & Keltner, 2001; Lerner et al., 2003; Mackie et al., 2000). These components of anger correspond with the psychological preconditions required to support aggression (see Halperin, 2010). Yet observations of the response tendencies associated with anger as well as findings from a study by Fischer and Roseman (2007) have indicated that while some angry people choose aggression and destruction as responses, others choose more constructive responses, such as education and efforts to achieve reconciliation. I will discuss this assumption as well as its relevant boundary conditions later in the chapter.

Implications of Anger on the Interpersonal Level: Conflicts, Negotiations, and Beyond

As an approach emotion that calls for an immediate action, anger has huge implications on various aspects of interpersonal relations. Focusing mainly on the realm of conflicts and negotiations, it would not be too far-reaching to state that anger is the central emotional player in motivating people to escalate interpersonal disputes, oftentimes leading them to threaten or even to implement aggressive actions. Additionally, due to its affective structure and motivational implications, anger has an effect on the way people process information during interpersonal interactions, decision making, and dilemmas. Finally, anger also influences the process and the results of interpersonal conflicts and negotiations due to its communicative power, which conveys both a message of relative strength as well as a message regarding the willingness to use that strength to promote one's own goals.

Fischer and Roseman (2007) have argued that anger belongs to an attack emotion family, suggesting that in the context of interpersonal conflicts, its main role is to motivate attack toward the other person to gain a better outcome or to correct a perceived wrongdoing (see also Roseman, Copeland, & Fischer, 2003; Roseman, Wiest, & Swartz, 1994). As such, it provides an approach tendency, focuses people on the target of that tendency, equips them with the needed (perceived) strength to implement that tendency, and even energizes them to face counterattacks or defensiveness. Accordingly, most research to date has dealt with anger's negative consequences for the object of one's anger, as is the case with physical, verbal, or social forms of aggression (e.g., Archer, 2000; Archer & Coyne, 2005; Berkowitz, 1993; Bushman, 2002).

At the same time, even when considered aggressive and at times violent, anger's motivational tendencies are perceived to be short-term and are aimed to change the target of the anger, as shown in studies dealing with marital conflicts (see e.g., Gottman & Levenson, 2002). In contexts of long-term relationships, side by side with its negative implications, anger also conveys two important messages: (1) it suggests that in spite of the current conflict, the relationship in general and the person who is the target of the anger are considered important; and (2) it suggests a strong belief in the ability of the target of the anger to improve. As such, studies have revealed positive effects of anger on interpersonal relations especially when it is expressed or regulated in less offensive and more constructive ways (Fischer & Roseman, 2007). Averill (1983) even has taken this notion one step further by suggesting that another possible behavior that may follow from a situation in which someone is angry at someone else is to reconcile with the person at whom one is angry (see also Fehr, Baldwin, Collins, Patterson, & Benditt, 1999; Kuppens, Van Mechelen, & Meulders, 2004). Kuppens et al. (2004) have found that such a pattern is more probable when the target of anger is of low status and when she is liked. Other studies have shown that such constructive implications of anger are possible only in very certain forms of anger communication, for example, by just telling someone you are angry, by expressing criticism verbally, by temporarily ignoring someone, or by merely venting your anger against inanimate objects (e.g., Archer & Coyne, 2005; Averill, 1982; Kuppens et al., 2004; Leary, Twenge, & Quinlivan, 2006; Wolf & Foshee, 2003).

But the effects of anger on interpersonal conflicts and negotiations are not limited to its role in motivating the behavior of the person who experiences it. According to functional approaches to emotions, anger, like other emotions, also can play a communicative role by providing information that others may use as input for their decisions and by eliciting affective reactions (Van Kleef, De Dreu, & Manstead, 2010). In line with its core appraisals, anger indicates that an unfair or even immoral event occurred involving a clear perpetrator (Frijda, 1986; Lazarus, 1991; for a review see Scherer, Schorr, & Johnstone, 2001). Additionally, anger communicates a motivation to attack or, at the very least, approach in a less violent way (Fischer, & Roseman, 2007; Frijda, 1986). Accordingly, studies have shown that angry bargainers are seen as tough negotiators who do not want to give in (e.g., Clark, Pataki, & Carver, 1996; Sinaceur & Tiedens, 2006, Van Kleef, De Dreu, & Manstead, 2004a, 2004b). In a competitive context, anger experience and expression have been found to promote successful confrontation and competition (Van Kleef, De Dreu, & Manstead, 2004b; Van Kleef, De Dreu, Pietroni, & Manstead, 2006). At the same time, these very same expressive utilities may lead to escalation of the conflict when the target of the anger feels unjustly accused of the difficulties in resolving the conflict and when it perceives the other side's limits (i.e., a minimal acceptable offer) as too high and inflexible. In these cases anger expressions can lead to an escalation of conflicts and to failed negotiations due to a simple process of reciprocal anger; namely, anger expressed by one side is answered with increased anger by the other side and so forth. The experience of (reciprocal) anger has been shown to elicit competitiveness (Forgas, 1998; Pillutla & Murnighan, 1996) and a desire for retaliation (Van Kleef & Côté, 2007), which typically is reflected in lower offers.

An interesting complexity that potentially determines the implications of anger communication in conflicts and negotiations is the relative strength of the involved parties. As already noted, anger usually is associated with experienced and perceived relative strength. This raises the question of anger communication's influence in asymmetrical conflicts and negotiations. Lelieveld, Van Dijk, Van Beest, and Van Kleef (2012) recently have tested that question and found that anger evoked a complementary emotion (fear) in targets when reported by a high-power bargainer but evoked a reciprocal emotion (anger) when reported by a low-power bargainer. In other words, while anger expressed by a high power negotiator was perceived as an indication of threat, anger communicated by a low power negotiator was perceived as inappropriate and as an unfulfilled wish for power by the weaker side and was therefore responded to by increased anger. Interestingly, in the latter case, this reciprocal anger led participants to offer less to low-power counterparts who reported anger. On the other hand, it helped high-power negotiators to morally justify their positions around the negotiation table. Thus, while anger expressed by the high-power side can serve their goals, the same anger communicated by low-power negotiators may backfire under some circumstances (see also Van Dijk, Van Kleef, Steinel, & Van Beest, 2008). This leaves low-power negotiators in a so-called catch-22 as anger may be their main emotional vehicle in their attempt to express their frustration and to motivate the counterpart to acknowledge their unjust position.

Interestingly, a recent line of research that is based on an instrumental approach to emotions and emotion regulation suggests that people have relatively accurate intuitions (or lay theories) regarding the instrumental benefits embedded in anger when they pursue confrontational goals. As described, the experience of anger has been found to promote successful confrontation and competition (Van Kleef, De Dreu, & Manstead, 2004a; Van Kleef, De Dreu, Pietroni, & Manstead, 2006). What is even more interesting, and to some extent even counterintuitive, are recent findings demonstrating that people are more motivated to increase their anger when expecting to confront another (e.g., Tamir & Ford, 2012a; Tamir, Mitchell, & Gross, 2008). However, anger is unlikely to offer instrumental benefits when one pursues nonconfrontational goals, and hence people were motivated to decrease rather than increase anger in collaborative settings. In the former case of pursuing confrontational goals, consistent with an instrumental account of emotion regulation, preferences for anger were mediated by the belief that anger would benefit performance: participants who were led to confront another were more likely to expect anger to be useful to them, which in turn, led to greater preferences for anger. This is somewhat counterintuitive because we tend to view emotions as driven mainly by hedonic considerations, namely, by the motivation to feel good (i.e., experience positive emotions) while avoiding negative feelings. The example of people motivated to experience anger in confrontational settings suggests that human motivations are more complex than just hedonic ones and also that people are quite impressive lay psychologists when it comes to their assessment of anger's role in different contexts.

Finally, anger can influence the dynamic of interpersonal conflicts and negotiations through its effect on the way people process information and make decisions in these contexts. Individually experienced anger has been established as leading people to use more heuristic and less systematic patterns of information processing and decision making. For example, Bodenhausen, Sheppard, and Kramer (1994) have shown that angry people were influenced by heuristic cues more than sad or neutral people (see also Forgas, 1995; Lerner, Goldberg, & Tetlock, 1998; Russell, 2003; Tiedens & Linton, 2001) and more recent work (Fischhoff, Gonzalez, Lerner, & Small, 2005; Lerner & Keltner, 2001) has demonstrated that angry people choose riskier strategies and objectives. In search for the underlying mechanisms of these anger effects, some scholars suggest that they can be attributed to the very high arousal associated with anger experiences (Berkowitz, 1990; Feldman, 1995; Henry, 1986; Walley & Weiden, 1973), while others suggest that it is because of the appraisals of certainty that anger entails (Tiedens & Linton, 2001).

From Interpersonal Anger to Group-Based Anger

When Eliot Smith, Diane Mackie, and their colleagues started developing the *intergroup emotions theory* (IET; e.g., Smith, 1993; Mackie et al., 2000), they chose group-based anger as one of their first selections to be studied in that framework. According to Rydell et al. (2008), one of the possible reasons is that "intergroup anger is repeatedly and reliably predictive of intergroup behavioral intentions directed both at the outgroup and ingroup" (p. 1142). In other words, intergroup anger is so extensively studied within the framework of IET because it has dramatic implications on intergroup relations in general and on the dynamic of intergroup conflicts more specifically.

The main role played by intergroup anger in intergroup conflicts is to direct the blame for perceived wrongdoing on a specific target and then to mobilize support for concrete actions (aggressive or not) vis-à-vis that target. In most cases the target will be the outgroup or its leaders, and then outgroup-directed anger predicts the desire to confront the outgroup in various ways (Mackie et al., 2000; Maitner, Mackie, & Smith, 2007; Smith, Seger, & Mackie, 2007). But intergroup anger also can be targeted at the ingroup, and in these cases it predicts the desire to have the ingroup right a perceived wrong (Maitner et al., 2007; Van-Zomeren, Spears, Fisher, & Leach, 2004). Altogether, regardless of its specific target, anger is well-known as a particularly potent motivator for group-based actions that potentially lead to relevant implications for ingroup–outgroup dynamics.

What follows is that intergroup anger is such an important target for research in social and political psychology due to its high impact on intergroup conflicts. But anger is not just an extremely powerful emotion in intergroup settings; it is also one of the most common or dominant of all emotions taking part in such conflicts. This dominancy of anger is not driven only by the nature of the events embedded within such conflicts but also, I would argue, by the way it serves the psychological needs of the involved groups.

In their *Needs-Based Model of Reconciliation* Shnabel and Nadler (2008) have suggested that experiencing and expressing intergroup anger nicely addresses the empowerment needs of the disadvantaged but not of the advantaged group in asymmetrical conflicts. I believe that in addition to serving empowerment needs, intergroup anger also serves other needs that are relevant to all involved parties (either advantaged or disadvantaged). Most importantly, as a moral emotion that is based on a strong sense of justness, it helps society members to hold on tightly to two of the most important themes of what Bar-Tal (2013) defines as the *ethos of conflict*—the belief in the ingroup's justness of goals and the belief in the positive image of the group. The experience of anger, which inherently involves the accusation of the outgroup of immoral actions and attributing the blame for the continuation of the conflict on the outgroup (both reflect the core appraisals of anger), serves as a glue that helps society members preserve some of their core identity themes, even in the face of seemingly immoral actions conducted by ingroup members.

To illustrate, think of an Israeli citizen who repeatedly faces Palestinians' and human rights organizations' accusations regarding Israel's immoral occupation as well as regarding its blame for the continuation of the Israeli-Palestinian conflict. That person is probably in search of a way to justify Israel's actions, which she sees as self-defense. Any Palestinian violent action or even a tough position in an ongoing negotiation may then lead to the experience of intergroup anger. The anger experience in turn, when amplified and ruminated personally and publicly, helps to serve personal and group needs of perceived justness and morality.

It is very clear, therefore, that anger plays an important role in intergroup conflicts. The question then is what exactly that role is or what the direct implications are of intergroup anger on people's attitudes and behaviors in political, intractable conflicts. As already suggested regarding other emotions (see, e.g., Chapter 3 on hatred), intergroup anger's implications on people's attitudes and behaviors are a direct by-product of anger's associated emotional goals coupled with some of its main characteristics. To simplify the description of these implications, I will start by focusing on the destructive implications of anger targeted at the outgroup and will then discuss potentially constructive implications of anger when targeted both at the ingroup and at the outgroup.

Destructive Implications of Anger Targeted at the Outgroup in Intergroup Conflict

As in research on the interpersonal level, the most direct implication of anger on the group level is the support of or willingness to initiate confrontational action against the outgroup. This was found in lab studies dealing with moderate, non-violent cases of intergroup conflicts (e.g., Mackie et al., 2000; Yzerbyt, Dumont, Wigboldus, & Gordin, 2003), but more interestingly, it has been revealed in the context of real-world violent conflicts (Halperin, 2011b; Huddy, Feldman, & Cassese, 2007; Lerner et al., 2003). The most important finding of these studies has been the ability to isolate anger's effects on support for confrontation from the effects of other negative emotions, like fear, hatred, and contempt. In line with a discrete emotion approach, these studies show that it is not mere negative emotional reaction that motivates people to attack the outgroup but a discrete group-based reaction of anger that yields such an effect.

To understand the process through which intergroup anger increases the support for military actions, it is important to point at some of its relevant psychological mechanisms. For example, researchers have found a direct association between intergroup anger and attribution of blame to the outgroup (Halperin, 2010; Small, Lerner, & Fischhoff, 2006). Other studies have found that individuals who feel group-based anger appraise future military attack as less risky (Lerner & Keltner, 2001) and forecast more positive consequences of such attack (Huddy, Feldman, & Cassese, 2007).

The immediate implications of these studies have been revealed in studies conducted in the US following the 9/11 attacks that found that priming of anger (but not fear or a neutral emotion) in response to the 9/11 attacks led to higher support for an American militant response in Iraq and elsewhere (Cheung-Blunden & Blunden, 2008; Lerner, Gonzalez, Small, & Fischhoff, 2003; Skitka, Bauman, Aramovich, & Morgan, 2006). Additionally, the central role of group-based anger in motivating conflict eruption and aggression yielded further support in recent studies conducted within the context of Serbian-Albanian relations in Serbia (Study 1) and Serbian-Bosniak intergroup relations in Bosnia (Study 2) (Spanovic, Lickel, Denson, & Petrovic, 2010). Interestingly, Spanovic et al. (2010) have been able to examine the role of anger in motivating intergroup aggression in the context of two different violent civil conflicts, one of which is largely resolved (Bosnia) and another that is still unfolding (Kosovo). In all of these studies (and others—e.g., Halperin, 2011b), anger's effects were compared to those of other negative emotions (on the group level), and in all of them, intergroup anger was found to be the single best predictor of support for violence.

The mirror image of intergroup anger's association with support for political aggression is its role in processes of negotiation and intergroup reconciliation. In later parts of this chapter, I will present a rather complex and nuanced view of that role, but for now I would like to focus on the more traditional approach. According to that approach, when group members believe that the outgroup has hurt them intentionally and unjustly, they lack the motivation to negotiate and reconcile with that group and instead search for ways to retaliate and at times even withdraw from the negotiation process. This was recently documented in regard to two different stages of intergroup reconciliation. First, in a study conducted by Sabucedo and colleagues (Sabucedo, Durán, Alzate, & Rodríguez, 2011) in the context of the ongoing conflict in the Basque country, intergroup anger was found to be the most powerful negative emotion associated with opposition to the Spanish government's declaration of its intention to negotiate a peace process with the terrorist group Euskadi Ta Askatasuna (ETA). Additionally, in the postconflict context in Northern Ireland, Tania Tam et al. (2007) have identified intergroup anger as an obstacle to intergroup forgiveness, which is considered particularly important in intergroup reconciliation processes. Altogether, these studies point at intergroup anger not just as an engine for intergroup aggression but also as a significant emotional barrier to negotiation, compromise, reconciliation, and forgiveness.

Finally, very similar to the role it plays on the interpersonal level, intergroup anger also can have implications for intergroup relations due to its expressive or communicative utilities. The study of emotional communication within an intergroup context is only at its first baby steps, but some indications regarding the implication of anger communication in that context already exist. One such study found that when powerful (but not powerless) groups communicate intergroup anger, outside observers tend to perceive the powerful group's aggressive tendencies as more justified (Kamans, Van-Zomeren, Gordijn, & Postmes, 2014).

How Can Intergroup Anger Play a Constructive Role in Intractable Conflicts?

One of intractable conflicts' main characteristics is that they are deemed irresolvable (Bar-Tal, 1998, 2007; Kriesberg, 1993, 1998). This general and consensual perception of the conflict's irresolvability drives feelings of hopelessness, a detrimental emotional state within the context of such conflicts. Over time, the feeling of hopelessness, experienced due to recurring and failed attempts to resolve the conflict, seeps into the national narrative (Bar-Tal, 2007), becoming an integral part of the psychological infrastructure of the conflict. This serves to remove responsibility for the disastrous situation and uphold positive perceptions of the ingroup as always aspiring for peace (Bar-Tal, 2000). When society members don't believe that peace is possible and when they don't see their group as holding any responsibility for such freezing, a sense of apathy rules the collective emotional climate. That apathy enables people to quietly accept the repeated damage caused by the continuation of the conflict and the violence without even entertaining the possibility of actively engaging in action to stop it.

In a nutshell, as already hinted at the outset of the chapter, my argument regarding the potentially constructive role of intergroup anger in intractable conflicts is that in these contexts, anger constitutes the opposite of apathy rather than the other side of empathy. Anger can be seen as the cure for apathetic societies mainly because it drives people to action. Oftentimes this action takes the form of joining or at the very least actively supporting militant forces. But as recently suggested by Cohen-Chen, Van-Zomeren, and Halperin (2015), collective action in an intractable conflict also can play a pivotal role in mobilizing societies and leaders alike to promote peace. *Collective action* typically is defined as any action that individuals engage in on the group's behalf to achieve group goals (Van-Zomeren & Iyer, 2009; Wright, Taylor, & Moghaddam, 1990). Indeed, individuals' engagements in collective action can change political agendas and instill values as well as empower members of nations and societies (e.g., the Civil Rights Movement). Put differently, collective action reflects people's capacity to create social change as a group, taking control of their destiny and pursuing the betterment of their position on a large scale.

But people's participation in collective action is very rare, and it is even less common when it comes to 'pro-peace' collective action in societies involved in intractable conflicts. This is mainly the result of the apathetic emotional climate already mentioned but also because 'pro-peace' activists many times are required to act and argue against their group's national narrative, which makes them seem to be deviants and to pay a high social price for it.

In line with this view of intergroup anger, according to the classic collective action literature, anger is considered the most powerful emotional engine of participation in such actions (Leach, Iyer, & Pedersen, 2006; Van-Zomeren et al., 2004; Van-Zomeren, Leach, & Spears, 2012). Van-Zomeren et al. (2004) have defined intergroup anger as the emotions-focused pathway to collective action. According to their view, if an event is appraised as unfair, group-based anger should be likely. This anger should, in turn, explain group members' tendencies to take collective action to address their collective disadvantage. Additionally, anger is closely related to other central mechanisms leading to collective action, like group efficacy, which amplifies its energetic role in that process. In the context of intractable conflicts, anger can be targeted at one's own government, which does not do enough to promote peace, or otherwise to the international community, or even to the adversary group leaders in a call for their actions. Finally, recent research by Tausch et al. (2011) conducted in three different contexts has found that whereas more extreme emotions like contempt predicted nonnormative or radical collective action, intergroup anger was related strongly to normative action but overall unrelated or less strongly related to nonnormative action. These findings correspond with the view of anger as a motivator for change rather than a motivator for destruction and further emphasize its potential role in conflict resolution and peace processes. Conflict resolution and peace making on the one hand require public action to unfreeze apathy and stability but on the other hand require caution against extreme actions that may lead to the conflict's reescalation. It seems that oftentimes intergroup anger is capable of providing the needed energy in the required intensity.

But the constructive role of anger is not limited to its influence on people's tendency to be engaged in collective action. Even more interestingly, recent studies reveal that even anger targeted at the adversary group itself would, under some circumstances, have positive implications (Halperin, 2011b; Halperin, Russel, Dweck, et al., 2011; Reifen Tagar et al., 2011). This is mainly due to the fact that anger, as an approach emotion, is associated with a feeling of strength and can potentially lead to risk-seeking behavior, optimistic forecasting, and a true belief in the capability to correct the situation, all of which are important requirements of a successful peace process.

In further detail, one can explain the pluripotentiality of anger by seeing it as an approach emotion (Harmon-Jones, 2003) whose specific manifestations (i.e., constructive vs. destructive) may vary across individuals and circumstances. This argument relies upon the distinction between general emotional goals and more specific attributions and response tendencies (Roseman, 1984; Roseman, Wiest, & Swartz, 1994). In line with appraisal theories, individuals who feel anger toward the outgroup will appraise the outgroup's behavior as unjust, and if the ingroup's relative power is high, these angry individuals will develop a similar emotional goal—they will wish to correct the behavior of the outgroup. Yet appraisal theories do not make any strong claims about the specific attributions associated with anger. In other words, anger is targeted at specific actions taken by individuals or groups but does not necessarily imply any negative internal characteristics of these groups or individuals. Hence, 'angry' people may differ in the way they translate that general goal into specific response tendencies. While some angry individuals gravitate toward achieving the required improvement using aggressive means, others with similar levels of anger may channel the anger into more constructive solutions such as education, negotiation, and even compromise.

The intriguing question therefore is what exactly can make anger constructive in such a context, or in other words, what are these specific circumstances under which anger would have positive rather than negative implications for conflict resolution. Our studies in recent years point to at least two such conditions. First, anger would lead to constructive rather than destructive consequences when the anger-inducing stimulus is followed immediately by constructive and feasible ways of operation (Reifen Tagar et al., 2011). In an experimental design, conducted among American students in the context of the ongoing US-Syrian negotiations (Reifen Tagar et al., 2011, Study 2), participants were subjected to an emotion manipulation raising either group anger, group hope, or no specific emotion and then were exposed to an offer to renew negotiations followed by items assessing their appraisals, emotions, and policy preferences. Results showed that American students who were led to experience anger toward the Syrians (compared to a control group) were supportive of policies that fall under the definitions of "positive risk taking" and "nonviolent policies" toward the Syrians in the context of intergroup conflict. These results suggest that at least in the context of efforts to deescalate a conflict, such as political negotiations, anger also is associated with support for nonviolent behaviors that appear to address the emotional goal of correcting the wrongdoing that produced the anger in the first place. Angry participants want to do something, and if the most available option to act happens to be constructive, they will probably take that route.

But that pattern probably does not apply to all people, as demonstrated in two additional studies that we have recently performed, this time in the context of Israeli-Palestinian negotiations (Halperin, Russel, Dweck, et al., 2011). In these studies we hypothesized that the specific results of an anger induction would be contingent on the presence or absence of long-term hatred sentiment. Because hatred, by its nature, leaves no opening for any constructive change, we believed that someone with a strong hatred sentiment would not be able to consider constructive action as a viable means to correct the perceived wrongdoing behind the anger and would consequently support aggression. However, we proposed the opposite would be true in the absence of a hatred sentiment. We found this to be true across two studies within the context of the Israeli-Palestinian conflict. The first showed that inducing Israeli Jews' anger toward Palestinians several weeks before the Annapolis peace summit increased support for making compromises in upcoming negotiations among those with low levels of hatred but decreased support for compromises among those with high levels of hatred. These findings were replicated in the next study, conducted just days before the summit.

Finally, another recent study revealed some positive effects of anger on intergroup relations, mainly due to its communicative utilities. In three experimental studies, de Vos, Van-Zomeren, and Postmes (2013) have shown that communicating group-based anger toward the outgroup can evoke empathy and thus reduce intergroup conflict. The authors have suggested that this process is driven by anger's communication ability to stress the value of maintaining a positive long-term intergroup relationship, thereby increasing understanding for the situation. Even more importantly, these positive implications occur only when anger is communicated purely, without contempt, which when it intervenes, totally diminishes these positive effects of anger communication.

Altogether, these studies show that intergroup anger is a much more nuanced phenomenon than what we usually tend to think. On the one hand, these findings lend credence to the argument that anger motivates *active, approach-oriented* steps towards the goal of addressing the wrongdoings that instigated the anger (e.g., Harmon-Jones & Sigelman, 2001). However, they also suggest that the substantive consequences of these psychological attributes of anger may depend in important ways on situational features of the conflict in question as well as on the unique characteristics of those experiencing the anger. So while an angered individual will be eager to act in some fashion and will perceive herself as more capable of acting effectively, the resulting action tendency will depend on various moderating factors.

Some Preliminary Thoughts on Anger Regulation

The complex findings regarding anger's role in intractable conflicts raise some important questions regarding the ways intergroup anger can be regulated to promote peace. In some ways they even question and challenge the need to downregulate anger. It might be the case that under certain circumstances, anger should be up- rather than downregulated if peace is desirable. Furthermore, rather than focusing on increasing or decreasing the magnitude of anger, attempts should be made to qualitatively regulate intergroup anger (see Halperin, Sharvit, et al., 2011), namely, to turn anger from being destructive to being constructive by changing the relevant context rather than by changing anger intensity.

Emotion regulation processes will be discussed in detail in Chapter 10, but on the simplest level, empirical evidence suggests that effective emotion regulation strategies, like cognitive reappraisal, can be used to decrease the experience of anger in the context of interpersonal relationships (e.g., Mauss, Cook, et al., 2007). More importantly, there is evidence suggesting that reappraisal decreases the anger experience over time (Ray, Wilhelm, & Gross, 2008) and might even decrease aggression (Barlett & Anderson, 2011). Finally, some of our recent studies have suggested that the traditional strategies of cognitive reappraisal also can be effective in regulating group-based anger and that this reduction in anger through reappraisal can in turn lead to changes in people's political reactions to dramatic political events (Halperin, Porat, Tamir, et al., 2013; Halperin, Pliskin, et al., 2014). This leaves us with the hope that anger can be either downregulated or alternatively channeled to be constructive.

5

SOCIETIES UNDER THREAT—COLLECTIVE FEAR AND ANGST AS BARRIERS AND (AT TIMES) CATALYSTS OF PEACE

For people who are living in societies involved in intractable conflicts, fear is much more than a powerful emotion. For most of them it is the dominant state of mind, governing the way they feel, think, act, and make important decisions in their lives. This is definitely true for members of disadvantaged or suppressed groups, but also, paradoxically, it is relevant to members of powerful groups as well. Returning to the theoretical framework I presented in the second chapter of the book, while I see anger as the most common emotional reaction in intractable conflicts, fear should be seen as the most powerful and most dominant long-term emotional sentiment. In other words, while anger is a pivotal engine driving people to (mainly aggressive) actions, fear takes over people's daily lives, their thoughts, dreams, concerns, and even their interpersonal relations.

Oftentimes I realize that this continuous and chronic feeling of personal and collective fear is difficult or even impossible for outsiders to understand. People who are not living in such contexts cannot really imagine how it feels to be concerned constantly about mere personal survival, that of your close ones, and sometimes even your entire society. When I try to explain this to some of my American friends and colleagues, I ask them to think about their personal as well as collective feelings in the few days or weeks following the 9/11 terror attacks and then to try to think of societies that experience these feelings continuously for dozens of years rather than just for a few days or weeks.

To anchor this view in empirical data, more than a decade ago Daniel Bar-Tal conducted an extensive analysis of Jewish Israeli society's collective emotional orientation of fear (Bar-Tal, 2001). He found that already in the early 1960s, fear was one of the dominant emotions expressed by Jews in Israel (Antonovsky & Arian, 1972). Years later, but still at the height of the intractable conflict, Israeli polls began to gauge Jewish Israelis' fears. Unsurprisingly, they showed that Israeli Jews felt threatened and expressed worries about the security situation. In 1970 and 1971 about 70 percent of Israeli Jews expressed high to very high security worries; in 1972 it was about 60 percent, and following the 1973 war, this rose to 90 percent (Stone, 1982). This trend has continued to rise as the Israeli–Palestinian conflict is still flaring. Surveys conducted in the last decade have found that the large majority of Israelis believe that ongoing terror attacks might cause a strategic and even existential threat to the State of Israel (Ben-Dor, Canetti-Nisim, & Halperin, 2007). In 2000, 85.5 percent of Israelis expressed this feeling, 86.6 percent in 2002, and 83 percent in 2006 (Ben-Dor, Canetti-Nisim, & Halperin, 2007). In addition, 80 percent of the Israeli public in 2006 expressed high levels of fear of a nuclear attack by Iran that would destroy the State of Israel (*Peace Index*, 2006). Finally, in late 2000, approximately 80 percent of the respondents expressed concern that they or a member of their family might become the victim of a terrorist attack, reaching a level of 92 percent in 2002 (Ben Meir & Bagno-Moldavsky, 2010).

These chronic and powerful feelings of fear are well grounded in people's reality. In many ways fear is inherent to the fundamental definition and conceptualization of intractable conflicts, and therefore the contexts of these conflicts define fear as the dominant emotional implication (see Bar-Tal & Halperin, 2013). When people are part of active violent conflict that lasts for more than two generations and revolves around core issues of their lives that are (perceived to be) constantly under threat, and when they feel that the conflict itself is threatening their very existence and that they may either win or be annihilated, they have good reasons to feel fear. Given that all these characteristics are embedded in the way we conceptualize intractable conflicts, the chronic experience of fear seems like the natural emotional reaction to such a context. Some would even claim that not feeling fear in these contexts should be considered an irrational or maladaptive response.

In further detail, people living in intractable conflicts often experience chronic fear at least on two levels, which feed and amplify each other. On the personal level, in intractable conflicts people often fear for their lives or for the lives of their close ones. Most intractable conflicts are not the kind that are handled by professional militant forces and take place in isolated areas, far away from civilian populations. Alternatively, civil populations in most cases take an active part in the fighting, either as bystanders or as members of the militant forces themselves. The implication is that each and every citizen in the involved societies has experienced personal harm, the loss of a close friend or a family member, or an immediate danger or threat to her life. Even in the rare cases of people who have not directly witnessed such horrors, they are exposed to them indirectly through the popular media and today also through social media. Therefore, feelings of fear are not abstract or vague, rather they are part of people's daily experience.

The repeated exposure to violence and its associated chronic sentiment of fear has grave consequences, including heightened anxiety, a reduced sense of safety, some clinical symptoms like those of PTSD, and a subjective sense of insecurity (e.g., Canetti, Halperin, Sharvit, & Hobfoll, 2009; Galea et al., 2002; Lavi & Solomon, 2005). Recent studies have begun exploring the effects of such traumatic exposure in conflict on threat perceptions and citizens' resultant political positions (Bonanno & Jost, 2006; Canetti, Halperin, Sharvit, et al., 2009). These repeated exposures to intergroup violence affect people's levels of fear not just directly but also indirectly through their influence on people's ability to regulate or cope with threatening events (this will be further discussed in Chapter 10).

On the collective level, people are exposed on a daily basis either to actual threats coming from adversarial leaders to destroy and annihilate their society or to repeated warnings of their own leaders suggesting that such danger is real and possible. These messages repeatedly are supported by concrete actions taken by the rival groups aiming to destroy their enemies. The immediate implication of these processes is that people feel that the mere existence of their group on a physical and symbolic way is at stake (e.g., Bar-Tal, 2001; Halperin, Bar-Tal, Nets-Zehngut, & Almog, 2008; Halperin, Porat, & Wohl, 2013; Wohl & Branscombe, 2008; Wohl, Squires, & Caouette, 2012).

These feelings of collective fear and angst are closely related to the societal beliefs of collective victimhood (Bar-Tal, Chernyak-Hai, Schori, & Gundar, 2009; Noor, Brown, & Prentice, 2008; Páez & Liu, 2011; Vollhardt, 2012a, 2013) and to its extreme configuration—siege mentality (Bar-Tal & Antebi, 1992). Collective victimhood denotes "a mindset shared by group members that results from a perceived intentional harm with severe and lasting consequences inflicted on a collective by another group or groups, a harm that is viewed as undeserved, unjust, and immoral and one that the group was not able to prevent" (Bar-Tal, Chernyak-Hai, Schori, & Gundar, 2009, p. 238). Recently, Schori-Eyal, Klar, Roccas, and McNeill (2015) have pointed to a more chronic and diffuse configuration of collective victimhood defined as *perpetual ingroup victimhood orientation* (PIVO), namely, the belief that one's group is a constant victim persecuted by different enemies (Schori-Eyal, Klar, Roccas, & McNeill, 2015). Examples of historical collective victimhood can be found among Poles (e.g., Jasiñska-Kania, 2007), Serbs (Volkan, 1997), and Jews (e.g., Bar-Tal & Antebi, 1992; Schori-Eyal, Klar, Roccas, & McNeill, 2015; Wohl & Branscombe, 2008) to name just a few. Based on an experience of considerable harm embedded in a society's collective memory as severe and unjust (Páez & Liu, 2011; Wertsch, 2002), it is a sense of unforgotten shared trauma and unjustified wrongdoing by others (e.g., Armenians carry in their collective memory the traumatic event of the genocide performed during World War I; see Wertsch, 2009). These memories and beliefs are powerful engines of contemporary fear reactions as they over-sensitize individuals and collectives to various threat cues.

But fear is so dominant in intractable conflicts not only because of the threatening reality or because of people's repeated exposure to violence and to other potentially harming stimuli. It is also dominant because of its functionality for individuals and collectives living in these situations. If an existential danger exists even to some degree, then the main purpose of individuals and collectives alike is to prepare themselves for the worst-case scenario. Fear, both on the individual and collective levels, adequately serves this goal. It prevents individuals and societies from taking risks and motivates them to take precautions. Accordingly, society members may become over-sensitized to cues that signal danger and exist in a state of constant readiness to defend themselves (Jarymowicz & Bar-Tal, 2006).

Oftentimes fear reactions, especially in situations of real conflict, may appear over-responsive (Nesse, 1990, 2005). According to evolutionary accounts of fear (e.g., Haselton & Ketelaar, 2006); however, rather than indicating irrationality, hypersensitivity to particular environmental cues, such as the ones common in intractable conflicts, may be due to error management (Haselton & Buss, 2000; Haselton & Nettle, 2006). Intractable conflicts are classic examples in which, according to the consensual view, the costs of expressing a defensive reaction are smaller than the consequences of failing to do so. When the future of the society in its entirely is at stake, it pays to err on the side of making false positive errors rather than false negative errors, even if this increases overall error rates (Bouskila & Blumstein, 1992; Haselton & Nettle, 2006; Nesse, 1990). As will be suggested later in this chapter, although this evolutionary approach can be functional when the conflict is at its peak, over-sensitivity to fear cues serves as a dramatic barrier to peace making when the context changes and when peace opportunities appear (Bar-Tal & Halperin, 2011; Halperin, 2011b).

The main goal of the current chapter is to illuminate the role played by personal and collective fear in determining people's attitudes and behaviors in the context of intractable conflicts. For that purpose the chapter begins with an in-depth discussion of the nature of fear on the personal and collective level, followed by a brief review of closely related constructs such as threat perception, collective angst, and terror management theory. Then, I turn to discuss fear's implications both generally and particularly in the context of intractable conflicts. Most importantly in that discussion I will highlight the less intuitive, more constructive implications fear can have on conflict resolution and peace making. Finally, some preliminary thoughts on fear regulation will be introduced.

In a nutshell, the main message of this chapter is that, given the dominancy of collective fear and its close associations both with the actual context and with the dominant ideologies in intractable conflicts, downregulating collective fear is an almost impossible mission. Alternatively, as will be demonstrated in the following paragraphs, collective fear sentiment can be channeled to promote peace rather than aggression. In that way, instead of trying to change people's core mental or emotional tendencies, we utilize these tendencies to promote peace.

The Nature of Fear

Prior to the discussion regarding the destructive as well as the potentially constructive implications of fear in intractable conflicts, a deeper understanding regarding the nature and the components of fear is required. Fear as a primary aversive emotion arises in situations of threat and danger to the organism (the person) and/or her environment (the society) and enables an adaptive response (Gray, 1989; Öhman, 1993; Plutchik, 1980; Rachman, 1978). It constitutes combined physiological and psychological reactions with the objective to maximize the probability of surviving in dangerous situations.

On the simplest level, fear is the affective reaction to situations in which people experience threat or danger, and they do not believe that they have the capabilities or skills to adaptively deal with that threat. It can be thought of as the emotional trade-off between the perceived threat and the perceived coping capabilities of each individual or society. There is no fear without perceived external or internal threat, but there is also no fear if one believes that she is fully protected from that threat. Think for example of the difference between encountering a tiger face-to-face on a jungle trip to Africa versus encountering the same tiger in a zoo on a weekend vacation with your kids. The threat in both cases is identical, while the coping capabilities are fundamentally different. So fear depends on levels of perceived threat coupled with perceived coping capabilities.

This rather intuitive account of fear is in line with findings of studies based on appraisal theories of emotions (Scherer, 1984; Roseman, 1984). According to their view, fear is associated with an appraisal of low strength and low control over the situation as well as with appraisals of surprise, low certainty, and high threat (Roseman, 1984). Importantly, different from other negative emotions that are targeted at a specific object (e.g., contempt or hatred) or at a specific action (e.g., anger), fear is targeted at a concrete, threatening situation. That is also the reason why people can be afraid of natural disasters, car accidents, and concrete actions of people or groups that elicit threat. The direct implication is that fear-associated emotional goals and action tendencies also are aimed at changing the concrete situation rather than impacting a certain object or group. As will be elaborated later in the chapter, this has dramatic implications on the way fear translates into political motivations in the context of intractable conflicts.

But fear is not always the result of a conscious appraisal process. In his seminal work, Robert Zajonc (1980) has demonstrated that at least in some cases, fear automatically arises and does not require any deliberate cognitive process. Consistent with that proposition, research has in fact revealed that unconscious presentation of facial stimuli is sufficient to evoke different aspects of fear and other emotional responses (e.g., Esteves, Dimberg, & Öhman, 1994; Murphy, & Zajonc, 1993; Whalen et al., 1998). It is possible, hence, to differentiate between two mechanisms of fear arousal: one via automatic and unconscious reactions and the other via conscious appraisal of the situation as threatening and dangerous (Goleman, 1995; LeDoux, 1996; Oatley & Jenkins, 1996; Zajonc, 1980). The former is based on automatic stimulus-reaction relations and the latter on cognitive evaluation.

Both automatic and cognitive-based fear experiences have the potential to elicit a cycle of fear in which each fear experience feeds into another. In these cases, information about threatening, or potentially threatening, stimuli is acquired through different modes of learning and then stored or coded as an emotional schema that in turn influences the appraisal of additional concrete situations (Lazarus, 1991). The stored information coupled with the fear schema provides a basis for further generalization of the fear situation to additional situations and conditions. This means that fear may operate irrationally and destructively because defensive reactions are not only evoked as a result of cues that directly imply threat and danger but also by conditioned stimuli that are nonthreatening in nature (LeDoux, 1996; Mowrer, 1960; Öhman, 1993; Rachman, 1978). Once fear on a high level is evoked, it limits the activation of other mechanisms of regulation and stalls consideration of various alternatives because of its egocentric and maladaptive patterns of reactions to situations that require creative and novel solutions for coping.

More specifically, according to Buss (2005), when the situation detector signals that the individual has entered the situation *possible stalking and ambush*, the following kinds of mental programs are entrained or modified: (a) there are shifts in perception and attention; (b) goals and motivational weightings change; (c) safety becomes a far higher priority; (d) information-gathering programs are redirected; (e) conceptual frames shift with the automatic imposition of categories such as *dangerous* or *safe*; (f) memory processes are directed to new retrieval tasks; and (g) specialized learning systems are activated as the large literature on fear conditioning indicates (e.g., LeDoux, 1995; Mineka & Cook, 1993; Pitman & Orr, 1995). In addition to these cognitive processes, various aspects of the physiological system change, and new behavioral decision rules are activated.

The behavioral implications of fear are related closely to its nature and appraisals. The core motivation of those who experience fear is to reduce the perceived threat and increase coping capabilities, namely, to change the balance of the two core appraisals of fear. As such, fear usually is associated with avoidance tendencies as well as with motivations to avoid taking risks and to create a safer environment (Frijda, Kuipers, & ter Schure, 1989; Halperin, Bar-Tal, Nets-Zehngut, & Drori, 2008). Importantly, that means that people who are dominated by fear are not directly motivated to hurt anyone. Instead, all of their energy and efforts are channeled into the core mission of threat reduction. Accordingly, the most common behavioral reaction to fear will be a defensive one. Only when defense and protection are not efficient may fear lead to aggressive acts against the perceived source of threat (Bandura & Walters, 1959). Thus, when in fear, human beings sometimes tend to cope by initiating a fight, even when there is little to be achieved by doing so (Blanchard & Blanchard, 1984; Eibl-Eibesfeldt & Sutterlin, 1990; Jarymowicz, 2002; Lazarus, 1991; Plutchik, 1990). Yet, as will be demonstrated later in the chapter, fight in these cases is first and foremost aimed at reducing or removing the perceived threat rather than at hurting the threatening object.

Collective (Perceived) Threat and Collective Fear

As noted threat perception constitutes the central cognitive building block of fear experience. The nature of that perceived threat, I would argue, also determines the kind of experienced fear. Perceived threat in cases of intergroup conflict may be defined as the cognitive evaluation of the extent to which outgroup members interfere with the achievement of individual or group goals (Canetti, Halperin, Sharvit, et al., 2009). Existing literature in social and political psychology emphasizes the multidimensional nature of perceived threat and points to the different natures of the various sources of threat.

Integrated threat theory (Stephan & Renfro, 2002; Stephan & Stephan 2000) specifically distinguishes between realistic and symbolic threats. *Realistic threat* refers mainly to potential harm to tangible or concrete objects (e.g., money, land, and human life), whereas *symbolic threat* includes various potential threats to relatively abstract aspects of the collective, such as threats to the ingroup's identity, value system, belief system, or worldview (e.g., language, religion, and morality) (Duckitt, 2001). In addition to this typology, scholars have pointed to the different nature and implications of personal versus collective or national threat in the context of intergroup conflicts and terrorism (Huddy, Feldman, Capelos, & Provost, 2002).

Extensive research has demonstrated that threatened individuals and groups commonly cope with threat by adopting hostile attitudes toward outgroups, attempting to reduce their relative power and supporting actions that potentially harm outgroup members in various ways (e.g., Duckitt & Fisher, 2003; Maddux, Galinsky, Cuddy, & Polifroni, 2008; Morrison & Ybarra, 2008; Pettigrew, 2003; Stephan & Renfro, 2002). More specifically, threat perceptions are consistently among the most important predictors of intergroup prejudice and hostility (e.g., Esses, Dovidio, Jackson, & Armstrong, 2001), exclusionism (Canetti-Nisim, Ariely, & Halperin, 2008; Canetti, Halperin, Sharvit, et al., 2009), political intolerance (Halperin et al., 2009; Quillian, 1995), political xenophobia (Canetti-Nisim & Pedahzur, 2003; Halperin, Canetti-Nisim, & Pedahzur, 2007), militarism (Bonanno & Jost, 2006), and support for aggressive national security policy (Huddy et al., 2005). Interestingly, with only a few exceptions (e.g., Halperin et al., 2009, 2011b), studies of threat perception do not refer to its most immediate emotional implication—fear. Nevertheless, from these studies, we definitely can infer both the nature and implications of fear in intergroup contexts.

Given that perceived threat is the most powerful predictor of fear, the literature on perceived threat in the intergroup context provides some important indications on the way fear appears in the social sphere. In the most simple way, and as already mentioned earlier in this chapter, people can experience personal fear within an intergroup context. When personal values (symbolic threat) or physical security (realistic threat) of individuals are at stake due to disagreements embedded within the intergroup conflict, then individual fear emerges. For example, if people's homes are located within the fighting zone, they feel personal fear. Given that its antecedents are rooted within the intergroup rivalry, such fear is not totally isolated from the group context. Yet it is more personal than group-based or collective fear because the target of (perceived) threat is the individual herself.

Very similar to other emotions, people also can experience group-based fear, namely, fear in the name of other members of their social group (Mackie, Devos, & Smith, 2000; Smith, 1993). In these cases, it can be an independent individual that is personally threatened by actions committed by others (outgroup members or not) that will elicit group-based fear. Such group-based fear is experienced by individuals who are not threatened either personally or collectively. For example, people can feel fear for other group members who have experienced a tsunami in a distant location or for other group members who have been victims of a terror attack committed by outgroup members. Importantly, given the local nature of these threats, they do not necessarily pose danger to the group in its entirety, so no collective fear actually is involved. In addition, when it comes to group-based fear, the source of threat does not have to be rooted in the dynamics of an intergroup conflict (e.g., the tsunami case), although it can be (e.g., the terror example).

But intergroup or collective fear can be experienced due to threats that go far beyond the individual level, and that is another reason why fear is experienced so frequently on the group or collective level. Parallel to the typology offered by the integrated threat theory, individuals can feel collective fear when their group as a collective is threatened on symbolic or realistic levels (Halperin et al., 2008; Jarymowicz & Bar-Tal, 2006). People, as part of groups, can feel fear for the physical existence of their group as well as fear that core interests or values of their group will be damaged. For example, one of the most dominant expressions of fear among Jews in Israel in recent years is the fear of what is sometimes defined as the *demographic threat*, namely, the fear of losing Jewish dominancy and majority among the Israeli population. This fear reflects serious concerns regarding the nature and culture of Israeli society and has huge implications on people's emotions and political decision making (Gayer, Landman, Halperin, & Bar-Tal, 2009).

Interestingly, while in some of these cases fear for the group in general already includes fear in the individual within that group, in other cases, fear for the group can be felt in isolation from individual concerns. Think for example of the collective fear about the very existence of Israel that is threatened by the Iranian atomic bomb as felt by an Israeli Jew who lives in the US. These feelings of fear, while not totally isolated from individual concerns (one can argue that Israel is the 'insurance' for all Jewish people worldwide), actually represent a more generalized experience of fear for the group itself rather than fear for the individual as part of the group.

A prototypical example for such a collective experience recently was defined by Wohl and Branscombe (2009) as collective angst. Angst involves the experience of anguish and dread at the thought of potential nonbeing or loss of personal existence (May, 1958). *Collective angst*, a future-oriented form of collective fear and anxiety, occurs when the future vitality of one's social group is believed to be under threat (e.g., Wohl & Branscombe, 2009; Wohl, Branscombe, & Reysen, 2010). Different from more traditional forms of collective fear in which specific aspects of the group's values and resources are threatened, collective angst is experienced when people feel that the possibility that their group will not survive becomes realistic.

In some ways, feelings of collective angst represent the collective equivalent of the notion of *mortality salience* originating in the well-established *terror-management theory* (TMT; e.g., Greenberg, Solomon, & Pyszczynski, 1997). TMT posits that all humans are predisposed biologically to want to continue living and at the same time are smart enough to realize that they are going to die and that it could happen at virtually any time for a wide variety of reasons. According to the theory, people are protected from the potential for anxiety that results from their awareness of the inevitability of death by an anxiety-buffering system consisting of their cultural worldviews and their self-esteem (for a recent review of TMT, see Kesebir & Pyszczynski, 2012). Both death anxiety on the individual level and an anxiety of the annihilation of the entire group are prominent in the context of violent conflicts (Pyszczynski et al., 2012).

Very similar to their view regarding their own lives, people also understand that social and ethnic groups can at some point stop existing. Looking at the history of human nature, this has happened to sports teams but also to ethnic groups. A growing body of research demonstrates that collective angst is elicited by diverse threats to the future vitality of one's group, such as the possibility that it will be significantly transformed from its present state, indistinct from salient outgroups or utterly nonexistent (see Wohl, Squires, & Caouette, 2012). One of the most common collective angst-inducing threats is the potential loss of ingroup distinctiveness (Wohl & Branscombe, 2008). For example, among French Canadians, collective angst is associated with the belief that French Canadian culture may, in subsequent generations, become indistinguishable from the surrounding English Canadian culture (Wohl, Giguère, Branscombe, & McVicar, 2011). People also may worry about their group's eventual disappearance due to physical threats such as environmental damage, disease, and interactions with hostile outgroups (Wohl & Branscombe, 2008, 2009). For example, historical and contemporary outgroup hostilities—the extreme case being genocide (e.g., the Rwandan genocide and the Armenian genocide initiated by the Ottoman Empire)—can be tremendously damaging to the perceived permanence of the victimized group (see Wohl et al., 2010). Within Israel, an omnipresent extinction threat is Iran. Specifically, Iranian leaders have called explicitly for the destruction of the Jewish state and have threatened the use of force to do so (Zisser, 2010). For this reason Israelis are concerned particularly with the possibility of a nuclear Iran to the extent that when this threat is salient, collective angst emerges (Halperin, Porat, & Wohl, 2013).

In real life, however, all these kinds of concerns coalesce to create a blend of perceived threat, fear, and anxiety on both individual and collective levels and in regard to the current situation of the group as well as to its future existence. The simultaneous and wide sharing of these emotions in societies involved in intractable conflicts turn these societies into entities that are characterized by fear orientation or by an emotional climate of fear (Bar-Tal, 2001; Brubaker & Laitin, 1998; Horowitz, 2001; Jarymowicz & Bar-Tal, 2006; Lake & Rothchild, 1996, 1998; Petersen, 2002; White, 1984). These experiences become embedded in the collective memory, are incorporated into cultural products, and are then disseminated via society's channels of communication (Bar-Tal, 2003; Páez, Basabe, & Gonzáles, 1997; Ross, 1995). In addition, fear also spreads via social contagion as group members empathetically absorb the fearful reaction of their co-patriots, and through behavioral patterns, as group members influence each other via modeling and imitation in various public situations.

Very similar to personal fear, collective fear cuts deeply into the psychic fabric of society members because fear is functional and adaptive for the group's goals. It prepares society members for better coping with the stressful situation on a very primary level (Collins, 1975; Lazarus & Folkman, 1984). This preparation is achieved in a number of ways (see Bar-Tal, 2013): (a) it mobilizes constant readiness for potential threats against unwished-for surprises; (b) it directs attention and sensitizes society to cues that signal danger and to information that implies threat; (c) it increases affiliation, solidarity, and cohesiveness among society members in view of the threat to individuals and to society at large; and (d) it mobilizes society members to act on behalf of the society, to cope with the threat, to act against the enemy, and to defend the country and society. At the same time, as will be demonstrated in the following section, it also constitutes a dramatic barrier to peace opportunities and conflict resolution processes.

Fear and Angst's Implications on Intractable Conflicts—The Defensive-Aggressive Aspect

Societies and individuals who experience high levels of threat, fear, and angst will take all possible preventive steps to protect themselves. This assumption is based on the understanding of these emotions' core emotional goals, namely, threat reduction at any price. This also means that this goal is prioritized over all other relevant goals and that information-processing patterns and judgment- and decision-making processes are influenced heavily by that motivation. Accordingly, although these feelings may be functional in protecting groups and individuals in violent situations, the immediate consequences of collective fear and angst in any attempt to resolve intractable conflicts are destructive.

According to Jarymowicz and Bar-Tal (2006), when the rival societies embark on the road to peace, the collective fear orientation plays a hindering role in this process. Being deeply entrenched in the psyche of society members, as well as in the culture, it inhibits the evolvement of the hope for peace by spontaneously and automatically flooding the consciousness. Society members then have difficulty freeing themselves from the domination of fear to construct hope for peace.

More specifically, as already mentioned in earlier parts of this chapter, dozens of studies in various societies and contexts show that experiences of threat and fear increase conservatism, prejudice, ethnocentrism, and intolerance (Duckitt & Fisher, 2003; Feldman & Stenner, 1997; Jost, Glaser, Kruglanski, & Sulloway, 2003b; Stephan & Stephan, 2000). Relevant to the negotiation process itself, fear is associated with a number of processes that usually hinder successful negotiation, such as strengthening of ingroup ties, cognitive freezing, risk-aversive political tendencies, and suppression of any creative ideas aimed at resolving the conflict. All of these implications will be discussed at length in the paragraphs to follow.

On the societal level, fear leads societies that are involved in intractable conflicts to stick to certain beliefs about the causes of threat, about the conflict, about the adversary, and about ways of coping with the dangers (Bar-Tal, 2013). Like individuals who are dominated by fear, societies in such situations have difficulties entertaining alternative ideas, solutions, or courses of action. As Maslow (1963) has noted, "[A]ll those psychological and social factors that increase fear cut impulse to know" (p. 124). This line of behaviors in the context of threat has also been demonstrated in experimental social psychological research (e.g., Corneille, Yzerbyt, Rogier, & Boudin, 2001; Mackie, Devos, & Smith, 2000; Rothgerber, 1997). In one such line of studies, Corneille et al. (2001) have examined the way threat and fear influence people's assessment of a group of voters. In two studies they showed that participants inferred relatively more extreme and more homogeneous attitudes among the members of a threatening group. As appraisals of extremity and homogeneity have dramatic influence on intergroup relations, this study nicely demonstrates the potential role of group-based fear in escalating intergroup conflicts.

But how exactly does fear amplify these attribution errors and other intergroup biases? One potentially relevant avenue is through biased and distorted information gathering and through processing of information regarding new opportunities for peace. In a recent study conducted among Jews in the context of the Israeli-Palestinian conflict, we examined the way fear was associated with the motivation to search for new information that could potentially shed new light on ways to promote the Israeli-Palestinian peace process (Cohen-Chen, Halperin, Porat, & Bar-Tal, 2014). Using a new computerized information processing simulator, assessing people's actual information search and processing patterns rather than self-report motivation to do so, we found that when faced with an opportunity for peace, long-term fear was associated with acquiring information that was biased toward rejecting the opportunity. Interestingly, fear was not associated with the amount of general information participants wanted to acquire but only with the kind of information they chose to absorb. Assuming that fear is the dominant sentiment among societies involved in intractable conflicts, one can only imagine the amount of potentially 'peace-promoting' information people miss or actively ignore in the course of the conflict.

These findings are in line with the findings of another recent study conducted by Gadarian and Albertson (2014) focusing on the role of fear and anxiety in shaping people's attitudes toward immigrants and immigration. In that study the authors sought to bridge the gap between two seemingly contradicting approaches to the role of fear and anxiety in information processing. On the one hand, studies, mainly in the tradition of the *affective intelligence theory* (e.g., Marcus & MacKuen, 1993; Marcus, Neuman, & MacKuen, 2000), suggest that anxiety motivates citizens to learn and pay more attention to news coverage. On the other hand, literature in psychology demonstrates that anxiety is associated with a tendency to pay closer attention to threatening information only. Integrating these two views, and in line with the findings of Cohen-Chen, Halperin, Porat, et al. (2014) the authors have found that anxious individuals exhibit biased information processing; they read, remember, and agree with threatening information on issues related to immigrants and immigration. Taken together, these studies show that people dominated by fear and anxiety are indeed more motivated than others to acquire new information, but they are open only to information focusing on the source of threat, which can be detrimental from the perspective of conflict resolution and peace processes.

Furthermore, according to Bar-Tal (2013), on a high level the collective fear orientation tends to limit society members' perspective by binding the present to past experiences related to the conflict and by building expectations for the future exclusively on the basis of the past. This seriously hinders the disassociation from the past needed to allow creative thinking about new alternatives that may resolve the conflict peacefully. These assumptions were supported by a study we have recently conducted (Halperin, Bar-Tal, Nets-Zehngut, & Drori, 2008) in which we found that individuals who tend to remember the very negative experiences of the Jewish people in the distant past tend also to experience fear about the future of the Jewish collective. This finding is of special importance because it shows that remembering traumatic Jewish experiences that took place in the remote past affects collective fear related to the Israeli-Arab conflict. Moreover, the results indicated that remembering the negative experiences in the Jewish distant past highly influences the results of interethnic meetings. For those who greatly remembered these experiences, meeting with an Arab triggered feelings of collective fear. This suggests that for them, an Arab serves as a generalized negative stimulus that elicits memories of past persecution. On the other hand, it appears that for people who are less flooded by traumatic national memories, interaction with the 'other' actually has managed to reduce perception of collective threat and feelings of fear. In line with these results, other studies show that fear is associated with great mistrust and delegitimization of the adversary (Bar-Tal, 2001; Maoz, & McCauley, 2008). Thus it may lead to stabilization of the violent context and escalation of the conflict and may prevent the launching of a peace-making process.

As an emotion meant to prepare individuals to protect or defend themselves, fear has complex relationships with people's support for aggression and militant actions. On the one hand, when possible, fear leads people to try and avoid new threats and risk taking and, thus, may be an obstacle to people's support for militant actions. In line with that idea, recent studies show that people who are dominated by fear prefer defensive over aggressive policies and pessimistically estimate the consequences of initiated militant actions. Therefore, fear may discourage group members from engaging in violent military activities due to elevated risk estimates and avoidance tendencies. Along these lines, several studies have found that fear reactions among Americans to the 9/11 terror attacks increased estimated risks of terrorism and war (Huddy et al., 2007; Lerner et al., 2003) and decreased support for military activities and the war in Iraq (Huddy et al., 2007). As such, under some circumstances fear may restrain military actions and aggression to prevent further threats (Huddy, Feldman, & Cassese, 2007; Lerner, Gonzalez, Small, & Fischhoff, 2003; Skitka, Bauman, Aramovich, & Morgan, 2006).

On the other hand, under different circumstances collective fear is a major cause of violence. This is mainly when levels of threat are very high, when a defensive solution seems less plausible, and when the fear experience is mixed with other emotions like hatred, contempt, and humiliation (see, e.g., Halperin et al., 2009). Fight is a habituated course of fear reaction based on past experience, and thus, a society again fixates on coping with threat in a conflictive way without trying new avenues of behavior that can break the cycle of violence (see Brubaker & Laitin, 1998; Lake & Rothchild, 1998; Petersen, 2002). The complexity of the fear–aggression relationship is demonstrated best in the study of Spanovic et al. (2010), already mentioned in Chapter 4. In that study, conducted in Serbia and Republika Srpska, the authors have found that fear of the outgroup was related to increased motivation for aggression in the context of an ongoing conflict but was related negatively to aggression in the context of a conflict that had been resolved. The authors explained this duality by the fact that, in the midst of mutual violence, aggression is perceived to be the ultimate threat reduction tool, whereas in a postconflict era, it is perceived as an unnecessary risk that potentially can bring about the reescalation of violent conflict.

Relatedly, studies in the tradition of terror management theory provide an excellent example of people's political and behavioral reactions to a situation of extreme threat to their lives when they feel that nothing constructive really can be done to reduce that threat (because death is inevitable). Experiments conducted in the recent decade or so (see Hirschberger & Pyszczynski, 2011, for a review) have shown that when Americans were primed with the possibility of death (i.e., mortality salience), their support for American military actions in Iraq increased (Landau et al., 2004). Very similar manipulations led Israelis to support a preemptive strike against Iran and the Hezbollah in Lebanon (Hirschberger, Pyszczynski, & Ein-Dor, 2009); led conservative Americans to support extreme military tactics to fight terrorism (Pyszczynski et al., 2006); led right-wing Israelis to support violent resistance against policies that threaten their worldview (Hirschberger & Ein-Dor, 2006); and led Iranians to increase their support for suicide bombing as a tactic to fight American imperialism (Pyszczynski et al., 2006).

Studies on collective angst have not yet tested its association with militant and aggressive tendencies, yet they provide some indications of the fact that such an association actually may exist. In general, according to Wohl, Hornsey, and Bennett (2012), collective angst functions to stimulate actions aimed at protecting the future vitality of the ingroup. Outside the context of intractable conflicts, Wohl et al. (2010) have demonstrated that the experience of collective angst among Jews elicited a desire to pursue ingroup strengthening behaviors, such as showing support for Jewish organizations and marrying a Jewish partner. In another set of studies, Jetten and Wohl (2012) have found that heightened collective angst among English participants led to greater opposition to immigration in England.

Although threats embedded within the context of intractable conflicts do not always imply an existential (personal or collective) threat, some of them definitely include an aspect of mortality salience. Thus, fear, on its most extreme levels, feeds the continuation of the intractable conflict, creating a vicious cycle of fear and violence. But this is not the only contribution fear may have to the continuation of these conflicts. It is well established today that it also plays a key role as a barrier to the resolution of conflicts when peace opportunities are on the table. Given fear's inhibitory nature and the avoidance tendencies associated with it, it is only natural that most conflict resolution scholars see fear as an extremely powerful barrier to peace (e.g., Bar-Tal, 2001).

Studies conducted in the context of the Basque conflict (Sabucedo et al., 2011) pointed at fear as one of the most powerful negative emotion associated with opposition to negotiation between ETA and the Spanish government. Other studies I have conducted in the midst of peace negotiations between Israelis and Palestinians revealed a slightly more complex picture (Halperin, 2011b). According to the results of these studies, fear was found to be the only emotional antecedent fostering opposition to taking risks during negotiations. This factor can be a crucial obstacle to any progress toward peace, which inherently requires mutual risk taking. In addition, fear reduced the support for making territorial compromises that might lead to security problems. However, it should be noted that although 'fearful' individuals do oppose compromises that may increase future risks, they do not oppose other types of compromise (e.g., symbolic ones). In line with these findings, we have found recently that collective angst elicited by an outside source (i.e., Iran) decreased Israeli's willingness to negotiate with Hamas on issues related to prisoner bargaining deals (Halperin, Porat, & Wohl, 2013, Study 1). Since the issue of the negotiation with Hamas potentially involves future risks (i.e., released Palestinian prisoners will go back to terrorism), these findings are congruent with the previous ones presented.

Fear and Angst's Implications on Intractable Conflicts—The Constructive Aspect

With all these observations it should be noted that because fear is associated with the emotional goal of reducing the threat (Halperin, 2008), the primary goal of fearful individuals (and societies) is to protect themselves and avoid threats and dangers rather than to hurt the source of the threat, namely, the outgroup. This is highly meaningful because it suggests that even when fear leads people to aggression or to opposition to compromises, such acts are meant only to ensure safety rather than to achieve other goals like revenge or dominancy. What follows is that if security and safety are guaranteed in other ways, aggression will no longer be the preferred option. To take this argument one step further, according to this logic, if conciliatory and peaceful actions can promote safety and reduce threat, they will probably be the preferred reaction for those dominated by fear (see, e.g., see Maoz & McCauley, 2009).

Thus, similar to anger, under the right circumstances, collective fear or angst can potentially promote the resolution of intractable conflicts. For example, in a set of three studies Gayer et al. (2009) have found that exposure to fear eliciting information about losses inherent in the continuation of the Israeli-Palestinian conflict induced higher willingness to acquire new information about possible solutions to the conflict, higher willingness to reevaluate current positions about it, and more support for compromises than the exposure to neutral information or to hope-eliciting information about possible gains derived from the peace agreement. The three studies by Gayer et al. (2009) were conducted in the framework of the debate within Jewish-Israeli society regarding the so-called demographic threat and the need to make compromises leading to the classic *two state solution* to cope with such a threat. Accordingly, this is a classic case in which political compromise is framed as a threat reduction tool and therefore is accepted as an ultimate cure for the threat.

Another interesting example of a very similar process was found in Study 2 of our research on collective angst and political compromise that was mentioned previously (Halperin, Porat, & Wohl, 2013). That study showed that in the context of negotiations with the Palestinian Authority—perceived inability to contend with the Iranian nuclear threat led to greater willingness to negotiate and compromise. Specifically, the extinction threat resulted in a heightening of collective angst and a belief that negotiating with the Palestinian Authority would reduce the Iranian threat. The outcome of this chain was a greater willingness to compromise with the Palestinian Authority to achieve a peace agreement between Israelis and Palestinians (in the West Bank).

Finally, a series of TMT studies also provide some preliminary indication for the potentially constructive role of existential threats in peace processes. These studies show that under some conditions, the salience of personal death leads people to reduce their endorsement of intergroup violence and increases their support for diplomacy and compromise (see Hirschberger & Pyszczynski, 2011). Most of these studies that encourage nonviolent responses to mortality salience activate predisposed pro-social moral commitments that are incompatible with violence. For example, Rothschild, Abdollahi, and Pyszczynski (2009) have found that priming compassionate teachings from the Bible or the Qur'an led Americans and Iranians to respond to mortality salience with less support for violent confrontation between these two nations. Motyl et al. (2007) have found that activating a sense of shared humanity by exposing participants to pictures or stories illustrating near universal family activities eliminated or reversed the tendency of mortality salience to increase prejudice. Pyszczynski et al. (2012) have found that having participants imagine the shared global consequences of dramatic climate change had a similar effect, redirecting the effect of mortality salience away from support for violent confrontation toward promoting peaceful coexistence and negotiation, presumably because focusing on a shared threat implied that diverse groups must cooperate and work together to counter it.

Some Thoughts on Fear Regulation—Qualitative Versus Quantitative Change

Given the duality of fear, as demonstrated in the previous pages, two fundamentally different questions should be asked in terms of its regulation. These two questions resonate with the distinction we (Halperin, Sharvit, & Gross, 2011) have made between qualitative (e.g., flight instead of fight response tendencies to fear) to quantitative (e.g., lower levels of fear) emotion regulation strategies. On the qualitative side of the spectrum, the main challenge of those trying to promote conflict resolution is to create the conditions under which those who already experience fear will choose flight policies rather than fight policies. This can be done either by highlighting the potential risk of the fight options or, alternatively, by framing the constructive, peace-promoting avenue as the most effective tool for threat reduction. Importantly, these qualitative fear regulation strategies are not expected to decrease levels of fear but instead to channel the existing fear into more constructive tendencies. Interestingly, when people accept the notion of compromise as a threat reduction tool, levels of fear should be increased rather than decreased.

On the quantitative side, while numerous studies examine ways to down-regulate fear on the individual level (for a review of the four main strategies, see Hartley & Phelps, 2010), to the best of my knowledge no studies have sought to do so on the collective level. Nevertheless, the basic principles that should guide attempts to downregulate collective fear and angst are rather simple. In line with fear's core appraisal themes, such regulation should focus either on revaluation of the actual external threats or on reappraisal of existing coping potential. The former can be done by reconsidering either the outgroup's intentions (e.g., maybe they too just want to feel secure rather than to destroy us) or its offensive capabilities (e.g., maybe they are not as powerful as we thought).

Reappraisal of existing coping potential also can be achieved in various ways. Most directly, we (Halperin, Porat, & Wohl, 2013) manipulated levels of collective angst by emphasizing Israeli's resilience and defensive capabilities vis-à-vis the Iranian threat. More sophisticated ways to downregulate collective fear can rely on increasing beliefs in group efficacy in the present (Mummendey, Kessler, Klink, & Mielke, 1999) or by highlighting the group's perceived collective continuity (PCC), namely, the group's ability to meet great challenges and survive throughout the years (Sani et al., 2007). These two simple interventions can provide people with the sense of current as well as future confidence that is required to reduce levels of fear in the face of outside threats.

6

IS PEACE REALLY AN OPTION? HOPE, DESPAIR, AND THE PEACE PROCESS

(Inspired by a PhD Dissertation by Smadar Cohen-Chen)

Introduction

That is where peace begins—not just in the plans of leaders, but in the hearts of people. . . . You must create the change that you want to see. I know this is possible. . . . Your hopes must light the way forward. Look to a future in which Jews, Muslims and Christians can all live in peace and greater prosperity in this Holy Land. . . . There will be many voices that say this change is not possible. . . . Sometimes, the greatest miracle is recognizing that the world can change.

US President Barack Obama speech in Jerusalem, March 21, 2013

As can be seen from this quote, on his first visit to Israel as American president, Barack Obama chose to focus his speech on inducing hope for change and for a better future among Israelis and Palestinians. By doing so he reflected two major insights he had regarding the current state of that conflict: (1) hope for peace is critical to promote change and progress toward peace; and (2) both Israelis and Palestinians share deep feelings of despair, do not believe that such change is possible, and therefore are not willing to act to promote the seemingly impossible change. Although President Obama, who extensively used the hope card in his first presidential election campaign ("Yes, we can"), is known as a big fan of hope, most people probably would agree with the two insights mentioned.

And indeed, recent data of a public opinion survey conducted in June 2013 among both Israelis and Palestinians revealed that only 20 percent of Israelis and 27 percent of Palestinians said that they truly believe that negotiations will be renewed and that violence will end in the near future (Palestinian Center for Policy and Survey Research, 2013). Additionally, more than two-thirds on both sides said that they do not believe that a Palestinian state will be established in the years to come. This means that huge majorities on both sides express great despair and very low levels of optimism and hope for peace in the Middle East. Interestingly, these results were obtained in a relatively nonviolent period and in the midst of intensive efforts by US Secretary of State John Kerry to renew the peace process. Even more interestingly, the widely shared feelings of despair seem to contradict the support most Israelis and Palestinians express (in this survey and in others) for the most critical compromises needed to promote peace. So, as can be found in many other conflicts worldwide, in the Israeli-Palestinian conflict most people are ready to make compromises for peace, but they just do not believe that it actually will promote such peace.

More generally regarding intractable conflicts, very similar to the case of fear, the widely shared feeling of despair seems like the most appropriate, though not necessarily the most functional, response to the actual events. Just think of Israelis and Palestinians who, throughout their lives, repeatedly experience failed attempts to promote peace, which are followed by repeated rounds of escalating violence. In each such attempt, people's hopes increase, but each and every time, these attempts fail to fulfil these hopes. Then, despair and hopelessness take over the dominant collective emotional orientations, and from one round of (failed) negotiations to another, it becomes harder and harder to make people believe that change is possible.

And indeed, one of intractable conflicts' main characteristics is that they are deemed irresolvable (Bar-Tal, 1998, 2007; Kriesberg, 1993, 1998). This general and consensual perception of the conflict's irresolvability drives feelings of hopelessness, a detrimental emotional state in the context of such conflicts. Over time, the lack of hope, experienced due to recurring and failed attempts to resolve the conflict, seeps into the national narrative, becoming an integral part of the psychological infrastructure of the conflict (Bar-Tal, 2007; Cohen-Chen, Halperin, Crisp, et al., 2014; Halperin, Bar-Tal, Nets-Zehngut, & Almog, 2008). In many cases, this widely shared feeling of despair paralyzes the entire political and social system by making the public apathetic to the conflict in general and to new opportunities for its resolution in particular. These feelings of despair and lack of hope also serve to remove responsibility for the disastrous situation and uphold positive perceptions of the ingroup as always aspiring for peace (Bar-Tal, 2000).

But why is hope so important to promote peace? As I will argue in the following chapter, most dynamics usually considered part of a successful conflict resolution process (e.g., openness, risk taking, and creativeness) are driven, at least to some extent, by some flavor of hope and optimism about the possibility of resolving the conflict. According to the existing psychological literature, *hope* facilitates goal setting, planning, use of imagery, creativity, cognitive flexibility, mental exploration of novel situations, and even risk taking (Breznitz, 1986; Snyder, 1994). While hope involves expectation and aspiration for a positive goal, as well as positive feelings about the anticipated outcome (Staats & Stassen, 1985), people who feel despair do not expect any positive change and thus also are not motivated to make any effort to promote such change.

What follows is that within the stressful context of intractable conflicts, hope allows members of groups involved in violent conflicts to imagine a future that is different from the past and to come up with creative solutions to the disputes at the core of the conflict (Jarymowicz & Bar-Tal, 2006). The belief that peaceful resolution of the conflict is possible is an essential step toward taking risks and compromising. These assumptions are in line with the results of previous studies that have found positive associations between hope and openness to positive information about peace opportunities (Cohen-Chen, Halperin, Porat, et al., 2014), support for making compromises toward peace (Cohen-Chen, Halperin, et al., 2014), willingness to forgive the adversary (Moeschberger, Dixon, Niens, & Cairns, 2005), and support for providing humanitarian aid to innocent members of the rivalry group (Halperin & Gross, 2011).

Altogether these findings highlight the central role played by hope in mobilizing public opinion to support peace as well as the destructive nature of despair as a fundamental barrier for peace. Hence, the goal of this chapter will be to reveal the origins, nature, and consequences of hope and despair in intractable conflicts with the hope that such deeper understandings of these emotional phenomena will create the platform for interventions aimed at increasing levels of hope and suppressing feelings of despair. Accordingly, in what follows I first will describe the nature of hope with special emphasis on its unique characteristics, appraisals, and motivational aspects. I will then briefly introduce the nature and role of hope in the intergroup arena followed by a detailed overview of its implications on people's attitudes and behaviors in intractable conflicts. Finally, some studies examining the various ways to induce hope in intractable conflicts will be presented, followed by some preliminary ideas about additional strategies for downregulation of despair and upregulation of hope in these conflicts.

The Nature of Hope and Despair

Although hope has not been defined as a basic emotion (Averill, 1994), it has been indicated as one of the core emotions needed for human survival (Stotland, 1969), and more importantly for human and social progress, since it drives goal-directed behavior. As a complex, secondary emotion hope is based on higher cognitive processing, requiring mental representations of positively valued abstract future situations (Breznitz, 1986; Clore, Schwarz, & Conway, 1994). It can be seen as an emotional state that requires development of new *scripts*: programs about future actions. According to Fromm (1968), hope requires conviction about the not yet proven and courage to resist temptation to compromise one's view of present reality for a better future.

People vary in their basic orientations of hope and despair, and this influences different aspects of their lives. That is mainly because hope requires a general tendency toward positive evaluations, even when the existing situation is far from ideal. As such, hope is an emotion that depends on human, intellectual capacities of two types: (1) the ability to anticipate particular states of future reality and (2) the ability to create programs that lead to the achievement of such states (Jarymowicz, 2015). Altogether, these dispositional tendencies toward hope (vs. despair) highly influence people's daily experiences. For example, individuals with high hope orientation are cognitively engaged in more positive events and in fewer negative events than individuals with low hope orientation. The former also spend more time thinking and were found to perform better on cognitive tasks (Snyder et al., 1991). Moreover, individuals with high hope orientation have greater problem-solving ability and a rational problem-solving style, and use less wishful thinking, self-blame, and social withdrawal strategies in comparison to individuals with low hope orientation (Chang, 1998; Snyder, Cheavens, & Michael, 1999).

But in addition to its function as a relatively stable emotional orientation or emotional trait, hope also can be experienced as a short-term emotion. That configuration of hope appears especially in reaction to meaningful, short-term events that provide indications for potential long-term positive change in the future. Averill, Catlin, and Chon (1990) have established the view of hope as an emotion rather than an attitude by comparing it to the more prototypical emotions of anger and love. By asking people to report their subjective experience of hope, they showed: (a) hope is difficult to control hence more like a passion than an action (e.g., "I couldn't help but hope"); (b) it is experienced at times in a non-rational way, in that people who hope for something important enough may convince themselves that chances of the outcome occurring are better than they actually are; and (c) like other emotions, hope motivates behavior. Their findings revealed that short-term experiences of hope play a dominant role in keeping people engaged with a future outcome.

The most common and well-accepted conceptualization of hope as a short-term emotion was introduced by Snyder (2000), suggesting that hope arises when a concrete positive goal is expected (Stotland, 1969), and this even includes yearning for relief from negative conditions (Lazarus, 1991). According to Snyder's approach, hope is defined as a two-dimensional construct that involves a person's determination to pursue goal-directed behavior (i.e., agency) and one's ability to find ways to meet those goals (i.e., pathways). Using a motivational account of emotions, hope is described as the motivation to attach oneself to positive outcomes or goals (Snyder et al., 1991). It consists of the cognitive elements of visualizing and expecting a better future as well as the affective element of feeling good about the expected events or outcomes (Staats & Stassen, 1985). The affective component of hope takes the form of subjective feelings based on goal-directed thinking, which combines goal-directed determination with planning to achieve this goal (Snyder, 1994, 2000). As such, although visualizing goal achievement inherently includes positive affect, the gestalt feeling of hope is more complex as it contains both positive and negative feelings since individuals may realize that the achievement of their final goal may involve struggles, costs, and endurance. Therefore, as Jarymowicz and Bar-Tal (2006) have suggested, hope can be depicted metaphorically as the light at the end of a dark tunnel. The awareness of such light provides the motivation to plan, act, and move toward the desired goal while also providing the directions toward which such motivation should be channeled.

On the other hand, according to that view, feeling despair and hopelessness can be seen as the difficult experience of a long, dark tunnel with no light in the end of it. Lazarus (1999) has stated that when there is a complete absence of hope, despair rises. As in the case of hope, despair is induced when attempting to think about and imagine the future. However, unlike hope, despair is rooted in feelings of uncertainty (Sallfors, Fasth, & Hallberg, 2002), futility, and an inability to imagine a better or even a positive future. The key appraisal and behavioral tendencies involved in both of these emotions are connected directly to envisioning or imagining the future. Whereas hope enables people to envision a better future and take risks and steps to achieve this future, despair creates an inability to think about a future that is different from the very negative present they are experiencing. Hence, looking at the complete process of hope, it can be seen as an emotion beginning with imagining a desired goal in the future that constitutes a positive change from the existing situation. This leads to positive affect regarding the desired goal, followed by behavioral tendencies characterized by cognitive flexibility and resourcefulness.

Accordingly, actual events that indicate to people that they will be able to achieve a certain goal provide a fertile ground for the appearance of hope (Nesse, 1999). On the other hand, events that indicate that the goal cannot be attained induce despair or hopelessness (Roseman, Spindel, & Jose, 1990). Averill et al. (1990) have pointed to four elements included in appraisals of hope. The first is that the goal must be perceived by one as realistically attainable, but there is no assurance that it will actually happen. While a goal that is sure to be achieved induces positive affect regarding the outcome, it is not hope for achievement but joy or happiness (Roseman et al., 1990). On the other hand, thinking about a goal that has no likelihood of being reached will induce despair. Thus, the probability of attainment involved in the appraisal of hope is intermediate.

This aspect also helps distinguish hope from optimism. In that view, hope is distinct from optimism by being an emotion representing more important but less likely outcomes (Bruininks & Malle, 2005). Averill et al. (1990) have found that hope extends to goals for which little control over the outcome is possible, such as other people's well-being. Bruininks and Malle (2005) have further supported that argument by empirically demonstrating that hope is characterized by a low perception of control as well as an intermediate level of subjective likelihood compared to other positive states such as joy, optimism, and wishing.

Second, according to Averill et al.'s (1990) conception, to elicit hope, the goal itself should be appraised as important and desired. As already mentioned, unlike other positive emotions that are generally experienced within positive contexts, hope often is experienced in negative situations and contexts (Roseman et al., 1990) while desiring a better situation in the future. For example, joy, happiness, and pride are triggered by a positive event, while hope often is induced in reaction to a negative event that the person imagines as improving in the future (Roseman et al., 1990). If the future goal is desirable and the envisioned situation in the future is perceived to be better than the current state (Beck, Weissman, Lester, & Trexler, 1974), it is followed by a positive change in mental state (Lazarus, 1999), namely, the occurrence of affective associations and positive feelings regarding the future goal (Beck et al., 1974; Snyder, 2000; Stotland, 1969). Thus, it is an imagined hypothetical and alternative situation in the future, which is different from the existing situation and considered to be better than the present and which both initiates and maintains the emotion of hope. At the same time, we can assume that hope will not be experienced as long as no positive indications appear within the experience of the negative event. So it is ambiguous situations in which negative current events are mixed with positive indications and expectations for better future that provide the platform for hope.

The third rule is that hope is experienced with regard to goals that are perceived as personally or socially acceptable. For example, people can be hopeful regarding academic or professional success, regarding love and caring romantic relationships, or regarding peaceful intergroup relations. However, if the goal is important and desired enough, it may override this aspect and lead people to hope for goals that may not be perceived as legitimate (Averill et al., 1990). Additionally, cultural and contextual differences may play an important role in defining what an acceptable or legitimate goal may be. For example, as already suggested in previous chapters, societies in protracted conflicts develop a sociopsychological infrastructure (Bar-Tal, 2007) that may involve goals that would not be perceived as legitimate or as justifying feelings of hope in other societies.

Last, the person should be willing to act to attain the goal, if action is possible. Though hope has not been associated with any direct physiological responses (Lazarus, 1999), it does have a cognitive manifestation of thinking and planning ways to achieve the imagined situation in question (Stotland, 1969). In line with that thought, Snyder (1995) has added agency (the perceived ability to achieve the desired aim) and pathways to attainment to the affective element (Snyder et al., 1991) and includes them in his definition of hope as a cognitive motivational system.

In terms of implications, hope's most unique motivational and behavioral role is in stimulating future thinking and planning as well as in encouraging extensive use of imagination, creative thinking, and optimistic evaluations. Imagery and mental simulations have proved highly effective in changing people's emotions, attitudes, and behaviors, such as decreasing stereotypes and creating social and behavioral change (Crisp, Birtel, & Meleady, 2011; Crisp & Turner, 2009; Galinsky & Moskowitz, 2000). The planning and development of pathways energizes and directs behavior (Staats & Stassen, 1985) and, when combined with a sense of agency regarding those paths, becomes action to achieve these goals (Snyder, 2000). This motivational factor is related to perceptions regarding the expectation and even willingness to change the current situation (Beck, Weissman, Lester, & Trexler, 1974). In a cyclical manner, achievement of goals as a result of the use of these planned pathways continues to strengthen and 'feed' future perception of pathways and agency in similar events in the future (Snyder, 2000).

But interestingly, hope can influence not just the way of thinking regarding future possibilities but also the content of these thoughts. According to Jarymowicz (2015), hope helps not only to perceive the large context of the reality but also to anticipate and create new visions of the future (Isen, 1999). It enables people to 'zoom out' from specific circumstances, looking at the events from a more abstract and less concrete perspective. As such, scholars of emotions often see hope as an attribute of the open mind. It helps to first visualize the end goal and only then to plan the way to achieve it, and accordingly, the open mind generates new ideas for the resolution of difficult problems.

Empirical research regarding hope's behavioral tendencies has found it to lead to cognitive flexibility and creativity (Breznitz, 1986; Clore et al., 1994; Fromm, 1968; Lazarus, 1991). Optimism regarding specific outcomes has been associated with a sense of power and found to mediate the effect of power on risk-taking behavior (Anderson & Galinsky, 2006). Hope has been identified as a predictor of achievements in sports as well as academics (Curry, Snyder, Cook, Ruby, & Rehm, 1997). Higher hope orientation (Snyder et al., 1991), the disposition toward hope held by different people, has been associated with better performance on cognitive tasks and problem-solving abilities (Chang, 1998; Snyder et al., 1996), and hopeful individuals tend to spend more time trying to solve problems (Snyder et al., 1996), which ultimately can lead to better outcomes and higher achievement. The state-related emotion of hope was found to improve both physical and psychological health (Cheavens, Michael, & Snyder, 2005; Nolen-Hoeksema & Davis, 2002; Tennen & Affleck, 2002) and has been pointed out as a central and important force that should be induced in therapeutic psychological processes for positive and long-lasting results (Cooper, Darmody, & Dolan, 2003; Hanna, 2002).

Hope and Despair in Intractable Conflicts

When living in the context of intractable conflicts, people can have many hopes of different kinds and for different things. In other words, people in such difficult situations can imagine various more positive scenarios that would make them feel hopeful. For example, many of them hope that their group will overpower the adversary group during the conflict and thus achieve their collective goals in the conflict. Yet when scholars of conflict resolution refer to collective hope in the context of long-term conflicts (e.g., Cohen-Chen, Halperin, Crisp, et al., 2014; Cohen-Chen et al., 2015a; Jarymowicz & Bar-Tal, 2003, 2006; Halperin, Bar-Tal, Nets-Zehngut, & Drori, 2008), they actually refer to people's experience of hope for a peaceful resolution to the conflict. More concretely, they refer to questions pertaining to people's ability to imagine a peaceful future, to their affective experience when they imagine such a future, and to their efforts to plan and then also pursue the pathways toward a better future.

Importantly, hope in the context of intractable conflicts refers to an improved or a better future not just on the personal level but also on the group-based or collective level. In this case, experiencing hope involves not only a better personal future but a desired future of security, prosperity, and peacefulness that is experienced on behalf of other members of the group (Lindner, 2006a; Petersen, 2002; Smith et al., 2007; Staub, 2005; Volkan, 1997). For example, those who may not be affected personally in everyday life by the conflict, due to geographical distance, still can desire the end of conflict for those who do experience the violence, based on a shared ingroup identity. To expand the scope even more, at least for some people (i.e., the more moderate or 'pro-peace' parts of the society), hope in the context of intractable conflict implies a better future for outgroup members and not just for ingroup members. So hope in these contexts goes beyond the individual level and at times even beyond the level of the ingroup.

But, as previously suggested by Bar-Tal, Halperin, and De Rivera (2007) feelings of hope and despair may go even beyond that level to be experienced as a more diffuse collective emotional climate. For example, Bellah (1967) has proposed that hope characterizes the American society: it is a central ingredient in what he called the "civil religion" of the United States. According to this view, for most Americans hope on the individual as well as on the collective level is "in the air"; namely, most members of the society attribute such feelings to their family members, friends, and even leaders. Importantly, while for Americans, hope is part of the 'American dream', its culture, and its collective orientations, for those who live in intractable conflicts, the same can be argued regarding despair.

Previous work in the field of conflict resolution has pointed toward hope as playing a crucial role in conflict resolution. Conceptual work has discussed the cognitive and attitudinal basis of hope within the context of conflict. Coleman and colleagues (Coleman, Vallacher, Nowak, & Bui-Wrzosinska, 2007) have described the paradoxical cycle of hope and despair in intractable conflicts, in which, though the situation is ever changing in its volatility, its very essence is seen as constant and unchanging. Subsequently, people and societies involved in the conflict adopt this perception of the specific conflict as stable, further feeding into its hopelessness and despair. This relates to Stotland's (1969) statement, according to which people involved in situations of long-term suffering do not only find it hard to hope for a better future but become afraid of experiencing hope itself.

Bar-Tal (2001) has added to Stotland's (1969) statement by suggesting that fear often overrides hope in situations of intractable conflicts. While hope is a secondary emotion that promotes orientation toward peace, fear is a primary emotion that inhibits conflict resolution by highlighting threatening information (Jarymowicz & Bar-Tal, 2003, 2006). According to Bar-Tal (2001), hope is critically important for conflict resolution since it involves conceiving of new paths and behaviors toward the positively viewed goal of ending the conflict, including motivating people to hold attitudes supportive of peace and compromises.

But why is it so difficult for people in intractable conflicts to experience hope? The first obstacle to hope is driven by the enduring nature of these conflicts. The fact that a huge part of the group knows no other situation but deep-rooted conflict makes the imagination of a different or a better future much more challenging than in other situations. Though yearning for a better future may exist in the public sphere and narrative, people tend to imagine situations they have experienced before or at least situations that are somewhat familiar to them. When most of the group has never experienced a peaceful context, it stands to reason that people will not have many accessible experiences regarding the end of conflict. Therefore, it may be harder to imagine a peaceful future when this reality is mostly alien and unknown.

An implication of the fact that people have never experienced anything but conflict is that many people in intractable conflicts also believe that conflicts of this kind simply cannot be resolved. Cohen-Chen and colleagues (Cohen-Chen, Halperin, Crisp, et al., 2014) recently have demonstrated that large sectors of Israeli society simply do not believe that conflicts like the ongoing one in the Middle East can be resolved. They also have demonstrated, based on both correlational and experimental studies, that this belief in the fixedness of the conflict is negatively associated with feelings of hope.

One might ask then, what happens when these people are exposed to real-world examples showing that very similar conflicts have been resolved in the past? According to recent studies (Kudish, Cohen-Chen, & Halperin, 2015), such new information will clash with another powerful belief held by many people in this context, namely, the belief that their conflict is unique and cannot be compared to any historical or ongoing conflict. The beliefs that the conflict is unique and that a conflict 'of this kind' cannot be resolved amplify feelings of hopelessness and despair, which are also supported repeatedly by the non-optimistic context and unfolding events.

Finally, hope is experienced so rarely in intractable conflicts because in addition to these non-dynamic views of the conflict itself, people also hold very similar views about the adversary group. If one believes that the outgroup is evil by nature and will never change (Halperin, 2008, 2011b), as already mentioned in the chapter about hatred, it only makes sense to also assume that the conflict itself cannot be solved peacefully. And indeed, recent analysis of political case studies (Halperin & Bar-Tal, 2007), as well as recent quantitative empirical data (Saguy & Halperin, 2014) have revealed that the *no partner* belief, namely, the belief that there is no one to talk to or seriously negotiate with on the other side, is associated closely with feelings of despair and lack of hope. Further support for that link was provided in a correlational study we conducted among Israeli Jews in 2008 (Halperin, Bar-Tal, Nets-Zehngut, & Drori, 2008) in which we found that hope for a peaceful resolution of the Israeli-Palestinian conflict was negatively correlated with tendencies to de-legitimize Palestinians.

Hope's Implications in Intractable Conflicts

Empirical evidence suggests that hope and despair influence people's attitudes and behaviors in almost every stage of the cycle of conflict, although their relative weight compared to other positive or negative emotions changes between these stages. For example, the findings regarding hope's role during conflict escalation and militant actions are ambiguous. Rosler, Cohen-Chen, and Halperin (in press) recently have found that when controlling for other positive and negative emotions (such as empathy, anger, and fear), hope had very minor influence on shaping Israelis' views regarding the extent to which Israel should use its military force in response to Palestinian provocations. At the same time, in a study conducted during a war in Gaza between Israelis and Palestinians, we (Halperin & Gross, 2011) found that those Israelis who managed to preserve hope for the resolution of the conflict also supported providing humanitarian aid to the Palestinians during the war. Hope led Israelis to a more nuanced or ambiguous position during the war. On the one hand, they wanted Israel to defeat the Palestinians, but on the other, they wanted to preserve the Palestinians' dignity to enable postwar reconciliation. As such, those Israelis who experienced relatively high levels of hope during the war supported policies like allowing the transfer of food and medicine to innocent Palestinians and providing medical care to injured Palestinian women and children in Israeli hospitals. So it seems that while hope may not be the most dominant and influential emotional phenomenon during wartime, it certainly plays some role even then.

On the other hand, during the deescalation or conflict resolution stages, the role of hope is much clearer, less ambiguous, and more central. At these times, hope allows the parties to imagine a different and better future, and the belief that a peaceful resolution is possible constitutes an essential step toward taking risks and making compromises. Furthermore, the essential component of pathway thoughts (Snyder 2000), which involves creating mental representations of routes to the desired target, can lead people to accept the compromises needed to achieve a peaceful solution to deep-rooted conflicts. As such, the most direct implication of hope in people's social and political behavior during intractable conflicts is its positive influence on their openness to new ideas and its constructive influence on their patterns of information seeking, processing, and decision making. By definition people who feel hope are more optimistic about the future, they tend to be less risk averse, and they are usually more open to new, even innovative ideas that can promote the better future they envision.

Accordingly, in a recent set of studies, Saguy and Halperin (2014) have found that experimentally induced hope led Jewish Israelis to be more open to the Palestinian perspective of the conflict. In more detail, those who were led to feel more hope for the resolution of the conflict expressed more willingness to "disseminate the Arab point of view of the conflict to the general Israeli public" as well as to "watch movies or read books which present the Palestinian point of view of the conflict". Interestingly, in these studies, hope was driven by the belief that "there is a partner" and that the outgroup is open to new ideas for peace. Perception of the outgroup as open-minded led to an increase in feelings of hope, which in turn led to more openness among ingroup members, providing further support for the close links among hope, flexible thinking, and openness.

Cohen-Chen and her colleagues (Cohen-Chen, Halperin, Porat, et al., 2014) expanded these findings by demonstrating that Jewish Israelis who feel hope regarding future relations between Israelis and Palestinians actively search for new information that can support their positive view of the future. Using a computerized simulator of information processing, we found that while levels of hope were not associated with the amount of information Israelis gathered regarding a new peace opportunity, hope was indeed positively associated with an inclination toward acquiring information that supports opportunities for peace making. Given that such information is by definition more ambiguous, less familiar, and more risky than the alternative information, the importance of hope in that regard cannot be overlooked.

Interestingly, a bulk of recent studies have shown that the effects of hope during a deescalation stage go beyond information processing to shaping concrete political attitudes regarding relevant compromises. In these studies the effect of hope on support for conciliatory policies in the context of peace processes remains significant even when taking into account other important predictors of these policies, such as political ideology (e.g., Halperin & Gross, 2011; Rosler et al., in press). This should not come as a surprise given that hope increases people's confidence in the fact that compromises on their side will lead to reciprocal compromises on the other side as well as to positive developments on the way to a better future. This hope by itself can provide people with the justifications and rationalizations required to support 'painful' compromises required for peace. Furthermore, given that hope motivates planning and implementing steps to promote a required goal, support for compromises seems to be the most immediate and reasonable step in that direction.

In terms of empirical evidence, outside the context of intractable conflicts, hope has been found to play a constructive role in reducing hostility and increasing problem-solving tendencies in negotiation contexts (Baron, Fortin, Frei, Hauver, & Shack, 1990). In the realm of intractable conflicts, Rosler et al. (in press) have pointed at hope as the most powerful positive emotion influencing people's attitudes regarding compromises for peace. In two studies, conducted during a peace summit between Israelis and Palestinians, the authors found that Israelis who expressed high levels of hope also supported the most critical compromises in an attempt to promote peace. Importantly, these associations remained significant even when controlling for other positive feelings toward the Palestinians and the conflict. Only recently these findings were further supported in a long series of studies in which Cohen-Chen and her colleagues (Cohen-Chen, Halperin, Crisp, et al., 2014; Cohen-Chen et al., 2015) experimentally induced hope in various ways among Jewish Israelis and found that this led to a significant increase in support for all relevant compromises for peace.

Furthermore, at least one study that I am aware of suggests that hope also can play a role in a postconflict or reconciliation process (Moeschberger, Dixon, Niens, & Cairns 2005). The authors conducted a study in the postconflict setting of Northern Ireland to examine psychological antecedents of willingness to forgive the outgroup for past atrocities. According to the authors, as forgiveness and reconciliation necessarily encompass the belief that controversial issues can be solved, hope should be considered a vital factor in the disposition for forgiveness. In line with that rationale, in a correlational study conducted among both Catholic and Protestant students, it was found that although the trait of hope was not directly associated with forgiveness, it had indirect relations with it through the dispositional trait characteristic dissipation or rumination.

But the experience of hope can influence the dynamics of conflicts and their resolutions not just by shaping public attitudes and information-processing patterns but also by providing the motivation for specific behavior. Most importantly, Cohen-Chen, Van-Zomeren, and Halperin (2015) recently have argued that hope for peace is necessary to motivate pro-peace collective action. As I have already mentioned in a previous chapter, the current literature on collective action focuses on intergroup anger as the most powerful emotional engine behind collective action. Yet at the same time, social identity theory (Tajfel, 1978; Ellemers, 1993) suggests that collective action should occur only under societal circumstances that allow for individuals' imagining a different future (thus enabling hope for the attainment of a fairer future) and a sense of instability and thus scope for social change (Tajfel, 1978; see also Ellemers, 1993; Mummendey et al., 1999; Van-Zomeren et al., 2012). This means that without hope and scope for social change, collective action will not occur. This also can explain why collective action is rare in intractable intergroup conflicts, namely, because such conflicts are defined by a lack of hope and scope for a positive change.

Outside the context of intractable conflicts, Greenaway, Cichocka, Van Veelen, Likki, and Branscombe (in-press) recently have demonstrated that hope is associated with greater support for social change in two countries with different political contexts (i.e., The Netherlands and the United States), that hope predicts support for social change over and above other emotions often investigated in collective action research, and even that experimentally induced hope motivates support for social change. Interestingly, in all four studies, the effect of hope was mediated by perceived efficacy to achieve social equality.

Within the context of an intractable conflict, a recent set of studies has suggested that the same mind-set that underlies feelings of hope (i.e., the world is dynamic, and the future can be different from the present) also drives motivation to take part in collective action (Cohen-Chen, Halperin, Saguy, & Van-Zomeren, 2014). The findings of these studies, based on both correlational and experimental designs conducted in Israel in the midst of large social protest, showed that inducing the belief that groups and situations can change increases the willingness to take part in collective action by inducing belief in group efficacy. This implies that finding a way to *upregulate* hope (e.g., Cohen-Chen et al., 2014) may remove an important barrier to collective action and translate an inactive state of affairs into a more active one. Indeed, it stands to reason that once hope is reinvigorated (or at least kept alive), the triad of motivations that predict the undertaking of collective action can be mobilized to increase chances of the occurrence of collective action. Put differently, hope may be an important *precondition* for individuals to be(come) motivated for pro-peace collective action in the first place.

Finally, while all of the abovementioned studies have tested the way feelings of hope shape people's attitudes and behaviors in intractable conflicts, an additional path through which hope can affect conflicts is through its expression by other group members. As mentioned in previous chapters, research on emotions as social information (EASI) (Van Kleef, 2009; Van Kleef et al., 2010) has shown that emotions provide information to observers (Hareli & Rafaeli, 2008; Steinel, Van Kleef, & Harinck, 2008; Van Kleef, 2009) about the expresser's feelings (Ekman, 1993), social intentions (Fridlund, 1994), and orientation toward other people (Knutson, 1996). Recently, Cohen-Chen and colleagues (Cohen-Chen, Crisp, & Halperin, 2015b) examined the effect of outgroup expressions of hope on ingroup hope and conciliatory attitudes in light of an opportunity for peace.

Ideally, we would want to believe that when group members absorb signals of hope for peace coming from the adversary group, it also will lead them to experience feelings of hope while strengthening their belief in the probability of peace. This is in line with ideas regarding emotional contagion, namely, a reciprocal emotional experience in which one might 'catch' other people's emotions

(Cheshin, Rafaeli, & Bos, 2011; Hatfield, Cacioppo, & Rapson, 1994). Yet in competitive settings, emotional contagion is less common. Instead, the fact that emotional expressions inform observers about the expresser's appraisals (Manstead & Fischer, 2001; Van Doorn, Heerdink, & Van Kleef, 2012) and interests (Van Kleef et al., 2010) may elicit a different emotional reaction when those interests and appraisals are perceived as directly opposed to one's own (Allred, Mallozzi, Matsui, & Raia, 1997; Ketelaar & Au, 2003; Sinaceur & Tiedens, 2006; Van Kleef et al., 2004a, 2004b; Van Kleef, De Dreu, & Manstead, 2006). For example, an outgroup's expressions of hope can be interpreted by ingroup members as a signal of belief that the outgroup has defeated or is about to defeat the ingroup or that the unfolding negotiation includes elements of fraud or deception. Additionally, in a context dominated by 'zero-sum-game' perceptions, the fact that outgroup members experience positive emotions such as hope is, in and of itself, a justification for the ingroup to experience negative emotions. Hence, the current literature provides rather ambiguous rationalizations regarding the potential role of hope expressions in conflict situations.

The first (and, to the best of my knowledge, the only) empirical examination of that question is Cohen-Chen et al.'s (2015b) studies that examined Israeli reaction to Palestinian expressions of hope. In their experimental studies, one group was informed that a large majority of Palestinians expressed high levels of hope in response to a new peace opportunity, while the other group was told that only a small minority of Palestinians felt this way. The first study provided some evidence for emotional contagion despite the competitive context of the intractable conflict. In that study, Jewish Israeli participants who learned that an agreement outline induced high hope among Palestinians were more hopeful and more willing to accept the agreement compared to those in the low hope condition. This was a rather surprising finding that led the authors to assume that the hope expression inherently includes, in addition to the affective feeling itself, an expression of support for the proposed agreement and that it is the expression of support rather than the affective or hopeful message that drives the positive effects. Therefore, in a subsequent study, the authors tried to isolate the effects of hope expressions from the ones of signals of support for the agreement by manipulating each of them independently. The results of that study revealed that expressions of Palestinian hope (high versus low) did not induce hope and support for the agreement among Israelis when Palestinian support for the agreement was presented as high. However, where hope did play an important role was when Palestinian support was presented as low. For these participants, high Palestinian hope induced hope and support for the agreement compared to those in the low Palestinian hope condition. Importantly, it is the low support condition that more accurately mirrors the context of an intractable conflict, in which the national narrative embodies the idea that the outgroup does not support opportunities for conflict resolution (Bar-Tal, 2007). Indeed, this research demonstrates the importance of outgroup hope expressions in conveying information that can be used to signal willingness to resolve conflict.

Turning Despair to Hope: Some Thoughts on Hope Regulation

Altogether, the writings and empirical findings reviewed in this chapter highlight the pivotal role played by despair (or the lack of hope) as a barrier to conflict resolution. Despair leads people to hopelessness and apathy and thus stabilizes the existing situation of an ongoing violent conflict. When people cannot imagine a future that is different and better than the current reality and when they do not really believe that a better future is possible, they try to maximize their well-being within the borders of the current (nonideal) situation rather than to break these borders to promise a better future for themselves and for their society. As such, they do not search for new information that potentially can promote alternative solutions and even ignore such information when it is presented to them. They also oppose relevant compromises for peace because they don't really believe that such compromises on their side will fundamentally change the reality on the ground. Finally, the apathetic sentiment prevents them from taking part in any individual or collective action meant to promote peace.

Given these observations, an important question is how hope can be induced to take over despair even in almost inherently hopeless situations such as intractable conflicts. We have recently initiated several studies with that goal in mind. Our basic assumption was that to transform despair to hope, the belief that a different, better future of the conflict is impossible since conflicts are fixed must be changed to a belief in peace as a possibility. This can be done either by pointing at signs of change or at least potential for change among outgroup members (e.g., Saguy & Halperin, 2014), by highlighting the malleable nature of the conflict itself (e.g., Cohen-Chen et al., 2014), or by providing a comparative perspective to other conflicts of the same kind that have been resolved in the past (e.g., Kudish et al., 2015).

Yet a direct manipulation referring to the conflict situation might prove to be ineffective and might even backfire since most people living in such situations already have lost faith in the possibility of positive change. Hence, to overcome negative reactions to direct references to the conflict, one would need to alter people's general beliefs about conflict malleability, which would be applied indirectly to the specific conflict by participants. In line with that rationale, Cohen-Chen and colleagues (Cohen-Chen, Halperin, Crisp, & Gross, 2014) have found that inducing a malleable belief regarding a conflict's ability to change, in general, induced hope regarding the future of the Israeli-Palestinian conflict, which subsequently led to support for conciliatory measures toward peace. Results from the first, correlational study indicated that participants who believe that conflict situations can change their nature in general (e.g., *"Under certain circumstances and if all core issues are addressed, the nature of conflicts can be changed"*) were also more hopeful regarding the end of the Israeli–Palestinian conflict specifically, and this was in turn associated with higher support for concessions regarding the peace process. The second study established the proposed model's causal direction: the authors successfully increased the participants' levels of hope by influencing beliefs regarding the malleability of conflicts, and this led them to be significantly more supportive of concessions for peace. Taken together, these two studies point to a distinct mechanism by which an increased belief in the malleability of conflict situations induces higher levels of hope regarding the end of the Israeli–Palestinian conflict in the future, and this in turn increases support for major concessions needed to promote peace. Thus, though the Israeli–Palestinian conflict, as well as the outgroup (i.e., the Palestinians) was in no way referred to, the mere reference to conflict situations as being able to change led participants to believe that the specific conflict could be resolved, and this led them to hold peace-making attitudes toward concession making.

One limitation of interventions, such as the one I have just described, focusing on the (malleable) nature of conflicts is that they might still be too concrete given that when people living in intractable conflicts hear about the malleability of conflicts in general, they automatically attribute it to their own conflict, and this can stimulate defensive reactions. To address this limitation, one such line of research (Cohen-Chen, Crisp, & Halperin, 2015a) indirectly regulated hope regarding conflict resolution by inducing a general mind-set and belief in a dynamic or changing (as opposed to unchanging) world. In these studies the manipulations did not include any reference to conflicts and instead focused on the dynamic nature of the world more generally.

Results from the first, observational study showed that when watching people describing the future of the Israeli–Palestinian conflict, coders who were blind to the study's initial hypotheses associated a belief in a changing world with hope for peace as well as higher support for concession making. In the second, correlational study, results indicated that participants who believed that the world was dynamic and ever changing were also more hopeful regarding the possibility of peace in the Israeli–Palestinian conflict. This was in turn associated with higher support for concessions regarding the negotiation process. Next, in two experimental studies in which the belief in a dynamic world was manipulated in two different ways, inducing a belief in a changing world led to greater support for concessions toward conflict resolution, and this effect was mediated by the experience of hope regarding peace. Taken together, these four studies point to a mechanism underlying hope for peace, in which an increased perception of the world's ever-changing nature indirectly turned into hope for peace, leading to changes in political attitudes required to promote peace.

Finally, another set of studies (Saguy & Halperin, 2014) related to hope showed that exposure to internal criticism within the outgroup can increase hope regarding the future of the conflict by instilling a sense of outgroup heterogeneity, implying that a change is possible in the future. Israelis who heard a Palestinian criticizing the Palestinian society were more hopeful about future relations with Palestinians, saw Palestinians as less homogeneous, and were, as a consequence, more open to the outgroup perspective. I believe that these effects were driven by an identification of a sign for potential change among outgroup members, which in turn increased the ingroup members' capability to imagine a different, better future.

The journey toward revealing ways to induce hope in intractable conflicts is only in its very first baby steps. We should keep in mind the fact that messages with that aim always have to confront the reality of the conflict that, in and of itself, often provides the contradicting messages. As such, another psychological mechanism that potentially can boost hope in such situations is an experience of group (Cohen-Chen, Halperin, Saguy, et al., 2014) or political efficacy and agency (e.g., Craig, Niemi, & Silver, 1990). When people feel that their group actually can influence the future dynamics of the conflict, they no longer feel hopelessness. Group efficacy interventions already have been implemented with relative success in other contexts (Sulitzeanu-Kenan & Halperin, 2013), and they definitely should be applied in the context of intractable conflicts as well, together with all other interventions that have been mentioned in this chapter.

7

MORAL EMOTIONS IN INTRACTABLE CONFLICTS

Group-Based Guilt, Conflict Resolution, and Reconciliation

Introduction

Ironically, I am writing this chapter on group-based guilt in intractable conflicts while another round of extreme violence between Israelis and Palestinians takes place just outside my office window. This round, which is called Operation Protective Edge or the third Gaza war by Israelis, highly involves civilians on both sides of the border. At this point, only six days into the war, more than 400 missiles already have been fired at large Israeli cities and other populated areas, and more than 160 Palestinians have been killed by Israeli Defense Forces (IDF) air strikes, at least 50 percent of them innocent civilians. The immediate threat to millions of Israelis and Palestinians is huge; sirens are sounded outside every few hours, and the traditional and social media are filled with messages of hate, fear, and aggression.

Interestingly enough, this round of violence began with two terrifying events, one on each side of the conflict. On June 12, 2014, three Israeli teenagers were kidnapped as they were hitchhiking to their homes, and they were immediately murdered in Gush Etzion on the West Bank. Then, two weeks later, a Palestinian boy, Mohammed Hussein Abu Khdeir, was kidnapped and then burned alive by three Israeli settlers who later confessed and declared that they had acted in revenge for the kidnapping and killing of the three Jewish teenagers. These two events, which later led to another round of extreme violence, were conducted by extremists on both sides who saw themselves as acting in the name of their groups. These two events raised fundamental moral questions among both Israelis and Palestinians regarding their group's moral responsibility for atrocities done by representatives of their groups as part of the vicious dynamic of the conflict. The events were condemned by official and lay citizens on both sides, offering apologies to the victims' families. These rather uncommon acts of acknowledgment of responsibility and expressions of guilt were undertaken even by those leaders who strongly support the goals of their group regarding the wider issues at the core of the conflict. At the same time, many others on both sides expressed support for these horrifying actions, justified them, and even encouraged the initiation of similar actions. In many ways these events capture the essence of the moral dilemma of societies involved in intractable conflicts as well as the potential role of group-based moral emotions, such as guilt, in breaking the vicious cycle of the conflict.

But these events, horrifying as they may be, are an inherent part of long-term, violent conflicts. Almost by definition, long-term intractable conflicts include repeated, mutual transgressions that are perceived by the victimized groups as immoral and unjust. These actions can sometimes take the form of exclusionism, discrimination, and negation of basic human rights. On other, more extreme occasions, they can take the form of mass killings of innocent civilians, genocide, and ethnic cleansing (Staub, 2011). As such, any process of conflict resolution, as well as a reconciliation process, must address the mutual psychological distress stemming from these past wrongdoings committed during the conflict (Bar-Tal & Bennink, 2004). Dealing with the past, and especially with the different views or narratives of the past, held by each group, is well-known in the literature of conflict resolution as one of the most powerful barriers to peace.

At the same time, in every society, there are some individuals who not only perceive their ingroup's structural advantage but judge it to be unfair (e.g., Schmitt, Behner, Montada, Muller, & Muller-Fohrbrodt, 2000). In cases of wrongdoings committed by groups, even in the case of the most extreme actions conducted by groups in human history, some individuals stood up against their groups and called for immediate change (Goldenberg, Saguy, & Halperin, 2014). The story of the White Rose in Nazi Germany nicely demonstrates this point. The six most-recognized members of the group were arrested by the Gestapo in 1943, and one of them was executed for his participation. Deviant group members serve as an opposition to the opinions of the majority and also can differ from the majority in their emotional experiences. When individuals include themselves in an ingroup that they perceive as unfairly advantaged or as treating outgroups in immoral ways, they should want systemic compensation as a goal (Leach, Snider, & Iyer, 2002).

The interesting question, therefore, is what psychological process potentially can drive such group members into action, which inherently includes risks on personal, social, and even physical levels. Recent developments in the study of moral emotions in the context of intergroup conflicts suggest that these emotions potentially can play such a role. It has been suggested that intergroup moral emotions like guilt, shame, and anger at one's own group, associated with these past atrocities, potentially can motivate society members to make compromises necessary to promote peace or to support reparative policies required for intergroup reconciliation. If society members feel that they are responsible for the (sometimes unnecessary) suffering of outgroup members, their political response tendencies may vary from pure defensiveness, resulting in opposition to any relevant compromise, to sincere willingness to offer an apology, or to compensate the outgroup. This can manifest itself in the form of compromises and gestures that potentially may promote peace. Hence, the goal of Chapter 7 will be to reveal the circumstances under which discrete moral emotions, and especially group-based guilt, will promote support for peace and other actions associated with reconciliation processes.

In a nutshell, the two most frequently studied moral emotions in the context of long-term conflicts are group-based shame and guilt. *Group-based guilt* is associated with appraised responsibility of one's ingroup for moral violations (Branscombe, 2004). Guilt is focused on the harmful acts and can motivate group members to rectify the wrongdoing and to compensate the victims (Brown, González, Zagefka, Manzi, & Čehajić, 2008; Čehajić, Effron, Halperin, Liberman, & Ross, 2011; Doosje, Branscombe, Spears, & Manstead, 1998; Iyer, Leach, & Crosby, 2003; Pagano & Huo, 2007; Wohl, Branscombe, & Klar, 2006; Zebel, Zimmermann, Tendayi Viki, & Doosje, 2008 but see Iyer, Schmader, & Lickel, 2007). *Group-based shame*, on the other hand, is associated with appraisals implying that a wrongdoing reflects fundamental characteristics of the perpetrator (Lickel, Schmader, & Barquissau, 2004; Tangney, 1991). In the intergroup context, shame leads to a desire to distance the ingroup from the shame-invoking situation (Iyer et al., 2007; Lickel, Schmader, & Barquissau, 2004), yet there are inconsistent findings regarding the role of shame in promoting support for compensating the outgroup (Allpress, Barlow, Brown, & Louis, 2010; Brown & Čehajić, 2008; Brown et al., 2008; Lickel, Schmader, Curtis, Scarnier, & Ames, 2005; Schmader & Lickel, 2006). Given the space limitation of the chapter and the relative superiority of group-based guilt over other moral emotions in terms of its ability to promote peace and reconciliation, the focus of the chapter will be on group-based guilt.

Accordingly, the chapter begins with a brief discussion of the nature and the implications of guilt on the individual and interpersonal level. Then, the nature and characteristics of guilt on the group level will be presented focusing mainly on its unique characteristics, the ones that distinguish it from other moral emotions such as shame or anger at one's own group. The third part of that chapter will be devoted to psychological processes that stimulate group-based guilt on the one hand and the ones that help society members to avoid feeling guilty on the other. This will be followed by a review of studies examining the constructive, but also some of the more destructive, implications of group-based guilt on intractable conflicts. Finally, some initial thoughts regarding avenues for upregulation of group-based guilt will be presented.

The Nature of Guilt

Guilt is considered an aversive emotion that arises as a consequence of a perceived immoral behavior committed by an individual that brings harm to another person, object, or group (e.g., Baumeister, Stillwell, & Heatherton, 1994; Devine & Monteith, 1993). According to self-discrepancy theory, guilt results from discrepancies between the actual self and the ought self (Higgins, 1987). This understanding of guilt is consistent with other discussions of this emotion, which define *guilt* as a negative feeling that arises when individuals' behavior violates standards or rules by which they believe they should abide (Lewis, 1993; Tangney & Fischer, 1995).

This means that, similar to other moral emotions, guilt arises when the individual believes that her behavior deviates from what she perceives to be the 'right', normative or moral behavior in a certain situation. An in-depth discussion of recent theoretical and empirical developments in the study of morality or moral behavior is beyond the scope of the current chapter, but it is important to distinguish between two very different approaches to these terms. According to the philosophical approach, there are objective standards that can differentiate right from wrong in any context. Moral judgments, according to that approach, are made with reference to 'universal' principles of justice rather than individual, group, or community standards (for discussions, see Blasi, 1990; Haidt & Kesebir, 2010). On the other hand, the social-psychological view of morality sees moral thought, feeling, and behavior as that which *individuals* subjectively consider right or wrong (for reviews, see Haidt & Kesebir, 2010; Leach, Bilali, & Pagliaro, 2013; Monin, & Jordan, 2009; Pagliaro, 2012). For example, in their work on people's *moral convictions*, Linda Skitka and her colleagues argue that moral conviction reflects the extent to which subjective evaluations of specific attitude targets are experienced in terms of fundamental right and wrong (Skitka, Bauman, & Sargis, 2005). Attitudes vested with moral conviction, or moral mandates, are a special class of strong attitudes (strong attitudes are extreme, important, central, and certain; Krosnick & Petty, 1995) that are distinct from otherwise strong but nonmoral attitudes (Skitka, Bauman, & Mullen, 2008).

This subjectively oriented view of morality fits nicely with appraisal theories of emotions, suggesting that moral emotions like guilt are elicited only to the extent that an individual subjectively believes that her actions have violated accepted moral values and norms. Yet, although necessary, the perceived violation of moral values is not sufficient to induce guilt. For that to happen, people have to acknowledge some kind of responsibility for the harm done. More specifically, responsibility means that they believe that they had some sort of control over the problematic act and even that they could have avoided acting this way had they wanted to do so. This means that only immoral behavior for which the individual holds herself responsible will elicit guilt.

The appraisal of personal responsibility for an immoral action that has caused harm leads those who feel guilt at the individual level to feel motivated to repair the damage done to the harmed person (Roseman, Wiest, & Swartz, 1994). This is consistent with more general research on guilt, which shows it to be linked to the abstract goal of compensation (for a review, see Baumeister, Stillwell, & Heatherton, 1994). In several studies in which individuals were asked to recall episodes in which they experienced individual guilt, they reported having wanted to make amends (Tangney, Miller, Flicker, & Barlow, 1996) and to undo what they had done (Frijda, Kuipers, & ter Schure, 1989, Study 1; Roseman et al., 1994). Ira Roseman et al. (1994) have compared the emotional goals associated with guilt with those of a variety of other emotions and found that guilt is distinguished by the goals of "wanting to make up for what was done" and "to be forgiven".

A more nuanced view of guilt motivations and emotional goals recently was introduced by Leach, Iyer, and Pederson (2006). According to their view, although guilt is indeed associated with a general tendency to be forgiven or to correct the wrongdoing, it lacks the kind of power and energy that is required to actually do so (which according to the authors can be found in anger toward oneself). These authors review several studies that demonstrate that the phenomenological experience of guilt is characterized by little of the physical agitation indicative of a readiness for action (Frijda et al., 1989). One notable example is the abovementioned Roseman et al. (1994) finding, in which those who recalled an episode of guilt reported experiencing less "blood rushing through the body", less feeling "that you'd explode", and less "heart pounding" than those recalling episodes of other emotions, such as anger, fear, or distress (for similar patterns of results, see Tangney, Miller, Flicker, & Barlow, 1996). Along the same lines, Frijda et al. (1989, Study 2) have found that, compared to recalling other emotions, people who recalled guilt episodes found it harder to indicate actual motivations like to "move against" or "move away". Similarly, Roseman et al. (1994) have found recalled guilt to be more weakly associated than other emotions such as anger with feeling "driven to do something" and feeling like yelling, kicking, "lashing out", or hitting someone.

One interesting question, though, is how exactly guilt-associated goals and action tendencies translate into actual behavior in the context of interpersonal bargaining and negotiation. In line with what we know about the nature of guilt, the natural expectation is that those who experience guilt in the process of bargaining and negotiation will feel that they owe something to the counterpart and, as such, will behave more constructively and maybe even make more generous offers compared to those who do not feel any guilt. Quite surprisingly, however, very little empirical work has been done with the goal of addressing that question. One recent study that actually did not focus on guilt (but rather on empathy and perspective taking during negotiation processes) found that guilt proneness predicted disapproval of false promises and misrepresentations in the negotiations

(Cohen, 2010). I find this result interesting because it suggests that the experience of guilt can have an effect not only on the concrete outcome of the negotiation or on the compromises the parties are willing to offer but also on the dynamic, the atmosphere, and the norms of the negotiation process itself.

Another interesting finding regarding the role of guilt in interpersonal bargaining was found in a study by Ketelaar and Au (2003) that examined the way experiencing guilt in the first round of a repeated social bargaining game would affect people's decisions in subsequent rounds of these games. In a set of two studies, using two different bargaining games (prisoner's dilemma and ultimatum game), Ketelaar and Au (2003) have found that those who experienced guilt after pursuing a noncooperative strategy in the first round of play displayed higher levels of cooperation in the subsequent rounds. That is an important finding for the purposes of the current book, given that long-term intractable conflicts are by all means 'repeated games' rather than a one-time encounter, and as such, these findings suggest that guilt experienced at a certain point in time potentially can improve future interactions (see also Carlsmith & Gross, 1969; Freedman, Wallington, & Bless, 1967 for similar patterns of results).

At the same time, from the guilty negotiator's opponent's perspective, it was found that since guilt induces the action tendency to repair wrongdoings, negotiators who face a guilty opponent expect her to offer them more concessions (Van Kleef, De Dreu, & Manstead, 2006). Thus, when receiving 'cues' of guilt from the counterpart, people tend to ask for more during negotiations and implement stricter negotiation strategies. Gerben Van Kleef, De Dreu, and Manstead (2006) nicely captured the ambiguous role of guilt in that context, saying that negotiators whose opponents appeared to experience emotions of appeasement (i.e., guilt or regret) developed a positive impression of their opponents, but they were non-conciliatory about the level of their demands (Van Kleef, De Dreu, & Manstead, 2006). In that regard, guilt expressions may lead to a more positive atmosphere and even improve relations, but it remains unclear if it actually will lead to more successful negotiation outcomes.

Finally, although this chapter focuses mainly on group-based guilt in intractable conflicts, it is important to distinguish guilt from other moral emotions and most importantly from shame. Most scholars agree that shame is linked to what is perceived as a failure of the self, whereas guilt is more often restricted to a failure of one's behavior (Tangney, Stuewig, & Mashek, 2007). Lewis (1971) has suggested that both emotions are self-conscious and negative, however with a difference in their focus: feeling guilty for one's wrongdoing is associated with a focus on specific behaviors and their consequences for the other ("I did this bad thing, and now the other is suffering as a result"), whereas feelings of shame involve a greater emphasis on the implications of the wrongdoing for the self ("I did this bad thing, and therefore I am a bad person"). This can be thought of in terms of distinguished attributions associated with each of these emotions; namely, whereas guilt is associated with attributions that are constrained to specific, controllable aspects of behavior, shame is associated with attributing some wrongdoing to internal, global, and stable aspects of the self (Tracy & Robins, 2006).

These different appraisals or attributions of guilt and shame naturally lead to fundamental differences in their associated motivations or action tendencies (e.g., Tangney & Fischer, 1995). Very similar to the distinction between anger and hatred made in previous chapters of the book, whereas attributions to internal or innate characteristics of the self (i.e., shame) lead to motivation to avoid, disengage, or withdraw, external attributions, focusing on specific wrong behavior, lead to motivation to restitute the victim (e.g., apology and reparations) (Lewis, 1971; Tangney & Fischer, 1995). More broadly, Sheikh and Janoff-Bulman (2010) have characterized this distinction as the extent to which each emotion is linked to self and moral regulatory systems that focus either on approach or avoidance motivations. In their view, shame is felt when we fail to do something we ought to have done, whereas guilt is felt when we fail to do something people are expected to do.

Given that most of the chapter will be devoted to guilt, it is important to mention that the debate regarding the exact nature and implications of shame is developing rapidly these days (see Gausel, Leach, Vignoles, & Brown, 2012; Giner-Sorolla, 2012). While some scholars still focus on the fact that shame results from some perceived flaw in one's essential character (Tangney, 1991; Tangney, Miller, Flicker, & Barlow, 1996), others suggest that it is distress caused by public exposure of the wrongdoing that best captures shame (Smith, Webster, Parrott, & Eyre, 2002). While the first approach focuses on the way an individual sees herself when acknowledging her involvement in an immoral behavior, the second approach highlights the damaged reputation or loss of respect and honor in the eyes of others (Crozier, 1998; Rodriguez Mosquera, Manstead, & Fisher, 2002; Smith et al., 2002). Of course, these two conceptions are not mutually exclusive, and in some cases one even can feed into and amplify the other. For example, repeated damage to one's dignity and reputation very easily can 'convince' a person that her actions are driven by innate, immoral characteristics. Importantly, both these processes probably will have the same motivational implications, namely, willingness to run away, hide, and avoid any relevant social interaction. It is mainly for this reason that I see guilt as more relevant than shame in terms of their potential contributions to conflict resolution processes.

Guilt in the Name of One's Group

More than 15 years ago, Doosje et al. (1998) have introduced the idea that people are capable of experiencing guilt for perceived immoral actions or wrongdoings committed by their group members, even if they were not personally involved in that action. Since then, a theoretically and empirically rich literature has developed, further examining the psychological processes behind that non-intuitive phenomenon (e.g., Branscombe, Slugoski, & Kappen, 2004; Brown, et al., 2008; Castano & Giner-Sorolla, 2006; Čehajić et al., 2011; Iyer et al., 2003; McGarty et al., 2005; Pagano & Huo, 2007; Wohl et al., 2006; Zagefka, Pehrson, Mole, & Chan, 2010; Zebel et al., 2008). This concept of group-based guilt is extremely relevant to the understanding of intergroup conflicts and conflict resolution processes for two main reasons: first, because most people in societies involved in intractable conflicts are not involved directly in most immoral actions committed by their group in the course of the conflict and, second, because of the repairing motivation embedded within guilt, which can potentially turn it into a pivotal affective player in conflict resolution and reconciliation processes.

But what kinds of situations hold the potential of eliciting group-based guilt? The simplest answer to that question is that people may feel guilty for actions they see as immoral that were conducted by their group as a whole or by representatives of the group in the name of that group. For example, I may feel group-based guilt for immoral military operations conducted by my country's army or for what I see as an immoral statement by the country's prime minister. In these cases, group-based guilt reactions seem almost automatic because the group itself or representatives of the group who symbolize the group as a whole are involved in what is perceived by the individual as an immoral occurrence.

But interestingly enough, current literature demonstrates that people can also feel guilt in reaction to specific actions of a specific fellow group member (e.g., racist comments made by a family member), even if that person does not represent the ingroup in any formal or even symbolic way. Furthermore, in other instances, people feel group-based guilt about their group's present or past history of behavior toward an outgroup (such as the policies seen as unfairly discriminating against a minority group; see Iyer & Leach, 2008). This means that people sometimes feel guilt in the name of their group, although it is clear that they could not have done anything to change their group's past behavior because they were not born when the perceived immoral actions were committed. This raises questions regarding the antecedents of guilt on the group level and, maybe even more importantly, regarding the boundaries of such feelings of guilt. In other words, it is interesting to explore what would lead people to experience guilt in the name of their group but also what would help people to avoid such an experience, which is typically encountered as aversive and involving some tangible or symbolic threats and costs.

The literature on group-based guilt generally has examined three main antecedents of guilt—acceptance of responsibility, identification with the group, and harm illegitimacy (see Ferguson & Branscombe, 2014). Yet, given the complexity of group-based guilt as a psychological phenomenon, each of these antecedents also includes some prominent boundary conditions. These complexities further amplify in intractable conflicts, given the unique physical and psychological nature of these conflicts, as will be discussed in the following paragraphs.

First, very similar to the case of guilt at the individual level, group-based guilt is associated with an appraisal that one's ingroup is responsible for actions that violate norms or values to which the group and the individual are committed (Branscombe, 2004; Roccas, Klar, & Liviatan, 2006). Contrary to the case of group-based shame, group-based guilt is driven by or associated with people's appraised responsibility for the wrongdoings and their consequences rather than the characteristics of the violator or the group itself (Branscombe, Doosje, McGarty, 2002; Leach et al., 2006). Yet, given that in most cases the individual who experiences the feelings of group-based guilt was not directly or personally involved in the wrongdoing, the question of the appraised responsibility for these wrongdoings is trickier.

Sabina Čehajić-Clancy (2012), who mainly has been studying the postconflict context in Bosnia and Herzegovina, has recently raised this question by asking whether, after commission of grave and mass atrocities, one can hold all members collectively and morally responsible for immoral actions and even crimes committed in their name. Are those who have not done anything wrong or those who were not even born yet automatically responsible for crimes committed by other members of *their* group? She raised the challenging question of whether they should feel responsible (and the subsequent emotion of guilt) even if they have not supported nor tolerated, not to mention were not actively engaged in, the commission of those crimes.

On the one hand, it would be inappropriate to expect people to accept the blame for something they neither did nor intended to do (Lewis, 1948). Take for example the two events I presented in the first part of the current chapter. Can we really expect all Palestinians to feel responsible for a specific action of two extremists who kidnapped and murdered three Israelis? This becomes even more complicated given that oftentimes people oppose and even speak out publicly against immoral actions conducted by their group members (see, e.g., Goldenberg et al., 2014). As such, expecting them to accept responsibility for these actions might be unrealistic and even unfair.

On the other hand, some scholars have regarded collective responsibility as a moral duty to respond to crimes committed in one's name and as a practical category that is a prerequisite for lasting reconciliation (Dimitrijevic, 2006). Čehajić-Clancy (2012) recently has offered a more nuanced approach, according to which the scope of expected responsibility depends primarily on the nature of the immoral actions committed and on the character of group identity. According to her approach, it is important to differentiate responsibility acceptance for collective immoral actions from individually committed wrongs, even if the latter were meant to be done in the name of the group. In Čehajić-Clancy's (2012) view, *collective immoral actions* or *crimes* are actions that have been committed by a significantly large number of people against other social groups and in the name of one's own group. According to Radzik (2001), these actions imply collective intent to commit specific acts, collective awareness of the nature of the intended actions, an organized effort to realize the intentions, and collective awareness of the consequences of the atrocities. Čehajić-Clancy (2012) has suggested that when all these criteria are met, acceptance of collective responsibility becomes more plausible, logical, and even expected.

This is in line with the approach taken by most scholars who have studied group-based guilt, focusing mainly on people's appraised responsibility for situations in which their group historically victimized outgroup members—events such as slavery, discrimination, and genocide (e.g., Doosje et al., 1998; Castano & Giner-Sorolla, 2006; Zebel et al., 2008)—or have benefitted from current discrimination of the outgroup in the present (e.g., Leach et al., 2003; Powell, Branscombe, & Schmitt, 2005). In these cases one can argue that a collective intent to commit specific acts was present, coupled with collective awareness of the nature of the actions. Moreover, in all of these cases, one could observe well-organized efforts aiming to realize the intention and at least some collective awareness of its inherent and unavoidable immoral consequences.

Even in the rare cases in which studies have tested collective responsibility for more specific, short-term actions by a small number of ingroup members (similar to the ones presented in the introduction of this chapter), they were tested within the broader context of a long-term oppression or a collective, well-orchestrated effort to confront and defeat the outgroup. For example, in a study we conducted in Israel, we tested Israelis' feelings of guilt and acceptance of responsibility in response to one specific event during a war between Israelis and Palestinians—the killing by a few Israeli soldiers of four innocent girls, the three daughters and a niece of Az-a-Din Abu El-Aish, a Palestinian physician who works at a large Israeli hospital (e.g., Čehajić et al., 2011, Study 2). In this specific case, three to four soldiers were involved in the action, which had not been planned by IDF commanders. Although this event does not meet all criteria mentioned, it cannot be considered as a sporadic action of independent Israelis but rather as part of a wider effort to suppress the Palestinian uprising. That is probably the reason that it induced collective responsibility, at least among some Israelis.

Second, in addition to perceived ingroup responsibility, for an individual to experience guilt in the name of a group, she has to affiliate herself with that group, to feel part of it, and to identify with it at least to some extent (Doosje et al., 1998). This is of course true for all group-based emotions (Mackie et al., 2000), but it is much more complicated in the case of group-based guilt, mainly because of the aversive nature of guilt and the way such an experience reflects on one's relationships with the group. Broadly speaking, people try to avoid feeling guilt, and as such, they will probably try to minimize their affiliation or identification with groups that are engaged in guilt-eliciting behavior. Furthermore, as suggested by Goldenberg et al. (2014), oftentimes feeling group-based guilt implies feeling guilt in the name of a group in which most group members do not share the same emotion. In that sense, group-based guilt differs substantially from other types of group-based emotions (e.g., anger or hatred) in which a large number of group members simultaneously experiences identical emotions. Accordingly, while other group-based emotions usually further connect people to their ingroup (i.e., I feel anger together with everyone else, so I feel more connected to them), the experience of group-based guilt often distances individuals from their ingroup, who see them (the individuals) as deviants or even traitors.

This complex process provides the basis for what can be described as the paradox of identity in group-based guilt (see Ferguson & Branscombe, 2014). On the one hand, group-based guilt can be experienced only by those who see themselves as part of the group. According to IET, the more people identify with a certain group, the more they feel emotions in the name of that group, especially when it comes to events or actions they were not personally engaged in (Mackie et al., 2000). On the other hand, people who strongly identify with their group are the ones who are most susceptible to blindness in the face of problematic or immoral group actions. Naturally, given that for these people the identification with the group plays a pivotal role in their self-image and identity, they may be most likely to be threatened by these negative characterizations of their social identity. As such, this identification can motivate people to find ways of exonerating their group from wrongdoing.

The first study to examine this paradox empirically was conducted by Doosje et al. (1998). In their study high identifiers who were presented with an ambiguous history of their country experienced less group-based guilt compared to low identifiers, presumably the result of selectively focusing on the positive outcomes as a means of justifying the more negative aspects of their country's past (see also Castano & Giner-Sorolla, 2006; Johns, Schmader, & Lickel, 2005; Myers, Hewstone, & Cairns, 2009). Although interesting, this pattern of results does not describe the full picture because, as already mentioned, a certain amount of group identification is necessary to enable group-based guilt. And indeed, other studies have revealed positive association between levels of identification and group-based guilt (e.g., Doosje, Branscombe, Spears, & Manstead, 2006), while some other studies have found no relations whatsoever between these variables (see McGarty et al., 2005)

One way to address this paradox was offered recently and empirically supported by Klein, Licata, and Pierucci (2011), who have revealed a curvilinear effect of identification on group-based guilt. These authors studied group-based guilt in the context of the Belgian colonization of Congo and found that group-based guilt about colonialism was affected nonlinearly by group identification, with higher guilt for mid-identifiers compared to low and high identifiers. These results suggest that while low identifiers have no real reason to experience guilt because they do not see themselves as an inherent part of the group, high identifiers, who probably feel high threat to their image, display defensive reactions that help them 'reject' potential feelings of guilt.

Another way to address the paradox of the identification–guilt relationships has been offered by Roccas et al. (2006). They studied Israeli feelings of guilt for historical events in which Israelis had committed harm against Palestinians. According to their view, two different aspects of group identification exist—glorification and attachment—and each of them is associated with guilt experience in a different way. Attachment to the ingroup had a positive relationship to guilt and glorification had a negative relationship to guilt. Roccas and colleagues also have found that defensive mechanisms in the form of exonerating cognitions mediated many of the relationships between the measures of identification and guilt. Interestingly, while Klein et al. (2011) have focused on the magnitude of identification with the group to explain the nonlinear identity–guilt association, Roccas et al. (2006) have highlighted qualitative differences between identification types as a potential moderator of these relationships (see also the work of Golec de Zavala, Cichocka, & Bilewicz, 2013; Golec de Zavala, Cichocka, Eidelson, & Jayawickreme, 2009, on collective narcissism).

Finally, the third necessary appraisal for group-based guilt is harm illegitimacy. People have to appraise their group's behavior as illegitimate to experience group-based guilt. In other words, harm caused by the ingroup to the outgroup will induce guilt only to the extent that it is perceived by ingroup members as unjust, immoral, or unfair. This is a tremendously high bar in terms of cognitive appraisals because groups, for various reasons, are motivated not to experience guilt and, therefore, seek to justify their group's behavior toward the outgroup. This is especially true in situations of ongoing (as opposed to past) conflicts, in which groups develop an ethos of conflict and a biased collective memory of the conflict that help them in justifying their ongoing actions (Bar-Tal, 2013).

That is even more challenging in asymmetrical conflicts in which dominant or advantaged groups often harm the subordinate groups and behave in ways that defy accepted norms and values to maintain their domination (Rosler, Bar-Tal, Sharvit, Halperin, & Raviv, 2009; Sidanius & Pratto, 1999). In such cases of long-term domination, the option of reducing experiences of guilt by engaging in the response tendencies with which they are associated (e.g., reparations and apologies) (Maitner, Mackie, & Smith, 2006) is less or not at all relevant because group members wish to maintain their domination. Hence, in these cases highly powerful societal and psychological mechanisms operate among advantaged group members to legitimize and justify the dominant group's behavior.

An interesting example of such a situation is Israel's prolonged occupation of the Palestinians in the West Bank. As we have described in an elaborate analysis of that situation (see Halperin, Bar-Tal, Sharvit, Rosler, & Raviv, 2010), given that most Israelis wish to preserve the status quo, they rationalize and justify the occupation in a way that portrays it as legitimate, and as such, it prevents them from feeling guilty for actions conducted in the name of the occupation. For example, most Israelis describe the occupation as a temporary situation forced on Israel due to security considerations stemming from the Palestinians' violence and their aspirations to annihilate Israel. As a result of that view, and given the dominant historical narrative in Israel, most Israelis even deny the mere definition of the situation as occupation. This enables Israelis, like other group members in similar contexts, to protect the group's positive identity and avoid negative emotions without changing the domination (Halperin et al., 2010, see also Bandura, 1999; Branscombe & Miron, 2004; Castano & Giner-Sorolla, 2006; Leach et al., 2002; Wohl et al., 2006).

Such exonerating cognitions may play a particularly important role in conflicts in which there is a history of harm and oppression directed at the blameworthy group itself. This historical narrative provides a basis for members of the group to frame any current offenses in ways that are protective of the group identity. In fact, research suggests that reminding people of their group's own victimization reduces feelings of guilt for intergroup conflict. For example, in research by Wohl and Branscombe (2008), when Americans were reminded of their own victimization on September 11 and the Pearl Harbor attack in 1941, they reported a reduced sense of guilt for America's involvement in Iraq. Other studies also have demonstrated how high perceived threat (e.g., Zagefka et al., 2010; Zebel et al., 2008) and perceived ingroup victimization (e.g., Myers et al., 2009) reduce the tendency to experience group-based guilt. In these cases people manage to justify their group's actions by turning their group from the perpetrator into the victim. In that sense, Massi Noor's concept of competitive victimhood (Noor, Shnabel, Halabi, & Nadler, 2012) and Johanna Vollhardt's (2012a) exclusive victimhood concept are extremely important because feeling as the ultimate victimized group in a certain situation helps group members to relegitimize the previously non-legitimate acts of their ingroup. Groups with a high sense of collective victimhood reason that to prevent a trauma from ever happening again, the ingroup is allowed to do everything within its power to prevent it (Bar-Tal, et al., 2009; Schori-Eyal, Klar, Roccas, & McNeill, 2015). Accordingly, any act that under other circumstances, potentially could elicit guilt, is considered legitimate in these cases.

Finally, in addition to justifying the immoral actions and portraying them as legitimate, group members often implement a denial mechanism to protect their positive self-image. People seem to be able to find ways to deny the meaning of what they or members of their group have done (Cohen, 2001). Literature on moral disengagement has identified a variety of mechanisms through which individuals can avoid negative self-sanctions while engaging in morally reprehensible behavior (Bandura, 1990, 1999). The most common mechanism in conflict situations is probably the delegitimization (Bar-Tal, 2013) or dehumanization

(Castano & Giner-Sorolla, 2006) of the outgroup. When outgroup members are not considered human beings, the most fundamental values that usually apply to other human beings become irrelevant, and therefore, even highly question-able actions (from a moral perspective) are perceived acceptable when it comes to these groups. The combination of delegitimization and collective victimhood can sometimes be interpreted as license to commit immoral and illegitimate acts (called *moral entitlement*), which in turn serve as barriers to guilt-inducing infor-mation (see Staub, 2003).

Group-Based Guilt's Implications on Intergroup (and Intractable) Conflicts

In the previous section, the processes that lead people to experience guilt in the name of their group have been reviewed, but more importantly, it has become clear that many obstacles stand in the way of implementing these processes. This makes the feeling of group-based guilt rather uncommon and usually experienced by a small minority in a certain society and only for a limited period of time. At the same time, group-based guilt's associated appraisals and emotional goals create high expectations that those who experience it actually will try to act personally and politically to repair what they have perceived as illegitimate wrongdoings conducted by their own group.

And indeed, most studies reveal patterns that adequately meet these expecta-tions. On a very basic level, numerous studies show that experience of group-based guilt predicts more positive attitudes toward victimized group members (e.g., Pedersen, Beven, Walker, & Griffiths, 2004; Powell et al., 2005; Stewart, Latu, Branscombe, & Denney, 2010). Along the same lines, Brown and Čehajić (2008) have found that higher levels of guilt on the group level for Serbians' treatment of Muslims during the Bosnian War was associated with higher levels of empathy for Bosnian Muslims.

But more importantly, an extensive line of studies show that feelings of guilt on behalf of one's group (i.e., group-based guilt) are associated with motivations to repair and compensate the victimized group. According to Čehajić-Clancy (2012), where personal or family resources and capacities are sufficient, these motivations lead some individuals who feel group-based guilt to endorse reparations on a personal level; namely, they are willing to contribute personally to repair the perceived wrongdoings. Yet, in most cases, these motivations are translated into collective reparations in the form of support for policies like, for example (but not limited to), monetary or symbolic compensations, apologies, and even support for further compromises during negotiations (e.g., Branscombe & Doosje, 2004; Brown et al., 2008; Čehajić, Effron, Halperin, Liberman, & Ross, 2011; Doosje et al., 1998; Iyer et al., 2003; McGarty et al., 2005; Pagano & Huo, 2007; Swim & Miller, 1999; Wohl, et al., 2006; Zebel et al., 2008).

Interestingly, evidence for the association between group-based guilt and support for reparative policies exists in different contexts and in different stages of conflicts. For example, McGarty et al. (2005) have found that group-based guilt felt by nonindigenous Australians was associated with support for official government policies to the indigenous community; Brown and Čehajić (2008) and also Čehajić et al. (2011, Study 3) have found that guilt felt by Serbian adolescents predicted endorsement for reparation policies to be offered to Bosnian Muslims; Iyer and colleagues (2003) have found that collective guilt among white Americans was associated with increased support for affirmative action for African Americans; Wohl, Matheson, Branscombe, and Anisman (2013) have found that greater collective guilt among European Canadians heightened the relations between perceived sincerity and positive expectations, whereas collective guilt assignment by Chinese Canadians heightened the relations between sincerity and forgiveness; and Doosje et al. (1998) have found that guilt elicited by a text dealing with Dutch colonialism in Indonesia was related to support for providing financial compensation to the victimized group.

Thus, there is a wide array of empirical evidence suggesting that group-based guilt can be an important factor motivating individuals to support policies aimed at compensating victimized groups and their society. Importantly, though, most of these studies were not conducted in contexts of violent, intractable conflicts, and among the few that were actually conducted in such contexts, most of them examined people's feelings and policy support in a postconflict rather than ongoing conflict era (e.g., Brown & Čehajić, 2008; Čehajić et al., 2011, Study 3; Myers et al., 2009). The very few exceptions are studies that have been conducted in recent years in the context of the Israeli-Palestinian conflict. For example, Sharvit et al. (2008) have found that guilt was highly associated with Israeli support for compensating Palestinians for Israeli actions in the occupied territories, and Čehajić et al. (2011) have found group-based guilt felt by Israelis in response to the killing of innocent Palestinians during a war in Gaza to be related to support for reparations offered to the families of these Palestinians and also to the Palestinian people more generally. Recently, Goldenberg et al. (2014) have replicated these results after another round of extreme violence between Israelis and Palestinians. As demonstrated by these findings, even when collective guilt researchers have studied ongoing conflicts, they have focused on support for reparations for past wrongdoings as their ultimate outcome variable. What is still left un-researched is the potential effect of group-based guilt on processes of ongoing negotiations and its predictive power of support for future compromises rather than reparations for past actions. This fits nicely with an emerging theme in the study of collective guilt that focuses on responsibility for future—rather than for historical—victimization (e.g., Ferguson & Branscombe, 2010; Caoutte, Wohl, & Peetz, 2012).

While most research reviewed in this section offers an encouraging view regarding the potential impact of group-based guilt on intractable conflicts, several recent lines of research present a more nuanced view regarding the utility of group-based guilt in such contexts. According to this rather skeptical approach, even in the rare cases that individuals experience and express group-based guilt, such feelings are not translated necessarily into reparative or constructive action. This is mainly because guilt is an aversive state that focuses attention on a person's own or a group's responsibility for wrongdoing, and as such, its motivation is targeted more at ameliorating the group's image than actually empathizing with or improving the outgroup's conditions. For example, Iyer et al. (2003) have compared the effects of a sympathy-inducing manipulation (i.e., outgroup focus) to a guilt-inducing manipulation (i.e., ingroup focus) and found that the sympathy framing was more effective in promoting support for non-compensatory efforts at promoting equality for African Americans, such as affirmative action programs.

Even more dramatically, recent studies by Colin Leach et al. (2006) have shown that although guilt is associated with the abstract goal of systemic compensation, it does not increase people's motivation to take part in collective action, meant to promote such compensation. Such motivation is driven primarily by anger at one's own group. In a way, Leach et al.'s (2006) findings have suggested that although group-based guilt orients people toward support for reparative policies, it lacks the fuel needed to mobilize people into real action. One explanation for these findings is that the abstract support for reparations already fulfils people's need not to feel guilt (self-focused need) and makes the actual action irrelevant.

Some Thoughts on Guilt Regulation

As described in the previous paragraphs, group-based guilt is not perfect. Yet, in the context of long-term, violent conflicts, it still should be seen as one of the most powerful and effective emotional engines for peace and especially for reconciliation. As such, those who are interested in promoting these processes constructively should search for ways to up regulate group-based guilt to promote its implicated attitudinal, motivational, and behavioral changes. For all the reasons mentioned, upregulation of group-based guilt is probably one of the most challenging tasks for those trying to promote conflict resolution and reconciliation. Individuals and societies involved in long-term conflicts have strong motivational reasons to reject any attempt to attribute guilt to their group and society. These motivational reasons encapsulate an ensemble of identity-based (i.e., the group's image) and more instrumental (i.e., the practical 'costs' of guilt) considerations of both individuals and groups.

Consequently, attempts to upregulate group-based guilt may face societal and institutional obstacles. For example, as suggested by Bar-Tal (2013), societies involved in long-term conflicts tend to reject any information that potentially might challenge group members' view of their group as moral and just.

Accordingly, attempts to introduce such guilt-eliciting information can back-fire because they often lead group members to hold more tightly to their initial (one-sided and biased) narrative and to come up with new rationalizations and justifications for their group's actions.

But even in those rare cases in which group members accept and internalize the criticism of their group, this can still backfire and lead to unwanted consequences. This can happen when individuals fully accept the conveyed message and attribute the misconduct and immoral behavior to the innate characteristics of their ingroup. In these cases, group-based shame will overcome guilt (Tangney, 1991; Tangney, Miller, Flicker, & Barlow, 1996), and as recent research has shown, its implications for peace and reconciliation processes also can be destructive. Given that shame is associated with more stable, negative, internal attributions of the ingroup's negative behavior, its influence on peace processes and reconciliation is less clear than that of guilt. Although evidence exists for positive effects of shame on constructive political tendencies (Brown & Čehajić, 2008; Brown et al., 2008), in most cases shame leads only to a desire to distance the ingroup from the shame-invoking situation (Iyer, Schmader, & Lickel, 2007; Sharvit et al., 2008). In that regard, not only is group-based shame not constructive, but it even can be considered a destructive emotion, enabling group members to avoid the situation rather than to deal with it.

It follows that, for group-based guilt to be upregulated, one should be exposed to information regarding illegitimate wrongdoing conducted by her own group but also be offered the necessary guarantees that such information will not reflect on the fundamental, moral characteristics of the individual and the group. In other words, to experience group-based guilt, individuals should believe that their group is fundamentally good and moral but also that the group itself or some representatives of it have caused unjust harm to members of the outgroup. This complex message potentially can lead group members to support constructive means like apology, reparations, and compensation.

Although most research on group-based guilt deals with its antecedents and consequences rather than with ways to amplify it, several recent attempts have taken up that important challenge. For example, in order to convey the complex message required to upregulate group-based guilt, we (Čehajić, Effron, Halperin, Liberman, & Ross, 2011) turned to self-affirmation theory (Sherman & Cohen, 2006; Steele, 1988), which stipulates that people can tolerate a threat to a specific aspect of their identity if they are able to secure or affirm other aspects of their positive self-image. Such self-affirmation can be accomplished by focusing on an important source of pride (McQueen & Klein, 2006). Prior research on self-affirmation has suggested that it can be efficacious in reducing ingroup bias (Sherman, Kinias, Major, Kim, & Prenovost, 2007) and can lead groups to admit negative ingroup traits like racism (Adams, Tormala, & O'Brien, 2006). In some cases, guilt can allow criticism against the ingroup (Cohen et al., 2007).

Using these findings as a background, we (Čehajić et al., 2011) hypothesized that affirming a positive aspect of the self would in fact enable people to accept responsibility and experience guilt while maintaining their (and their group's) positive identity. To examine this idea and its applicability to the context of violent intergroup conflicts, a self-affirmation manipulation was applied within the realm of two violent conflicts. In the first two studies Jewish Israeli students were presented with a simple self-affirmation manipulation and were prompted to describe a personal success, how it made them feel, and its reflection upon them (vs. a control group, who wrote about what they planned to pack for a long trip). Following this manipulation, all participants read an article that described a highly infamous event that occurred during the war in Gaza between Israel and the Palestinian movement of Hamas during 2008. The event involved the three daughters and niece of a Palestinian physician who were killed in his home by the Israeli army. An internal investigation conducted by the Israeli army confirmed that there had been no military justification for targeting his house. Results showed that participants in the self-affirmation condition experienced more guilt compared to those in the control condition. Furthermore, those in the self-affirmation group were more willing to make reparations to the Palestinians, compared to those in the control condition, and group-based guilt partially mediated the effect of the self-affirmation manipulation on support for reparation policies. Importantly, a third study yielded very similar patterns of results among Serbian participants within the context of the Srebrenica genocide that took place in Bosnia and Herzegovina in 1995.

Outside the context of intractable conflicts, Miron, Branscombe, and Biernat (2010) have extended our findings by demonstrating that enabling individuals to affirm the positive image of their group (rather than of themselves) can have very similar effects. These authors demonstrated that when white American participants affirmed their American identity (vs. a control), they set lower evidential standards for ingroup immorality and felt greater collective guilt for racial inequality. In 2011, Gunn and Wilson revealed very similar patterns when studying Canadians' guilt feelings over the mistreatment of Aboriginals and men's guilt feelings about gender inequalities.

Two additional approaches have proposed ways to upregulate collective guilt by overcoming its previously described obstacles. The first was offered by Peetz, Gunn, and Wilson (2010) (see also Ferguson & Branscombe, 2014), who have found that reducing temporal distance increases collective guilt, especially for those more likely to accept inclusive categorization with the victimized group. Their study was conducted in the context of Germans' memories of the Holocaust, trying to overcome defensive reactions by altering temporal distance. According to the study's results, this intervention is useful in upregulating group-based guilt, particularly for past (Peetz et al., 2010) or for future (Ferguson & Branscombe, 2014) wrongdoings but seems less relevant when it comes to wrongdoings done in the present. For example, in Peetz et al.'s (2010) study, non-defensive Germans induced to view the Holocaust as closer reported more collective guilt and willingness to compensate.

Finally, we (Goldenberg et al., 2014) recently have managed to upregulate feelings of group-based guilt among Jews in Israel, in the context of the Israeli-Palestinian conflict, by providing Jewish Israelis with information regarding the low levels of guilt experienced by other group members facing a situation in which feelings of guilt seemed normative and even required. Participants who perceived the collective as experiencing less guilt than it should have felt (according to their perceptions) expressed a greater need to experience group-based guilt to advance action relative to those who perceived the collective as experiencing a proper level of guilt. Thus, according to that view, when the collective fails to experience the emotions that are appropriate for the event (in this case guilt), individuals seem to take on the burden of feeling that very emotion. This offers a new way to regulate group-based emotions in general and guilt in particular by manipulating or highlighting the emotion felt by other group members.

8

EMPATHY AS A PEACE CATALYST IN INTRACTABLE CONFLICT

Is It Feasible? Is It Enough?

More than two and a half centuries ago, Adam Smith (1759) set an extremely high standard for what he viewed as genuine interpersonal caring and sympathy. In his classical contribution *The Theory of Moral Sentiments*, he wrote that, "Though our brother is upon the rack, as long as we ourselves are at our ease, our senses will never inform us of what he suffers". Smith has argued that what makes people moral is our ability to "place ourselves in his situation . . . and become in some measure the same person with him, and hence form some idea of his sensations, and even feel something which, though weaker in degree, is not altogether unlike them".

Smith's quote very nicely captures the way contemporary psychologists define empathy. According to Batson, one of the leading figures in the study of empathy, it is generally conceived of as an other-oriented cognitive and emotional response elicited by and congruent with the perceived welfare of someone in need (Batson., Chang, Orr, & Rowland, 2002). In terms of the involved processes, "empathy comprises related but distinct processes through which 'perceivers' (individuals focusing on another person's internal states) relate to 'targets' (individuals who are the focus of perceivers' attention)" (Zaki & Ochsner, 2012, p. 675). More specifically, feeling empathy means being moved emotionally by others' suffering, which often can result in feeling compassion, sympathy, or consideration for the other (Čehajić-Clancy, 2011). As a result, empathy induces a desire to help others, do justice to them, and improve their conditions (Batson et al., 2002; Iyer, Leach, & Crosby, 2003; Pagano & Huo, 2007; Zhou, Valiente, & Eisenberg, 2003).

Accordingly, it should not be too surprising that for many of us, empathy is conceived of as the ideal emotional response in the context of interpersonal and intergroup relations. What could be more desirable in the context of any kind of relationship than stepping into the other's shoes, understanding her point of view, and even experiencing her feelings? This looks like the ultimate recipe for interpersonal harmonies as well as intergroup relations. And indeed, relationships, of any kind that are dominated by mutual empathic concerns are much healthier, less susceptible to destructive conflicts, and more resilient in dealing with difficulties of different kinds.

Along the same lines, for many years, scholars of intergroup conflicts have treated intergroup empathy as a desired goal, capable of dramatically improving the probability of reaching an agreement leading to sustainable peace. In a way, intergroup empathy is conceived by academicians and practitioners of conflict resolution alike as the ultimate cure for the disease called intractable or violent conflicts. For example, Ralph White, a former US Information Agency official, later a leading political scientist and psychologist, wrote that "[e]mpathy is the great corrective for all forms of war-promoting misperception. . . . [I]t (means) simply understanding the thoughts and feelings of others . . . imagining being in another's skin, imagining how you might feel about what you experienced" (White, 1984, p. 160).

This view, which is widely shared by other prominent conflict resolution scholars (e.g., Kelman 1998; Kriesberg & Dayton, 2012), has shaped the themes of various conflict resolution interventions, primarily the ones involving intergroup contact, dialogue, and peace education. A simple Google search targeting the mission statements and core values of conflict resolution intervention programs in the context of the Israeli–Palestinian conflict reveals that increasing empathy is mentioned as a central goal in most if not all of those programs. Looking at the 'peace industry' from a financial perspective reveals that most funding invested in that industry finds its way to programs that try to bring rival group members together with the aim of increasing empathy and decreasing dehumanization of the other.

Apparently, investing the resources and time in trying to increase intergroup empathy can be seen as the right way to go, given that studies evaluating the effectiveness of peace education endeavors have shown that empathic engagement converts stereotypes and turns fear into humanness. It is also in line with studies in the framework of the contact hypothesis demonstrating that the effectiveness of intergroup contact in improving intergroup relations may stem in part from outgroup empathy or outgroup perspective taking (Pettigrew, 1998).

Accordingly, throughout the years, extensive research and practice has sought to reveal new ways to increase intergroup empathy, either by imbuing people with the skills needed to take the perspective of the other or by providing them with the platform to get to know the other more deeply, with the assumption in mind that such acquaintance with the 'other' will boost levels of empathy (see Hameiri, Bar-Tal, & Halperin, 2014 for a review of interventions). Altogether, these empathy-focused peace education and dialogue programs have created high expectations for fundamental improvements in areas of intergroup intractable conflicts. The rationale behind these expectations is in the spirit of Ralph White's quote presented earlier, namely, that by instilling empathy in people from both sides of the conflict, they will better understand the 'other side', and in turn such understanding will make them riper for the dramatic social and political compromises required for peace.

But in recent years it has become apparent that these high expectations too often are met with disappointment. In May 2013, Paul Bloom published an intriguing and even controversial article in the *New Yorker*, making the case against empathy. In the most powerful lines of that piece he pointed out that "[t]his enthusiasm (about empathy) may be misplaced, however. Empathy has some unfortunate features—it is parochial, narrow-minded, and innumerate. We're often at our best when we are smart enough not to rely on it". Although, like many others, I cannot accept all aspects of the argument offered by Bloom, I find it extremely stimulating and challenging. Moreover, as will be argued in later parts of the current chapter, some of the more problematic aspects of empathy, as expressed in the *New Yorker* piece, play a central role particularly in the context of long-term, violent conflicts, and therefore, Bloom's approach might be more relevant in that context than in any other.

From a more empirical perspective, we now know that even in conflicts in which huge efforts have been made to increase intergroup empathy, the results have not always been as encouraging as expected. Furthermore, recent empirical evidence regarding the role of empathy and perspective taking in promoting successful negotiation and conflict resolution also yield mixed results (e.g., Pierce, Kilduff, Galinsky, & Sivanathan, 2013; Rosler et al., in press). It follows that what has been considered the ultimate cure for intractable conflicts—intergroup empathy—does not seem to be so magical anymore. Importantly, I do not argue that intergroup empathy cannot be constructive in terms of conflict resolution but only that the picture is much more complicated than it looks at first glance.

The following chapter, thus, deals with the ambiguous role played by empathy in intergroup conflicts. I will make the case that although there is much merit in promoting intergroup empathy in intractable conflicts, such an endeavor might turn out to be less effective than expected for several reasons. First, given the motivational nature of empathy (see Cameron & Payne, 2011; Zaki, 2014), under certain circumstances inducing intergroup empathy is extremely difficult and at times even impossible. Second, even when empathy is induced among members of two rivalry groups, it will not translate necessarily into constructive action. Third, in those cases that empathy translates into action, it will drive people to offer humanitarian aid or to restrain intergroup aggression (Kaukiainen et al., 1999; Mehrabian, 1997; Richardson, Hammock, Smith, Gardner, & Signo, 1994) but not necessarily to support political compromises required for peace (Rosler et al., in press). And finally, even when mutual empathy is induced, like in the case of successful intergroup encounters, this harmony can serve as a barrier rather than as a catalyst of peace because it undermines the disadvantaged group's motivation to become engaged in pro-peace collective action (e.g., Saguy, Tausch, Dovidio, & Pratto, 2009).

In what follows I will start by broadly defining empathy, focusing on its three main components as well as on its motivational underpinnings. Then a more elaborated discussion of empathy on the intergroup level will be presented, followed by a review of studies dealing with intergroup biases in empathy. I will then discuss the role of empathy in intergroup conflict resolution, emphasizing side by side both its positive and negative implications on such processes. Finally, some preliminary thoughts on empathy regulation will be presented, focusing mainly on ways that can make intergroup empathic concerns more useful in the attempt to promote the resolution of long-term conflicts.

The Nature of Empathy

Even after so many years of research, there is no consensus regarding the way empathy should be defined. As pointed out by Wispe (1986) and more recently by Zaki (2014), there are nearly as many definitions of empathy as there are scientists who study this phenomenon (Duan & Hill, 1996; Preston & De Waal, 2002). At the same time, most current approaches agree that empathy is comprised of two primary components: affective and cognitive (Batson, 2009; Blair, 2005; Davis, 1983; Dziobek et al., 2008; Singer, 2006). Zaki and Ochsner's (2012) classification has added what they consider to be a third subcomponent of empathy, prosocial concern (here termed *empathic concern*): expressing motivation to improve targets' experiences. The following paragraphs briefly discuss each of these three components of empathy.

The cognitive aspect of empathy—also labeled as *mentalizing, perspective taking, mind reading,* or *theory of mind*—refers to one's ability to recognize, identify, and possibly understand another person's feelings (e.g., Davis, 1980; Hoffman, 1977; Zaki & Ochsner, 2012). Cognitive empathy involves imagining yourself in someone else's shoes (Batson et al., 2003) or entertaining the points of view of others (Davis, 1983), and it focuses exclusively on the cognitive processes while ignoring the emotional reactions to others' feelings (Cassels, Chan, Chung, & Birch, 2010). As such, taking the perspective of the other refers mainly to the ability to read the other's thoughts accurately but not necessarily to mirror her feelings. These thoughts are composed of many different aspects and this makes mentalizing a complex and multilayered process, targeting the other's intentions, beliefs, and emotions based on lay theories concerning how events affect others' experiences (Baker, Saxe, & Tenenbaum, 2009; Frith & Frith, 2012; Heider, 1958; Mitchell, 2009; Zaki, 2014). Although perspective taking or mentalizing usually is considered a constructive process in terms of interpersonal or intergroup conflicts, it also constitutes the basis for the modus operandi of military intelligence agencies.

For them, perspective taking and mentalizing are necessary tools that help predict future behavior of leaders and nations alike.

Although perspective taking or mentalizing also may offer a view into the target's affective or emotional experience, this does not lead necessarily to an identical affective experience in the observer. For example, when people experience schadenfreude, they cognitively realize that the other feels distress or sadness, but they actually feel good about that. In a way, they go through a cognitive process that is very similar to perspective taking, whereas their emotional experience is as far as one can imagine from empathy.

On the other hand, the affective aspect of empathy (also called *emotional empathy*) refers to one's vicarious emotional response to another person's emotion or situation, that is, feeling the way another feels or having a congruent emotion because the other feels that way (Eisenberg & Miller, 1987; Feshbach, 1975; Hoffman, 1977). Accordingly, the affective aspect of empathy can be defined as an affective reaction caused by, and congruent with, another person's inferred or forecasted emotions (Eisenberg, Shea, Carlo, & Knight, 1991), that is, feeling good in response to someone experiencing a positive event (e.g., when Rich wins a competition) and feeling bad in response to someone experiencing a negative event (e.g., when Rich's proposal is declined). Interestingly, this can be done even in the absence of an in-depth understanding regarding the target's cognitive appraisal of the situation; namely, one can feel emotional empathy without knowing the causes, interpretations, and thoughts of the other.

Although, no doubt, the cognitive and affective aspects of empathy can appear simultaneously, existing research demonstrate that these processes are dissociable in terms of the dominant brain systems involved (Gobbini, Koralek, Bryan, Montgomery, & Haxby, 2007; Keysers & Gazzola, 2007; Uddin, Iacoboni, Lange, & Keenan, 2007; Zaki, 2013). It also can be assumed that while emotional empathy requires at least some sense of connectedness, perceptions of similarity, or even attachment to the target person or object, cognitive empathy can take place even when the target of empathy is considered dissimilar and isolated from the source.

Both cognitive and affective components relate to a third empathic subcomponent referred to as *empathic concern* (termed *prosocial concern* by Zaki & Ochsner, 2012), which is the motivation to alleviate the suffering of another (Batson, 2011; de Waal, 2008; Harbaugh, Mayr, & Burghart, 2007; Waytz, Zaki, & Mitchell, 2012; Zaki & Ochsner, 2012). For example, a perceiver may witness another person's pain and experience cognitive empathy (imagine herself in that person's shoes) and/or affective empathy (feel what the other is feeling), but these two experiences may not motivate the perceiver to do anything to help relieve the suffering of the target (the subject of the perceiver's focus). This is where empathic concern comes in—it is the motivation to do something to help the target. Considering empathic concern as part of the comprehensive experience of empathy is in line with traditional component models of emotions, which see the emotional goals or motivations as an inherent part of the emotional experience itself (e.g., Scherer, 2004).

While empathic concern provides the motivation to help the target of empathy, it does not always translate into actual behavior, mainly due to limitations in terms of time, resources, attention, and capabilities. Yet research demonstrates that in many cases empathic concern results in helping behaviors (Batson, 2011; de Waal, 2008; Harbaugh, Mayr, & Burghart, 2007; Waytz, Zaki, & Mitchell, 2012), as indicated by the vast research showing a significant positive correlation between empathy and prosocial behavior (e.g., Batson & Coke, 1981; Eisenberg & Miller, 1987; Knight, Johnson, Carlo, & Eisenberg, 1994). In more detail, existing research has shown that empathic concern motivates prosocial actions such as providing the target with situation-specific emotional support (Lepore, 1992) and comforting messages (Burleson, 1985), increased willingness to volunteer time and money to help individuals facing hardship (Batson et al., 1991; Coke, Batson, & McDavis, 1978; Dovidio, Allen, & Schroeder, 1990), reduced egocentrism (Savitsky, Van Boven, Epley, & Wight, 2005), and more objective judgments of fairness (Epley, Caruso, & Bazerman, 2006).

The link between empathic concerns and pro-social behavior has some interesting implications in the context of interpersonal relations and more specifically in the context of interpersonal conflict resolution. For example, research conducted in the mid-1990s has shown that empathy plays a vital role in one's social-emotional health and well-being and is thought to be a highly functional trait for the development of high-quality connections with others (Litvack-Miller, McDougall, & Romney, 1997; Oswald, 1996). Empathy also has been linked to successful conflict management strategies, such as support for constructive responses including problem solving, obliging, and calm discussion (Davis, 1996; de Wied, Branje, & Meeus, 2007). Studies also have shown that higher levels of empathy predict positive outcomes, such as better emotion management and relationships and heightened valuation of others' welfare and well-being (Batson, Turk, Shaw, & Klein, 1995; Cassels, Chan, Chung, & Birch, 2010; Eisenberg, Shea, Carlo, & Knight, 1991; Eisenberg & Fabes, 1998). Finally, Björkqvist, Österman, and Kaukiainen (2000) have found that empathy was linked positively to peaceful conflict resolution and withdrawal and negatively to various types of aggression.

While there seems to be a link between empathic concern and pro-social behavior, there is a significant debate regarding the precise nature of the motivation (altruistic vs. egoistic) empathic concern elicits (Batson et al., 1995; Cialdini, 1991). Researchers from the altruism perspective, led by Daniel Batson, suggest that empathic concern evokes *altruistic motivation*—motivation with the ultimate goal of increasing the welfare of the person for whom empathy is felt—and hence is primarily selfless (Batson, 1991, 1998; Batson, Bolen, Cross, & Neuringer-Benefiel, 1986; Batson, Duncan, Ackerman, Buckley, & Birch, 1981). In contrast, researchers from the egoistic perspective suggest that empathy for another leads to a greater sense of self–other overlap, with the consequence that helping is not selfless but is directed toward both the other person and the self (i.e., to make oneself feel better) (Cialdini, Brown, Lewis, Luce, & Neuberg, 1997; Maner et al., 2002) and hence is primarily selfish. Although interesting, this debate is more theoretical or academic than practical and in many ways less relevant for us who are trying to reveal the role of empathy in intractable conflicts.

Automatic Versus Motivated Empathy

One of the most important questions, when thinking of the role played by empathy in processes of conflict resolution, is whether or to what extent empathy should be considered as an automatic reaction to exposure to the other's suffering or distress or, alternatively, to what extent it is a motivated and regulated experience. This question is important because it touches upon the essence of the ambiguity of empathy in intergroup conflicts. On the one hand, we all understand that intergroup empathy potentially can lead to more positive intergroup emotions, attitudes, and even behavior. On the other hand, it is also rather clear that from an instrumental perspective people have (or at least think that they have), all good reasons not to feel empathy toward outgroup members in the midst of violent conflict.

To clarify that idea, it is important to think more broadly about the way instrumental considerations play a role in people's emotional experiences and emotion regulation processes (see also a discussion of the instrumental approach to anger in Chapter 4). We know that through emotion regulation processes, people are capable of influencing the way they feel (Gross, 1998). In the last two decades, Maya Tamir and her colleagues have demonstrated repeatedly that the direction in which people regulate their emotions depends on what they want to feel (e.g., Mauss & Tamir, 2014; Tamir, 2009). Dominated by hedonic considerations, people typically want to experience pleasant emotions and avoid unpleasant ones. However, according to the instrumental approach to emotion regulation (e.g., Bonanno, 2001; Parrott, 1993; Tamir, 2009), this is not always the case. Individuals may be motivated to experience emotions that are instrumental in pursuing their goals, even when these emotions are unpleasant (e.g., Tamir & Ford, 2012a; Tamir, Mitchell, & Gross, 2008).

Instrumental emotion regulation occurs when people want to experience emotions to attain their instrumental (vs. immediate hedonic) benefits. Focusing on the fact that emotions influence performance, research on instrumental motives in emotion regulation has demonstrated that people are motivated to experience emotions that are expected to promote desired performance on subsequent tasks. For example, people are motivated to experience anger when they are preparing for a task that requires aggression (e.g., Tamir, Mitchell, & Gross, 2008) but fear when they are preparing for a task that requires avoidance (e.g.,

Tamir & Ford, 2009). Such cases of motivated emotion regulation were mediated by the expectation that emotions would have beneficial effects on performance. For example, people who believed that anger would improve their performance in a negotiation were motivated to increase their anger (Tamir & Ford, 2012b).

Going back to the case of empathy, given that intergroup empathy may motivate actions and policies that are not always in line with the group's main goals in the context of a violent conflict, instrumental consideration might lead people to downregulate empathy in that context. On the other hand, if empathy is an automatic reaction to the other's suffering, then instrumental considerations will play only a marginal role, if any, in the experience of empathy in conflict situations. In that case (i.e., that empathy is an automatic reaction), all that needs to be done is to make sure that groups in conflicts are exposed extensively to information and visuals presenting the suffering of the other.

Initial indications for the motivational underpinnings in the development of empathy were presented in a set of studies by Cameron and Payne (2011), who have demonstrated that people who thought that feeling intense emotions in response to mass suffering would lead to undesirable personal consequences were more motivated to initiate emotion regulation in an attempt to reduce the intensity of their emotional experiences. According to their findings, people respond with more empathy to an individual's suffering compared to group suffering because they expect the needs of large groups to be potentially overwhelming. Moreover, according to Cameron and Payne (2011), only people who can control their emotions skillfully show this effect—so emotion regulation seems to matter as well. What follows is that people who are motivated not to experience empathy, and who are capable of empathy regulation, will decrease empathy successfully when they believe it has instrumental costs.

A more elaborate theoretical framework recently was introduced by Jamil Zaki (2014) of Stanford University, who published an influential piece directly addressing this question. Zaki has offered a nuanced view of empathy development. According to that view, "although empathy *can be* automatic, by no means is it *always* automatic" (p. 1608). The clearest evidence for that is that empathy is context dependent; namely, people will experience empathy in one case but will fail to experience empathy in response to the very same event in a different context. According to the motivated account of empathy offered by Zaki, three main motives drive people to avoid feeling empathy—suffering, material costs, and interference with competition—while three other motives—positive affect, affiliation, and social desirability—drive them to *approach* empathy. It is not too difficult to notice that when thinking of intergroup empathy in the context of violent conflicts, while the restraining forces are highly prevalent, the supporting ones are rarely found. This in a nutshell is the explanation of why intergroup empathy is so uncommon in such conflicts. In the following section I will discuss empathy's failures in the intergroup context in more depth.

Empathy in Intergroup Context

One of the biggest and probably most important challenges of human society is to expand empathic concerns beyond the intragroup level into individuals from other groups and the suffering of other groups more generally (i.e., not just as individuals). In his 2010 book, James Rifkin argued that moral progress involves expanding our concern from the family and the tribe to humanity as a whole. And indeed, in the context of intergroup tensions and conflicts, several studies show that feelings of empathy can underpin the development of positive attitudes toward outgroups, whereas failure of empathy is associated with negative attitudes and behavior toward outgroups (for a review, see Dovidio et al., 2009). Even more interestingly, studies have found that eliciting empathy for one outgroup member can generalize into more positive feelings and attitudes for the entire outgroup (Batson, Early, & Salvarini, 1997; Clore & Jeffery, 1972).

Thus, much of the research into empathy and intergroup relations has focused on the potential of empathy-generating interventions (such as perspective taking) for improving intergroup attitudes, reducing intergroup bias, and increasing pro-social behavior. Previous literature has shown that taking the perspective of another negates the impact of privately held negative stereotypes on the evaluations of outgroups. For example, Batson et al. (1997) have managed to improve attitudes toward moderately stigmatized groups (i.e., people with AIDS and homeless people) by simple empathy induction manipulation. Interestingly, the same empathy manipulation failed to change negative fundamentally attitudes toward a more extreme stigmatized group (i.e., convicted murderers). Another interesting example is a study by Stephan and Finlay (1999), which has found that Whites who were instructed to empathize with a Black person showed lower levels of bias in their evaluations of Whites versus Blacks compared to those in a control condition who were given no instruction to empathize. Finally, Vescio, Sechrist, and Paolucci (2003) also have used the Batson et al. (1997) perspective-taking manipulation and found that participants who focused on how a Black interviewee felt subsequently reported more positive attitudes toward Blacks as a group than did those who adopted an objective perspective while listening to the interview.

Recent studies show that the effects of empathic concerns and predominantly its cognitive aspect (i.e., perspective taking) can go beyond its influence on intergroup attitudes and emotions to change the motivation to actually help the outgroup. These studies show that perspective taking elicits outgroup helping via the activation of a pro-social motive of empathy (Batson, Chang, Orr, & Rowland, 2002; Batson et al., 1997; Batson, van Lange, Ahmad, & Lishner, 2007; Mashuri, Hasanah, & Rahmawati, 2012). Interestingly, these effects recently were found to be moderated by the outgroup's perceived status. Mashuri et al. (2012), who studied effects of cognitive empathy on help motivations in a neutral (non-conflict) context (i.e., Vietnam and Indonesia), have found that empathy motivated outgroup helping more efficiently when the outgroup (as the help recipient) is portrayed as having a lower status than the ingroup (Mashuri et al., 2012).

Empathic perspective taking, however, also can have opposite consequences and lead to a more negative construal of the outgroup. When the setting is highly competitive, when people very strongly identify with their group, and when people have ideologically based or other group-based motivations not to sympathize with the outgroup, perspective taking equips them with necessary tools to fight the outgroup in a more effective way. In simple terms, it enables them to better 'know their enemy'. This notion is supported by several recent empirical studies. For example, when native Dutch participants were confronted with their group's past mistreatment of outgroups, manipulated perspective taking significantly increased guilt among lower identifiers but decreased guilt among higher identifiers (Zebel, Doosje, & Spears, 2009; see also Tarrant, Calitri, & Weston, 2012). Another example of the limitations of perspective taking in a highly conflictual setting is a field experiment conducted by Princeton psychologist Elizabeth Paluck (2010) in the Democratic Republic of Congo (an area replete with intergroup conflict). Among other things, in this fascinating field study Paluck tested the effects of perspective taking on attitudes toward outgroups. Results indicated that people who were exposed to the perspectives of outgroups indicated less tolerance of the outgroup and were less likely to help them than if they had not been exposed to their perspectives (Paluck, 2010).

Altogether these studies suggest that intergroup empathy potentially can result in more positive attitudes and emotions as well as constructive intergroup relations but only if it is experienced by the right people, at the right time, and under very specific circumstances. This last sentence, backed by the reviewed empirical findings, offers an important boundary condition to the effectiveness of empathy in long-term intergroup conflicts that are dominated by highly competitive environments and by highly ideological participants. The following paragraphs deal with another important boundary condition, namely, people's difficulty in experiencing empathy toward outgroup members.

Intergroup Biases in Empathy

We know from our daily lives that people do not respond with the same amounts of empathy to the suffering of all others. One common experience is hearing the news of some horrible accident in which people were injured or even killed but not yet aware of who these people were. Then, usually later in the day, when the identities of the involved individuals are revealed, our empathic response toward their friends and close ones changes, sometimes dramatically, in direct correlation with our perceived closeness or identification with these people. The closer they are to us in terms of geographical location, gender, ethnicity, and even political or religious views, the more empathy we feel toward their suffering.

This is just one example of the fact that empathy is not a universal response and that the same situations may elicit different empathy responses, based on people's distinct levels of identification with the target of the empathy. This phenomenon, which usually is termed the *intergroup empathy bias* suggests that people often feel less empathy for strangers who belong to a different racial, political, or social group compared to strangers who are described as belonging to the same group (Batson & Ahmad, 2009; Davis, 1996; Hornstein, 1978). According to Cikara, Bruneau, and Saxe (2011), most previous research in this area has focused on documenting intergroup empathy bias among real social groups, such as racial groups (e.g., Dovidio et al., 2009) and academic, athletic, or political rivals (e.g., Combs, Powell, Schurtz, & Smith, 2009; Leach, Spears, Branscombe, & Doosje, 2003; Tarrant, Dazeley, & Cottom, 2009).

Recently, Cikara, Bruneau, Van Bavel, and Saxe (2014) have replicated these findings among novel groups and also demonstrated how changing the relational structures between groups and perceptions of group entitativity can significantly can moderate intergroup empathy bias. Other studies along the same lines show that children randomly assigned to groups (e.g., the red team or the blue team) show greater empathy for ingroup members than for outgroup members who are socially rejected (Masten, Gillen-O'Neel, & Brown, 2010).

But intergroup empathy bias can go beyond a simple empathy failure when it comes to outgroup members. Rather than just not feeling empathy toward a suffering outgroup member, some people even feel pleasure in such situations. Accordingly, distressed ingroup members typically elicit empathy (Batson & Ahmad, 2009), whereas competitive rivals' pain even may elicit positive emotions, sometimes referred to as *schadenfreude* (Cikara et al., 2014; Smith, Powell, Combs, & Schurtz, 2009). Indeed, the more distant the group is, the more competitive the setting is, and the more the historical relations of the groups are characterized by mutual victimization, the higher the probability of group members experiencing schadenfreude as a result of the other's suffering.

Although this phenomenon is not surprising, it still challenges some naïve views of human nature, according to which, people feel empathy when they identify suffering, and the specific group affiliation of the suffered object or group should be less relevant. But why do people experience such failures of empathy when it comes to the suffering of outgroup members? One plausible reason for this, according to social identity theory (e.g., Turner, Hogg, Oakes, Reicher, & Wetherell, 1987), is that when a specific group membership is salient, people come to perceive ingroup members (including the self) as similar to one another. It is this perception of increased similarity among ingroup members that leads to increased feelings of empathy toward other ingroup members compared to outgroup members. Importantly, this process of group-based similarity leading to increased empathy can be automatic and does not require any involvement of motivational mechanisms. This more automatically based nature of the intergroup empathy bias phenomenon is supported by physiological and neural studies showing that outgroup members reliably elicit diminished perceptions of suffering among ingroup members and fail to elicit equivalent physiological and affective empathic responses compared with ingroup members (Avenanti, Sirigu, & Aglioti, 2010; Cikara, Bruneau, & Saxe, 2011). For example, functional magnetic resonance imaging (fMRI) studies found that the *shared neural circuit for pain* was more active in White participants when viewing White versus Asian faces being pricked with a needle (Xu, Zuo, Wang, & Han, 2009).

But there are other ways that can explain nicely the intergroup empathy bias. For example, people holding Paul Bloom's view of empathy as a finite resource suggest that given that people cannot feel empathy regarding all suffering everywhere around the globe, they consciously or unconsciously prioritize the empathic energy they are willing to invest in each person or group. Naturally, if that is the case, people will locate their friends and close ones at the top of the list and their ultimate enemies at the very bottom of that list. This process also involves intergroup attentional biases; namely, people pay more attention to the suffering of their close ones (or their ingroup members) and as a result also feel more empathy toward them.

Another valuable perspective to understand intergroup empathy bias is the one applying some principles originating in the instrumental approach of emotion regulation (Tamir, 2009) into the intragroup and intergroup domains. From a purely instrumental approach, it is more adaptive to feel empathy toward ingroup members than to outgroup members because people are usually more interested in cooperation with ingroup members, and empathic concerns can promote successful cooperation (de Waal, 2008). At the same time, especially from within an advantaged or high-powered group, feelings of empathy toward the disadvantaged group potentially can challenge current hierarchy and act against people's motivations to preserve unequal power relations (e.g., as expressed in social dominance orientation theory—Sidanius & Pratto, 2001) and more broadly against their motivation to justify the discriminatory system (Jost & Banaji, 1994).

These motivational underpinnings of empathy become even more influential when groups are involved in long-term conflict and even more so when the suffering of one group is caused, intentionally or not, by the actions of the other group. In these cases, feeling empathy toward the outgroup has direct costs to the ingroup, both psychological and at times even tangible or political ones. On the psychological level, feeling empathy toward outgroup members as a result of a suffering caused by the ingroup may challenge the group's positive self-image and potentially can raise doubts regarding some of the core beliefs usually held by societies in conflict (e.g., we are the moral side, and we are the ultimate victims; Bar-Tal, 2013). Additionally, on a more practical level, empathic concerns drive motivations to help the outgroup, which may lead to support for concrete compromises, for providing humanitarian aid, or for restraining the military force.

Altogether, the awareness of the potential psychological and tangible costs of intergroup empathy may motivate group members to downregulate their empathy toward the outgroup and its members. And indeed, in a series of studies, Porat Halperin, and Tamir (2015) recently have demonstrated that most Israelis explicitly admit being motivated not to experience empathy toward Palestinians even in the face of dramatic Palestinian suffering. This raises serious doubts regarding the feasibility and not just the effectiveness of intergroup empathy in the context of intractable conflicts.

Empathy in Intractable Conflicts—The Full but Also the Empty Half of the Glass

The previous paragraphs suggest that it is difficult for people to experience empathy in the context of intergroup conflict, and it is probably even more difficult and at times even impossible for intergroup empathy to be experienced in the context of long-term violent conflict. Yet we know that even in these extremely difficult situations, at least some group members experience some levels of empathy toward the suffering of the outgroup or at least toward the suffering of specific members of the outgroup.

For example, in the case of the Palestinian gynecologist and peace advocate Dr. Izzeldeen Abuelaish, whose three daughters and niece were killed by the IDF (previously described in Chapter 7), many Israelis indeed felt empathy toward the doctor's suffering, even though the Israeli army was the one responsible for that suffering and despite the fact that the event occurred in the midst of a violent war between Israelis and Palestinians. According to Ofer Shelah, then an Israeli Channel 10 news anchor, and now an Israeli parliament member, "Dr. Abuelaish's tragedy changed Israeli attitudes" (Associated Press, 2009). Shelah states that while Israeli public support for the [Gaza] offensive remained strong, as a justified response to years of rocket fire, the story of Abuelaish caused Israelis really to empathize for the first time with a Gaza (Palestinian) civilian. The story of Dr. Abuelaish exemplifies that even in the context of an ongoing intergroup conflict, ingroup members are capable of empathizing with the suffering of *individuals* from the outgroup. But how would such empathy influence people's attitudes and behaviors in intractable conflict? I would like to argue that experienced empathy indeed can have an effect on some aspects of the conflict but also that this effect does not necessarily translate into attitudes and actions that can contribute directly to conflict resolution.

Let me start with the full half of the glass. Existing research in areas of violent conflicts has pointed to at least three conflict-related outcomes that are influenced directly by people's levels of empathy toward the outgroup. First, empathy has been found consistently to be associated negatively with aggressive tendencies as well as with support for aggressive policies (Kaukiainen, Björkqvist, Lagerspetz,

Österman, Salmivalli, et al., 1999; Mehrabian, 1997; Richardson, Hammock, Smith, Gardner, & Signo, 1994), even in the context of intractable conflict (Shechtman & Basheer 2005). A recent example has been found in studies conducted by Rosler et al. (in press), who utilized two nationwide surveys of representative samples of Jewish Israelis and found that among all other positive emotions, empathy was the most powerful predictor of opposition to aggressive Israeli policies toward the Palestinians. In these studies, those who reported experiencing empathy toward Palestinians also strongly disagreed with items such as *"Only an attack in Gaza will restore Israel's deterrence capabilities"*.

Second, another bulk of studies has suggested that those who feel empathy toward the outgroup, quite naturally, also tend to support policies that promote the offering of humanitarian aid to that group. Outside the context of intractable conflicts, Gault and Sabini (2000) have found that trait empathy was associated positively with support for human service actions. Similar patterns were discovered by Mashuri, Hasanah, and Rahmawati (2012) who have found that empathic concern for the outgroup motivated support for political action to increase the welfare and decrease the suffering of the outgroup. Within a context of violent conflict, Pagano and Huo (2007) have found that American students who were higher in empathy (toward the outgroup) were more supportive of a variety of humanitarian actions intended to enhance the welfare of the Iraqi people. These students, who experienced empathy more than others, also expressed strong agreement with items such as "We should pull our resources together to make sure that, at the very least, the humanitarian needs of the Iraqi people for food, medical assistance, and shelter are met".

Third, when conflicts are over, at least formally, empathy has been revealed as an important fuel driving the parties toward reconciliation. For example, Brown and Čehajić (2008) have found that Serbian adolescents who felt empathy for the suffering of Bosnian Muslims, which was caused by their own group, were more ready to support reparation policies to be offered by their group, such as issuing an apology or providing material compensation to the victims. From a victim group's perspective, Čehajić, Brown, and Castano (2008) asked Bosnian Muslims to report their readiness to forgive the misdeeds committed by Bosnian Serbs during the 1992–1995 war in Bosnia and Herzegovina. They found that frequent and good-quality contact with members from the perpetrator group predicted forgiveness (positively) and desire for social distance (negatively) and that these relationships were mediated by empathy toward the outgroup (as well as by trust and perceived outgroup heterogeneity). Similarly, in the postconflict setting in Northern Ireland, affective empathy toward the "other community" was found to be the most powerful predictor of support for forgiveness of the "other community" (Moeschberger, Dixon, Niens, & Cairns, 2005; see also Tam et al., 2007).

Finally, empathy can have positive effects on intractable conflicts not just when it is experienced but also as a message conveyed to the outgroup. For example, in two studies Nadler and Liviatan (2006) have exposed Israeli Jewish participants to a Palestinian leader who either expressed or did not express empathy toward Israelis. Results showed that empathy induced forgiveness and a willingness to reciprocate empathy to Palestinian suffering caused by Israelis but only among individuals who were high on trust in the Palestinians. In a more recent study, Gubler, Halperin, and Hirshberger (2015) have revealed that expressed empathy can induce more positive intergroup attitudes among all people (and not just those with high trust) as long as the empathy-inducing stimulus is unrelated to the conflict. In their study, an op-ed author—identified by name and location as a Palestinian citizen of Israel—expressed empathy for outgroup (Jewish Israeli) suffering *not caused by his ingroup*, in this case suffering caused by the Holocaust. These results provide an interesting indication not just of the fact that expressed empathy can lead to positive consequences but also to the specific content of empathy that can be most effective in doing so. Real-world evidence for the role of empathy in reconciliation processes is described by Gobodo-Madikizela (2003), who has suggested that in the context of the Truth and Reconciliation Committees in South Africa, the offender's expression of empathy for the victim's suffering was a necessary condition for reconciliation.

But turning to the empty half of the glass, in spite of its obvious virtues, empathy has some meaningful limitations that raise serious questions regarding its actual role in promoting peace during intractable conflicts. For example, even in cases in which empathy is experienced (which are not so common in intractable conflicts), this does not motivate group members to become engaged in pro-peace collective action, which is a highly important factor in the transition from conflict to peace. Montada and Schneider (1989), for example, have found that empathy did not predict willingness to engage in political action to help change the situation of victims of injustice. This was replicated more recently in an experiment that found that empathy did not predict willingness to engage in active political action such as writing a letter to political representatives (de Rivera, Gerstmann, & Maisels, 2002). In the concluding paragraph of their paper, Joe de Rivera and his colleagues have argued that: "While some may be able to take political action out of compassion, many may require the energy of righteous anger in order to overcome the challenge posed by uncaring governments, and to avoid the political passivity implicit in assuming that the world is just" (pp. 18–19). In other words, empathy has the potential of leading people to support policies that directly reduce the suffering of the other (e.g., humanitarian aid or reduced aggression), but it lacks the required energy to actually mobilize people to act in the name of the acknowledged suffering.

Even more importantly, recent studies, conducted mainly in the framework of the contact hypothesis, suggest that it is not only that intergroup empathy does not contribute to collective action, but in some cases, it even can undermine the motivation for such action. In their highly influential piece titled "The Irony of

Harmony", Tamar Saguy, Tausch, Dovidio, and Pratto (2009) have demonstrated how harmonious encounters between rival group members decrease a disadvantaged group member's motivation to get engaged in collective action aimed at changing the discriminatory status quo (see also Dixon, Tropp, Durrheim, & Tredoux, 2010; Saguy & Chernyak-Hai, 2012; Wright & Lubensky, 2009). In one of their studies, Palestinians citizens of Israel (a disadvantaged minority) who reported on positive contact they experienced with Jews also expressed an increased perceptions of Jews as fair, which in turn predicted decreased support for social change (Saguy et al., 2009). Importantly, although these studies did not directly measure empathy, their basic rationale heavily relies on intergroup empathy as a barrier to collective action. The main conclusion of these studies is that in the context of unequal power relations, empathetic encounters often increase understanding of discriminatory policies and actions, which in turn reduce the motivation to partake in actions aiming at changing the status quo (Saguy & Chernyak-Hai, 2012).

Finally, and probably most relevant for the purposes of the current chapter, contemporary research has offered mixed results (at best) regarding the role played by intergroup empathy in promoting support for compromises for peace. On the one hand, Maoz and McCauley (2005) have found in the past that sympathy of Jewish Israelis toward Palestinians predicted support of compromises. Unfortunately, items mentioning liking and empathy were combined together in that study to measure sympathy, hence weakening distinction between specific positive emotional phenomena.

In an attempt to untangle this ambiguity, we recently have tested the association between empathy and support for compromises in the context of the Israeli-Palestinian conflict while controlling for various other factors, including other positive emotions (Rosler et al., in press). The results were very clear. When other relevant variables were controlled, we did not find any meaningful associations between the extent to which Israelis feel empathy toward Palestinians, on the one hand, and the extent to which they support compromises, on the other.

The null associations can be explained in various ways. First, the emotional goal of empathy is to reduce the suffering of the other, and unlike other policies (e.g., support for humanitarian aid), political compromises are not always conceived as directly serving this goal. Second, given the highly competitive nature of these conflicts and their zero-sum nature, motivational mechanisms may influence the outcomes of empathy and not just its experience. Hence, people can feel affective empathy toward outgroup members, but given instrumental considerations, this empathy will not result in increased support for making compromises.

Some Thoughts on Empathy Regulation

One important conclusion drawn from the previous parts of the chapter is that for empathy regulation to be effective in the context of long-term, intractable conflicts, both quantitative and qualitative tactics of regulation should be utilized (Halperin, Sharvit, & Gross, 2011). In other words efforts should be made in two, complementary paths: first, to quantitatively increase the magnitude of the experienced intergroup empathy and, second, to change qualitatively the actions driven by that empathy in the context of the conflict. In the case of empathy, the second path is critical, given that we know that people can feel empathy, but it will not necessarily be translated into constructive action.

In terms of quantitative upregulation of empathy, the most obvious first step is to make sure that group members constantly are exposed to the suffering of the outgroup. Yet extensive research suggests that even that exposure should be done cautiously and selectively. For example, in their work on the *Identified Victim Effect*, Kogut and Ritov (2005) have demonstrated that people would increase their donations dramatically for developing lifesaving drugs when the child's name, age, and even pictures were provided. Even more relevant for our purposes, Kogut and Ritov (2005) have found that the identified victim effect is restricted largely to situations with a single victim. A single identified victim elicited higher contributions than a non-identified individual, while a group of eight identified individuals did not elicit significantly higher contributions than a group of unidentified individuals.

Another rule of thumb regarding effective exposure can be found in Paul Slovic's (2007) work on the *collapse of compassion* (2007). The title of Slovic's work is inspired by a statement by Mother Teresa: "If I look at the mass I will never act. If I look at the one, I will". According to Slovic, people tend to experience empathy and compassion in response to one individual in need of aid, and this sometimes translates into a strong desire to help. But people's experienced empathy as well as their desire to help surprisingly do not increase when there are many individuals in need of help (Slovic, 2007). Altogether it seems that exposure to suffering is an important tool in empathy regulation, but one should focus on a limited number of identified victims rather than on a large number of anonymous ones (see Cameron & Payne, 2011, for a motivated account of this phenomenon).

Yet exposure to suffering is not enough. Upregulation of empathy can be achieved only if those who are exposed to suffering also are capable of taking the outgroup's perspective. And indeed, numerous studies in recent years have shown that simple training of perspective taking can induce empathy significantly and decrease animosity and hostility toward the rival group (e.g., Galinsky & Moskowitz, 2000; Todd, Bodenhausen, Richeson, & Galinsky, 2011). In a typical perspective-taking intervention, a participant is presented with a photograph of a member of the outgroup and is instructed to write a short essay from the perspective of this member, as if the participant were her. In situations of conflict, perspective taking is a key skill that can open a window to the suffering of the rival, to perceive her also as a victim, and to understand her needs and goals (see Brown & Čehajić, 2008; Nadler & Liviatan, 2006).

Yet recent studies show that perspective-taking training often fails to induce empathy among those who are highly motivated not to experience it (Levinas, 2015). Furthermore, as already mentioned in earlier parts of the current chapter, when individuals are requested to take the rival's perspective, or to empathize with her, it can backfire and lead to resistance and self-serving behavior (e.g., Epley, Caruso, & Bazerman, 2006; Galinsky, Ku, & Wang, 2005; Galinsky, Maddux, Gilin, & White, 2008; Vorauer & Sasaki, 2009). Finally, perspective taking, as well as other peace-promoting interventions in general, can take their toll even when they are successful as "[individuals] on one side of the conflict can lose credibility with their in-group if they attempt to understand the other side" (Paluck, 2010, p. 1172).

In addition to ordinary perspective-taking skills, another strategy that can contribute to upregulation of intergroup empathy is the minimization of intergroup bias. One way to do that is by emphasizing intergroup similarities rather than differences in various aspects. Enabling individuals to see similarities between themselves and members of other groups was a key element of the contact hypothesis proposed by Allport (1954). Much of the subsequent research focused on interpersonal similarity in attitudes and values (for a review, see Brown & Lopez, 2001). For instance, extensive research has demonstrated that individuals are evaluated more negatively when they differ in attitudes and beliefs than when they differ in racial group membership (reviewed in Insko, Nacoste, & Moe, 1983). Other domains of similarity are also effective in reducing intergroup bias, such as creating an environment in which individuals from different groups share the same goal (Aronson & Patnoe, 1997; Sherif, Harvey, White, Hood, & Sherif, 1961). Finally, shared subjective experiences (e.g., reacting to something with laughter at the same moment) increases interpersonal liking even more than objective similarities between individuals (Pinel, Long, Landau, Alexander, & Pyszczynski, 2006). While perspective-taking training quantitatively may increase empathy because it provides people with the skills needed to do that, highlighting intergroup similarities may contribute to empathy by increasing the motivation to experience empathy toward the outgroup. Importantly, such motivation can be provided in other ways as well, for example, by emphasizing the instrumental benefits of harmonious relations or by highlighting the potential contribution of experiencing intergroup empathy in terms of self-esteem and positive self-image.

But we know that increasing experience of intergroup empathy might not be efficient because it would not necessarily be translated into constructive action. What needs to be done, then, is to change the motivation stemming from the empathy experience in addition to changing the magnitude of the experience itself. One way to do that is by reframing the nature of the required political compromises to make sure they better fit the motivation naturally drawn from the experience of empathy. For example, if compromises are construed as humanitarian aid or as a restriction of aggression toward innocent civilians, rather than as a just or moral-based concession, its association with experienced empathy may increase.

Having said all that, we should be very realistic regarding the plausibility and the effectiveness of empathy in long-term, intergroup conflicts. As I see it, empathy is plausible and it can be effective, but only in limited cases, for a limited time and for a small number of people. It definitely can help in restricting violence, but it shouldn't be expected to mobilize the masses to support for peace. And maybe, as offered by Ralph White (1984) in the following paragraph, empathy has other positive side effects that make it so valuable in conflict situations:

> *Most of all it means trying to look at one's own group's behavior honestly, as it might appear when seen through the other's eyes, recognizing that his eyes are almost certainly jaundiced, but recognizing also that he has the advantage of not seeing our group's behavior through the rose-colored glasses that we ourselves normally wear. He may have grounds for distrust, fear and anger that we have not permitted ourselves to see. That is the point where honesty comes in. An honest look at the other implies an honest look at oneself.*

(p. 161)

9

THE CATCH-22 OF INTRACTABLE CONFLICTS

The Role of Pride and Humiliation in Conflicts and Peace Processes

(Inspired by a paper by Saulo Fernandez, Saguy, & Halperin, 2015)

One of the most important contributions of social identity theory (Tajfel & Turner, 1986) to the understanding of group processes is the idea that people's self-image and self-esteem are derived heavily from their identification with certain social groups. In other words, the identification with positively evaluated social groups helps people to maintain positive views of themselves. Given the central role intractable conflicts play in the lives of the involved individuals, the main target for the identification of those individuals is the social, ethnic, or national group that reflects their position within that conflict. As such, this relevant group constitutes the main group-based source for positive self-esteem, based on group affiliation. This raises the question of the emotional processes that contribute to the induction or reduction of that positive image throughout the dynamics of intractable conflicts. In the current chapter I focus on two of the most powerful players in that game, intergroup pride and humiliation, suggesting that both play a central role in preventing people and societies from making meaningful progress toward the resolution of intractable conflicts.

The Israeli government launched Operation Cast Lead on December 27, 2008, in what most Israelis saw as an Israeli response to ongoing and prolonged rocket fire by Hamas in Gaza, on the western Negev and Gaza vicinity communities. Israel's then-prime minister, Benjamin Netanyahu, was interviewed on the first day of the war and said, "I will not accept this situation. . . . I can't think of any other country that would do nothing when faced with constant rocket fire. We have to go from a policy of compliance to one of assault. We have to restore our national pride" (Branovsky, 2009). Interestingly, just three years later, in a different context, the Turkish prime minister Recep Tayyip Erdogan used the exact same terminology, this time against Israel, saying that he had decided to suspend defense trade with Israel as a matter of national pride. Erdogan added that he did not care if trade sanctions cost $15 or $150 million (Kate 2011).

Although political leaders do not so frequently use such explicit 'pride' terminology as used by Netanyahu and Erdogan, there is wide consensus regarding the destructive role it plays in intractable conflicts. *Pride* is commonly defined as a positive feeling that emerges as a consequence of a successful evaluation of action or performance. Pride involves experiences of joy, pleasure, and satisfaction as a result of praise by others or independent self-reflection (Lewis, 1993; Tracy & Robins, 2004). A feeling of collective pride requires strong identification with the group, and as such, pride often has been included in the assessment of patriotic feelings of society members (de Figueiredo & Elkins, 2003; Mummendey, Klink, & Brown, 2001; Smith & Kim, 2006). Intractable conflicts, and especially repeated acts of fighting, create a fertile ground for the evolvement of collective pride (Brewer, 2001) based mainly on heroic behaviors, overcoming ostensibly more powerful enemies, or holding to some moral values even in the face of violent war and seemingly immoral actions conducted by the outgroup. In the current chapter I argue that these processes potentially can lead groups and societies to become more psychologically invested in the conflict and less keen to resolve it because it serves the important goal of preserving the group's and, as such, also the individual's positive self-image.

On the other side of the spectrum, humiliation is probably the most extreme form of violation of collective pride, and it also has dramatic implications on the dynamics of conflicts. In a speech in October 2003, Malaysia's then-departing prime minister Mahathir Mohamad said:

> I will not enumerate the instances of our humiliation. . . . We are all oppressed. We are all being humiliated. . . . Today we, the whole Muslim [community], are treated with contempt and dishonor. . . . There is a feeling of hopelessness among the Muslim countries and their people. They feel they can do nothing right. . . . Our only reaction is to become more and more angry. Angry people cannot think properly.
>
> *(Friedman, 2003)*

Mohamad's words nicely capture the way humiliation is viewed in contemporary psychological literature, namely, as an extreme feeling of subjugation and harm to dignity. In terms of appraisals, those who feel humiliated see themselves as unjustly downgraded and devalued as a result of intentional behavior of the other (Hartling & Luchetta, 1999; Lindner, 2001, 2002, 2006b, 2009; Statman, 2002). During conflicts, humiliation is evoked as a result of continuous negative behaviors imposed by a strong group toward a weaker group. This can include discrimination, oppression, or occupation in the conflict situation. But in other cases, a strong group also can be humiliated, meaning that it loses dignity and self-respect by an act or acts of another group. Examples include a defeat in battle or a harsh terror attack that hits the center of another group. Lindner (2002) has suggested that humiliation leads to a desire for retribution and therefore motivates violence. Others (e.g., Ginges & Atran, 2008) have found that humiliation is associated with a tendency toward inaction that suppresses rebellious or violent action. In the current chapter I postulate that repeated experiences of group humiliation may hurt the positive view of the ingroup in a way that would not enable group members to be open, generous, or cooperative as required to promote peace, at least until they restore their positive self-image in another way. Thus, humiliation does not only constitute fuel leading to intergroup violence and aggression, but it also can hinder processes aspiring to promote peace.

Integrating these two themes, namely, the need to preserve a credible, reliable, and fertile source of pride, together with the desire to restore the positive image damaged by one-time or repeated humiliating events, may hold back society members from making progress toward peace. Finally, it will be suggested that to overcome the abovementioned obstacles, people's feelings of pride and humiliation, and maybe more importantly, their desire to preserve self and group positive image must be taken into account in any proposed path for peace.

In what follows I will start by broadly defining pride and humiliation, first on the individual level. Then a more elaborated discussion of pride and humiliation on the intergroup level will be presented, followed by a review of studies dealing with the implications of these emotions on intragroup processes and intergroup relations. I will then discuss the way both pride and humiliation constitute barriers to conflict resolution, focusing on the unique processes that make it difficult to overcome each of them. Finally, some preliminary thoughts will be offered on the way these two emotional processes should be addressed properly for a conflict resolution process to lead to stable peace and potentially also to reconciliation.

The Nature of Pride and Humiliation

People experience pride when they appraise a certain action they have committed to be successful, to meet high standards or norms, to reflect supreme moral values or ideologies, or to be superior to parallel actions conducted by others (Lewis, 1993; Tracy & Robins, 2004). These pride-eliciting events make people believe that they are responsible for a socially valued outcome or that they are a socially valued person (Barrett, 1995; Mascolo & Fischer, 1995). Such an appraisal naturally is followed by positive feelings of joy, happiness, and satisfaction as well as by a significant boost in self-esteem, forming a more positive self-image in the short and in the long run. According to Tracy and Robins (2004), pride seems to include judgments about the consistency of one's behavior with a valued identity, and the more the actions align to such identity, the more pride the person experiences. People can experience acute feelings of pride that disappear after a short period of time, but they also can experience quiet satisfaction, which they would probably define as pride in retrospect, years after an event (Sullivan, 2007a). In the last two decades, as part of the attempts to define pride more accurately and to isolate it from other discrete emotions, researchers have identified particular facial and bodily expressions of pride taking the form of the head raised, arms in the air, a small smile (Tracy & Robins, 2003), or even making a fist (Schubert & Koole, 2009), which is highly common in pride events that occur during public sports events.

Pride is considered central in understanding human behavior due to its wide implications on the way people regulate their intra- and interpersonal psychological functioning and due to its implications on people's well-being. On the positive side of the spectrum, inherent in pride is its significant contribution to people's self-esteem to the extent that some scholars have argued that pride is the emotion that gives self-esteem its affective kick (Brown & Marshall, 2001). More interestingly, pride was found to reinforce pro-social behaviors such as altruism and adaptive behaviors such as achievement (Weiner, 1985). On the other side of the same coin, sometimes the loss of pride is part of what provokes aggression and other antisocial behaviors in response to ego threats (Bushman & Baumeister, 1998).

But while pride, or at least certain types of pride, contributes to the development of a deep-rooted sense of self-esteem and even promotes positive behaviors in the achievement domain (Herrald & Tomaka, 2002), in other cases, it can be harmful and even destructive. As such, extreme levels of pride have been associated with narcissism (Lewis, 2000) and labeled the deadliest of the Seven Deadly Sins (Dante, 1308–1321/1937). Along these lines studies focusing on what frequently has been described as "the dark side of pride" have revealed its causal relations with maladaptive attitudes and behaviors like aggression and hostility, relationship conflict, and interpersonal difficulties (Bushman & Baumeister, 1998; Campbell, 1999; Morf & Rhodewalt, 2001; Paulhus, Robins, Trzesniewski, & Tracy, 2004).

Interestingly, when scholars of pride have tried to bridge the gap between the positive and the negative implications pride has on our lives, they have come to a very similar conclusion to that of researchers studying other self-conscious emotions (e.g., guilt and shame). According to that view, the pride that results from a specific achievement or pro-social behavior might be distinct from the pride people tend to experience as a result of a more general view they hold on the global self. Tracy and Robins (2007) have suggested that two facets of pride can be distinguished by their associated core appraisals or subsequent attributions. In their words "*authentic*, or *beta*, pride (*I'm proud of what I did*) might result from attributions to internal, unstable, controllable causes (*I won because I practiced*), whereas pride in the global self (*I'm proud of who I am*), referred to as *hubristic*, or *alpha*, pride (M. Lewis, 2000; Tangney, Wagner, & Gramzow, 1989), might result from attributions to internal, stable, uncontrollable causes (*I won because I'm always great*)" (p. 507).

More importantly, the implications and consequences of these two types of pride differ significantly. Authentic pride might accompany and fuel high self-esteem and as such provide an adaptive psychological reaction, whereas hubristic pride might be the basis of narcissists' feeling state (Lewis, 2000; Tracy & Robins, 2003). According to Tracy, Weidman, Cheng, and Martens (2014), individuals high in dispositional authentic pride tend to be low in depression, trait anxiety, social phobia, aggression, hostility, and rejection sensitivity and high in life satisfaction, relationship satisfaction, dyadic adjustment, and social support, and typically they are attached securely to their relationship partners. In contrast, individuals high in dispositional hubristic pride are more likely to experience chronic anxiety; engage in aggression, hostility, and a range of other antisocial misbehaviors (e.g., drug use and petty crime); and report lower dyadic adjustment and social support (Orth, Robins, & Soto, 2008; Tracy, Cheng, Robins, & Trzesniewski, 2009).

If pride is the affective kick of self-esteem, humiliation, which is by all means no less powerful than pride, can be considered as the affective opponent of positive self-esteem. According to Eveline Lindner (2002), one of the most important scholars of humiliation, *humiliation* is

> [e]nforced lowering of a person or group, a process of subjugation that damages or strips away their pride, honor or dignity. . . . To be humiliated is to be placed, against your will and often in a deeply hurtful way, in a situation that is greatly inferior to what you feel you should expect. Humiliation entails demeaning treatment that transgresses established expectations. . . . The victim is forced into passivity, acted upon, made helpless.
>
> *(p. 126)*

Despite the relevance that humiliation has in human relationships, there is still no clear consensus about what unique characteristics define this emotional phenomenon and differentiate it from other related ones. While there is general agreement that humiliation implies a feeling of having been demeaned or put down by others (Torres & Bergner, 2012; Walker & Knauer, 2011), the existing empirical evidence about the core appraisals that characterize humiliation and distinguish it from other related emotions is scarce and not sufficient (see Leidner, Sheikh, & Ginges, 2012; Elison & Harter, 2007, for a similar argument).

The existing literature, however, seems to highlight two basic appraisals that underlie humiliation: the assimilation of *a devalued identity* as a consequence of the actions of others and the appraisal that those actions that have caused the devaluation of the self are *unjust* (Ginges & Atran, 2008; Harling & Luchetta, 1999; Klein, 1991; Leidner et al., 2012; Walker & Knauer, 2011). Regarding the first appraisal, which can very easily be seen as the mirror image of pride core appraisal themes, Torres and Berger (2012) have highlighted that humiliation implies damage to *the victim's identity* produced by a loss of status forced by someone who has the necessary position to reject the humiliated victim. This idea of damaging the victim's identity via a hostile process has been emphasized by other authors, such as Klein (1991), who has defined humiliation as "what one feels when one is ridiculed, scorned, held in contempt, or otherwise disparaged for what one *is* rather than what one *does*" (p. 117, emphasis added). According to our recent findings (Fernández et al., 2015), the damage to the victim's identity must be driven by an appraisal of interiorizing, assimilating, or accepting the devaluation posited by others. Interestingly, this specific appraisal of humiliation overlaps with core appraisals of shame, but according to Torres and Bergner (2012), these two emotions differ in the extent to which the self's perceived deficiency is revealed to others. If the deficiency is made public, humiliation arises; if it is not, the person will feel only ashamed but not humiliated.

Another appraisal that separates humiliation from shame is that of perceived injustice, which is also highlighted in most discussions of humiliation. For instance, Walkner and Knauer (2011) have argued that humiliation implies negative feelings about oneself such as feeling small, insignificant, weak, or stupid, which are a result of a fundamental appraisal of being the victim of a damage of the self *unjustly* inflicted by others. Similarly, Hartling and Luchetta (1999) have defined humiliation as a "deep dysphoric feeling associated with being, or perceiving oneself as being, unjustly degraded, ridiculed or put down" (p. 264). Other scholars also have discussed the extent to which humiliation implies a *public* devaluation of the self (Elison & Harter, 2007; Torres & Berger, 2012). Finally, some recent findings also connect humiliation with a feeling of helplessness on the part of victimized individuals or groups (Leidner et al., 2012). The injustice appraisal creates some overlap between humiliation and anger, yet while angry individuals reject the (perceived) unjust criticism, humiliated individuals interiorize it, at least to some extent. A second important difference between humiliation and anger maintains that anger is associated with feeling powerful (Peterson & Harmon-Jones, 2012; Tiedens, 2001), while humiliation implies a sense of powerless (Leidner et al., 2012).

In regard to action tendencies, humiliation has been associated with two opposing kinds of behavioral motivations: approach action tendencies in the form of aggression and desire for revenge (Elison & Harter, 2007; Thomaes, Stegge, Olthof, Bushman, & Nezlek, 2011; Torres & Bergner, 2012) as well as withdrawal action tendencies in the form of inaction and helplessness (Ginges & Atran, 2008; Leidner et al., 2012). According to Fernández and colleagues (2015), these two seemingly conflicting motivations encapsulate the paradoxical nature of humiliation, which shares characteristics with two fundamentally different emotions such as anger (a clear approach emotion) and shame (a clear avoidance emotion). For example, Leidner, Sheikh, and Ginges (2012) have found that humiliating experiences were associated with intense, other-directed outrage. However, they also found that humiliating events were characterized by a feeling of powerlessness. Indeed, these authors describe the experience of humiliation as a mix of outrage and powerlessness. This interesting mixture finds expression in what was defined by Ginges and Atran (2008) as an "inertia effect". Based on research conducted among Palestinians in the context of the Israeli-Palestinian conflict, they found that humiliating experiences did not foster violent aggressions but led to apparent inertia: "[H]umiliation was typically negatively related to cognitive and emotional support for suicide attacks against Israelis and was never positively related to such support" (p. 291). Torres and Bergner (2012) also have emphasized a tendency toward hopelessness, helplessness, and suicide among victims of humiliation. However, these authors also have argued that experiencing humiliation can lead to "powerless rage" and extreme aggressive behavior. Thomaes et al. (2011) have found that when their participants reappraised shameful events as caused by *others*, they experienced what they called "humiliated fury", defined as the anger people experience when they are shamed.

Pride and Humiliation in the Intergroup Context

People feel pride in response to success they have had, but they also can feel pride because of the perceived success of another group member or even of the group in its entirety. Obviously, people feel pride when they see their group as moral (e.g., Leach, Ellemers, & Barreto, 2007) or when a group effort materializes into a significant group achievement (e.g., winning of a national sports team or high rank in worldwide education survey). Interestingly, people sometimes feel pride when another, unknown group member does something that is considered valuable or moral (e.g., when our group member contributes to poor people on another continent), even if the group itself has not done anything to make this happen. In many ways, feeling proud in the success or moral behavior of other (unknown) group members can be considered the purest form of group-based emotional experience.

When pride is experienced simultaneously by many group members, we see it as collective pride. In these cases, the feeling of pride is the widespread positive feeling of a crowd in response to a specific collective or even national triumph, which can be sports based, culturally based, or even political (Sullivan, 2014). According to Gavin Sullivan (2014), who writes extensively on collective pride, this collective emotion is experienced when people believe (or are led to believe) that the successful event says something positive about their group more generally. Sullivan (2014) also has argued that to thoroughly capture the interactional, multilevel experience of pride, both individual and group-based forms of pride must be taken into account simultaneously. This approach is also grounded in social identity theory, which sees the social and the individual identities as part of the same psychological ensemble.

In conflict situations or competitive contexts, groups rely heavily on collective pride as a mobilization vehicle and as glue that brings group members together to serve important group goals. Interestingly, in these contexts the source of the collective pride usually is derived from themes relevant to the conflict itself. During long-lasting, intractable conflicts, actions characterized as victories, heroism, resilience, successful persistence, sacrifice, or extensive mobilization are examples of successes that may result in collective pride. For example, Bar-Tal (2013) has described the unequivocal and very rapid Israeli victory in the Six-Day War in June 1967 over the Egyptian, Syrian, and Jordanian armies as arousing exhilarated feelings of pride among Israeli Jews. In this vein, Devine-Wright (2001) has reported that in the Northern Ireland context that Protestants who commemorate their past victories in parades view them with great pride, seeing them as symbolic reminders of successful moments of historical events that fuel their sense of social identity. Pride also may be experienced as a result of the ability to withstand a strong rival in the conflict who has military and economic superiority. Palestinians often express pride in their ability to cope with the objectively more powerful and well-equipped Israeli army. In the Jewish tradition, only a few ideas are as deeply ingrained in Israeli culture as the one summed up by the Hebrew phrase *Meatim Mul Rabim*, or "the few against the many". Rooted in the story of Hanukkah, Jewish Israelis often express pride in the Jewish people's ability to contend with much more powerful forces.

Interestingly, according to Bar-Tal (2013), groups in conflicts tend to feel pride not only because of their courage, creativity, and determination in the battlefield but also due to their perceived moral behavior during these violent episodes. This leads to a paradoxical situation in which groups are proud of their perceived moral behavior regarding contemporary or historical wrongdoings. For example, as mentioned by Doosje and colleagues (1998), some Dutch citizens are proud of the advanced educational system and the solid legal system the Dutch bequeathed to Indonesia during the Dutch colonization of that country. Similarly, many Israelis are proud of the way Israel treats Palestinians in the occupied territories. For years, the Israeli mainstream defined it as an enlightened occupation (in Hebrew, *Kibush Naor*), and the main theme has been that the Palestinian's situation would have been much worse had they been under the sovereignty of other Arab countries (see Halperin, Bar-Tal, Sharvit, Rosler, & Raviv, 2010).

It seems, therefore, that collective pride helps society members to preserve a positive group image in the context of intergroup tensions. This may lead to a group member's refusal to accept any responsibility for their group's immoral actions. Additionally, recent work conducted outside the context of intractable conflicts demonstrated that the more individuals are proud of their ingroup achievements, the less willing they are to share resources with dissimilar others (Harth, Kessler, & Leach, 2008; Leach et al., 2007). To illustrate, Harth and colleagues (2008) have found that students who were proud of their ingroup refused to share athletic facilities with a disadvantaged group when they were led to believe that they enjoyed an advantage in athletic facilities over immigrants of the same age.

These findings are consistent with the notion of pride as a rank-related emotion (Oveis, Horberg, & Keltner, 2010), which enables individuals and groups to create distance between the self and the other (Kitayama, Markus, & Kurokawa, 2000; Kitayama, Mesquita, & Karasawa, 2006) or between the ingroup and the outgroup. Within an intergroup setting, the pride-boosted distance also enables groups to preserve social hierarchies with their group being perceived as superior to other groups. At the same time, though, pride can have more constructive implications on intergroup relations since it provides people with sufficient self- and/or group esteem that potentially can enable them to acknowledge the group's wrongdoings and even to accept responsibility for these actions (see Čehajić et al., 2011). We (Schori-Eyal, Reifen Tagar, Saguy, & Halperin, 2015) have recently found that inducing conflict-related, group-based pride among high glorifiers can increase group-based guilt for group actions during the same conflict, effectively regulating one group-based emotion by regulating another. Additionally, as pride is a source of happiness and other positive affective reactions, it can have positive implications on the way people think and act in the context of intergroup tensions.

The gap between the destructive and the more constructive implications of collective pride has been addressed in the literature in various ways; all fit very nicely with the distinction between authentic and hubristic pride that has been offered mostly by scholars who studied pride on the individual level. On the national level, political scientists (e.g., de Figueiredo & Elkins, 2003) have pointed to the distinction between patriotism and nationalism. According to their theorization and findings, while nationalists have a strong predilection for hostility toward outgroups of different kinds (e.g., immigrants), patriots who share the same connectedness and affection toward their country as do nationalists show no more prejudice than does the average citizen (see also Mummendey, Klink, & Brown, 2001; Smith, & Kim, 2006).

In social psychology, Sonia Roccas, Klar, and Liviatan (2006) and Roccas, Sagiv, Schwartz, Halevy, and Eidelson (2008) have made a similar, although not identical, distinction between ingroup attachment, on the one hand, and ingroup glorification, on the other hand. While attachment refers to extending one's self-concept to include the nation, feeling emotionally attached to the nation and wanting to contribute to it, ingroup glorification highlights the superiority of the nation over others. Ingroup glorification overlaps to some extent with the notion of *collective narcissism*, which is defined as an emotional investment in a belief in the unparalleled greatness of an ingroup (Golec de Zavala, Cichocka, Eidelson, & Jayawickreme, 2009). Although the work of Roccas et al. (2006) and Roccas et al. (2008) has not dealt directly with the feeling of collective pride, but rather with various aspects of group identity, their conceptualization provides the identity-based platform for the emergence of different kinds of collective pride.

Even more importantly, these very different aspects of collective identity and pride naturally yield distinct implications on attitudes and behaviors in intergroup settings. While those who are strongly attached to their group (but do not glorify it) see themselves as responsible for the group's (immoral) actions due to their strong commitment to the group (Roccas et al., 2006), glorification is associated with increased support for aggression against the outgroup (Dugas et al., 2015); a shift in morality toward a focus on loyalty and authority when under threat (Leidner & Castano, 2012); less demand for justice after reading about mistreatment of prisoners and civilians by coalition troops in the Iraq war (Leidner, Castano, Zaiser, & Giner-Sorolla, 2010); and reduced group-based guilt (Roccas, Klar, & Liviatan, 2006). These associations are echoed in the work on collective narcissism, which also is associated with a similar negative impact on intergroup relations (e.g., de Zavala, 2011; de Zavala, Cichocka, Eidelson, & Jayawickreme, 2009; Golec de Zavala, Cichocka, & Bilewicz, 2013).

To sum up, when collective pride is driven mainly by people's connectedness to their own group and their happiness in its success, rather than by the need to degrade other groups, this can play an important role in maintaining a positive group image, creating group solidarity and cohesion and even enabling group members to acknowledge the ingroup's wrongdoings. Yet nationalistic, hubristic, or glorification-based pride might have destructive implications on intergroup conflicts. Still another potentially destructive implication of collective pride on intergroup conflicts stems from the centrality of conflict-related themes in the formation of collective pride of societies in conflict. According to that view, if the conflict has been such a fertile ground for collective pride induction, societies will be reluctant to 'give up' the conflict itself. As such, societies in conflict might be motivated to maintain the conflict in spite of its obvious costs not to give up their main source of pride.

But people might not be willing to give up conflicts not only because of the need to preserve a pride-based positive group image but also because they feel an urgent need to restore group pride that was damaged during the years of the conflict. This can happen mainly if the group has gone through repeated or even one dramatic episode of collective humiliation. Humiliation as noted at the beginning of the chapter is defined as feelings of subjugation and harm to dignity that occurs when a person feels unjustly downgraded and devalued as a result of intentional behavior of the other (Hartling & Luchetta, 1999; Lindner, 2001, 2002; Statman, 2002). Very similar to other group-based emotions, people can feel group-based or collective humiliation even if they were not personally humiliated in any way. For example, group-based humiliation can be felt when another group member has been unjustly devaluated by outgroup members. People also can feel group-based humiliation if they perceive an action or statement of an outgroup representative to unjustly and intentionally offend the ingroup in its entirety.

Although people try to avoid humiliation, it is endogenous to the dynamics of intergroup conflicts and, therefore, is more common in these settings than in others. Interestingly, as most intergroup conflicts are asymmetrical in nature and include an inherent gap in power among the groups, the source and the nature of humiliation differ significantly between high and low power groups in conflicts. While sporadic, short-term events can cause humiliation for both high- and low-power groups, there are differences in the nature of the more common appearances of humiliation for each type of group.

For low-power groups, humiliation is often a result of continuous negative behaviors imposed by the high-power outgroup, such as discrimination, oppression, or occupation in the conflict situation. These acts of humiliation are embedded within the fundamental structure of the relations between the groups, and they can be amplified by concrete, high-intense humiliating actions of specific group members. For example, for most Palestinians living in the West Bank, the mere fact that they live under Israeli occupation is humiliating, and the daily encounters with the Israeli soldiers who enforce that situation further highlight the feeling of humiliation. Adding to that, a specific provocative statement or violent behavior by a young Israeli soldier toward an elderly or pregnant Palestinian woman can amplify the feeling of humiliation even more. In these cases, acts that cause humiliation are inflicted because the other group has more power and can carry them out. In such an asymmetrical conflict, one group has the power to carry out acts of humiliation that intentionally demean, harm, subjugate, and/or downgrade the rival group.

But humiliation also can be experienced by high-power groups in spite of the fact that the structure of the relations themselves does not enable low-power groups constantly and repeatedly to humiliate the high-power group. In these cases, high-power groups can feel humiliated due to concrete actions of the outgroup that break or challenge the acceptable intergroup hierarchy or challenge the high-power group's image as superior to the low-power outgroup. For example, if one group is perceived by all parties to be the more capable in terms of military strength, any act by the low-power group that violates the status quo can be perceived as humiliating as it hurts the dignity and self-respect of the high-power group. These acts are unpredictable, and being hurt, the society feels that it has lost its dignity unjustly. An example of this type of humiliation was experienced by Russians when between 40 and 50 Chechens seized a crowded Moscow theatre on October 23, 2002. They took hostages and demanded the withdrawal of Russian forces from Chechnya. At the end of this dramatic terror attack, more than 130 hostages were killed together with most of the attackers. Another example is the experience of Jewish Israelis after the Second Lebanon War, which ended with no clear victory by either side. Given Israel's alleged superiority, such a military draw was perceived humiliating by most Israelis.

The common denominator in all types of collective humiliation, among high- and low-power groups alike, is the fact that it causes fundamental harm to the group's positive image. If group members accept or internalize what they define as an unjustified and intentional devaluation of their group, some damage to positive group identification is caused. Given that positive identification with the group is what motivated people to belong to social groups in the first place, challenging that positive identification must have implications on people's action tendencies in social and political domains.

The most immediate implication of such a challenge to positive group identification is an increase in motivation to fight back, hurt, and probably also humiliate the humiliating outgroup. Although there is no strong empirical support for that idea, it is well rooted in psychoanalytic theory (Steinberg, 1991) and has substantial anecdotal support (Hassan, 2007). For example, Ginges and Atran (2008) have described a long series of interviews that they and others have conducted with members of different terror organizations and other militant groups, in which the interviewees attributed their own violent acts to personal or collective humiliation experienced at the hands of their oppressors (Atran & Stern, 2005; Fontan, 2006). The same approach is also demonstrated in a fascinating line of studies, based mainly on in-depth interviews conducted by Eveline Lindner (2002) in Somalia, Rwanda, and Burundi in which she found that, according to people's lay understanding of their own and other's actions, humiliation leads to a wish for retribution and therefore motivates violence.

From a macro perspective, Thomas Scheff (2003) has echoed a widely discussed notion according to which the humiliation that befell Germany after World War I led Hitler and the German public to become trapped in an ongoing cycle of humiliation, rage, and vengeful aggression, which ultimately resulted in the perpetration of the atrocities of the Holocaust. In an attempt to reveal the psychological underpinnings of the Cuban missile crisis, Steinberg (1991) has described the way the experience of being humiliated, the fear of humiliation, and the wish to retaliate by inflicting humiliation on the other motivated aggressive behavior by Khrushchev and President Kennedy. In her words, the feelings of humiliation and shame often are followed by narcissistic rage that is expressed in acts of aggression in an attempt to alleviate the painful emotions and to increase feelings of self-worth. That entire approach is encapsulated in the words of Osama Bin Laden (as cited by Wright, 2006, p. 150) that provide a humiliation-based explanation for Al-Qaeda's major attacks against the Western world: "They [the United States] have attacked our brothers in Palestine as they have attacked Arabs and Muslims elsewhere. The blood of Muslims is shed. It has become too much. . . . We are only looked upon as sheep, and we are very humiliated".

With very similar rationale in mind, Ginges and Atran (2008) also have explained why humiliation may constitute a barrier to mutually beneficial compromises in intergroup conflicts. They base their thesis on the fact that in intractable conflicts, people often see the core issues at the heart of the conflict as "holy" or "sacred" (Tetlock, 2003; Ginges, Atran, Medin, & Shikaki, 2007). When issues or values are attributed as such, any compromise or even the entertainment of such compromise may be seen as potentially humiliating. Accordingly, the experience or the fear of humiliation suppresses support for political compromise. These authors also offer sophisticated ways to overcome that barrier, but these will be discussed in later parts of this chapter.

A recent study by Ginges and Atran (2008), which has already been mentioned in earlier parts of this chapter, has provided support for their thesis and also revealed a more nuanced picture regarding the role played by humiliation in shaping people's support for aggressive policies in intractable conflicts. Importantly, Ginges and Atran's (2008) study is one of the first actually to test ideas regarding the role of humiliation in a quantitative, empirical set of studies conducted in the midst of a real intractable conflict. According to the authors, using such an approach enabled them to disentangle what humiliation really does in conflicts from what people think or report that it does. These authors carried out two studies among Palestinians residing in the West Bank and Gaza Strip in 2005 and 2006. First, they found that a high percentage of Palestinians reported being humiliated by Israelis. This is no big surprise given the structural differences in power between these parties. Second, they found that humiliation produces an *inertia effect*, a tendency toward inaction that suppresses rebellious or violent action but that paradoxically also suppresses support for acts of intergroup compromise when such compromise is perceived to be humiliating. Palestinians who felt more humiliated by the Israeli occupation were less likely to support suicide attacks against Israelis but also expressed high reservations about the peace-making process. Interestingly, Palestinians who felt humiliated by peace deals involving compromises over Palestinian sacred values showed less support for those deals, although they did not show greater support for violent opposition to those deals.

Pride and Humiliation Regulation on the Way to Sustainable Peace

According to the philosopher Avishai Margalit (2002), *humiliation* is a formative experience that has the power to shape how individuals view themselves, their group, and their environment. Margalit has discussed at length the possibility that parties may reach what he defines as humiliating solutions, namely, solutions in which human beings are treated as nonhumans on the way to peace. In his view, such solutions are non-legitimate even if they potentially can save some lives in the short term (Margalit, 1996, 2002). Accordingly, from a normative perspective, parties should search for a non-humiliating, pride-preserving (or even pride-boosting) solution to conflicts.

But even if we put aside the strict normative approach, from a practical point of view that takes into account the main themes embedded in social identity theory, sustainable peace is not possible if emotions tied to group identity, such as pride and humiliation, are not properly addressed. Given that both pride on issues related to the conflict itself and humiliation stemming from provocative outgroup's actions are inherent aspects of intractable conflicts, they should be addressed in an integrative way, in both inter- and intragroup processes, to promote peace.

In terms of intergroup processes, at least two valuable ideas can be found in the existing literature that can address the abovementioned goal. The first, already mentioned in Chapter 8, is the expression of counter-empathy. Results of the studies by Nadler and Liviatan (2006) as well as studies by Gubler, Halperin, and Hirshberger (2015) have revealed that expressed empathy by the outgroup can induce more positive intergroup attitudes among ingroup members. Such empathy is commonly seen as an important component of reconciliation processes, given that it conveys an important message of respect and caring between the previously rival groups. Although there is no direct empirical evidence indicating that the outgroup's empathy can help the ingroup members to overcome past feelings of humiliation, that idea constitutes the essence of the rapidly developing literature on intergroup reconciliation (Čehajić, Brown, & Castano, 2008; Moeschberger et al., 2005; Tam et al., 2008).

The second process that is also deeply rooted in recent writings and research on reconciliation processes is intergroup apologies. At its most basic, the collective apology (akin to the interpersonal apology) is an acknowledgement of harms committed and an expression of remorse for those harms (Lazare, 2004). Indeed, theorists have positioned the collective apology as a central facilitator of forgiveness and reconciliation in the aftermath of intergroup harm (Lazare, 2004; Staub, 2006; Tutu, 1999). According to Nadler and Liviatan (2006), historical harms obstruct intergroup relations, and the collective apology helps trim down that obstruction. This is accomplished via successful completion of an *apology–forgiveness cycle* (Tavuchis, 1991)—a cycle that entails a social exchange whereby the perpetrator group creates a debt by apologizing that is removed only when the victimized group forgives (Shnabel & Nadler, 2008). This is by all means a process that takes into account the goal of restoring group-based pride in the context of past humiliation.

Although some empirical studies have demonstrated the constructive implications of intergroup apologies for intergroup reconciliation (e.g., Leonard, Mackie, & Smith, 2011; Philpot & Hornsey, 2008; Blatz, Day, & Schryer, 2014), current research in social and political psychology offers a more nuanced picture. First, experimental and correlational work by Philpot and Hornsey (2008, 2011) failed to find a reliable apology–forgiveness link (see also Blatz, Schumann, & Ross, 2009). Second, two sets of studies by Michael Wohl, Hornsey, and Bennett (2012) and Wohl et al. (2015) have demonstrated that intergroup apologies would be effective only under very unique circumstances. Specifically, they will be effective only when accompanied by primary emotions (Wohl et al., 2012) and when offered to individuals holding incremental beliefs about groups (Wohl et al., 2015). But third and maybe most importantly, intergroup apologies yield some psychological costs for the perpetrator or apologizing group, costs that also may involve loss of pride, and the apology might backfire if not properly regulated.

Another strategy, still in the intergroup-communicative realm, has been offered by Geremy Ginges, Scott Atran, Medin, and Shikaki (2007). Their fundamental assumption is that efforts to decrease humiliation will increase the prospects of support for compromise. In their view, which was tested and supported empirically, violent opposition to compromises on perceived sacred values that potentially can induce feelings of humiliation can be reduced if the other party makes simultaneous symbolic compromises over one of their own sacred values (Ginges et al., 2007; Atran, Axelrod, & Davis, 2007). This relatively simple reciprocal process that touches upon some of the most sensitive beliefs of society members was demonstrated in a series of experiments carried out with Palestinian and Israeli participants. In all these studies violent opposition to compromise over issues considered sacred was increased by offering material incentives to compromise (i.e., monetary compensation) but was decreased when the adversary made symbolic compromises over what they perceived to be their own sacred values (Ginges et al., 2007). It seems that while the material incentives were perceived as furthering humiliation, suggesting that the ingroup was willing to trade its fundamental values for monetary compensation, the symbolic compromises were absorbed as a sign of pride-preserving, non-humiliating agreement. It follows, therefore, that the reciprocity embedded in any peace agreement should not focus exclusively on material exchange but should also take into account psychological, identity, and image-based assets.

As important as these may be, to address feelings of humiliation and loss of pride, societies need to do more than just absorbing relevant messages communicated by the outgroup. Given that during the years of the conflict, the group's successes and failures regarding the conflict become the most fertile source of group pride and disappointment, fundamental intragroup processes are required to compensate for the loss of that source. One possible way to address that gap is for groups to identify an alternative source of group pride and to highlight it during the transition between violent conflict and stable peace and reconciliation. Such an alternative source should focus on either national triumph (e.g., international sports events) or on unique aspects of the nation and society that can help society members to feel proud of their nation in a domain unrelated to the conflict (see group and self-affirmation studies that were reviewed in Chapter 7: Čehajić et al., 2011; Cohen et al., 2007; Miron, Branscombe, & Biernat, 2010; Sherman, Kinias, Major, Kim, & Prenovost, 2007). For example, in Israel in recent years the idea of Israel being a "start-up nation" (Senor & Singer, 2009) permeated into Israeli society's discourse and at least to some extent constituted a source of pride, replacing the "good old" notions of pride based on the most powerful army in the Middle East and the most moral army in the world.

But more important, and to a very large extent also much more challenging, is the need for societies to substitute the belief system that provides the source of pride during the conflict (i.e., the "ethos of conflict"—Bar-Tal, 2013) with an alternative belief system, which is more suitable to times of peace but also can elicit pride in the hearts and minds of society members. To do that, societies need to develop an 'ethos of peace' that will address all psychological needs previously addressed by the ethos of conflict and at the same time will provide the epistemic justifications for recent conciliatory policies initiated by the ingroup. According to Bar-Tal and Halperin (2014), this requires the penetration of the alternative beliefs supporting peace making into societal institutions and channels of communication, such as the formal political system, the educational system, cultural products, and the mass media. In fact, in this phase, an alternative narrative about the necessity of peace making is well established. It contains beliefs that contradict the established collective memory and ethos of conflict and serve as the foundations for an ethos of peace, which sheds new light on reality. This ethos refers to adoption and internalization by society members of values, beliefs, attitudes, emotions, norms, and practices that cherish peace, justice, respect of human rights, cooperation, trust, sensitivity, and consideration of the other party's needs, interests, goals, equality of relations, and acceptance and respect of cultural differences—all as foundations of the culture of peace. Such a culture of peace provides group members with a new source of pride and dignity, which on the one hand does not negate historical actions of the group during the conflict but, on the other hand, glorifies the new values and policies that promote and sustain the peaceful situation.

10

CHANGING FEELINGS TO PROMOTE PEACE

Emotion Regulation as a New Path to Conflict Resolution

The first nine chapters of this book concentrated on revealing the unique role played by each intergroup emotion in conflicts and peace processes. These nine chapters have provided relatively strong evidence to support that discrete intergroup emotions play a significant causal role in mobilizing people toward or away from support for policies that promote peace and reconciliation processes by forming attitudes, biasing attention and action, and shaping reactions to conflict-related events (e.g. Bar-Tal, 2001; Batson et al., 1997; Čehajić, Brown, & González, 2009; Cohen-Chen et al., 2014; Halperin, 2008, 2011b; Halperin & Gross, 2011; Huddy, Feldman, Taber, & Lahav, 2005; Lerner et al., 2003; Mackie et al., 2000; Pliskin, Bar-Tal, Sheppes, & Halperin, 2014; Reifen Tagar et al., 2011; Sabucedo et al., 2011; Spanovic et al., 2010; Stephan & Finlay, 1999; Sternberg, 2003; Tam et al., 2007, 2008; Volkan, 1997; Wohl et al., 2006, 2010). Importantly, this evidence also suggests that the effects of emotions on aggressive and conciliatory political attitudes are evident above and beyond other prominent factors such as ideology, situational factors, and socioeconomic conditions (e.g., Halperin, Russell, Dweck, & Gross, 2011; Spanovic et al., 2010).

However, from my perspective as a researcher, but also as someone who has been living in a society involved in violent conflict for decades, those of us who study violent, destructive conflicts do not have the privilege of studying such a critical social phenomenon for the sole purpose of general understanding as in the 'good old' basic science tradition. Instead, we are obligated to use such knowledge to search for new, innovative approaches to promote peace and prevent the continuation of mass killings and violence. As such, the research on the role of emotions in conflicts constitutes only the first step toward the desired goal of finding new ways of utilizing that knowledge to contribute to the promotion of peace. Hence, the main challenge, addressed in the tenth chapter of this book and which constitutes the center of my work in recent years, is to utilize the aggregated knowledge about emotions in conflicts to pave the way for new, emotion-focused, conflict resolution interventions.

Interestingly however, although the central role played by emotions in conflict has long been recognized by many of the scholars who study ethnic conflicts and conflict resolution (e.g., Bar-Tal et al., 2007; Horowitz, 1985; Lindner, 2006b; Petersen, 2002; Staub, 2005; Volkan, 1997), most of these scholars tended to express a rather deterministic view regarding the existence and implications of intense, negative emotions in long-term conflicts. According to this view, intense negative emotions, such as fear, anger, and contempt, are an inherent part of political and violent conflicts. As such, studying them can promote the understanding of these conflicts, but it can do very little to promote their resolution. This approach led to a disconnection between the writing and the empirical work on emotions in conflicts and the actual attempts on the ground to promote conflict resolution. In most cases, these interventions lacked a focused attempt to address the emotional aspects of people's worldviews. This gap has become more and more problematic in recent years given the rapid development in the study of emotions in conflicts.

To bridge that gap, we recently have introduced a different approach to the study of emotion and emotion regulation in political conflicts (e.g., Halperin, Sharvit, & Gross, 2011; Halperin, 2014; Halperin & Pliskin, 2015). According to this new approach, developments in the psychological study of discrete emotions (e.g., Roseman, Spindel, & Jose, 1990; Smith & Ellsworth, 1985), as well as the rapid developments in the growing field of emotion regulation (e.g., Gross, 2007), should be better integrated and have more of an impact on the way scholars of conflict resolution study emotions in conflicts, and of no less importance, they should have an impact on the way conflict resolution interventions are structured and implemented. Together with my colleagues (e.g., Gross, Halperin, & Porat, 2013; Halperin, Sharvit, & Gross, 2011; Halperin, Cohen-Chen, et al., 2014), I have argued that doing so would greatly advance theory and practice in conflict resolution by providing scholars and practitioners with effective emotionally based tools to change people's attitudes and behaviors in the context of long-term conflicts. Additionally, this approach would contribute substantially to the understanding of core processes in emotion and emotion regulation in (at least) three key ways. First, it would enable an examination of the effects of emotion and emotion regulation processes on the intergroup level rather than just on the interpersonal level (see Goldenberg et al., in press). Second, it would enable emotion and emotion regulation scholars to examine their theories in one of the most ideologically driven, intense, and highly emotional settings and in the face of an ongoing stream of negative information and destructive events (e.g., Halperin, Porat, Tamir, et al., 2013). Finally, the proposed framework would enable the examination of the effects of emotion regulation strategies not only on affective reactions but on political ones as well (e.g., Halperin, Pliskin, et al., 2014).

In a nutshell, *emotion regulation* refers to processes engaged when individuals try to influence the type or amount of emotion they (or others) experience, when they (or others) have them, and how they (or others) experience and express these emotions (Gross, 1998, 2007). To promote people's support for peace and other conciliatory policies, emotion regulation should be utilized in the context of intractable conflicts to (1) downregulate (decrease) destructive emotions like hatred and despair; (2) upregulate (increase) constructive emotions like hope, empathy, and guilt; and (3) qualitatively regulate (i.e., channel from destructive to constructive; see Halperin, Sharvit, & Gross, 2011) ambiguous emotions like anger and fear. In the previous chapters I already have provided some preliminary indications for emotion regulation strategies of discrete intergroup emotions. The current chapter will provide a more comprehensive approach to the study of emotion regulation in intractable conflicts, aspiring to provide a review of existing findings but, more importantly, to introduce an organizational framework for future work along these lines.

To address these goals, the chapter will begin with a brief review of dominant conceptualizations of emotion regulation, focusing both on emotion regulation strategies as well as on emotion regulation goals. I will then review recent empirical work on emotion regulation in intractable conflicts, distinguishing between two different ways to consider, study, and apply emotion regulation strategies to real-life conflict resolution processes—the direct and the indirect emotion regulation approaches. I will then move to discuss the unique implementation of emotion regulation strategies within the context of intractable conflicts, focusing mainly on the reciprocal relations between emotion regulation processes, on the one hand, and conflict unique characteristics (e.g., the intergroup settings, ideologically driven goals, and the violent and threatening context), on the other. The end of the chapter will offer an optional road map for future studies on emotion regulation in various intergroup settings.

Emotion Regulation—A Conceptualization

The entire approach of the current chapter is predicated on the idea that even powerful emotions can be modified and, maybe more importantly, that oftentimes people have strong motivations to modify their and others' emotions. Almost naturally, when emotions threaten to "drag down their victim with the weight of stupidity" (Nietzsche, 1889/1998, p. 10), we often try to regulate these emotions and change their trajectories in ways that help us to achieve our goals (Gross, 1998). Because emotions are multi-componential processes that unfold over time, emotion regulation may involve changes in various components of the emotional process, including the latency, rise time, magnitude, duration, or offset of responses in behavioral, experiential, or physiological domains (Gross & Thompson, 2007). Emotion regulation may increase or decrease the intensity and/or duration of either negative or positive emotions.

Even though many emotional responses may in themselves involve some conscious or unconscious attempt by the responder to regulate them, emotion regulation is a unique emotional process in that it always serves a regulatory goal (Sheppes & Gross, 2011). That is also what differentiates emotion regulation processes from emotion generation ones. I can feel anger in response to the outgroup's provocation, but anger will be regulated only if I intentionally try to increase or decrease my anger experience. A regulatory goal, hence, denotes a desire to influence the experienced emotion or its possible expressive or behavioral consequences and can be distinguished from the emotional goal associated with an emotion, which is not concerned with the emotion itself but rather with the emotion-provoking stimulus and its relation to the self or group. In the case of intrinsic emotion regulation processes (i.e., I regulate my own emotions), the regulatory process is guided by the individual's own goals, whereas in the case of extrinsic processes of emotion regulation (i.e., I regulate another individual's emotions), people regulate others' emotions to achieve their own goals.

Recent studies on emotion regulation at the intrapersonal level have shown that what people want to feel influences both the direction and the outcome of emotion regulation (e.g., Tamir, Bigman, Rhodes, Salerno, & Schreier, 2015). Therefore, people's desired emotional states or their regulatory goals are critical factors in determining their emotional experience. But what exactly do people want to feel? For many decades, the common assumption has been that people's emotion regulation processes are driven mainly by hedonic goals or considerations; namely, people would like to increase their experience of positive emotions and to decrease the experience of negative emotions. Yet recent evidence draws a more nuanced picture of people's emotional motivations. According to the instrumental approach to emotion regulation (e.g., Bonanno, 2001; Parrott, 1993; Tamir, 2009), already mentioned in previous chapters of this book, people are sometimes motivated to experience an emotion that might be instrumental to them, even if that emotion does not elicit positive feelings in the immediate time frame. Accordingly, people may be motivated to experience even unpleasant emotions when they expect these emotions to promote the attainment of their goals. For instance, consistent with the idea that anger can promote successful confrontation (e.g., Frijda, 1986; Parrott, 2001), people were more motivated to experience anger when their goal was to confront others (e.g., Tamir & Ford, 2012a; Tamir, Mitchell, & Gross, 2008) and when they expected anger to be useful to them (Ford & Tamir, 2012). Similarly, consistent with the idea that fear promotes successful avoidance (e.g., Frijda, 1986; Öhman, 1993), people were more motivated to experience fear when their goal was to avoid a threat (Tamir & Ford, 2009).

If what people want to feel or their regulatory goals represents the steering wheels of emotion regulation processes, the strategies used to modify the emotions should be seen as the engine of that change. As such, of equal importance to the question of *why* people regulate their emotions is the question of *how* they do so. Theory and research on emotion regulation has identified multiple strategies individuals may use to influence emotions that they perceive to be unhelpful (and therefore seek to decrease) or that they perceive to be helpful (and therefore seek to increase). The emotion regulation strategies that people employ may be automatic or controlled, conscious or unconscious, intrinsic or extrinsic, and may have effects at one or more points in the emotion generation process.

The process model of emotion regulation, first introduced by James Gross in 1998 (see also Gross, 2008), is considered today as the most dominant and influential model in that field. This model offers a framework for describing different regulatory strategies and outlines different families of strategies that focus on the regulation of each stage (situation, attention, appraisal, and response) in the emotion-generative process (Gross & Thompson, 2007). The process model provides a broad framework that focuses on individuals' personal emotion regulation strategies. Our modest contribution in recent years is to investigate different ways to apply some aspects of the well-established process model of emotion regulation to the context of intergroup processes (e.g., Goldenberg et al., in press) and, more specifically, intractable conflicts (Halperin, Porat, Tamir, et al., 2013, Halperin, Cohen-Chen, et al., 2014; Halperin & Pliskin, 2015). I will now very briefly review the five main families of emotion regulation strategies, as presented in Gross's classic model.

Emotion regulation often is seen as targeting the emotional process once it is already in motion. However, some efficient regulation strategies involve preemptively avoiding situations in which unwanted emotions may occur. *Situation selection*, the earliest strategy in the process model, involves acting to make it more likely that we will be in situations we expect will give rise to desired emotions (or less likely that we will be in situations we expect will give rise to undesired emotions). This strategy occurs before entering into the emotion-eliciting situation and is the most forward-looking approach to emotion regulation. It does not refer to all of our decisions about future actions but only to the choices that are taken with consideration, at least in part, of the future consequences of our actions for our emotional responses (Baumeister, Vohs, DeWall, & Zhang, 2007; Gross, 2008). A typical example of a situation selection strategy is a person who chooses to avoid watching horror movies to regulate the fear that she usually experiences in these movies. On the other hand, choosing to watch a comedy can be considered as an intentional attempt to upregulate happiness and joy. In the context of intergroup conflict, the choice not to be present in areas in which the probability of encountering outgroup members is high and, in that way, downregulating intergroup anxiety, can be considered as a situation selection strategy.

Assuming that an individual has entered into the emotional situation, she can invest efforts to modify the situation in a way that will alter its emotional impact. The ability to modify situations even slightly can serve as a useful tool to regulate the emotion. *Situation modification* is a very potent form of emotion regulation as it demands a sense of agency from the individual. Using the example of the horror film, assuming that the person was forced to sit in front of the television, she could turn on the light, turn down the volume, or even switch to a different channel. All of these actions may affect her emotional response. Using the example of the anxiety-inducing intergroup encounter, a person may choose to take off all clothing items (e.g., a T-shirt or a hat) that potentially can identify her as a member of specific group and, by that, decrease levels of intergroup anxiety. Alternatively, she can choose to walk only with other ingroup members escorting her as an additional situation modification strategy of emotion regulation.

Situation selection and modification focus on influencing the situation that elicits the emotion or the individual's role in the situation. Other strategies, which refer to later stages of the emotion generation process, focus on regulating emotions by affecting the experience of the individual without changing the environment. *Attentional deployment*, the strategy associated with the attention phase in the process model, includes the shift of one's attention to or away from the emotion-eliciting event (Gross & Thompson, 2007). Distraction has been found to be effective in changing an emotional reaction after the emotional response already has evolved (Sheppes, Catran, & Meiran, 2009; Sheppes & Meiran, 2007). Using the previous example, an attentional deployment strategy would be to shift attention away from the television screen during scary parts of the movie, focusing on aspects of the movie other than the plot, such as the set and costumes, or even thinking of a funny joke. The same strategy can be used in the example of the intergroup potentially threatening encounter in which people can make active efforts to pay attention to items in the environment other than to the identity of outgroup members themselves.

As stated by appraisal theories of emotions (e.g., Roseman, 1984; Scherer, 2004), after the situation has received attention, to proceed with the emotional process, the individual must go through a (consciousness or unconsciousness) cognitive evaluation of the situation. *Cognitive change* involves (re)thinking about the situation in a way that will alter the emotional response. The most commonly researched method of cognitive change is *cognitive reappraisal*, which involves thinking about a situation in a way that can change its meaning (for a review, see Webb, Miles, & Sheeran, 2012; see also Van-Zomeren et al., 2012). Reappraising the meaning of the situation can of course increase or decrease the emotional experience, but naturally, most studies on reappraisal have focused on ways it can help to downregulate negative emotions. One example of a reappraisal strategy that was found useful in doing so is to try to take an outsider's view of a situation and analyze it with greater distance. Reappraisal methods have been successfully used to change the way people construe upsetting situations to decrease their aversion (Richards, Butler, & Gross, 2003), and people who use reappraisal more frequently to regulate their emotions report significantly fewer negative emotions before entering a negative situation (Jackson, Malmstadt, Larson, & Davidson, 2000). Using the example of the scary movie, the person can decrease suspension of disbelief by telling herself that the characters are merely actors and that scary movies will use any possible trick to increase fear. In the intergroup setting, an individual can tell herself that, like her, all outgroup members really want is to feel secure and unthreatened, and therefore there is no reason to feel threatened by the situation.

The next family of strategies, *response modulation*, occurs later in the emotional process and is focused on modifying the emotional responses themselves, once they have arisen. Attempts to regulate the psychological and experiential aspects of emotion include physical relaxation and suppression of the expressive behavior of the emotion. These regulatory strategies seem to have mixed effects on the actual emotional experience and may even increase it (Gross, 1998). Response modulation strategies are more linked to psychopathology than strategies that are used earlier in the emotional process (Aldao, Nolen-Hoeksema, & Schweizer, 2010; Bloch, Moran, & Kring, 2010). Using the previous examples (both the scary movie and the intergroup encounter), the person can regulate the expressions of fear during the movie and suppress them to the extent that her friends cannot detect that she is actually scared.

For some years, it has been argued that some emotion regulation strategies (e.g., reappraisal) are more adaptive and more effective than others (e.g., expressive suppression). However, recent studies in the field focusing on some of these strategies have shown that different strategies are implemented and lead to positive consequences under different circumstances and in response to different emotion-eliciting events (e.g., Bonanno, Papa, Lalande, Westphal, & Coifman, 2004; Sheppes, Scheibe, Suri, & Gross, 2011). Therefore, it is important to use the right strategy at the right time and in the context of the relevant or right emotion. For example, on the one hand, reappraisal has been hailed as particularly important, with countless studies demonstrating the positive effects of teaching people to use the strategy on the experience and expression of emotion (see Gross, 2007, for a review) and even on aggression (Barlett & Anderson, 2011). On the other hand, because this strategy allows for extensive engagement with the stimulus, it may be less effective for emotion regulation under circumstances of high emotional intensity. In these cases other emotion regulation strategies, such as attention deployment, may be more effective (Sheppes et al., 2011) because they tackle the emotion at an earlier point in its temporal development (Sheppes & Gross, 2011). Other than levels of engagement or effectiveness, these and other emotion regulation strategies may differ in the amount of cognitive effort they demand, their appropriateness for different situations, and the different motivations associated with them (Sheppes et al., 2014).

Most of the research on emotion regulation has thus far focused on individuals or dyads. Additionally, research on emotion regulation has focused largely on direct forms of emotion regulation by which people are given explicit instructions or strategies to modify aspects of their emotional experiences. I argue that many of the insights from such research are applicable to the context of intergroup conflicts. Furthermore, I maintain that because of motivational factors that may hinder the effectiveness of explicit strategies of direct emotion regulation, the study of emotion regulation in the context of intractable conflict must also consider methods of *indirectly* prompting the regulation of emotions. Both of these lines of research are discussed next.

Emotion Regulation in Intractable Conflicts—Existing Evidence

Research into direct forms of emotion regulation has recently begun applying this construct to intergroup conflicts and the group-based emotions that emerge in their wake (Halperin & Gross, 2011, Halperin, Pliskin, et al., 2014; Halperin, Porat, Tamir, & Gross, 2013; Lee, Sohn, & Fowler, 2013). By now, most of the studies along these lines have focused on cognitive reappraisal, although recent correlational studies in the context of prejudice against Muslims in the US utilized other emotion regulation strategies, such as rumination (Steele, Parker, & Lickel, 2015).

Together with James Gross we (Halperin & Gross, 2011) have obtained the first evidence linking reappraisal with conciliatory attitudes in the context of conflict in a correlational study conducted in the midst of the war between Israelis and Palestinians in Gaza in 2008 and 2009. A nationwide survey of Jewish Israelis was sampled to test whether individual differences in the use of reappraisal were associated with conciliatory political reactions during war. To do that, we used Gross's classic measure of Emotion Regulation Questionnaire (ERQ), with minor adjustments to the context of the conflict. We found that Israelis who reported a greater tendency to use reappraisal when dealing with negative emotional experiences were also more supportive of providing humanitarian aid to Palestinian citizens. Most importantly, these associations were not conditioned by people's political ideologies, meaning that effective use of cognitive reappraisal was associated with support for providing humanitarian aid to Palestinians among both leftists and rightists. This is especially important given the results of recent studies by Lee et al. (2013) demonstrating that individual differences in emotion regulation styles (and particularly in reappraisal) predict variation in political orientations and support for conservative policies.

Then, a few years later, in an attempt to examine whether reappraisal played a causal role, we conducted a pair of studies in which we manipulated, rather than measured, cognitive reappraisal and estimated its effects on emotional reactions and political attitudes related to a long-term intergroup conflict (Halperin,

Pliskin, et al., 2014). Using the intra-societal Israeli context, we examined whether very brief training in cognitive reappraisal would decrease Jewish Israelis' political intolerance toward various minorities in Israel. In Study 1, we presented Jewish Israeli participants with either neutral or reappraisal instructions (i.e., instructions to read the following text from an external, analytical viewpoint) before they read a text inducing a range of negative emotions toward Palestinian citizens of Israel (PCIs). We found that Israelis with a rightist political orientation (but not those with leftist orientation), which in Israel is linked with intolerance for PCIs, expressed lower levels of both negative emotions (average across the several negative emotions measured) and political intolerance toward PCIs after reading reappraisal (vs. neutral) instructions. Negative emotions mediated the effect of the reappraisal manipulation on levels of intolerance. The fact that the effect of reappraisal on experienced negative emotions and political intolerance was found only among rightists was explained by the very low baseline levels of these emotions and of intolerant attitudes among leftists. In other words, for an emotion regulation strategy to be effective, the target of the emotion regulation intervention must experience the relevant emotions, at least on medium if not high levels to start with.

Study 2 employed a similar methodology, but participants were asked to select their least-liked group in Israel and respond to a stimuli and questions specifically addressing their outgroup of choice. For example, whereas most rightists selected Palestinians or radical leftists as their least-liked group, leftists in Israel chose "settlers in the occupied territories" as their most hated group. This allowed us to test our hypothesis among all participants, and not just those with a right-wing ideology, and increased the external validity of our findings. Results were clear: collapsing across all selected least-liked groups, we found lower levels of political intolerance among participants in the reappraisal condition compared to those in the control condition. This effect was again mediated by negative emotions and was not moderated by the selected group.

These findings led us to wonder whether the effect of reappraisal would hold not only for an internal intergroup conflict but also in the more extreme case of an intractable conflict and, outside the laboratory, in conflict related events in the real world. To seriously test the latter question, we had to wait for a predictable real-world event to occur, the kind of event that would allow us to train participants in cognitive reappraisal prior to its actual occurrence. To address this question, we presented a reappraisal manipulation, this time in the form of a reappraisal (vs. neutral) 15- to 20-minute training session to Jewish Israeli participants one week prior to the Palestinian United Nations bid in September 2011. We then measured emotional and political reactions one week later and then five months later (Halperin, Porat, Tamir, & Gross, 2013, Study 2). In the reappraisal training, participants were handed anger-inducing pictures and were asked to respond to them as if they were looking at them as outsiders, like scientists, objectively and analytically—to try to think about them in a cold and detached manner (see Richards & Gross, 2000). The experimenter explained how to use reappraisal in response to the first picture, and participants were then asked to apply the technique in response to each of four additional pictures. The experimenter ensured that participants applied the technique appropriately. Although the reappraisal training session provided several general tools for reappraising one's emotions that were not targeted at a specific emotion or at the context at hand, we found that participants trained to reappraise showed greater support for conciliatory rather than aggressive political policies toward Palestinians both one week and five months post-training and that these effects were mediated by changes in anger.

However successful, there is still much work to be done in terms of applying direct emotion regulation strategies into the context of intractable conflicts. Most importantly, emotion regulation strategies other than cognitive reappraisal should be tested and then used in practice to provide people with a more diverse tool kit in their attempt to regulate their emotions in the context of conflicts. This is especially true given recent findings, already mentioned, showing that reappraisal is less effective than other emotion regulation strategies (e.g., distraction) when it comes to high magnitude emotional events (Sheppes et al., 2011). By all means, intractable conflicts offer such repeating highly emotional stimulus, and therefore, cognitive reappraisal might not be the optimal strategy in that context.

But beyond the question of the specific strategy used to regulate destructive emotions, the basic decision to use direct emotion regulation may pose challenges in its application outside the laboratory. Since most direct emotion regulation interventions take some time to learn and may require personal training, it would seem harder to broaden its scope to the societal level. An additional, related limitation is the fact that for people to utilize these methods spontaneously and continuously, they must be motivated to regulate their emotions in the first place (Tamir, 2009). Within the context of extreme and violent conflicts, in which people adhere to certain values and ideologies regarding the outgroup, it is doubtful that the majority of people will be motivated internally to transform their negative emotions toward the adversary outgroup. To overcome both of these obstacles, we (see Halperin, Cohen-Chen, & Goldenberg, 2014, for a review) recently started developing methods to transform emotions without providing people with direct instructions to do so in the form of *indirect* emotion regulation. These methods are based on focused messages that are aimed at transforming discrete emotions and that can be used easily through educational or media-based platforms.

The indirect approach to emotion regulation involves, first and foremost, identifying the target action tendency associated with the desired conflict-related process (e.g., contact motivation, compromises, and support for providing humanitarian aid, among others). Given the specificity of the emotion–action tendency association (Frijda, 1986), the next step would be connecting the target action tendency to a discrete emotion. For example, to motivate the conflicting parties into the negotiation room, a relevant target emotion for downregulation would be fear associated with withdrawal tendencies. If the goal is to increase support for providing humanitarian aid to the adversary outgroup, however, a more useful target emotion may be intergroup empathy. To successfully influence the selected emotion, the next step is to identify the emotion's core appraisal theme (e.g., Roseman, 1984; Scherer, 1984), which constitutes the basis for its motivational and behavioral implications. By changing this core appraisal theme, the associated emotion can be regulated, leading to a transformation in emotional goals as well as action tendencies related to the conflict (see Figure 10.1). One such target action tendency may be, for example, an unwillingness to make any concessions to the adversary in a conflict, which may answer the destructive emotional goal associated with intergroup hatred. Once hatred is identified as the driving emotion, we can examine its core appraisal themes, finding a central one to be the belief that the outgroup's evil nature is inherent and stable. Finding an intervention that may tackle this appraisal theme directly would complete the process illustrated in Figure 10.1.

Indeed, several studies have demonstrated the great promise contained in this indirect approach to emotion regulation. Along the lines of the example presented, we conducted a series of studies with the aim of reducing intergroup hatred and the destructive attitudinal outcomes of this emotion. In these studies we (Halperin, Russell, Trzesniewski, Gross, & Dweck, 2011) began by identifying its core appraisal—namely, the perception of stable negative characteristics in the outgroup and the belief in the outgroup's inability to undergo positive change (Halperin, 2008). We hypothesized that this appraisal is based on a more fundamental belief that groups in general hold some stable, innate characteristics that cannot change in a meaningful way. This belief has been described as an "entity" (or fixed) implicit theory about the malleability of groups, standing in opposition to an "incremental" (or malleable) view of group natures (e.g., Rydell, Hugenberg, Ray, & Mackie, 2007).

Then, drawing on a growing body of literature suggesting that implicit beliefs about the malleability of groups (e.g., Rydell et al., 2007) can be changed, we decided to examine whether an intervention designed to promote an incremental view of the malleability of groups would also lead to reduced hatred and increased support for compromises. Participants belonging to different groups living in an

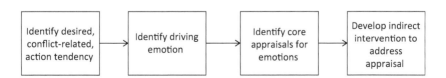

FIGURE 10.1 Indirect emotion regulation in intractable conflicts

intractable conflict (i.e., Jewish Israelis, PCIs, and West Bank Palestinians) read an informative text indicating that research shows groups in general can (vs. cannot) change over time. Results showed that teaching people that groups have a malleable (vs. fixed) natures led them to express less hatred-related appraisals toward their respective outgroups compared to those who learned that groups have fixed natures. This further led people to be more willing to make concessions at the core of the conflict. Thus, in all cases and for all groups, the indirect implementation of the idea of a malleable nature among groups in general led to a transformation in the appraisal of the specific outgroup as fixed, decreasing hatred appraisals and increasing support for compromises required for peace (Halperin, Russell, Trzesniewski, et al., 2011). Importantly, in the past two years we have examined the influence of this indirect approach to hatred reduction outside the laboratory by using educational workshops and longitudinal designs among the general Israeli population. Although the study is still in progress and no conclusive inferences can be drawn, preliminary data analysis has shown that the basic findings of the lab studies also persist in a real-world setting, and maybe more interestingly, they hold even when people are exposed to difficult conflict-related events, such as war or terror attacks.

The same principles, based on very similar processes, were applied to other group-based emotions. As reported in Chapter 7, using simple self-affirmation techniques (Steele, 1988), we (Čehajić et al., 2011) enabled people in Israel and in Bosnia to secure or affirm other aspects of their positive self-image and, by that, managed to upregulate guilt and promote support for offering the outgroup compensation for perceived wrongdoing. Although the target action tendencies (i.e., support for compensation and reparations) as well as the target group-based emotion (i.e., guilt) are fundamentally different from the ones examined in the hatred-malleability studies (Halperin, Russell, Trzesniewski, et al., 2011), the basic process of indirect emotion regulation, as presented in Figure 10.1, is practically identical. That is also the process that has been applied in the studies aimed to upregulate hope in a conflict (see Chapter 6; Cohen-Chen, Halperin, Crisp, et al., 2014; Cohen-Chen et al., 2015a), to downregulate collective angst (see Chapter 5: Halperin, Porat, & Wohl, 2013), and to upregulate intergroup empathy (see Chapter 8; Gubler, Halperin, & Hirschberger, 2015).

Importantly, in all these indirect emotion regulation attempts, people are not aware of the fact that the message they absorb or the process they go through is aimed at regulating their emotions, and as such, no concrete motivation is required for the emotion regulation process to take place. Additionally, most of these interventions have been designed in a way that the specific conflict or the specific outgroup is not mentioned at all, the rationale being that direct attempts to change people's emotions in conflict while confronting them with facts or information regarding their outgroup can backfire very easily. As such, the indirect approach to emotion regulation utilizes contemporary knowledge in affective science to regulate group-based emotions while overcoming motivational and conflict- or context-related obstacles. Given that the indirect approach focuses on changing the emotional experience (and the subsequent attitudes and behaviors) through changing the emotion's core appraisal themes, it also can be considered as a unique type of motivation-free cognitive reappraisal. Thinking of it in that way enables a conceptual as well as a practical integration of direct and indirect approaches to regulating emotions in conflicts.

Emotion Regulation in a Unique Context—The Regulation of Emotions in an Intergroup Conflict Setting

As previously demonstrated, in recent years we have implemented some well-established emotion regulation strategies in context of intractable conflicts, which were previously used mainly in intra- or interpersonal settings. Although this implementation proved to be rather successful in terms of its influence on people's emotional and even political reactions to difficult conflict-related events, I believe that all these previous studies share one fundamental limitation. In all of them, the emotion regulation strategies were used exactly in the same format as they were used in previous work outside the intergroup conflict setting. I see this as a limitation mainly due to the dramatic power I attribute to the context itself and more specifically to the power I attribute to the interaction between the psychological processes on the one hand and contextual factors on the other. As such, to properly utilize the potential of emotion regulation strategies in promoting people's support for peace and conciliatory policies, various aspects of the emotion regulation process should be adjusted to different aspects of the unique context of intergroup, violent conflicts.

Most important, probably, is the fact that the target emotion we have been seeking to regulate in these contexts is a group-based rather than a 'classic' individual-based emotion. This requires some adjustments and modifications that, unfortunately, did not exist in our or in any other previous work on emotion regulation in conflicts. With this understanding in mind, we (Goldenberg et al., in press) have recently introduced a new process model of group-based emotion that offers an integration of intergroup emotion and emotion regulation perspectives. Thus far, emotion regulation research has focused mainly on regulation strategies in which the individual is (implicitly) self-categorized as a separate, independent unit, thus reacting to situations that have relevance to the *personal* self (e.g., Markus & Kitayama, 1991; Turner et al., 1987). However, intergroup emotions theory suggests that individuals can categorize themselves as group members rather than as unique individuals (Ellemers, 2012; Smith, 1993; Turner et al., 1987) and, via this psychological mechanism, experience emotions on behalf of the group. Our new processes model has aimed to address a series of important questions, including these: are similar emotion regulation strategies equally useful when it comes to regulating group-based or non-group-based emotions? Do the (instrumental or hedonic) goals people may have in regulating their emotions extend to group-based emotions? Unfortunately, the scope of the current book is limited, so the more comprehensive approach to the study of emotion regulation of group-based emotions cannot be presented. Yet I will try to highlight some of the main principles we have identified.

In an attempt to pinpoint the appropriate implementation of the process model into the intergroup domain, we have highlighted two core points of synergy between theorizing about group-based emotions and emotion regulation (Goldenberg et al., in press). First, in the group-based emotion domain, we extend the analysis of group-based emotion by identifying and specifying the role of regulatory processes that prevent a view of emotion as uncontrolled responses to personally relevant events. Especially useful for the achievement of this goal, we argue, is identifying and specifying the goals and strategies involved in group-based emotion regulation (Gross, 1998). Second, in the emotion regulation domain, our intention was to incorporate the notion of self-categorization (Mackie et al., 2000; Smith, 1993; Smith, Seger, & Mackie, 2007; Turner et al., 1987) into existing models of emotion regulation. This fits with insights from a broader literature indicating that individuals' construals of themselves in a given situation (e.g., as an individual or as a group member) has a strong influence on how they view that situation and act on it (Van-Zomeren, Postmes, & Spears, 2008; Van-Zomeren et al., 2012). Taken together, we argue that a synthesis between these two influential lines of thought potentially can deepen our understanding of the role of emotions in intergroup relations and provide a broader view of emotion regulation in general.

Hedonic and Instrumental Motivations for Regulating Group-Based Emotions

Even before dealing with the question of how people regulate their group-based emotions, it is important to ask what unique factors shape the way people want to feel in intergroup contexts. Although it probably makes sense to assume that similar to individual emotions, group-based emotions also are driven both by hedonic and instrumental considerations, it also would make sense to assume that the nature of these considerations would be at least slightly different when it comes to group-based emotions. It would be different because people have unique goals when it comes to intergroup settings but also because what makes people feel good in an intergroup setting is different from what makes them feel good in an interpersonal setting.

From a hedonic point of view, it would make sense to assume that beyond the simple goal of feeling positive emotions, in a group setting, people also want to feel emotions that echo those they believe other members of their group are feeling at the moment. We know that emotions serve an important function in defining the relationship between individuals and their groups (Heerdink, Van Kleef, Homan, & Fischer, 2013; Totterdell, Kellett, Teuchmann, & Briner, 1998; Van-Zomeren, Spears, Fischer, & Leach, 2004). This leads to the assumption that oftentimes, people will be motivated to experience even what we usually call negative emotions because they simply believe that feeling these emotions simultaneously with other group members will make them feel good or will benefit their well-being in other related ways. Being a sports fan of a losing team will not provide hedonic pleasure in winning, yet the experience of feeling sad together with other fans may facilitate bonding and provide some hedonic value (Crisp, Heuston, Farr, & Turner, 2007). Recent work on conformity using functional neuroimaging shows that conformity is associated with brain regions responsible for subjective positive value (Zaki, Schirmer, & Mitchell, 2011). This suggests that merely experiencing conformity in certain contexts may lead to positive emotions. It can be argued, therefore, that oftentimes the negative value of unpleasant emotions is trumped by any positive valuation of conformity. Notable examples for such experiences are collective rituals, public ceremonies, and memorial days (Hochschild, 1979; Kanyangara, Rimé, Philippot, & Yzerbyt, 2007). Studies focusing on these situations suggest that given the simple dissemination and synchrony of strong emotions among group members who simultaneously experience the same events (Gallese, 2001; Hatfield, Cacioppo, & Rapson, 1994; Rimé, 2007), people's connections to their group members intensify. They get to believe that "we feel the same, we are the same, we are one" by this token, massively reinforcing group identification (Collins, 2004, Rossano, 2012; von Scheve & Ismer, 2013). The result is that people may be motivated to experience even negative emotions if they believe these will make them feel better regarding their connection with their group.

In a recent set of empirical studies, conducted right before and during Israel's Memorial Day, we (Porat, Halperin, Mannheim, & Tamir, in press) directly tested this assumption. The study demonstrated that the more people want to connect to their group, the more motivated they are to experience group-based sadness, even when it is unpleasant to experience. Importantly, these studies have not shown emotional contagion (i.e., that people of the same group share the same emotions simultaneously), but rather they have demonstrated how people are motivated to upregulate a seemingly negative emotion like sadness to feel good as an integral part of their ingroup. The first two studies (1a and 1b) have shown that people with a higher need to belong to Israeli society expected that the experience of group-based sadness on Israeli Memorial Day would make them feel better in better connecting them to Israeli society. This expectation in turn, was associated with a stronger preference to experience group-based sadness. In Studies 2 and 3, we demonstrated that social motives might play a causal role in shaping preferences for group-based emotions. We found that participants with a stronger need to belong to Israeli society expected group-based sadness to better connect them to their group and, as a result, wanted to experience more sadness in connection with Israeli Memorial Day. People's motivations in these studies can be seen both as hedonic (i.e., feeling part of the group makes me feel happier) or as instrumental (i.e., my goal is to be part of the group, and therefore I want to share emotions with other group members), but in both cases they are highly informative in terms of our understanding of people's motivations to regulate their emotions in an intragroup context.

What follows from these studies is that people's motivation to experience certain group-based emotions is driven, at least to some extent, by the way they perceive what the majority of their group members feel at a certain moment. That idea, which differentiates regulatory processes of group-based emotions from those of other emotions, has been explored in another series of studies we have conducted recently (Goldenberg, Saguy, & Halperin, 2014; see also Chapter 7). In these studies, participants were led to experience group-based emotion (guilt or anger) by reading a newspaper report, and their perception of the collective emotion (guilt or anger) was manipulated. In one condition, Israeli participants read that 81 percent of Israelis who read the article reported experiencing strong emotion. In a second condition, Israeli participants read that 81 percent of Israeli who read the article did not feel any emotion at all. In cases in which it was clear that guilt was the appropriate emotion to feel, participants responded with stronger guilt when learning that others did not feel guilt at all. This increased sense of guilt was mediated by negative emotion toward the ingroup (as suggested by the social identity model of collective action) as well as by participants' sense of obligation to express emotion to promote action. Furthermore, an increased sense of guilt led to higher willingness to support conciliatory actions. In other cases, in which the appropriate emotional reaction to the scenario was less clear, people responded in conformity with their group—namely, people expressed higher levels of guilt when their group expressed an increase in collective guilt. These research findings suggest that people's perceptions of the collective emotion are used as an internal source of motivation for the regulation of group-based emotion, a source of motivation that is unique to group-based emotions. Furthermore, they offer a more nuanced view of the relationships between collective and group-based emotions, suggesting that although sometimes people conform to what they perceive to be the collective emotion (i.e., what most people feel) (Leonard, Moons, Mackie, & Smith, 2011; Moons, Leonard, Mackie, & Smith, 2009), at other times they do not and even respond in what we have defined as emotional compensation.

In addition to hedonic goals, regulation of group-based emotions also can serve instrumental goals that go beyond both the group and the individual's immediate pleasure. Oftentimes, instrumental goals motivate people to experience short-term negative emotions in the service of long-term group goals. For example, group members may be willing to experience negative group-based emotions (like fear and anxiety) and support a war, hoping that this will lead to better future outcomes for the group. Porat, Halperin, and Tamir (2015) have shown that in supporting a country's battle with another country, citizens may be willing to undergo extreme negative emotions if they believe this will lead to a calmer and better future for themselves, their children, and other members of their group.

The regulation of group-based emotions also may serve the instrumental goal of communicating loyalty to one's group (Brewer, 1999) and motivating group members to be willing to sacrifice for the sake of the group's goals (Bar-Tal, 2013). For example, a country involved in an intractable conflict needs tremendous resources to survive, and to draw on these resources, people must put aside their individual aspirations and interests. For people to be willing to do so, they must feel a very strong connection and commitment to their group. Therefore, it is important for the group and its leaders to instill strong positive emotions toward the group, such as pride, as well as negative emotions, such as hate and anger, toward the outgroup (Bar-Tal, Halperin, & De Rivera, 2007) to mobilize group members to support the group's goals. Although this process is familiar to anyone who is interested in conflicts and social processes, looking at it through the lens of instrumental goals for emotion regulation may provide some new, interesting insights.

We now know that the choice between instrumental and hedonic goals is not necessarily the result of a conscious process (Bargh, 1996; Barrett et al., 2007; Mauss, Bunge, & Gross, 2007). In many cases, the activation of a goal may occur without awareness (Kruglanski et al., 2002; Suri, Sheppes, & Gross, 2013). For example, in Porat et al. (2015), Israeli participants preferred to read anger-inducing newspaper articles before addressing a negotiation regarding the Israeli-Palestinian conflict. They did so because they believed that it would serve their goals when approaching negotiation decisions. That being said, these choices were made without participants' awareness that reading such a newspaper article would necessarily induce anger and that anger necessarily influence negotiation decisions.

An interesting question, therefore, is what guides people's instrumental motivations to regulate their group-based emotions in the context of intractable conflicts. A reasonable assumption would be that people's basic goals in a certain context guide the instrumental considerations they have to regulate certain emotions. Along that line of thought, Porat et al. (2015) recently have theorized and then showed empirically that people's ideological convictions may serve as such guiding signals. *Political ideology* refers to "an interrelated set of attitudes and values about the proper goals of society and how they should be achieved" (Tedin, 1987, p. 65). It involves motivational components that help explain why people do what they do in the group context (Jost, 2006). Therefore, especially in the context of long-term intergroup conflict, political ideology reflects central group goals. As such, people may be motivated to experience certain emotions either to justify and support their ideology (i.e., leftists want to feel hope even when there is no sign of peace) or to promote policies that potentially can serve their ideological goals (i.e., leftists would like to feel hope because they believe that if many people expressed hope, leaders would feel obliged to adopt peace promoting actions). Hence, to the extent that people are motivated to experience emotions that are consistent with their group-based goals, what people want to feel in the political context should depend on their political ideology.

Political ideology often has been classified into two contrasting poles—right-wing and left-wing ideology. This formulation contains two interrelated aspects: advocating versus resisting social change and rejecting versus accepting inequality (Jost, 2006; Jost, Glaser, Kruglanski, & Sulloway, 2003a, 2003b). Whereas right-wing ideology is associated with resistance to change and the acceptance of inequality, left-wing ideology is associated with advocating change and the rejection of inequality (Jost, Federico, & Napier, 2009). According to the moral foundations theory (Graham, Haidt, & Nosek, 2009; Haidt & Graham, 2007; Haidt & Joseph, 2004), rightists and leftists also differ with respect to the moral values they endorse. While left-wing ideology pertains to fairness and care, right-wing ideology pertains to loyalty, authority, and purity. If ideology indeed encapsulates people's instrumental motivations to experience group-based emotions, then the abovementioned values and goals should indicate the kinds of emotions people will be motivated to experience in the context of their ideology.

According to that view, right-wingers would be more motivated than left-wingers to experience emotions that maximize power inequality and less motivated than left-wingers to experience emotions that minimize it. In line with the notion that anger can preserve power and promote social dominance (e.g., Frijda, 1986; Roseman, 2001, Scherer, 1999), Porat and colleagues (2015) have found in a series of studies that people who adhere to right-wing ideology are more motivated than leftists to experience anger toward outgroup members, especially during conflict. In contrast, they also found that because empathy facilitates helping and compromising with others (Batson, 1991, 1998), right-wingers were less motivated than leftists to experience empathy toward outgroup members. Even more importantly, Porat and colleagues (2015) have demonstrated the downstream effects of these ideological motivations, showing that those who were more motivated to feel group-based anger (or less motivated to feel empathy) actually responded with more anger (or less empathy) to conflict-related events, and that in turn, these emotional reactions significantly influenced their political reactions in the expected direction. These results demonstrate that at least some of the influence of people's ideologies on their concrete political reactions can be explained by the extent to which these ideologies instrumentally motivate them to experience certain group-based emotions and not to experience others.

Finally, instrumental goals for regulating group-based emotions often conflict with either hedonic goals or with other instrumental goals. As already mentioned, long-term instrumental goals might include immediate negative emotions such as sadness or anger, which are accepted under the assumption that their benefit will exceed the costs associated with the immediate negative experience. For example, although fear is not a pleasant emotion, people are sometimes motivated to experience group-based fear because they believe that it will help their group's preparation for future attacks (Lerner et al., 2003; Skitka, Bauman, & Mullen, 2004).

Another interesting conflict exists between personal and group goals for regulating certain emotions. Going back to the fear example, I may wish to down-regulate fear to better cope with personal difficulties, but at the same time, I may want to feel group-based fear to experience my group as weak to support the perception of collective victimhood and justify acts of violence committed by my group (Bar-Tal, Chernyak-Hai, Schori, & Gundar, 2009). Goldenberg et al. (in press) have recently argued that when goals at the two levels conflict with each other, they may lead to changes in one emotion regulation strategy at the expense of the other. For example, a motivation not to be fearful on a personal level may interfere with a motivation to feel fear at the group-based level. This conflict may lead to a change in goals at one of the levels, which in turn will change my emotional experience.

Emotion Regulation Strategies for Regulating Group-Based Emotions

Given that group-based emotions are a subcategory of individual emotions, the strategies used to regulate them should not be fundamentally different from the ones used to regulate individual emotions. People can use situation selection, situation modification, distraction, cognitive change, and other strategies to regulate group-based emotions as well as individual ones. Yet, given that group-based emotions appear within a certain intra- and intergroup context and given that they involve various mechanisms of group identification and dis-identification, the way they are regulated can be slightly different from that of individual emotions. Unfortunately, the scope of the current chapter is too limited to introduce a systematic overview of these differences, but I will try to briefly highlight the most important ones as I see them.

First, and maybe most importantly, when it comes to group-based emotions, people sometimes try to regulate their own emotions (I want to feel less anger in the name of my group), but they also try to regulate the emotions of other members of their group (I want other group members to feel angrier toward the outgroup) or even the emotions of outgroup members (I want outgroup members not to experience anger toward my ingroup to avoid outgroup aggression).

Whereas the first falls into what previously has been defined as intrinsic emotion regulation, the latter two capture two kinds of extrinsic regulation processes.

In terms of the regulation strategies themselves, given that the events that elicit group-based emotions are mostly in the public rather than in the private sphere, the strategy of situation selection may be seen as less relevant in that case. That is mainly because individuals usually have rather limited ability to select the situations that may elicit group-based emotions. Likewise, given that emotional experiences within the group context often are followed by an inherent need of the group for emotional sharing (Luminet IV, Bouts, Delie, Manstead, & Rimé, 2000; Rimé, Mesquita, Boca, & Philippot, 1991), avoiding events such as public ceremonies, or even attempts not to be exposed to the news, might be very difficult. It is even more difficult as long as people want to remain part of the group and not go through a group dis-identification process (Becker, Tausch, Spears, & Christ, 2011). Additionally, as group-based emotions can be elicited by the actions of many different group members, individuals have a limited ability to identify when group-based emotion-eliciting situations may occur and therefore limited ability to use situation selection strategies.

At the same time, on an extrinsic level, situation selection is used quite frequently to up- or downregulate group-based emotions. As already mentioned, groups often use communal rituals, collective holidays, and memorial events to elicit emotions that serve their goals (Harris & Sutton, 1986; Hochschild, 1979; Radcliffe-Brown, 1993). An example of such situations is the memorial siren, which is activated every year on Israel's Memorial Day. The siren reminds people of the significance of the day, eliciting emotions like sadness and empathy as well as increasing the sense of unity with the group. Another form of extrinsic situation selection occurs via education (Bar-Tal, 2007). For example, sending students to a tolerance museum can serve as a positive emotion regulator toward the outgroup. On the other hand, sending them to visit monuments of past wars can have the opposite effects by upregulating fear and group anxiety. Such examples of extrinsic emotion regulation are very common in societies and often serve to increase a sense of nationality, unity, and identity, leading to positive emotions toward the ingroup and negative emotions toward the outgroup.

If situation selection is rather difficult, situation modification is a more plausible strategy for regulating group-based emotions. This can be done in two very different ways—either by modifying the actual social situation, which is the source of the emotion (also defined in social psychology as collective action (see Van-Zomeren et al., 2012) or by modifying the source of exposure to the collective event, such as a news outlet or a friend. These two types of strategies differ both in the ways they are conducted and in the ease of their implementation.

In the first case, the viability of situation modification of the actual events depends on the magnitude of the situation and the size of the group. According to resource mobilization theory (Jenkins, 1983; McCarthy & Zald, 1977), the success of situation modification is dependent on the number of agents, their level of unity, the availability of resources, and the ability to attract others' support. In situations of small-scale intergroup conflicts (e.g., conflict between two families), changing the actual situation may be feasible and require few resources. However, in large-scale conflicts (e.g., conflict between societies or states), it is much more difficult for individuals or even groups to gather the appropriate resources to change the dynamic of the collective event itself (Khawaja, 1993). In cases in which fundamental change of the context is impossible, situation modification strategies often include symbolic gestures such as choosing to wear a certain outfit at a group rally or deciding not to hang the national flag on one's porch for Independence Day. These actions are considered to be situation modification inasmuch as they include the individual's involvement in actively changing the nature of the situation to regulate group-based emotions.

Given the limited influence people have on modifying group-based events, situation modification strategies are often focused on influencing the communication of the information regarding events rather than on changing the events themselves. As group-based situations often are not directly experienced by the individual, but rather mediated by various means of communication, the individual has the ability to modify the sources of information to meet her needs. An example of such attempts is described in Noelle-Neumann's (1974) idea of the spiral of silence. According to this theory, group members aspire to stop the flow of certain information by influencing other group members not to express it. By censoring information, people are not only regulating their own emotions but also extrinsically regulating others' emotions and especially unpleasant, moral, group-based emotions such as group-based guilt (Branscombe & Doosje, 2004) and shame (Allpress, Barlow, Brown, & Louis, 2010). These processes involve both intrinsic and extrinsic regulation strategies, given that group members not only have the tendency to censor interpretations that may elicit unpleasant emotions but also tend to punish individuals who expose such information (Schachter, 1951; Sears & Funk, 1991).

The third family of strategies, attentional deployment, is used uniquely in regard to group-based emotions because its most basic process is in many ways embedded within the contours of social identity theory. According to the theory, a common strategy used by individuals to maintain a positive sense of the group is defined as "social creativity" (Turner & Reynolds, 2001), in which individuals focus their attention on aspects of the group that emphasize its positivity. Similar to the case of situation modification, intrinsic attentional deployment strategies can focus on either the situation or the channels of communication regarding the situation. Focusing first on attentional shifts from the situations themselves, distracting oneself from emotional situations may be very challenging in the case of group-based emotions. For example, shifting attention away from a memorial day in Israel is almost an impossible task, considering the fact that it is a national holiday during which a siren is heard all over the country.

Yet this still can be done sometimes by individuals as well as by groups. For example, denial is an extreme case of attentional deployment in which people and groups simply eliminate (psychologically) the existence of evidence of certain emotion-eliciting events. Holocaust deniers, for example, may oppose the facts of the Holocaust to decrease group-based guilt (Edelstein, Nathanson, & Stone, 1989). The Turkish government, which refuses to publicly acknowledge the Armenian genocide, is another example (Hovannisian, 1999) in which societal formal and informal mechanisms help society members to distract themselves from the troubling event. Again, this is done both in intrinsic (I choose not to be exposed or think of certain information) and extrinsic ways (the government conceals certain evidence so the public will not experience guilt) (Bar-Tal, 2007; George, 2000). Additionally, given that group-based emotions are boosted when group identification is salient, extrinsic attentional deployment can be instantiated merely by focusing group members' attention on their group membership (Gordijn, Yzerbyt, Wigboldus, & Dumont, 2006; Wohl & Branscombe, 2005).

Looking at the general literature on emotion regulation, the fourth family of strategies, cognitive change, is by all means the most studied and also the one that generally is considered the most effective. As such, it is only natural that it is the first (and by now also the only) strategy that has been tested empirically in the context of intractable conflicts (Halperin, Porat, Tamir, et al., 2013; Halperin, Cohen-Chen et al., 2014). As in attentional deployment, cognitive change resonates well with the strategy defined by social identity theory as *social creativity*, in which the individual finds interpretations that will maintain positive emotions toward one's group. When applied to group-based emotions, cognitive change can be achieved in two different ways—either by changing the meaning of the situation (as in individual emotions) or by changing one's level of categorization. Whereas the first is well studied in the literature on emotion regulation and therefore will not be discussed at length here, the second is unique to group-based emotions and therefore more intriguing.

The idea that changing the individual's self-categorization with the group can serve as a useful regulatory strategy is well supported by literature on group-based emotions (Mackie et al., 2000; Smith, 1993; Smith et al., 2007). However, in most of these studies, self-categorization was either measured (Gordijn et al., 2006; Maitner, Mackie, & Smith, 2007; Pennekamp, Doosje, Zebel, & Fischer, 2007; Van-Zomeren, Postmes, & Spears, 2008; Van-Zomeren et al., 2012; Yzerbyt et al., 2003) or manipulated to prove the existence of group-based emotions (Mackie et al., 2000; Seger, Smith, & Mackie, 2009). Considering self-categorization as an intentional emotion regulation strategy is rather new.

Effectively regulating negative emotions by altering one's self-categorization can be executed by perceiving oneself as an independent individual or by shifting the salience of one self-categorization to more inclusive levels (which is called *recategorization*). This idea was exemplified by Wohl and Branscombe

(2005), who have shown that changing participants' categorization from a national to a universal level influenced their willingness to forgive outgroup inequities. Although these findings did not focus on group-based emotions, they did suggest that outgroup attitudes are dependent on one's self-categorization. These findings emphasize that people are members of various groups and have the ability to recategorize themselves according to different contexts (Gaertner, Dovidio, Anastasio, Bachman, & Rust, 1993; Turner, Oakes, Haslam, & McGarty, 1994). These shifts can be horizontal (a shift among different groups within the group: American to academic) as well as vertical in both time (a Y generation and a teenager) and space (i.e., the size of group, such as Americans or humans).

On the extrinsic level, leaders or others who are interested in changing public opinion use cognitive change in the form of reframing public events to alter people's emotional reactions to these events (Niven, Totterdell, Stride, & Holman, 2011; Rimé, 2007; Zaki & Williams, 2013). In terms of changing the meaning of the situation itself, leaders often attribute malevolent intentions to the other group's unintentional behavior in ways that lead to elicitation of negative group-based emotions (Halperin, 2008). This is especially common in cases of intractable conflicts in which leaders frame the outgroup's provocations as stemming from innate characteristics to justify and mobilize support for ingroup's counterviolence. Additionally, the extrinsic regulation of group-based emotions can occur by changing the other's self-categorization in ways that lead to the regulation of different emotions. Inclusion and exclusion of others in a specific group have been found to have a crucial effect on these people's motivations regarding their group (Baumeister, DeWall, Ciarocco, & Twenge, 2005). Again, the phenomenon itself is not new, but its analysis through the framework of extrinsic emotion regulation is rather innovative.

The final type of emotion regulation strategy described by the process model is response modulation. Here the individual tries to directly control behavioral and physiological responses during emotional experience. Due to the fact that response modulation is focused mainly on changing the physiological and facial responses of an individual, there is no reason to expect huge differences between the way it is done on the individual versus the group level. At the same time, it is reasonable to assume that individual's emotional responses (modulated or not) would have an effect on other group members' emotional reactions. Emotions serve a very important functional role in communicating an individual's thoughts and intentions (Ekman, 1992; Keltner & Gross, 1999; Le Bon, 1960/1895; Van Kleef, 2009; Van Kleef, De Dreu, & Manstead, 2010). In group-based emotion, this function is extremely important as it facilies group unity and leads group members to act together (Bar-Tal, 2007). Group-based emotional responses also serve as communication to outgroups regarding the intentions of the group as a whole (Kamans, Van-Zomeren, Gordijn, & Postmes, 2014).

To sum up, people's regulation of group-based emotions is not fundamentally different from the way they regulate individual emotions, but some differences do exist. Among the more important ones are the centrality of group goals and ideologies in guiding regulation goals, the relative efficacy of different strategies, preferences for one strategy over another, and the specific content of cognitive change. These differences result from several key factors, among them the fact that people have less personal control and more limited direct exposure to group-based events, the central role played by identity and categorization processes in the generation and regulation of group-based emotions, and the emotional dynamic of many group members simultaneously experiencing group-based events and expressing similar or dissimilar emotions.

Repeated Exposure to Violence and Emotion Regulation Processes

One last thing that must be taken into account in attempting to create a deeper understanding of emotion regulation processes in intractable conflicts is the psychological or mental health characteristics of the individuals who are the target of that regulation. In that regard, emotion regulation in the context of intractable conflict is fundamentally different from the regulation of emotions in nonviolent, more standard intergroup conflicts. That is mainly due to the fact that the conditions of intractable conflict involve repeated exposure to violence, often directly. In extreme cases, such exposure can lead to posttraumatic stress disorder (PTSD) (American Psychiatric Association, 2013), but even in the absence of such a clear clinical diagnosis, research has shown repeated exposure to have effects on psychological outcomes such as the processing and learning of new information (e.g., Levy-Gigi & Richter-Levin, 2014). Given that acute trauma disorders are highly prevalent in societies living in such conflicts (e.g., Canetti, Hall, Rapaport, & Wayne, 2013; Muldoon & Lowe, 2012), many of the clinical symptoms of PTSD (including avoidant behavior, negative alterations in cognition or mood, and autonomic hyperarousal; American Psychiatric Association, 2013) are also highly prevalent in such societies. But even beyond these, the repeated exposure to violence carries substantial psychological consequences for all society members, even for those who were not exposed directly to violence and who do not report on any symptomatic experiences related to trauma. In fact, in his classical conceptualization of intractable conflict, Peter Colman already has referred to acute trauma as a characteristic of such realities (Coleman, 2003), and numerous accounts of the harsh realities of intractable conflict have since identified the clinical consequences of exposure to violence as a central element within societies involved in this reality (e.g., Bar-Tal, Chernyak-Hai, Schori, & Gundar, 2009; Hamama-Raz, Solomon, Cohen, & Laufer, 2008; Muldoon & Trew, 2000).

On a personal level, the repeated exposure to violence in the context of conflict can have grave consequences, including heightened anxiety, a reduced sense of safety, the symptoms previously listed, and a subjective sense of insecurity (e.g., Canetti, Halperin, Sharvit, & Hobfoll, 2009; Galea et al., 2002; Lavi & Solomon, 2005). Recent studies have begun exploring the effects of such traumatic exposure in conflict on threat perceptions and citizens' resultant political positions (Bonanno & Jost, 2006; Canetti, Halperin, Sharvit et al., 2009). However, this psychological distress also has major effects on the collective level as it is a motivator and entrencher of conflict-supporting beliefs and also leads to aggressive, non-conciliatory intergroup attitudes (Canetti, Muldoon, Hirsch-Hoefler, & Rapaport, 2011).

Relevant to the present discussion, trauma-related clinical symptomology is implicated significantly in emotional processes (e.g., Etkin & Wager, 2007; Litz & Gray, 2002). The nature of the resulting abnormalities in emotional processing, however, has been the source of conflicting theoretical and empirical accounts (Litz & Gray, 2002; Wolf, Miller, & McKinney, 2009). Indeed, some empirical findings have indicated that repeated exposure to violence may lead to higher negative emotionality (Amdur et al., 2000; Wolf et al., 2009), whereas others document emotional numbing in individuals exposed to traumatic events (Glover, 1992; Litz & Gray, 2002; Wolf et al., 2009). Recent neuroimaging studies focusing on emotional areas of the brain such as the amygdala have provided support for the former explanation over the latter: even those who report emotional numbing following repeated exposure to traumatic events tend to experience greater emotional intensity in response to negative stimuli (e.g., Etkin & Wager, 2007; Wolf et al., 2009).

Because of these findings, it is important to understand how repeated exposure to violence might influence attempts to regulate emotions in the context of intractable conflict. In such realities, not only are trauma-related clinical disorders prevalent, but the trauma leading to them originates from events of the conflict, and such conflict-related events and information are omnipresent. Therefore, emotions are experienced by a significant portion of society members at very high levels—higher than the emotions trauma-less individuals would have in response to identical stimuli. One common result of that process that is highly relevant for our discussion is the frequent use of suppression as an emotion regulation strategy.

In fact, suppression has received much interest in the literature on emotion regulation as a largely counter-effective strategy to regulate emotional experiences (Gross, 2007). The research linking emotion regulation to the clinical consequences of exposure to violence, however, goes far beyond reference to suppression, and much research in the past few years has focused on emotion regulatory processes among individuals with trauma-related disorders (e.g., Benoit, Bouthillier, Moss, Rousseau, & Brunet, 2010; Tull, Barrett, McMillan, & Roemer, 2007). For example, many studies examining the relationship between PTSD and emotion regulation difficulties have found symptom severity to be associated with several hindering factors for successful regulation: lack of emotional acceptance, difficulty engaging in goal-directed behavior when upset, impulse control difficulties, limited ability to employ effective emotion regulation strategies or to choose appropriate strategies to employ, and lack of emotional clarity (e.g., Cloitre, Miranda, Stovall-McClough, & Han, 2005; Ehring & Quack, 2010; Levy-Gigi, Richter-Levin, Shapiro, Kéri, & Sheppes, in press). Recently, supporting evidence also has been offered by a neuroimaging study (Etkin & Wager, 2007).

Because the clinical consequences of repeated exposure to violence play a decisive role in emotion regulation strategies, rendering them significantly less effective, it is highly important to acknowledge the high prevalence of such clinical features in the context of intractable conflicts. Specifically, it follows that for many individuals living in societies in conflict, strategies of direct emotion regulation may not be effective in modifying emotional experiences and that such strategies generally should be less effective in such societies compared to societies living in nonviolent realities. It remains to be examined whether indirect methods of emotion regulation focusing on the core cognitive appraisals of the emotion rather than on the emotion itself, would be more effective than direct strategies for individuals suffering from repeated exposure to violence. As we have argued recently (Halperin & Pliskin, 2015), such a finding would be important not only for the study of conflicts and their resolution but potentially also for the creation of better treatments for trauma-related psychological disorders such as PTSD, promoting emotional coping by focusing on the cognitive rather than the affective features of the relevant emotions.

Concluding Remarks

Although the study of emotions and emotion regulation in conflicts is developing incrementally, there is still a long way to go before the potential embedded within the integration of these two fields can be utilized fully. One pivotal challenge on the way toward achieving this goal is to knit together several communities of scholars, educating conflict scholars about the potential contribution of the study of emotion and emotion regulation and educating emotion scholars about conflict studies. Among emotion scholars, it is not uncommon to see scholars who are apprehensive about research conducted outside the laboratory and especially in such uncontrolled environments. In addition, emotion scholars are not always enthusiastic about adjusting their 'good-old' conceptualizations and methodological approaches to different contexts and situations. Among conflict resolution scholars, on the other hand, one can still identify general biases against the emotional approach, hesitations about the actual ability to change people's emotions in such long-term violent conflicts, and even some level of uncertainty about whether changing people's emotions can in fact promote peace. Upon bridging these interdisciplinary gaps, scholars of both fields will face some theoretical, empirical, and applied challenges that are described in the following section.

Theoretical and Empirical Challenges for the Scientific Communities

The first challenge of those who seek to study emotion in conflicts is to move beyond the 'immediate suspects' in terms of the emotions that are being studied. I often identify a gap between emotions that are studied in the tradition of emotion or affective science, on the one hand, and the emotions that are more central to conflict situations, on the other hand. While numerous studies have examined the role of anger, fear (e.g., Cheung-Blunden, & Blunden, 2008; Huddy et al., 2007; Lerner et al., 2003; Skitka et al., 2006), and moral emotions (e.g., Branscombe & Doosje, 2004; Čehajić et al., 2011; Iyer et al., 2003; McGarty et al., 2005) in conflict situations, empirical research studying the role of other relevant emotions such as despair, contempt, and hatred is not as common and definitely does not mirror the dominance of these emotions in conflict zones. Undoubtedly, empirical research into the nature and implications of some of these emotions in conflict situations can be challenging because it will require the development of new conceptualizations and measurements that were not used previously among emotion scholars. But it is necessary to form a comprehensive picture of the affective map involved in conflict situations.

The same principle of going beyond the most common and most studied emotions should be applied to the selection of the emotion regulation strategies studied. As already mentioned, while most studies so far on emotion regulation in conflicts have utilized cognitive reappraisal as the sole emotion regulation strategy, other emotion regulation strategies like suppression or even situation selection might be relevant and should be studied in this context. Studying these emotion regulation strategies must go beyond the simple utilization of existing strategies in a new context and should use knowledge about group processes and conflict situation to improve the effectiveness of emotion regulation strategies among those living in intractable conflicts.

On a related issue, future studies should seek to reveal not only the effective emotion regulation strategies that potentially can promote peace but also the emotion regulation strategies (e.g., suppression) that help people ignore conflict-related events while avoiding any real confrontation with the problems inherent in conflict situations. In many cases, these emotion regulation strategies serve as peace barriers rather than peace catalysts, and as such, they should be studied with scrutiny. These processes stabilize or freeze conflict situations because they help people to avoid feeling group-based emotions, like guilt or shame, which potentially can promote peace. This can be seen as the 'dark side' of effective emotion regulation strategies in conflict situations, an issue that should be studied in depth in the future.

Finally, an important theoretical and empirical challenge for scholars from both communities is to adjust current knowledge regarding effective regulatory processes to the unique characteristics of societies involved in long-term, intractable conflict. An attempt to regulate negative emotions among those who are, on the one hand, absolutely convinced of the justness of their ideological goals and, on the other hand, suffer from repeated events of personal and collective trauma, deserves a nuanced theoretical and empirical treatment. In this regard, the suggested model and findings constitute the first baby steps of a much larger scholarly endeavor.

From the Lab to the Field: Future Challenges in Implementing a New Approach

Extending our understanding of the role and dynamics of emotional processes in conflicts is an admirable goal. Yet the ultimate goal of such a scientific endeavor definitely should be to contribute to the actual resolution of these destructive conflicts. To address this goal, knowledge based on scientific methodologies should be transferred, adjusted, and then properly utilized by those in the field who try to promote the peaceful resolution of conflicts. Such progress requires true faith in the potential benefits of the emotional approach by practitioners but also extensive investment by the scientific community to translate the aggregated knowledge into clear and workable materials that can be transferred to the general public through various channels.

In many ways, the 'million dollar question' is how we can use this knowledge to mobilize public opinion for peace or how we can increase the scale and scope of existing emotion regulation strategies. The simplest answer to these questions lies in the intersection between research and education or, in this case, peace education. Peace education programs should focus on more concrete messages based on scientific knowledge about the implications of discrete emotions and the way to change them by altering their core appraisal themes (i.e., indirect emotion regulation). Simultaneously, other programs can teach efficient emotion regulation strategies (i.e., direct emotion regulation) and connect them to emotional experiences during conflict-related events. This can be suited to situations in which explicit reference to promoting peace is not welcomed in the political and societal atmosphere, and more indirect strategies, in which the actual conflict is rarely mentioned, are thus more feasible (see Bar-Tal & Rosen, 2009).

Finally, a huge potential for disseminating these ideas is embedded within media channels in general and the social media more specifically. Some efforts have been made in recent years to use media channels to reduce prejudice and promote peace (e.g., Paluck, 2009; Singhal, Cody, Rogers, & Sabido, 2004). New technological developments and the huge popularity of new social media create a fertile ground for building new bridges that may assist people to regulate their negative emotions in the midst of long-term conflicts. Such regulation, as seen in the studies reviewed in this paper, can help in forming more constructive reactions and potentially promoting more conciliatory policies with the aim of ending the conflict.

REFERENCES

Adams, G., Tormala, T. T., & O'Brien, L. T. (2006). The effect of self-affirmation on perception of racism. *Journal of Experimental Social Psychology, 42*(5), 616–626.

Al Ramiah, A., & Hewstone, M. (2013). Intergroup contact as a tool for reducing, resolving, and preventing intergroup conflict: Evidence, limitations, and potential. *American Psychologist, 68*(7), 527–542.

Aldao, A., Nolen-Hoeksema, S., & Schweizer, S. (2010). Emotion regulation strategies across psychopathology: A meta-analysis. *Clinical Psychology Review, 30,* 217–237.

Alicke, M. D. (2000). Culpable control and psychology of blame. *Psychological Bulletin, 126*(4), 556–574.

Allport, G. W. (1954). *The nature of prejudice.* Reading, MA: Addison-Wesley.

Allpress, J. A., Barlow, F. K., Brown, R., & Louis, W. R. (2010). Atoning for colonial injustices: Group-based shame and guilt motivate support for reparation. *International Journal of Conflict and Violence, 4*(1), 75–88.

Allred, K., Mallozzi, J. S., Matsui, F., & Raia, C. P. (1997). The influence of anger and compassion on negotiation performance. *Organizational Behavior and Human Decision Processes, 70*(3), 175–187.

Amdur, R. L., Larsen, R., & Liberzon, I. (2000). Emotional processing in combat-related post-traumatic stress disorder: A comparison with traumatized and normal controls. *Journal of Anxiety Disorders, 14*(3), 219–238.

American Psychiatric Association. (2013). *Diagnostic and statistical manual of mental disorders (DSM-5®).* Author.

Anderson, C., & Galinsky, A. D. (2006). Power, optimism, and risk-taking. *European Journal of Social Psychology, 36*(4), 511–536.

Antonovsky, A., & Arian, A. (1972). *Hopes and fears of Israelis: Consensus in a new society.* Jerusalem, Israel: Jerusalem Academic Press.

Archer, J. (2000). Sex differences in aggression between heterosexual partners: A meta-analytic review. *Psychological Bulletin, 126*(5), 651–680.

Archer, J., & Coyne, S. M. (2005). An integrated review of indirect, relational, and social aggression. *Personality and Social Psychology Review, 9*(3), 212–230.

Arnold, M. B. (1960). *Emotion and personality.* New York: Columbia University Press.

Aronson, E., & Patnoe, S. (1997). *The jigsaw classroom* (2nd ed.). New York: Longman.

Associated Press. (2009, May 21). Gaza doctor whose family were killed by IDF fundraises for Israeli hospital. *Haaretz.* Retrieved from: http://www.haaretz.com/news/gaza-doctor-whose-family-were-killed-by-idf-fundraises-for-israeli-hospital-1.276449

Atran, S., Axelrod, R., & Davis, R. (2007). Sacred barriers to conflict resolution. *Science, 317,* 1039–1040.

Atran, S., & Stern, J. (2005). Small groups find fatal purpose through the web. *Nature, 437,* 620.

Avenanti, A., Sirigu, A., & Aglioti, S. M. (2010). Racial bias reduces empathic sensorimotor resonance with other-race pain. *Current Biology, 20*(11), 1018–1022.

Averill, J. R. (1980). A constructivist view of emotion. In R. Plutchik & H. Kellerman (Eds.), *Emotion: Theory, research and experience* (Vol. 1, pp. 305–339). New York: Academic Press.

Averill, J. R. (1982). *Anger and aggression: An essay on emotion.* New York: Springer-Verlag.

Averill, J. R. (1983). Studies on anger and aggression. *American Psychologist, 38*(11), 1160–1145.

Averill, J. R. (1984). The acquisition of emotions during adulthood. In C. Z. Malatesta & C. Izard (Eds.), *Affective processes in adult development* (pp. 23–43). Beverly Hills, CA: Sage.

Averill, J. R. (1994). Emotions are many splendored things. In P. Ekman & R. J. Davidson (Eds.), *The nature of emotion* (pp. 99–102). New York: Oxford University Press.

Averill, J. R., Catlin, G., & Chon, K. K. (1990). *Rules of hope.* New York: Springer-Verlag.

Baker, C., Saxe, R., & Tenenbaum, J. B. (2009). Action understanding as inverse planning. *Cognition, 113*(3), 329–349.

Bandura, A. (1990). Selective activation and disengagement of moral control. *Journal of Social Issues, 46*(1), 27–46.

Bandura, A. (1999). Moral disengagement in the perpetration of inhumanities. *Personality and Social Psychology Review, 3*(3), 193–209.

Bandura, A., & Walters, R. H. (1959). *Adolescent aggression.* New York: Ronald.

Barbalet, J. M. (1998). *Emotions, social theory, and social structure: A macrosociological approach.* Cambridge, UK: Cambridge University Press.

Bargh, J. A. (1996). Automaticity in social psychology. In E. T. Higgins & W. A. Kruglanski (Eds.), *Social psychology: Handbook of basic principles* (pp. 169–183). New York: Guilford.

Barlett, C. P., & Anderson, C. A. (2011). Reappraising the situation and its impact on aggressive behavior. *Personality and Social Psychology, 37*(12), 1564–1573.

Baron, R. A., Fortin, S. P., Frei, R. L., Hauver, L. A., & Shack, M. L. (1990). Reducing organizational conflict: The role of socially-induced positive affect. *International Journal of Conflict Management, 1*(2), 133–152.

Barrett, K. (1995). A functionalist approach to shame and guilt. In J. P. Tangney & K. W. Fischer (Eds.), *Self-conscious emotions* (pp. 25–63). New York: Guilford.

Barrett, L. F. (2006). Solving the emotions paradox: Categorization and the experience of emotion. *Personality and Social Psychology Review, 10*(1), 20–46.

Barrett, L., Mesquita, B., Ochsner, K., & Gross, J. J. (2007). Emotional experience. *Annual Review of Psychology, 58*(7), 373–403.

Barrett, L. F., & Russell, J. A. (1999). The structure of current affect: Controversies and emerging consensus. *Current Directions in Psychological Science, 8,* 10–14.

Bar-Tal, D. (1998). Societal beliefs in times of intractable conflict: The Israeli case. *International Journal of Conflict Management, 9*(1), 22–50.

Bar-Tal, D. (2000). *Shared beliefs in a society: Social psychological analysis.* Thousand Oaks, CA: Sage.

Bar-Tal, D. (2001). Why does fear override hope in societies engulfed by intractable conflict, as it does in the Israeli society? *Political Psychology, 22*(3), 601–627.

Bar-Tal, D. (2003). Collective memory of physical violence: Its contribution to the culture of violence. In E. Cairns & D. Roe (Eds.), *The role of memory in ethnic conflict* (pp. 77–93). Houndmills, England: Palgrave Macmillan.

Bar-Tal, D. (2007). Sociopsychological foundations of intractable conflicts. *American Behavioral Scientist, 50*(11), 1430–1453.

Bar-Tal, D. (2013). *Intractable conflicts: Socio-psychological foundations and dynamics.* Cambridge, UK: Cambridge University Press.

Bar-Tal, D., & Antebi, D. (1992). Beliefs about negative intentions of the world: A study of the Israeli siege mentality. *Political Psychology, 13*, 633–645.

Bar-Tal, D., & Bennink, G. H. (2004). The nature of reconciliation as an outcome and as a process. In Y. Bar-Siman-Tov (Ed.), *From conflict resolution to reconciliation* (pp. 11–38). New York: Oxford University Press.

Bar-Tal, D., Chernyak-Hai, L., Schori, N., & Gundar, A. (2009). A sense of self-perceived collective victimhood in intractable conflicts. *International Red Cross Review, 91*(874), 229–277.

Bar-Tal, D., & Halperin, E. (2011). Socio-psychological barriers to conflict resolution. In D. Bar-Tal (Ed.), *Intergroup conflicts and their resolution: Social psychological perspective* (pp. 217–240). New-York: Psychology Press.

Bar-Tal, D., & Halperin, E. (2013). The psychology of intractable conflicts: Eruption, escalation and peacemaking. In L. Huddy, D., O. Sears, & J. S. Levy (Eds.), *Oxford handbook of political psychology* (pp. 923–956). New York: Oxford University Press.

Bar-Tal, D., & Halperin, E. (2014). Socio-psychological barriers for peace making and ideas to overcome them. *Revista de Psicología Social, 29*(1), 1–30.

Bar-Tal, D., Halperin, E., & De Rivera, J. (2007). Collective emotions in conflict: Societal implications. *Journal of Social Issues, 63*(2), 441–460.

Bar-Tal, D., & Hammack, P. L. (2012). Conflict, delegitimization, and violence. In L. R. Tropp (Ed.), *The Oxford handbook of intergroup conflict* (pp. 29–52). New York: Oxford University Press.

Bar-Tal, D., & Rosen, Y. (2009). Peace education in societies involved in intractable conflicts: Direct and indirect models. *Review of Educational Research, 79*(2), 557–575.

Batson, C. D. (1991). *The altruism question: Toward a social-psychological answer.* Hillsdale, NJ: Lawrence Erlbaum.

Batson, C. D. (1998). Altruism and prosocial behavior. In D. T. Gilbert, S. T. Fiske, & G. Lindzey (Eds.), *The handbook of social psychology* (4th ed., Vol. 2, pp. 282–316). Boston: McGraw-Hill.

Batson, C. D. (2009). These things called empathy: Eight related but distinct phenomena. In J. Decety, & W. Ickes (Eds.), *The social neuroscience of empathy* (pp. 3–15). Cambridge, MA: MIT Press.

Batson, C. D. (2011). *Altruism in humans.* New York: Oxford University Press.

Batson, C. D., & Ahmad, N. Y. (2009). Using empathy to improve intergroup attitudes and relations. *Social Issues and Policy Review, 3*(1), 141–177.

Batson, C. D., Batson, J. G., Slingsby, J. K., Harrell, K. L., Peekna, H. M., & Todd, R. M. (1991). Empathic joy and the empathy-altruism hypothesis. *Journal of Personality and Social Psychology, 61*(3), 413–426.

Batson, C. D., Bolen, M. H., Cross, J. A., & Neuringer-Benefiel, H. E. (1986). Where is the altruism in the altruistic personality? *Journal of Personality and Social Psychology, 50*(1), 212–220.

Batson, C. D., Chang, J., Orr, R., & Rowland, J. (2002). Empathy, attitudes and action: Can feeling for a member of a stigmatized group motivate one to help the group. *Personality and Social Psychology Bulletin, 28*(12), 1656–1666.

Batson, C. D., & Coke, J. S. (1981). Empathy: A source of altruistic motivation for helping. In J. P. Rushton & R. M. Sorrentino (Eds.), *Altruism and helping behavior* (pp. 167–187). Hillsdale, NJ: Lawrence Erlbaum.

Batson, C. D., Duncan, B. D., Ackerman, P., Buckley, T., & Birch, K. (1981). Is empathic emotion a source of altruistic motivation? *Journal of Personality and Social Psychology, 40*(2), 290–302.

Batson, C. D., Early, S., & Salvarini, G. (1997). Perspective taking: Imagining how another feels versus imagining how you would feel. *Personality & Social Psychology Bulletin, 23*(7), 751–758.

Batson, C. D., Lishner, D. A., Carpenter, A., Dulin, L., Harjusola-Webb, S., Stocks, E. L., . . . Sampat, B. (2003). ". . . As you would have them do unto you": Does imagining yourself in the other's place stimulate moral action? *Personality & Social Psychology Bulletin, 29*(9), 1190–1201.

Batson, C. D., Sager, K., Garst, E., Kang, M., Rubchinsky, K., & Dawson, K. (1997). Is empathy-induced helping due to self—other merging? *Journal of Personality and Social Psychology, 73*(3), 495–509.

Batson, C. D., Turk, C. L., Shaw, L. L., & Klein, T. R. (1995). Information function of empathic emotion: Learning that we value the other's welfare. *Journal of Personality and Social Psychology, 68*(2), 300–313.

Batson, C. D., Van Lange, P. A., Ahmad, N., & Lishner, D. A. (2007). Altruism and helping behavior. In M. A. Hogg & J. Cooper (Eds.), *Sage handbook of social psychology* (pp. 279–295). London: Sage.

Baumeister, R. F., DeWall, C., Ciarocco, N. J., & Twenge, J. M. (2005). Social exclusion impairs self-regulation. *Journal of Personality and Social Psychology, 88*, 589–604.

Baumeister, R. F., Stillwell, A. M., & Heatherton, T. F. (1994). Guilt: An interpersonal approach. *Psychological Bulletin, 115*(2), 243–267.

Baumeister, R. F., Vohs, K. D., DeWall, C. N., & Zhang, L. (2007). How emotion shapes behavior: Feedback, anticipation, and reflection, rather than direct causation. *Personality and Social Psychology Review, 11*, 167–203.

Beck, A. T., Weissman, A., Lester, D., & Trexler, L. (1974). The measurement of pessimism: The hopelessness scale. *Journal of Consulting and Clinical Psychology, 42*(6), 861–865.

Becker, J. C., Tausch, N., Spears, R., & Christ, O. (2011). Committed dis(s)idents: Participation in radical collective action fosters disidentification with the broader in-group but enhances political identification. *Personality and Social Psychology Bulletin, 37*, 1104–1116.

Bellah, R. N. (1967). Civil religion in America. *Daedalus*, 1–21.

Ben Meir, Y., & Bagno-Moldavsky, O. (2010). The second intifada and the Israeli public opinion. *Strategic Assesement, 13*(3), 71–83.

Ben-Dor, G., Canetti-Nisim, D., & Halperin, E. (2007). *The social aspect of national security: Israeli public opinion and the second Lebanon war.* Haifa, Israel: National Security Studies Center.

Benoit, M., Bouthillier, D., Moss, E., Rousseau, C., & Brunet, A. (2010). Emotion regulation strategies as mediators of the association between level of attachment security and PTSD symptoms following trauma in adulthood. *Anxiety, Stress & Coping, 23*(1), 101–118.

Ben-Zeev, A. (1992). Anger and hate. *Journal of Social Philosophy, 23*(2), 85–110.

Berkowitz, L. (1990). On the formation and regulation of anger and aggression: A cognitive-neoassociationistic analysis. *American Psychologist, 45*(4), 494–503.

Berkowitz, L. (1993). *Aggression: Its causes, consequences and control.* Philadelphia, PA: Temple University Press.

Björkqvist, K., Österman, K., & Kaukiainen, A. (2000). Social intelligence – empathy = aggression? *Aggression and Violent Behavior, 5*(2), 191–200.

Blair, R. J. (2005). Applying a cognitive neuroscience perspective to the disorder of psychopathy. *Developmental Psychopathology, 17*(3), 865–891.

Blanchard, D. C., & Blanchard, R. J. (1984). Affect and aggression: An animal model applied to human behavior. In R. J. Blanchard, & D. C. Blanchard (Eds.), *Advances in the study of aggression* (Vol. 1, pp. 2–62). New York: Academic Press.

Blasi, A. (1990). How should psychologists define morality? or, The negative side effects of philosophy's influence on psychology. In T. Wren (Ed.), *The moral domain: Essays on the on-going discussion between philosophy and the social sciences* (pp. 38–70). Cambridge, MA: MIT Press.

Blatz, C. W., Day, M. V., & Schryer, E. (2014). Official public apology effects on victim group members' evaluations of the perpetrator group. *Canadian Journal of Behavioural Science, 46,* 337–345.

Blatz, C. W., Schumann, K., & Ross, M. (2009). Government apologies for historical injustices. *Political Psychology, 30*(2), 219–241.

Bloch, L., Moran, E. K., & Kring, A. M. (2010). On the need for conceptual and definitional clarity in emotion regulation research on psychopathology. In A. M. Kring & D. M. Sloan (Eds.), *Emotion regulation and psychopathology: A transdiagnostic approach to eitiology and treatment.* (pp. 88–107). New York: Guildford.

Bodenhausen, G. V., Sheppard, L. A., & Kramer, G. P. (1994). Negative affect and social judgment: The differential impact of anger and sadness. *European Journal of Social Psychology, 24*(1), 45–62.

Bonanno, G. A. (2001). Emotion self-regulation. In T. J. Mayne, & G. A. Bonanno (Eds.), *Emotions: Current issues and future directions* (pp. 254–285). New York: Guilford.

Bonanno, G. A., & Jost, J. T. (2006). Conservative shift among high-exposure survivors of the September 11th terrorist attacks. *Basic and Applied Social Psychology, 28*(4), 311–323.

Bonanno, G. A., Papa, A., Lalande, K., Westphal, M., & Coifman, K. (2004). The importance of being flexible: The ability to both enhance and suppress emotional expression predicts long-term adjustment. *Psychological Science, 15,* 482–487.

Bouskila, A., & Blumstein, D. T. (1992). Rules of thumb for predation hazard assessment: Predictions from a dynamic model. *American Naturalist, 139,* 161–176.

Branovsky, Y. (2008). Bibi: Israel must restore national pride. Ynetnews.com. Retrieved from http:// http://www.ynetnews.com/articles/0,7340,L-3643740,00.html

Branscombe, N. R. (2004). A social psychological process perspective on collective guilt. In R. Branscombe & B. Doosje (Eds.), *Collective guilt: International perspectives* (pp. 320–334). New York: Cambridge University Press.

Branscombe, N. R., & Doosje, B. (2004). *Collective guilt: International perspectives.* Cambridge, UK: Cambridge University Press.

Branscombe, N. R., Doosje, B., & McGarty, C. (2002). Antecedents and consequences of collective guilt. In D. M. Mackie & E. R. Smith (Eds.), *From prejudice to intergroup emotions: Differentiated reactions to social groups* (pp. 49–66). Philadelphia, PA: Psychology Press.

Branscombe, N. R., & Miron, A. M. (2004). Interpreting the ingroup's negative actions towards another group: Emotional reactions to appraised harm. In L. Z. Tiedens & C.

W. Leach (Eds.), *The social life of emotions* (pp. 314–355). Cambridge, UK: Cambridge University Press.

Branscombe, N. R., Slugoski, B., & Kappen, D. M. (2004). Collective guilt: What it is and what it is not. In N. R. Branscombe & B. Doosje (Eds.), *Collective guilt: International perspectives* (pp. 16–34). Cambridge, UK: Cambridge University Press.

Brewer, M. B. (1999). The psychology of prejudice: Ingroup love and outgroup hate? *Journal of social issues, 55*(3), 429–444.

Brewer, M. B. (2001). Ingroup identification and intergroup conflict: When does ingroup love become outgroup hate. In R. D. Ashmore, L. Jussim, & D. Wilder (Eds.), *Social identity, intergroup conflict, and conflict reduction* (pp. 17–41). New York: Oxford University Press.

Breznitz, S. (1986). The effect of hope on coping with stress. In M. H. Appley & R. Trumbull (Eds.), *Dynamics of stress: Physiological, psychological and social perspectives* (pp. 295–306). New York: Plenum.

Briggs, J. L. (1970). *Never in anger: Portrait of an Eskimo family.* Cambridge, MA: Harvard University Press.

Brown, J. D., & Marshall, M. A. (2001). Self-esteem and emotion: Some thoughts about feelings. *Personality and Social Psychology Bulletin, 27*(5), 575–584.

Brown, L. M., & Lopez, G. E. (2001). Political contacts: Analyzing the role of similarity in theories of prejudice. *Political Psychology, 22*(2), 279–292.

Brown, R., & Čehajić, S. (2008). Dealing with the past and facing the future: Mediators of the effects of collective guilt and shame in Bosnia and Herzegovina. *European Journal of Social Psychology, 38*(4), 669–684.

Brown, R., González, R., Zagefka, H., Manzi, J., & Čehajić, S. (2008). Nuestra Culpa: Collective guilt and shame as predictors of reparation for historical wrongdoing. *Journal of Personality and Social Psychology, 94*(1), 75–90.

Brubaker, R., & Laitin, D. D. (1998). Ethnic and nationalist violence. *Annual Review of Sociology, 24*, 423–452.

Bruininks, P., & Malle, B. F. (2005). Distinguishing hope from optimism and related affective states. *Motivation and Emotion, 29*(4), 327–355.

Burleson, B. R. (1985). The production of comforting messages: Social-cognitive foundations. *Journal of Language and Social Psychology, 4*(3–4), 253–273.

Bushman, B. J. (2002). Does venting anger feed or extinguish the flame? Catharsis, rumination, distraction, anger, and aggressive responding. *Personality and Social Psychology Bulletin, 28*(6), 724–731.

Bushman, B., & Baumeister, R. (1998). Threatened egotism, narcissism, self-esteem, and direct and displaced aggression: Does self-love or self-hate lead to violence? *Journal of Personality and Social Psychology, 75*(1), 219–229.

Buss, D. M. (2005). *The murderer next door: Why the mind is designed to kill.* New York: Penguin.

Cacioppo, J. T., & Gardner, W. L. (1999). Emotion. *Annual Review of Psychology, 50*, 191–214.

Cameron, C. D., & Payne, B. K. (2011). Escaping affect: How motivated emotion regulation creates insensitivity to mass suffering. *Journal of Personality and Social Psychology, 100*(1), 1–15.

Campbell, W. K. (1999). Narcissism and romantic attraction. *Journal of Personality and Social Psychology, 77*(6), 1254–1270.

Canetti, D., Galea, S., Hall, B. J., Johnson, R. J., Palmieri, P. A., & Hobfoll, S. E. (2010). Exposure to prolonged socio-political conflict and the risk of PTSD and depression among Palestinians. *Psychiatry, 73*(3), 219–231.

Canetti, D., Hall, B. J., Rapaport, C., & Wayne, C. (2013). Exposure to political violence and political extremism: A stress-based process. *European Psychologist, 18*(4), 263–272.

Canetti, D., Halperin, E., Hobfoll, E., Shapira, O., & Hirsch-Hoefler, S. (2009). Authoritarianism, perceived threat and exclusionism on the eve of the disengagement: Evidence from Gaza. *International Journal of Intercultural Relations, 33*(6), 463–74.

Canetti, D., Halperin, E., Sharvit, K., & Hobfoll, S. E. (2009). A new stress-based model of political extremism personal exposure to terrorism, psychological distress, and exclusionist political attitudes. *Journal of Conflict Resolution, 63*(3), 363–389.

Canetti, D., Muldoon, O., Hirsch-Hoefler, S., & Rapaport, C. (2011). *The politics of threat in Israel-Palestine and in Northern Ireland: How exposure to political conflict poisons compromise for peace.* Paper presented at the annual meeting of the International Society of Political Psychology, Istanbul, Turkey.

Canetti, D., Rapaport, C., Wayne, C., Hall, B., & Hobfoll, S. (2013). An exposure effect? Evidence from a rigorous study on the psycho-political outcomes of terrorism. In S. J. Sinclair & D. Antonius (Eds.), *The political psychology of terrorism fears* (pp. 193–212). New York: Oxford University Press.

Canetti-Nisim, D., Ariely, G., & Halperin, E. (2008). Life, pocketbook, or culture: The role of perceived security threats in promoting exclusionist political attitudes toward minorities in Israel. *Political Research Quarterly, 61*, 90–103.

Canetti-Nisim, D., & Pedahzur, A. (2003). Contributory factors to political xenophobia in a multicultural society: The case of Israel. *International Journal of Intercultural Relations, 27*(3), 307–333.

Caouette, J., Wohl, M. J., & Peetz, J. (2012). The future weighs heavier than the past: Collective guilt, perceived control and the influence of time. *European Journal of Social Psychology, 42*(3), 363–371.

Carlsmith, J. M., & Gross, A. E. (1969). Some effects of guilt on compliance. *Journal of Personality and Social Psychology, 11*(3), 232–239.

Carnevale, P. J., & Isen, A. M. (1986). The influence of positive affect and visual access on the discovery of integrative solutions in bilateral negotiation. *Organizational Behavior and Human Decision Processes, 37*(1), 1–13.

Carver, C. S., & Harmon-Jones, E. (2009). Anger is an approach-related affect: Evidence and implications. *Psychological Bulletin, 135*(2), 183–204.

Cassels, T. G., Chan, S., Chung, W., & Birch, S. (2010). The role of culture in affective empathy: Cultural and bicultural differences. *Journal of Cognition and Culture, 10*(3), 309–326.

Castano, E., & Giner-Sorolla, R. (2006). Not quite human: Infra-humanization as a response to collective responsibility for intergroup killing. *Journal of Personality and Social Psychology, 90*(5), 804–818.

Čehajić, S., Brown, R., & Castano, E. (2008). Forgive and forget? Antecedents and consequences of intergroup forgiveness in Bosnia and Herzegovina. *Political Psychology, 29*(3), 351–367.

Čehajić, S., Brown, R., & González, R. (2009). What do I care? Perceived ingroup responsibility and dehumanization as predictors of empathy felt for the victim group. *Group Processes & Intergroup Relations, 12*(6), 715–729.

Čehajić, S., Effron, D., Halperin, E., Liberman, V., & Ross, L. (2011). Affirmation, acknowledgment of ingroup responsibility, group-based guilt, and support for reparative measures. *Journal of Personality and Social Psychology, 101*(2), 256–270.

Čehajić-Clancy, S. (2011). Empathy, intergroup: Regarding the suffering of others. In *The encyclopedia of peace psychology* (pp. 405–408). Malden, MA: Wiley-Blackwell.

Čehajić-Clancy, S. (2012). Coming to terms with the past marked by collective crimes: Collective moral responsibility and reconciliation. In O. Simić, Z. Volčič, & C. R. Phipot (Eds.), *Peace psychology in the Balkans: Dealing with a violent past while building peace* (pp. 235–244). New York: Springer.

Chang, E. C. (1998). Hope, problem-solving ability, and coping in a college student population: Some implications for theory and practice. *Journal of Clinical Psychology, 54*(7), 953–962.

Cheavens, J. S., Michael, S. T., & Snyder, C. R. (2005). The correlates of hope: Psychological and physiological benefits. In J. A. Eliott (Ed.), *Interdisciplinary perspectives on hope.* (pp. 119–132). Hauppauge, NY: Nova Sciences.

Cheshin, A., Rafaeli, A., & Bos, N. (2011). Anger and happiness in virtual teams: Emotional influences of text and behavior on others' affect in the absence of non-verbal cues. *Organizational Behavior and Human Decision Processes, 116*(1), 2–16.

Cheung-Blunden, V., & Blunden, B. (2008). The emotional construal of war: Anger, fear, and other negative emotions. *Peace and Conflict, 14*(2), 123–150.

Chipman, K. J., Palmieri, P. A., Canetti, D., Johnson, R. J., & Hobfoll, S. E. (2011). Predictors of posttraumatic stress-related impairment in victims of terrorism and ongoing conflict in Israel. *Anxiety, Stress & Coping: An International Journal, 24*(3), 255–271.

Cialdini, R. B. (1991). Altruism or egoism? That is (still) the question. *Psychological Inquiry, 2*(2), 124–126.

Cialdini, R., Borden, R., Thorne, A., Walker, M., Freeman, S., & Sloan, L. (1976). Basking in reflected glory: Three (football) field studies. *Journal of Personality and Social Psychology, 34*(3), 366–375.

Cialdini, R. B., Brown, S. L., Lewis, B. P., Luce, C., & Neuberg, S. L. (1997). Reinterpreting the empathy-altruism relationship: When one into one equals oneness. *Journal of Personality and Social Psychology, 73*(3), 481–494.

Cikara, M., Bruneau, E. G., & Saxe, R. R. (2011). Us and them: Intergroup failures of empathy. *Current Directions in Psychological Science, 20*(3), 149–153.

Cikara, M., Bruneau, E., Van Bavel, J. J., & Saxe, R. (2014). Their pain gives us pleasure: How intergroup dynamics shape empathic failures and counter-empathic responses. *Journal of Experimental Social Psychology, 55*, 110–125.

Clark, M. S., Pataki, S. P., & Carver, V. H. (1996). Some thoughts and findings on self-presentation of emotions in relationships. In G. J. Fletcher, & J. Fitness (Eds.), *Knowledge structures in close relationships: A social psychological approach* (pp. 247–274). Mahwah, NJ: Erlbaum.

Cloitre, M., Miranda, R., Stovall-McClough, K. C., & Han, H. (2005). Beyond PTSD: Emotion regulation and interpersonal problems as predictors of functional impairment in survivors of childhood abuse. *Behavior Therapy, 36*(2), 119–124.

Clore, G. L., & Jeffery, K. M. (1972). Emotional role playing, attitude change, and attraction toward a disabled person. *Journal of Personality and Social Psychology, 23*(1), 105–111.

Clore, G. L., Schwarz, N., & Conway, M. (1994). Affective causes and consequences of social information processing. In R. S. Wyer & T. K. Srul (Eds.), *Handbook of social cognition* (2nd ed., Vol. 1, pp. 323–417). Hillsdale, NJ: Erlbaum.

Cohen, G. L., Sherman, D. K., Bastardi, A., Hsu, L., McGoey, M., & Ross, L. (2007). Bridging the partisan divide: Self-affirmation reduces ideological closed-mindedness and inflexibility in negotiation. *Journal of Personality and Social Psychology, 93*(3), 415–430.

Cohen, S. (2001). *States of denial: Knowing about atrocities and suffering.* Cambridge, MA: Polity Press.

Cohen, T. R. (2010). Moral emotions and unethical bargaining: The differential effects of empathy and perspective taking in deterring deceitful negotiation. *Journal of Business Ethics, 94*(4), 569–579.

Cohen-Chen, S., Crisp, R., & Halperin, E. (2015a). Perceptions of changing world induce hope and promote peace in intractable conflicts. *Personality and Social Psychology Bulletin, 41*(4), 498–512.

Cohen-Chen, S., Crisp, R., & Halperin, E. (2015b). *Observing outgroup hope promotes peace and reconciliation in intractable conflicts.* Manuscript in preparation.

Cohen-Chen, S., Halperin, E., Crisp, R. J., & Gross, J. J. (2014). Hope in the Middle East: Malleability beliefs, hope, and the willingness to compromise for peace. *Social Psychological and Personality Science, 5*(1), 67–75.

Cohen-Chen, S., Halperin, E., Porat, R., & Bar-Tal, D. (2014). The differential effects of hope and fear on information processing in intractable conflict. *Journal of Social and Political Psychology, 2*(1), 11–30.

Cohen-Chen, S., Halperin, E., Saguy, T., & Van-Zomeren, M. (2014). Beliefs about the malleability of immoral groups facilitate collective action. *Social Psychological and Personality Science, 5*(2), 203–210.

Cohen-Chen, S., Van-Zomeren, M., & Halperin, E. (2015). Hope(lessness) and (in)action in intractable intergroup conflict. In E. Halperin & K. Sharvit (Eds.), *The social psychology of intractable conflicts—Celebrating the legacy of Daniel Bar-Tal.* New York: Springer.

Coke, J. S., Batson, C. D., & McDavis, K. (1978). Empathic mediation of helping a two-stage model. *Journal of Personality and Social Psychology, 36*(7), 752–766.

Coleman, P. T. (2003). Characteristics of protracted, intractable conflict: Towards the development of a metaframework—I. *Peace and Conflict: Journal of Peace Psychology, 9*(1), 1–37.

Coleman, P. T., Vallacher, R. R., Nowak, A., & Bui-Wrzosinska, L. (2007). Intractable conflict as an attractor: A dynamical systems approach to conflict escalation and intractability. *American Behavioral Scientist, 50*(11), 1454–1475.

Collins, F. S. (2004). What we do and don't know about "race", "ethnicity", genetics, and health at the dawn of the genome era. *Nature Genetics, 36*(11), S13–S16.

Collins, R. (1975). *Conflict sociology.* New York: Academic Press.

Combs, D. J., Powell, C. A., Schurtz, D. R., & Smith, R. H. (2009). Politics, schadenfreude, and ingroup identification: The sometimes happy thing about a poor economy and death. *Journal of Experimental Social Psychology, 45*(4), 635–646.

Conejero, S., & Etxebarria, I. (2007). The impact of the Madrid bombing on personal emotions, emotional atmosphere and emotional climate. *Journal of Social Issues, 63*(2), 273–287.

Cooper, S., Darmody, M., & Dolan, Y. (2003). Impressions of hope and its influence in the process of change: An international e-mail trialogue. *Journal of Systemic Therapies, 22*(3), 67–78.

Corneille, O., Yzerbyt, V. Y., Rogier, A., & Boudin, G. (2001). Threat and the group attribution error: When threat elicits judgments of extremity and homogeneity. *Personality and Social Psychology Bulletin, 27*(4), 437–446.

Cosmides, L., & Tooby, J. (2000). Evolutionary psychology and the emotions. In M. Lewis & J. M. Haviland-Jones (Eds.), *Handbook of emotions* (2nd ed., pp. 91–115). New York: Guilford.

Craig, S. C., Niemi, R. G., & Silver, G. E. (1990). Political efficacy and trust: A report on the NES pilot study items. *Political Behavior, 12*(3), 289–314.

Crisp, R. J., Birtel, M. D., & Meleady, R. (2011). Mental simulations of social thought and action: Trivial tasks or tools for transforming social policy? *Current Directions in Psychological Science, 20*(4), 261–264.

Crisp, R. J., Heuston, S., Farr, M. J., & Turner, R. N. (2007). Seeing red or feeling blue: Differentiated intergroup emotions and ingroup identification in soccer fans. *Group Processes & Intergroup Relations, 10*, 9–22.

Crisp, R. J., & Turner, R. N. (2009). Can imagined interactions produce positive perceptions? Reducing prejudice through simulated social contact. *The American Psychologist, 64*(4), 231–240.

Crozier, W. (1998). Self-conscious in shame: The role of the "other". *Journal for the Theory of Social Behavior, 28*(3), 271–286.

Curry, L. A., Snyder, C. R., Cook, D. L., Ruby, B.C., & Rehm, M. (1997). The role of hope in student-athlete academic and sport achievement. *Journal of Personality and Social Psychology, 73*(6), 1257–1267.

Dante, A. (1937). *The divine comedy.* London: J. M. Dent. (Original work published 1308–1321)

Darley, J. M. (1992). Social organization for the production of evil. *Psychology Inquiry, 3*(2), 199–218.

Davidson, R. J., Jackson, C. D., & Kalin, N. H. (2000). Emotion, plasticity, context, and regulation: Perspectives from affective neuroscience. *Psychological Bulletin, 126*(6), 890–909.

Davis, M. H. (1980). A multidimensional approach to individual differences in empathy. *Catalog of Selected Documents in Psychology, 10*, 85–103.

Davis, M. H. (1983). Empathic concern and the muscular dystrophy telethon: Empathy as a multidimensional construct. *Personality and Social Psychology Bulletin, 9*, 223–229.

Davis, M. H. (1994). *Empathy: A social psychological approach.* Boulder, CO: Westview.

Davis, M. H. (1996). *Empathy: A social psychological approach.* Madison, WI: Westview.

de Figueiredo, R. J., & Elkins, Z. (2003). Are patriots bigots? An inquiry into the vices of ingroup pride. *American Journal of Political Science, 47*(1), 171–188.

de Quervain, D. J., Fischbacher, U., Treyer, V., Schellhammer, M., Schnyder, U., Buck, A., & Fehr, E. (2004). The neural basis of altruistic punishment. *Science, 305*, 1254–1258.

De Rivera, J. (1992). Emotional climate: Social structure and emotional dynamics. In K. T. Strongman (Ed.), *International review of studies on emotion* (Vol. 2, pp. 199–218). New York: John Wiley.

De Rivera, J., Gerstmann, E., & Maisels, L. (2002). Acting righteously: The influence of attitude, moral responsibility, and emotional involvement. In M. Ross, & D. T. Miller (Eds.), *The justice motive in everyday life* (pp. 271–288). New York: Cambridge University Press.

De Rivera, J., & Páez, D. (2007). Emotional climate, human security, and cultures of peace. *Journal of Social Issues, 63*(2), 233–253.

de Vos, B., Van-Zomeren, M., Gordijn, E. H., & Postmes, T. (2013). The communication of "pure" group-based anger reduces tendencies toward intergroup conflict because it increases out-group empathy. *Personality and Social Psychology Bulletin, 39*(8), 1043–1052.

de Waal, F. B. (2008). Putting the altruism back into altruism: the evolution of empathy. *Annual Review of Psychology, 59*, 279–300.

de Wied, M., Branje, S., & Meeus, W. (2007). Empathy and conflict resolution in friendship relations among adolescents. *Aggressive Behavior, 33*(1), 48–55.

de Zavala, A. G. (2011). Collective narcissism and intergroup hostility: The dark side of "in-group love". *Social and Personality Psychology Compass, 5*(6), 309–320.

de Zavala, A. G., Cichocka, A., Eidelson, R., & Jayawickreme, N. (2009). Collective narcissism and its social consequences. *Journal of Personality and Social Psychology, 97*(6), 1074–1096.

Deutsch, M. (1985). *Distributive justice: A social psychological perspective.* New Haven, NJ: Yale University Press.

Devine, P. G., & Monteith, M. J. (1993). The role of discrepancy associated affect in prejudice reduction. In M. D. Mackie & D. L. Hamilton (Eds.), *Affect, cognition, and stereotyping: Interactive processes in intergroup perception* (pp. 317–344). San Diego, CA: Academic Press.

Devine-Wright, P. (2001). History and identity in Northern Ireland: An exploratory investigation of the role of historical commemorations in contexts of intergroup conflict. *Peace and Conflict: Journal of Peace Psychology, 7*(4), 297–315.

Dimitrijevic, N. (2006). Moral responsibility for collective crime. *Belgrade Circle Journal, 1–4,* 25–44.

Dixon, J., Tropp, L., Durrheim, K., & Tredoux, C. (2010). "Let them eat harmony": Prejudice reduction strategies and attitudes of historically disadvantaged groups. *Current Directions in Psychological Science, 19*(2), 76–80.

Doosje, B. E., Branscombe, N. R., Spears, R., & Manstead, A. S. (1998). Guilty by association: When one's group has a negative history. *Journal of Personality and Social Psychology, 75*(4), 872–886.

Doosje, B. E., Branscombe, N. R., Spears, R., & Manstead, A. S. (2006). Antecedents and consequences of group-based guilt: The effects of ingroup identification. *Group Processes and Intergroup Relations, 9*(3), 325–338.

Dovidio, J. F., Allen, J. L., & Schroeder, D. A. (1990). The specificity of empathy-induced helping: Evidence for altruistic motivation. *Journal of Personality and Social Psychology, 59*(2), 249–260.

Dovidio, J. F., Johnson, J. D., Gaertner, S. L., Pearson, A. R., Saguy, T., & Ashburn-Nardo, L. (2009). Empathy and intergroup relations. In M. Mikulincer & P. R. Shaver (Eds.), *Prosocial motives, emotions, and behavior: The better angels of our nature* (pp. 393–408). Washington, DC: American Psychological Association.

Duan, C., & Hill, C. (1996). Current state of empathy research. *Journal of Counseling Psychology, 43*(3), 261–274.

Duckitt, J. (2001). A dual-process cognitive-motivational theory of ideology and prejudice. In M. Zanna (Ed.), *Advances in experimental social psychology* (Vol. 3, pp. 41–113). San Diego, CA: Academic Press.

Duckitt, J., & Fisher, K. (2003). The impact of social threat on worldview and ideological attitudes. *Political Psychology, 24*(1), 199–222.

Dugas, M., Schori-Eyal, N., Kruglanski, A. W., Touchstone-Leonard, K., McNeill, A., & Gelfand, M. J. (2015). *The hurt justifies the means: Perceived ingroup victimhood and group glorification as motivated by cognitive need for closure.* Manuscript in preparation.

Dziobek, I., Rogers, K., Fleck, S., Bahnemann, M., Heekeren, H. R., Wolf, O. T., & Convit, A. (2008). Dissociation of cognitive and emotional empathy in adults with Asperger syndrome using the Multifaceted Empathy Test (MET). *Journal of Autism and Developmental Disorders, 38*(3), 464–473.

Edelstein, E. L., Nathanson, D. L., & Stone, A. M. (Eds.). (1989). *Denial: A clarification of concepts and research.* New York: Plenum.

Ehring, T., & Quack, D. (2010). Emotion regulation difficulties in trauma survivors: The role of trauma type and PTSD symptom severity. *Behavior Therapy, 41*(4), 587–598.

Eibl-Eibesfeldt, I., & Sutterlin, C. (1990). Fear, defence and aggression in animals and man: Some ethological perspectives. In P. F. Brain, S. Parmigiani, R. J. Blanchard, & D. Mainardi (Eds.), *Fear and defense* (pp. 381–408). London: Harwood.

Eisenberg, N., & Fabes, R. A. (1998). Prosocial development. In W. Damon & N. Eisenberg (Eds.), *Handbook of child psychology, vol. 3: Social, emotional, and personality development* (5th ed., Vol. 3, pp. 701–778). New York: John Wiley.

Eisenberg, N., & Miller, P. (1987). The relation of empathy to prosocial and related behaviors. *Psychological Bulletin, 101*(1), 91–119.

Eisenberg, N., Shea, C. L., Carlo, G., & Knight, G. (1991). Empathy-related responding and cognition: A "chicken and the egg" dilemma. In W. Kurtines & J. Gewirtz (Eds.), *Handbook of moral behavior and development* (Vol. 2, pp. 63–88). Hillsdale, NJ: Erlbaum.

Ekman, P. (1992). Facial expressions of emotion: New findings, new questions. *Psychological Science, 3*(1), 34–38.

Ekman, P. (1993). Facial expression and emotion. *American Psychologist, 48*(4), 384–392.

Elison, J., & Harter, S. L. (2007). Humiliation: Causes, correlates, and consequences. In J. L. Tracy, R. Robins, & J. P. Tangney (Eds.), *The self-conscious emotions: Theory and research* (pp. 310–329). New York: Guilford.

Ellemers, N. (1993). The influence of socio-structural variables on identity enhancement strategies. *European Review of Social Psychology, 4*(1), 27–57.

Ellemers, N. (2012). The group self. *Science, 336*, 848–852.

Epley, N., Caruso, E. M., & Bazerman, M. H. (2006). When perspective taking increases taking: Reactive egoism in social interaction. *Journal of Personality and Social Psychology, 91*(5), 872–889.

Er-rafiy, A., & Brauer, M. (2013). Modifying perceived variability: Four laboratory and field experiments show the effectiveness of a ready-to-be-used prejudice intervention. *Journal of Applied Social Psychology, 43*(4), 840–853.

Esses, V. M., Dovidio, J. F., Jackson, L. M., & Armstrong, T. L. (2001). The immigration dilemma: The role of perceived group competition, ethnic prejudice, and national identity. *Journal of Social Issues, 57*(3), 389–412.

Esteves, F., Dimberg, U., & Öhman, A. (1994). Automatically elicited fear: Conditioned skin conductance responses to masked facial expressions. *Cognition and Emotion, 8*(5), 393–413.

Etkin, A., & Wager, T. D. (2007). Functional neuroimaging of anxiety: A meta-analysis of emotional processing in PTSD, social anxiety disorder, and specific phobia. *American Journal of Psychiatry, 164*(10), 1476–1488.

Fehr, B., Baldwin, M., Collins, L., Patterson, S., & Benditt, R. (1999). Anger in close relationships: An interpersonal script analysis. *Personality and Social Psychology Bulletin, 25(3)*, 299–312.

Feldman, L. A. (1995). Valence focus and arousal focus: Individual differences in the structure of affective experience. *Journal of Personality and Social Psychology, 69*, 153–166.

Feldman, S., & Stenner, K. (1997). Perceived threat and authoritarianism. *Political Psychology, 18*, 741–770.

Ferguson, M. A., & Branscombe, N. R. (2010). Collective guilt mediates the effect of beliefs about climate change on willingness to engage in mitigation behavior. *Journal of Environmental Psychology, 30*, 135–142.

Ferguson, M. A., & Branscombe, N. R. (2014). The social psychology of collective guilt. In C. von Scheve & M. Salmela (Eds.), *Collective emotions: Perspectives from psychology, philosophy, and sociology* (pp. 251–265). Oxford, UK: Oxford University Press.

Fernández, S., Saguy, T., & Halperin, E. (2015). The paradox of humiliation: The acceptance of an unjust devaluation of the self. *Personality and Social Psychology Bulletin, 41*(7), 976–988.

Feshbach, N. D. (1975). Empathy in children: Some theoretical and empirical considerations. *The Counseling Psychologist, 4*, 3–25.

Fischer, A. H., & Roseman, I. J. (2007). Beat them or ban them: The characteristics and social functions of anger and contempt. *Journal of Personality and Social Psychology, 93(1)*, 103–115.

Fischer, A. H., Rotteveel, M., Evers, C., & Manstead, A. S. (2004). Emotional assimilation: How we are influenced by other's emotions. *Current Psychology of Cognition, 22,* 223–246.

Fischhoff, B., Gonzalez, R. M., Lerner, J. S., & Small, D. A. (2005). Evolving judgments of terror risks: Foresight, hindsight, and emotion. *Journal of Experimental Psychology: Applied, 11,* 124–139.

Fitness, J., & Fletcher, G. J. (1993). Love, hate, anger, and jealousy in close relationships: A prototype and cognitive appraisal analysis. *Journal of Personality and Social Psychology, 65*(5), 942–958.

Fontaine, J. R., Scherer, K. R., Roesch, E. B., & Ellsworth, P. C. (2007). The world of emotions is not two-dimensional. *Psychological Science, 18(12),* 1050–1057.

Fontan, V. (2006). Polarization between occupier and occupied in post-Saddam Iraq: Colonial humiliation and the formation of political violence. *Terrorism and Political Violence, 18,* 217–238.

Ford, B. Q., & Tamir, M. (2012). When getting angry is smart: Emotional preferences and emotional intelligence. *Emotion, 12,* 685–689.

Forgas, J. P. (1995). Mood and judgment: The affect infusion model (AIM). *Psychological Bulletin, 117,* 39–66.

Forgas, J. P. (1998). On feeling good and getting your way: Mood effects on negotiator cognition and behavior. *Journal of Personality and Social Psychology, 74,* 565–577.

Freedman, J. L., Wallington, S. A., & Bless, E. (1967). Compliance without pressure: The effects of guilt. *Journal of Personality and Social Psychology, 7,* 117–124.

Fridlund, A. J. (1994). *Human facial expression: An evolutionary view.* San Diego, CA: Academic Press.

Friedman, T. L. (2003, November 9). The humiliation factor. *The New York Times,* Section 4, p. 11.

Frijda, N. H. (1984). Toward a model of emotion. In C. D. Spielberger, I. G. Sarason, & P. Defares (Eds.), *Stress and anxiety* (Vol. 9, pp. 3–16). Washington, DC: Hemisphere.

Frijda, N. H. (1986). *The emotions.* Cambridge, UK: Cambridge University Press.

Frijda, N. H. (1994). Varieties of affect: Emotions and episodes, moods, and sentiments. In P. Ekman & R. J. Davidson (Eds.), *The nature of emotion: Fundamental question* (pp. 59–66). New York: Oxford University Press.

Frijda, N. H. (2004). Emotions and action. In S. R. Manstead, N. Frijda, & A. Fischer (Eds.), *Feeling and emotions: The Amsterdam symposium* (pp. 158–173). Cambridge, UK: Cambridge University Press.

Frijda, N. H., Kuipers, P., & ter Schure, E. (1989). Relations among emotions, appraisal, and emotional action readiness. *Journal of Personality and Social Psychology, 57*(2), 212–228.

Frijda, N. H., Markam, S., Sato, K., & Wiers, R. (1995). Emotions and emotion words. In J. A. Russel, J. Fernández-Dols, A. S. Manstead, & J. C. Wellenkamp (Eds.), *Everyday conceptions of emotion* (pp. 121–143). Dordrecht, the Netherlands: Kluwer Academic.

Frith, C. D., & Frith, U. (2012). Mechanisms of social cognition. *Annual Review of Psychology, 63,* 287–313.

Fromm, E. (1968). *The revolution of hope.* New York: Bantam.

Gadarian, S. K., & Albertson, B. (2014). Anxiety, immigration, and the search for information. *Political Psychology, 35*(2), 133–164.

Gaertner, S. L., Dovidio, J. F., Anastasio, P. A., Bachman, B. A., & Rust, M. C. (1993). The common ingroup identity model: Recategorization and the reduction of intergroup bias. *European Review of Social Psychology, 4*(1), 1–26.

Galea, S., Ahern, J., Resnick, H., Kilpatrick, D., Bucuvalas, M., Gold, J., & Vlahov, D. (2002). Psychological squeal of the September 11 terrorist attacks in New York City. *New England Journal of Medicine, 346*, 982–987.

Galinsky, A.D., Ku, G., & Wang, C. S. (2005). Perspective-taking and self-other overlap: Fostering social bonds and facilitating social coordination. *Group Processes and Intergroup Relations, 8(2)*, 109–124.

Galinsky, A. D., Maddux, W. W., Gilin, D., & White, J. B. (2008). Why it pays to get inside the head of your opponent: The differential effects of perspective taking and empathy in negotiations. *Psychological Science, 19*, 378–384.

Galinsky, A. D., & Moskowitz, G. B. (2000). Perspective-taking: Decreasing stereotype expression, stereotype accessibility, and in-group favoritism. *Journal of Personality and Social Psychology, 78*, 708–724.

Gallese, V. (2001). The "shared manifold" hypothesis: from mirror neurons to empathy. *Journal of Consciousness Studies, 8*(5–7), 33–50.

Gault, B. A., & Sabini, J. (2000). The roles of empathy, anger, and gender in predicting attitudes toward punitive, reparative, and preventative public policies. *Cognition and Emotion, 14*, 495–520.

Gausel, N., Leach, C. W., Vignoles, V. L., & Brown, R. (2012). Defend or repair? Explaining responses to in-group moral failure by disentangling feelings of shame, rejection, and inferiority. *Journal of Personality and Social Psychology, 102*, 941–960.

Gayer, C., Landman, S., Halperin, E., & Bar-Tal, D. (2009). Overcoming psychological barriers to peaceful conflict resolution: The role of arguments about losses. *Journal of Conflict Resolution 53*(6), 951–975.

Gaylin, W. (2003). *Hatred: The psychological descent into violence*. New York: Public Affairs.

George, J. M. (2000). Emotions and leadership: The role of emotional intelligence. *Human Relations, 53*(8), 1027–1044.

Gibson, J. L. (2006). Enigmas of intolerance: Fifty years after Stouffer's communism, conformity, and civil liberties. *Perspectives on Politics, 4*, 21–34.

Giner-Sorolla, R. (2012). *Judging passions: Moral emotions in persons and groups*. London: Psychology Press.

Ginges, J., & Atran, S. (2008). Humiliation and the inertia effect: Implications for understanding violence and compromise in intractable intergroup conflicts. *Journal of Cognition and Culture, 8*, 281–294.

Ginges, J., Atran, S., Medin, D., & Shikaki, K. (2007). Sacred bounds on rational resolution of violent political conflict. *Proceedings of the National Academy of Sciences of the United States of America, 104*, 7357–7360.

Glover, H. (1992). Emotional numbing: A possible endorphin-mediated phenomenon associated with post-traumatic stress disorders and other allied psychopathic states. *Journal of Traumatic Stress, 5*, 643–675.

Gobbini, M. I., Koralek, A. C., Bryan, R. E., Montgomery, K. J., & Haxby, J. V. (2007). Two takes on the social brain: A comparison of theory of mind tasks. *Journal of Cognitive Science, 11*, 1803–1814.

Gobodo-Madikizela, P. (2003). *Human being died that night: A South African story of forgiveness*. Boston: Houghton Mifflin.

Goldberg, J. H., Lerner, J. S., & Tetlock, P. E. (1999). Rage and reason: The psychology of the intuitive prosecutor. *European Journal of Social Psychology, 29(56)*, 781–795.

Goldenberg, A., Halperin, E., Van-Zomeren, M., & Gross, J. J. (in press). The process model of group-based emotion: Integrating intergroup emotion and emotion regulation perspectives. *Personality and Social Psychology Review*.

Goldenberg, A., Saguy, T., & Halperin, E. (2014). How group-based emotions are shaped by collective emotions: Evidence for emotional transfer and emotional burden. *Journal of Personality and Social Psychology, 107*(4), 581–596.

Golec de Zavala, A., Cichocka, A., & Bilewicz, M. (2013). The paradox of ingroup love: Differentiating collective narcissism advances understanding of the relationship between ingroup and outgroup attitudes. *Journal of Personality, 81*(1), 16–28.

Golec de Zavala, A., Cichocka, A., Eidelson, R., & Jayawickreme, N. (2009). Collective narcissism as and its social consequences. *Journal of Personality and Social Psychology, 97*, 1074–1096.

Goleman, D. (1995). *Emotional intelligence.* New York: Bantam.

Gordijn, E. H., Yzerbyt, V., Wigboldus, D., & Dumont, M. (2006). Emotional reactions to harmful intergroup behavior. *European Journal of Social Psychology, 36*, 15–30.

Gottman, J. M., & Levenson, R. W. (2002). A two-factor model for predicting when a couple will divorce: Exploratory analyses using 14-year longitudinal data. *Family Process, 41*, 83–96.

Graham, J., Haidt, J., & Nosek, B. A. (2009). Liberals and conservatives rely on different sets of moral foundations. *Journal of Personality and Social Psychology, 96*, 1029–1046.

Gray, T. S. (1989). Autonomic neuropeptide connections of the amygdala. In Y. Tache, J. E. Morley, & M. R. Brown (Eds.), *Neuropeptides and stress.* (pp. 92–106). New York: Springer-Verlag.

Greenaway, K. H., Cichocka, A., Van Veelen, R., Likki, T., & Branscombe, N. R. (in press). Feeling hopeful inspires support for social change. *Political Psychology.*

Greenberg, J., Solomon, S., & Pyszczynski, T. (1997). Terror management theory of self-esteem and cultural worldviews: Empirical assessments and conceptual refinements. *Advances in Experimental Social Psychology, 29*, 61–139.

Griffiths, P. E. (2013). Current emotion research in philosophy. *Emotion Review, 5*(2), 215–222.

Gross, J. J. (1998). The emerging field of emotion regulation: An integrative review. *Review of General Psychology, 2*(3), 271–299.

Gross, J. J. (2002). Emotion regulation: Affective, cognitive, and social consequences. *Psychophysiology, 39*, 281–291.

Gross, J. J. (2007). *Handbook of emotion regulation.* New York: Guilford.

Gross, J. J. (2008). Emotion regulation. In M. Lewis, J. M. Haviland-Jones, & L. F. Barrett (Eds.), *Handbook of emotions* (3rd ed., pp. 497–512). New York: Guilford.

Gross, J. J. (Ed.). (2014). *Handbook of emotion regulation* (2nd ed.). New York: Guilford.

Gross, J. J., Halperin, E., & Porat, R. (2013). Emotion regulation in intractable conflicts. *Current Directions in Psychological Science, 22*(6), 423–429.

Gross, J. J., & Thompson, R. A. (2007). Emotion regulation: Conceptual foundations. In J. J. Gross (Ed.), *Handbook of emotion regulation* (pp. 3–24). New York: Guilford.

Gross, K. (2004). Frames, emotional response and policy opinion. *Political Psychology, 25*, 1–38.

Gubler, J., Halperin, E., & Hirschberger, G. (2015). Humanizing the outgroup in contexts of protracted intergroup conflict. *Journal of Experimental Political Science, 2*(1), 36–46.

Gunn, G., & Wilson, A. E. (2011). Acknowledging the skeletons in our closet: The effect of group-affirmation on collective guilt, collective shame, and reparatory attitudes. *Personality and Social Psychology Bulletin, 37*(11), 1474–1487.

Haidt, J., & Graham, J. (2007). When morality opposes justice: Conservatives have moral intuitions that liberals may not recognize. *Social Justice Research, 20*, 98–116.

Haidt, J., & Joseph, C. (2004). Intuitive ethics. *Dædalus, 133*, 55–66.

Haidt, J., & Kesebir, S. (2010). Morality. In S. T. Fiske, D. Gilbert, & G. Lindzey (Eds.), *Handbook of Social Psychology* (5th ed., pp. 797–832). Hoboken, NJ: Wiley.

Halperin, E. (2008). Group-based hatred in intractable conflict in Israel. *Journal of Conflict Resolution, 52*, 713–736.

Halperin, E. (2010). The emotional roots of intergroup violence—The distinct role of anger and hatred. In M. Mikulincer & P. R. Shaver (Eds.), *Human aggression and violence: Causes, manifestations, and consequences* (pp. 315–331). Washington, DC: American Psychological Association.

Halperin, E. (2011a). Intergroup hatred: Psychological dimensions. In D. J. Christie (Ed.), *Encyclopedia of peace psychology* (pp. 557–561). Malden, MA: Wiley-Blackwell.

Halperin, E. (2011b). Emotional barriers to peace: Emotions and public opinion of Jewish Israelis about the peace process in the Middle East. *Peace and Conflict: Journal of Peace Psychology, 17*, 22–45.

Halperin, E. (2014). Emotion, emotion regulation, and conflict resolution. *Emotion Review, 6*(1), 68–76.

Halperin, E., & Bar-Tal, D. (2007). The fall of the peace camp in Israel: The influence of Prime Minister Ehud Barak on Israeli public opinion—July 2000–February 2001. *Conflict & Communication Online, 6*(2), 1–18.

Halperin, E., Bar-Tal, D., Nets-Zehngut, R., & Almog, E. (2008). Fear and hope in conflict: Some determinants in the Israeli-Jewish society. *Peace and Conflict: Journal of Peace Psychology, 14*, 1–26.

Halperin, E., Bar-Tal, D., Nets-Zehngut, R., & Drori, E. (2008). Emotions in conflict: Correlates of fear and hope in the Israeli-Jewish society. *Peace and Conflict: Journal of Peace Psychology, 14*, 233–258.

Halperin, E., Bar-Tal, D., Sharvit, K., Rosler, N., & Raviv, A. (2010). Socio-psychological implications for occupying society: The case of Israel. *Journal of Peace Research, 47*(1), 59–70.

Halperin, E., Canetti-Nisim, D., & Hirsch-Hoefler, S. (2009). Emotional antecedents of political intolerance: The central role of group-based hatred. *Political Psychology, 30*, 93–123.

Halperin, E., Canetti-Nisim, D., & Kimhi, S. (2012). In love with hatred: A longitudinal study on the political consequences of group based hatred. *Journal of Applied Social Psychology, 42*(9), 2231–2256.

Halperin, E., Canetti-Nisim, D., & Pedahzur, A. (2007). Threatened by the uncontrollable: Psychological and socio-economic antecedents of social distance toward labor migrants in Israel. *International Journal of Inter-Cultural Relations, 31*, 459–478.

Halperin, E., Cohen-Chen, S., & Goldenberg, A. (2014). Indirect emotion regulation in intractable conflicts: A new approach to conflict resolution. *European Review of Social Psychology. 25*(1), 1–31.

Halperin, E., Crisp, R., Husnu, S., Dweck, C., & Gross, J. (2012). Promoting intergroup contact by changing Beliefs: Group malleability, intergroup anxiety and contact motivation. *Emotion, 12*(6), 1192–1195.

Halperin, E., & Gross, J. J. (2011). Intergroup anger in intractable conflict: Long-term sentiments predict anger responses during the Gaza war. *Group Processes and Intergroup Relations, 14*(4), 477–488.

Halperin, E., & Pliskin, R. (2015). Emotions and emotion regulation in intractable conflict: Studying emotional processes within a unique context. *Advances in Political Psychology, 36*(1), 119–150.

Halperin, E., Pliskin, R., Saguy, T., Liberman, V., & Gross, J. J. (2014). Emotion regulation and the cultivation of political tolerance: Searching for a new track for intervention. *Journal of Conflict Resolution, 58*(6), 1110–1138.

Halperin, E., Porat, R., Tamir, M., & Gross, J. J. (2013). Can emotion regulation change political attitudes in intractable conflict? From the laboratory to the field. *Psychological Science, 24*, 106–111.

Halperin, E., Porat, R., & Wohl, M. (2013). Extinction threat and reciprocal threat reduction: Collective angst predicts willingness to compromise in intractable intergroup conflicts. *Group Processes and Intergroup Relations, 16*(6), 797–813.

Halperin, E., Russell, A. G., Dweck, C. S., & Gross, J. J. (2011). Anger, hatred, and the quest for peace: Anger can be constructive in the absence of hatred. *Journal of Conflict Resolution, 55*(2), 274–291.

Halperin, E., Russell, A. G., Trzesniewski, H. K., Gross, J. J., & Dweck, S. C. (2011). Promoting the peace process by changing beliefs about group malleability. *Science, 333*, 1767.

Halperin, E., Sharvit, K., & Gross, J. J. (2011). Emotion and emotion regulation in conflicts. In D. Bar-Tal (Ed.), *Intergroup conflicts and their resolution: Social psychological perspective* (pp. 83–103). New York: Psychology Press.

Hamama-Raz, Y., Solomon, Z., Cohen, A., & Laufer, A. (2008). PTSD symptoms, forgiveness, and revenge among Israeli Palestinian and Jewish adolescents. *Journal of Traumatic Stress, 21*(6), 521–529.

Hameiri, B., Bar-Tal, D., & Halperin, E. (2014). Challenges for peacemakers: How to overcome the socio-psychological barriers. *Policy Insights From the Behavioral and Brain Sciences, 1*, 164–171.

Hanna, F. J. (2002). Therapy with difficult clients: Using the precursors model to awaken change. In F. J. Hannah (Ed.), *Building hope for change* (pp. 265–273). Washington, DC: American Psychological Association.

Harbaugh, W., Mayr, U., & Burghart, D. R. (2007). Neural responses to taxation and voluntary giving reveal motives for charitable donations. *Science, 316*(5831), 1622–1625.

Harbom, L. S., Hogbladh, S., & Wallensteen, P. (2006). Armed conflict and peace agreements. *Journal of Peace Research, 43*, 617–631.

Hareli, S., & Rafaeli, A. (2008). Emotion cycles: On the social influence of emotion in organizations. *Research in Organizational Behavior, 28*, 35–59.

Harmon-Jones, E. (2003). Clarifying the emotive functions of asymmetrical frontal cortical activity. *Psychophysiology, 40*, 838–848.

Harmon-Jones, E., & Sigelman, J. (2001). State anger and prefrontal brain activity: Evidence that insult-related relative left prefrontal activity is associated with experienced anger and aggression. *Journal of Personality and Social Psychology, 80*, 797–803.

Harris, S., & Sutton, R. (1986). Functions of parting ceremonies in dying organizations. *Academy of Management Journal, 80*, 5–30.

Harth, N. S., Kessler, T., & Leach, C. W. (2008). Advantaged group's emotional reactions to intergroup inequality: The dynamics of pride, guilt, and sympathy. *Personality and Social Psychology Bulletin, 34*, 115–129.

Hartley, C. A., & Phelps, P. A. (2010). Changing fear: The neurocircuitry of emotion regulation. *Neuropsychopharmacology, 35*(1), 136–146.

Hartling, L. M., & Luchetta, T. (1999). Humiliation: Assessing the impact of derision, degradation, and debasement. *Journal of Primary Prevention, 19*(5), 259–278.

Haselton, M. G., & Buss, D. M. (2000). Error management theory: A new perspective on biases in cross-sex mindreading. *Journal of Personality and Social Psychology, 78*, 81–91.

Haselton, M. G., & Ketelaar, T. (2006). *Affect in social thinking and behavior.* New York: Psychology Press.

Haselton, M. G., & Nettle, D. (2006). The paranoid optimist: An integrative evolutionary model of cognitive biases. *Personality and Social Psychology Review, 10*(1), 47–66.

Haselton, M. G., Nettle, D., & Andrews, P. W. (2005). The evolution of cognitive bias. In D. M. Buss (Ed.), *The handbook of evolutionary psychology* (pp. 724–746). Hoboken, NJ: Wiley.

Hassan, N. (2007). Suicide terrorism. In L. Richardson (Ed.), *The roots of terrorism* (pp. 29–44). New York: Routledge.

Hatfield, E., Cacioppo, J. T., & Rapson, R. L. (1994). *Emotional contagion.* Cambridge, UK: Cambridge University Press.

Heerdink, M. W., van Kleef, G. A., Homan, A. C., & Fischer, A. H. (2013). On the social influence of emotions in groups: Interpersonal effects of anger and happiness on conformity versus deviance. *Journal of Personality and Social Psychology, 105,* 262–284.

Heider, F. (1958). *The psychology of interpersonal relations.* New York: Wiley.

Henry, J. P. (1986). Neuroendocrine patterns of emotional response. In R. Plutchik & H. Kellerman (Ed.), *Emotion: Theory, research, and experience* (Vol. 3, pp. 37–60). San Diego, CA: Academic Press.

Herrald, M. M., & Tomaka, J. (2002). Patterns of emotion-specific appraisal, coping, and cardiovascular reactivity during an ongoing emotional episode. *Journal of Personality and Social Psychology, 83,* 434–450.

Higgins, E. T. (1987). Self-discrepancy: A theory relating self and affect. *Psychological Review, 94,* 319–340.

Hirschberger, G., & Ein-Dor, T. (2006). Defenders of a lost cause: Terror management and violent resistance to the disengagement plan. *Personality and Social Psychology Bulletin, 32,* 761–769.

Hirschberger, G., & Pyszczynski, T. (2010). An existential perspective on ethno-political violence. In M. Mikulincer, & P. R. Shaver (Eds.), *Understanding and reducing aggression, violence and their consequences* (pp. 297–314). Washington, DC: American Psychological Association.

Hirschberger, G., & Pyszczynski, T. (2011). Killing with a clean conscience: Existential angst and the paradox of mortality. In M. Mikulincer, & P. R. Shaver (Eds.), *Social psychology of morality: Exploring the causes of good and evil* (pp. 331–348). Washington, DC: American Psychological Association.

Hirschberger, G., Pyszczynski, T., & Ein-Dor, T. (2009). Vulnerability and vigilance: Threat awareness and perceived adversary intent moderate the impact of mortality salience on intergroup violence. *Personality and Social Psychology Bulletin, 35,* 597–607.

Hobfoll, S. E., Canetti-Nisim, D., & Johnson, J. R. (2006). Exposure to terrorism, stress-related mental health symptoms, and defensive coping among Jews and Arabs in Israel. *Journal of Consulting and Clinical Psychology, 74*(2), 207–218.

Hochschild, A. R. (1979). Emotion work, feeling rules, and social structure. *American Journal of Sociology, 85,* 551–575.

Hoffman, M. L. (1977). Sex differences in empathy and related behaviors. *Psychological Bulletin, 84,* 712–722.

Hornstein, H. A. (1978). Promotive tension and prosocial behavior: A Lewinian analysis. In L. Wispé (Ed.), *Altruism, sympathy, and helping: Psychological and sociological principles* (pp. 177–207). San Diego, CA: Academic Press.

Horowitz, D. L. (1985). *Ethnic groups in conflict.* Berkeley: University of California Press.

Horowitz, D. L. (2001). *The deadly ethnic riot.* Berkeley: University of California Press.

Hovannisian, R. G. (1999). Denial of the Armenian genocide in comparison with Holocaust denial. In R. G. Hovannisian (Ed.), *Remembrance and denial: The case of the Armenian genocide* (pp. 201–236). Detroit, MI: Wayne State University Press.

Huddy, L., Feldman, S., Capelos, T., & Provost, C. (2002). The consequences of terrorism: Disentangling the effects of personal and national threat. *Political Psychology, 23,* 485–509.

Huddy, L., Feldman, S., & Cassese, E. (2007). On the distinct political effects of anxiety and anger. In A. Crigler, M. MacKuen, G. Marcus, & W. R. Neuman (Eds.), *The dynamics of emotion in political thinking and behavior* (pp. 202–230). Chicago, IL: Chicago University Press.

Huddy, L., Feldman, S., Taber, C., & Lahav, G. (2005). Threat, anxiety, and support of antiterrorism policies. *Journal of Political Science, 49,* 593–608.

Iacoboni, M. (2009). Imitation, empathy, and mirror neurons. *Annual Review of Psychology, 60,* 653–670.

Insko, C. A., Nacoste, R. W., & Moe, J. L. (1983). Belief congruence and racial discrimination: Review of the evidence and critical evaluation. *European Journal of Social Psychology, 13,* 153–174.

Isen, A. M. (1999). Positive affect. In *Handbook of Cognition and Emotion* (pp. 521–539). Chichester, UK: Wiley.

Iyer, A., & Leach, C. W. (2008). Emotion in inter-group relations. *European Review of Social Psychology, 19*(1), 86–125.

Iyer, A., Leach, C. W., & Crosby, F. L. (2003). White guilt and racial compensation: The benefits and limits of self-focus. *Personality and Social Psychology Bulletin, 29,* 117–129.

Iyer, A., Schmader, T., & Lickel, B. (2007). Why individuals protest the perceived transgressions of their country: The role of anger, shame, and guilt. *Personality and Social Psychology Bulletin, 33*(4), 572–587.

Jackson, D. C., Malmstadt, J. R., Larson, C. L., & Davidson, R. J. (2000). Suppression and enhancement of emotional responses to unpleasant pictures. *Psychophysiology, 37,* 515–522.

James, W. (1884). What is an emotion? *Mind, 9*(34), 188–205.

Janoff-Bulman, R. (1992). *Shattered assumptions.* New York: The Free Press.

Jarymowicz, M. (2002). Human aggressiveness in the light of knowledge about human emotions. In S. Amsterdamski (Ed.), *Human beings and aggression* (pp. 173–189). Warszawa, Poland: Wydawnictwo SIC.

Jarymowicz, M. (2015). Fear and hope in intractable conflicts: The automatic vs. reflective bases of collective emotional orientation. In E. Halperin & K. Sharvit (Eds.), *Understanding the social psychology of intractable conflicts: The Israeli-Palestinian case and beyond. A tribute to the legacy of Daniel Bar-Tal.* New York: Springer.

Jarymowicz, M., & Bar-Tal, D. (2003). The dominance of fear over hope—Can it be changed? In R. Jacoby & G. Keinan (Eds.), *Between stress and hope* (pp. 105–122). Westport, CT: Greenwood.

Jarymowicz, M., & Bar-Tal, D. (2006). The dominance of fear over hope in the life of individuals and collectives. *European Journal of Social Psychology, 36,* 367–392.

Jasini, A., & Fischer, A. H. (2015). *Hate: Charateristics and consequenses.* Manuscript in preperation.

Jasińska-Kania, A. (2007). Bloody revenge in "God's Playground": Poles' collective memory of relations with Germans, Russians, and Jews. *International Journal of Sociology, 37,* 30–42.

Jenkins, C. (1983). Resource mobilization theory and the study of social movements. *American Review of Sociology, 9*, 527–553.

Jervis, R. (1976). *Perception and misperception in international politics* (Vol. 49). Princeton, NJ: Prinston University Press.

Jetten, J., & Wohl, M. J. (2012). The past as a determinant of the present: Historical continuity, collective angst, and opposition to immigration. *European Journal of Social Psychology, 42*, 442–450.

Johns, M., Schmader, T., & Lickel, B. (2005). Ashamed to be American? The role of identification in predicting vicarious shame for anti-Arab prejudice after 9–11. *Self and Identity, 4*, 331–348.

Jost, J. T. (2006). The end of the end of ideology. *American Psychologist, 61*(7), 651–670.

Jost, J. T., & Banaji, M. R. (1994). The role of stereotyping in system-justification and the production of false consciousness. *British Journal of Social Psychology, 33*, 1–27.

Jost, J. T., Federico, C. M., & Napier, J. L. (2009). Political ideology: Its structure, functions and elective affinities. *Annual Review of Psychology, 60*, 307–337.

Jost, J. T., Glaser, J., Kruglanski, A. W., & Sulloway, F. (2003a). Exceptions that prove the rule: Using a theory of motivated social cognition to account for ideological incongruities and political anomalies. *Psychological Bulletin, 129*, 383–393.

Jost, J. T., Glaser, J., Kruglanski, A. W., & Sulloway, F. J. (2003b). Political conservatism as motivated social cognition. *Psychological Bulletin, 129*, 339–375.

Kahneman, D., & Tversky, A. (1996). On the reality of cognitive illusions. *Psychological Review, 103*(3), 582–591.

Kamans, E., Van-Zomeren, M., Gordijn, E. H., & Postmes, T. (2014). Communicating the right emotion makes violence seem less wrong: Power-congruent emotions lead outsiders to legitimize violence of powerless and powerful groups in intractable conflict. *Group Processes & Intergroup Relations, 17*(3), 286–305.

Kanyangara, P., Rimé, B., Philippot, P., & Yzerbyt, V. (2007). Collective rituals, emotional climate, intergroup perceptions: Participation in "Gacaca" tribunals and assimilation of the Rwandan Genocide. *Journal of Social Issues, 63*, 387–403.

Kate. (2011). Turkey expels Israeli ambassador, cuts military ties and promises further legal action following UN flotilla report. *Mondoweiss.* Retrieved from http://mondoweiss.net/2011/09/turkey-expels-israeli-ambassador-cuts-military-ties-and-promises-further-legal-action-following-un-flotilla-report

Kaukiainen, A., Björkqvist, K., Lagerspetz, K., Österman, K., Salmivalli, C., Rothberg, S., & Ahlbom, A. (1999). The relationships between social intelligence, empathy, and three types of aggression. *Aggressive Behavior, 25*(2), 81–89.

Kelman, H. C. (1998). Social-psychological Contributions to peacemaking and peacebuilding in the Middle East. *Applied Psychology, 47*, 5–29.

Keltner, D., & Gross, J. J. (1999). Functional accounts of emotion. *Cognition and Emotion, 13*, 467–480.

Kesebir, P., & Pyszczynski, T. (2012). The role of death in life: Existential aspects of human motivation. In R. M. Ryan (Ed.), *The Oxford handbook of human motivation* (pp. 43–64). New York: Oxford University Press.

Ketelaar, T., & Au, W. T. (2003). The effects of guilty feelings on the behavior of uncooperative individuals in repeated social bargaining games: An affect-as information interpretation of the role of emotion in social interaction. *Cognition and Emotion, 17*, 429–453.

Keysers, C., & Gazzola, V. (2007). Integrating simulation and theory of mind: From self to social cognition. *Trends in Cognitive Sciences, 11*, 194–196.

Khawaja, M. (1993). Repression and popular collective action: Evidence from the West Bank. *Sociological Forum, 8*, 47–71.

Kitayama, S., Markus, H. R., & Kurokawa, M. (2000). Culture, emotion, and well-being: Good feelings in Japan and the United States. *Cognition and Emotion, 14*, 93–124.

Kitayama, S., Mesquita, B., & Karasawa, M. (2006). Cultural affordances and emotional experience: Socially engaging and disengaging emotions in Japan and the United States. *Journal of Personality and Social Psychology, 91*, 890–903.

Klein, D. C. (1991). The humiliation dynamic: Viewing the task of prevention from a new perspective. *Journal of Primary Prevention, 12*(2), 93–121.

Klein, O., Licata, L., & Pierucci, S. (2011). Does group identification facilitate or prevent collective guilt about past misdeeds? Resolving the paradox. *British Journal of Social Psychology, 50*, 563–572.

Kleinginna Jr., P. R., & Kleinginna, A. M. (1981). A categorized list of emotion definitions, with suggestions for a consensualdefinition. *Motivation and Emotion, 5*(4), 345–379.

Knight, G. P., Johnson, L. G., Carlo, G., & Eisenberg, N. (1994). A multiplicative model of the dispositional antecedents of a prosocial behavior: Predicting more of the people more of the time. *Journal of Personality and Social Psychology 66*(1), 178–183.

Knutson, B. (1996). Facial expressions of emotion influence interpersonal trait inferences. *Journal of Nonverbal Behavior, 20*, 165–182.

Kogut, T., & Ritov, I. (2005). The "identified victim" effect: An identified group, or just a single individual? *Journal of Behavioral Decision Making, 18*, 157–167.

Kriesberg, L. (1993). Intractable conflicts. *Peace Review, 5*(4), 417–421.

Kriesberg, L. (1998). Intractable conflicts. In E. Weiner (Ed.), *The handbook of interethnic coexistance* (pp. 332–342). New York: Continuum.

Kriesberg, L., & Dayton, B. W. (2012). *Constructive conflicts: From escalation to resolution* (4th ed.). Lanham, MD: Rowman & Littlefield.

Krosnick, J. A., & Petty, R. E. (1995). Attitude strength: An overview. In R. E. Petty & J. A. Krosnick (Eds.), *Attitude strength: Antecedents and consequences* (pp. 1–24). Mahwah, NJ: Erlbaum.

Kruglanski, A. W., Shah, J. Y., Fishbach, A., Friedman, R., Chun, W. Y., & Sleeth-Keppler, D. (2002). A theory of goal-systems. In M. Zanna (Ed.), *Advances in experimental social psychology* (Vol. 34, pp. 331–376). New York: Academic Press.

Kudish, S., Cohen-Chen, S., & Halperin, E. (2015). Increasing support for concession-making in intractable conflicts: The role of conflict uniqueness. *Peace and Conflict: Journal of Peace Psychology, 21*(2), 248–263.

Kuppens, P., Van Mechelen, I., & Meulders, M. (2004). Every cloud has a silver lining: Interpersonal and individual differences determinants of anger-related behaviors. *Personality and Social Psychology Bulletin, 30*(12), 1550–1564.

Kuppens, T., Yzerbyt, V. Y., Dandache, S., Fischer, A. H., & Van Der Schalk, J. (2013). Social identity salience shapes group-based emotions through group-based appraisals. *Cognition and Emotion, 27*(8), 1359–1377.

Lake, D. A., & Rothchild, D. S. (1996). Containing fear: The origins and management of ethnic conflict. *International Security, 21*(2), 41–75.

Lake, D. A., & Rothchild, D. S. (1998). *The international spread of ethnic conflict: Fear, diffusion, and escalation.* Princeton, NJ: Princeton University Press.

Landau, M. J., Solomon, S., Greenberg, J., Cohen, F., Pyszczynski, T., Arndt, J., . . . Cook, A. (2004). Deliver us from evil: The effects of mortality salience and reminders of 9/11 on support for President George W. Bush. *Personality and Social Psychology Bulletin, 30*, 1136–1150.

Lang, P. J. (1995). The emotion probe: Studies of motivation and attention. *American Psychologist, 50*(5), 372–385.

Larsen, R. J., & Diener, E. (1992). Promises and problems with the circumplex model of emotion. In M. S. Clark (Ed.), *Review of personality and social psychology: Emotion* (Vol. 13, pp. 25–59). Thousand Oaks, CA: Sage.

Lavi, T., & Solomon, Z. (2005). Palestinian youth of the Intifada: PTSD and future orientation. *Journal of the American Academy of Child & Adolescent Psychiatry, 44*(11), 1176–1183.

Lazare, A. (2004). *On apology*. Oxford, UK: Oxford University Press.

Lazarus, R. S. (1982). Thoughts on the relations between emotion and cognition. *American Psychologist, 37*(9), 1019–1024.

Lazarus, R. S. (1991). *Emotion and adaptation*. New York: Oxford University Press.

Lazarus, R. S. (1999). Hope: An emotion and a vital coping resource against despair. *Social Research, 66*, 653–678.

Lazarus, R. S., & Folkman, S. (1984). *Stress, appraisal and coping*. New York: Springer.

Le Bon, G. (1960). *The crowd*. New York: Viking Press. (Original work published 1895)

Leach, C. W., Bilali, R., & Pagliaro, S. (2013). Groups and morality. In J. Simpson, & J. F. Dovidio (Eds.), *APA handbook of personality and social psychology. Interpersonal relationships and group processes* (Vol. 2, pp. 123–149). Washington, DC: American Psychological Association.

Leach, C. W., Ellemers, N., & Barreto, M. (2007). Group virtue: The importance of morality (vs. competence and sociability) in the positive evaluation of in-groups. *Journal of Personality and Social Psychology, 93*(2), 234–249.

Leach, C. W., Iyer, A., & Pedersen, A. (2006). Anger and guilt about ingroup advantage explain the willingness for political action. *Personality and Social Psychology Bulletin, 32*(9), 1232–1245.

Leach, C. W., Snider, N., & Iyer, A. (2002). "Poisoning the consciences of the fortunate": The experience of relative advantage and support for social equality. In I. Walker & H. J. Smith (Eds.), *Relative deprivation: Specification, development and integration* (pp. 136–163). New York: Cambridge University Press.

Leach, C. W., Spears, R., Branscombe, N. R., & Doosje, B. (2003). Malicious pleasure: Schadenfreude at the suffering of another group. *Journal of Personality and Social Psychology, 84*(5), 932–943.

Leary, M. R., Twenge, J. M., & Quinlivan, E. (2006). Interpersonal rejection as a determinant of anger and rejection. *Personality and Social Psychology Review, 10*, 111–132.

LeDoux, J. E. (1995). Emotion: Clues from the brain. *Annual Review of Psychology, 46*, 209–235.

LeDoux, J. E. (1996). *The emotional brain*. New York: Simon and Schuster.

Lee, J. J., Sohn, Y., & Fowler, J. H. (2013). Emotion regulation as the foundation of political attitudes: Does reappraisal decrease support for conservative policies? *PLOS ONE, 8*(12), article e83143. doi:10.1371/journal.pone.0083143

Leidner, B., & Castano, E. (2012). Morality shifting in the context of intergroup violence. *European Journal of Social Psychology, 42*(1), 82–91.

Leidner, B., Castano, E., Zaiser, P., & Giner-Sorolla, R. (2010). Ingroup glorification, moral disengagement, and justice in the context of collective violence. *Personality and Social Psychology Bulletin, 36*(8), 1115–1129.

Leidner, B., Sheikh, H., & Ginges, J. (2012). Affective dimensions of intergroup humiliation. *PLOS ONE, 7*(9), 1–6.

Lelieveld, G. J., Van Dijk, E., Van Beest, I., & Van Kleef, G. A. (2012). Why anger and disappointment affect other's bargaining behavior differently: The moderating role of power and the mediating role of reciprocal and complementary emotions. *Personality and Social Psychology Bulletin, 38*(9), 1209–1221.

Leonard, D. J., Mackie, D. M., & Smith, E. R. (2011). Emotional responses to intergroup apology mediate intergroup forgiveness and retribution. *Journal of Experimental Social Psychology, 47*(6), 1198–1206.

Leonard, D. J., Moons, W. G., Mackie, D. M., & Smith, E. R. (2011). We're mad as hell and we're not going to take it anymore: Anger self-stereotyping and collective action. *Group Processes and Intergroup Relations, 14*, 99–111.

Lepore, S. J. (1992). Social conflict, social support, and psychological distress: Evidence of cross-domain buffering. *Journal of Personality and Social Psychology, 63*, 857–867.

Lerner, J. S. (2005). Negotiating under the influence: Emotional hangovers distort your judgment and lead to bad decisions. *Negotiation, 8*, 1–3.

Lerner, J. S., Goldberg, J., & Tetlock, P. (1998). Sober second thought: The effects of accountability, anger, and authoritarianism on attributions of responsibility. *Personality and Social Psychology Bulletin, 24*, 563–574.

Lerner, J. S., Gonzalez, R. M., Small, D. A., & Fischhoff, B. (2003). Effects of fear and anger on perceived risks of terrorism: A national field experiment. *Psychological Science, 14*(2), 144–150.

Lerner, J. S., & Keltner, D. (2000). Beyond valence: Toward a model of emotion—specific influences on judgement and choice. *Cognition and Emotion, 14*(4), 473–493.

Lerner, J. S., & Keltner, D. (2001). Fear, anger, and risk. *Journal of Personality and Social Psychology, 81*, 146–159.

Levenson, R. W., Ekman, P., & Friesen, W. V. (1990). Voluntary facial action generates emotion-specific autonomic nervous system activity. *Psychophysiology, 27*(4), 363–384.

Levinas, S. (2015). *Does perspective taking translate into empathy In the context of Intractable Conflicts: The moderating role of delegitimization.* (MA thesis). IDC Herzliya, Isreal.

Levy, J. S. (1988). Domestic politics and war. *Journal of Interdisciplinary History, 18*(4), 653–673.

Levy-Gigi, E., & Richter-Levin, G. (2014). The hidden price of repeated traumatic exposure. *Stress, 17*(4), 343–351.

Levy-Gigi, E., Richter-Levin, G., Shapiro, A. R., Kéri, S., & Sheppes, G. (in press). Emotion regulatory flexibility sheds light on the elusive relationship between repeated traumatic exposure and post-traumatic stress disorder symptoms. *Clincal Psychological Science.*

Lewin, K. (1951). Behavior and development as a function of the total situation. In D. Cartwright (Ed.), *Field theory in social science: Selected theoretical papers* (pp. 238–303). New York: Harper & Row.

Lewis, H. B. (1971). *Shame and guilt in neurosis.* New York: Universities Press.

Lewis, H. D. (1948). Collective responsibility. *Philosophy, 23*(84), 3–18.

Lewis, M. (1993). Self-conscious emotions: embarrassment, pride, shame and guilt. In M. Lewis & J. M. Haviland (Eds.), *Handbook of emotions* (pp. 623–636). New York: Guilford.

Lewis, M. (2000). Self-conscious emotions: Embarrassment, pride, shame, and guilt. In M. Lewis & J. M. Haviland-Jones (Eds.), *Handbook of emotions* (2nd ed., pp. 623–636). New York: Guilford.

Lewis, M., Haviland-Jones, J. M., & Barrett, L. F. (2008). *Handbook of emotions* (3rd ed.). New York: Guilford.

Lickel, B., Schmader, T., & Barquissau, M. (2004). The evocation of moral emotions in intergroup contexts: The distinction between collective guilt and collective shame. In N. Branscombe & B. Doojse (Eds.), *Collective guilt: International perspectives* (pp. 35–55). Cambridge, UK: Cambridge University Press.

Lickel, B., Schmader, T., Curtis, M., Scarnier, M., & Ames, D. R. (2005). Vicarious shame and guilt. *Group Processes & Intergroup Relations, 8*(2), 145–157.

Lindner, E. G. (2001). Humiliation and the human condition: Mapping a minefield. *Human Rights Review, 2*(2), 46–63.

Lindner, E. G. (2002). Healing the cycles of humiliation: How to attend to the emotional aspects of "unsolvable" conflicts and the use of "humiliation entrepeneurship". *Peace and Conflict: Journal of Peace Psychology, 8*(2), 125–139.

Lindner, E. G. (2006a). Emotion and conflict: Why it is important to understand how emotions affect conflict and how conflict affects emotions. In M. Deutch, P. T. Coleman, & E. C. Marcus (Eds.), *The handbook of conflict resolution* (pp. 268–293). San Francisco, CA: Jossey-Bass.

Lindner, E. G. (2006b). *Making enemies: Humiliation and international conflict*. Westport, CT: Greenwood and Praeger.

Lindner, E. G. (2009). *Emotion and conflict: How human rights can dignify emotion and help us wage good conflict*. Westport, CT: Praeger/Greenwood.

Litvack-Miller, W., McDougall, D., & Romney, D. M. (1997). The structure of empathy during middle childhood and its relationship to prosocial behavior. *Genetic, Social, and General Psychology Monographs, 123*, 303–324.

Litz, B. T., & Gray, M. J. (2002). Emotional numbing in posttraumatic stress disorder: Current and future research directions. *Australian and New Zealand Journal of Psychiatry, 36*(2), 198–204.

Luminet IV, O., Bouts, P., Delie, F., Manstead, A., & Rimé, B. (2000). Social sharing of emotion following exposure to a negatively valenced situation. *Cognition and Emotion, 14*(5), 661–688.

Mackie, D. M., Devos, T., & Smith, E. R. (2000). Intergroup emotions: Explaining offensive action tendencies in an intergroup context. *Journal of Personality and Social Psychology, 79*, 602–616.

Mackie, M. D., & Smith, E. R. (2000). *Social psychology* (2nd ed.). Singapore: Psychology Press.

Maddux, W. W., Galinsky, A. D., Cuddy, A. J., & Polifroni, M. (2008). When being a model minority is good . . . and bad: Realistic threat explains negativity toward Asian Americans. *Personality and Social Psychology Bulletin, 34*(1), 74–89.

Maitner, A. T., Mackie, D. M., & Smith, E. R. (2006). Evidence for the regulatory function of intergroup emotion: Emotional consequences of implemented or impeded intergroup action tendencies. *Journal of Experimental Social Psychology, 42*(6), 720–728.

Maitner, A. T., Mackie, D. M., & Smith, E. R. (2007). Antecedents and consequences of satisfaction and guilt following ingroup aggression. *Group Processes & Intergroup Relations, 10*(2), 223–237.

Maner, J. K., Luce, C. L., Neuberg, S. L., Cialdini, R. B., Brown, S., & Sagarin, B. J. (2002). The effects of perspective taking on motivations for helping: Still no evidence for altruism. *Personality and Social Psychology Bulletin, 28*(11), 1601–1610.

Manstead, A. S., & Fischer, A. H. (2001). Social appraisal: The social world as object of and influence on appraisal processes. In K. R. Scherer, A. Schorr, & T. Johnstone (Eds.), *Appraisal processes in emotion: Theory, methods, research. Series in affective science* (pp. 221–232). New York: Oxford University Press.

Manstead, A. S., & Tetlock, P. E. (1989). Cognitive appraisals and emotional experience: Further evidence. *Cognition and Emotion, 3*(3), 225–239.

Maoz, I., & McCauley, C. (2005). Psychological correlates of support for compromise: A polling study of Jewish-Israeli attitudes toward solutions to the Israeli-Palestinian conflict. *Political Psychology, 26*(5), 791–808.

Maoz, I., & McCauley, C. (2008). Threat, dehumanization, and support for retaliatory aggressive policies in asymmetric conflict. *Journal of Conflict Resolution, 52*(1), 93–116.

Maoz, I., & McCauley, C. (2009). Threat perceptions and feelings as predictors of Jewish–Israeli support for compromise with Palestinians. *Journal of Peace Research, 46*(4), 525–539.

Maoz, I., Ward, A., Katz, M., & Ross, L. (2002). Reactive devaluation of an 'Israeli' vs. 'Palestinian' peace proposal. *Journal of Conflict Resolution, 46*(4), 515–546.

Marcus, G. E., & MacKuen, M. B. (1993). Anxiety, enthusiasm, and the vote: The emotional underpinnings of learning and involvement during presidential campaigns. *American Political Science Review, 87*(3), 672–685.

Marcus, G. E., Neuman, W. R., & MacKuen, M. (2000). *Affective intelligence and political judgment.* Chicago, IL: University of Chicago Press.

Margalit, A. (1996). *The decent society.* Cambridge, MA: Harvard University Press.

Margalit, A. (2002). *The ethics of memory.* Cambridge, MA: Harvard University Press.

Markus, H., & Kitayama, S. (1991). Culture and the self implications for cognition, emotion, and motivation. *Psychological Review, 98*, 224–253.

Maroney, T. A., & Gross, J. J. (2014). The ideal of the dispassionate judge: An emotion regulation perspective. *Emotion Review, 6*, 142–151.

Mascolo, M. F., & Fischer, K. W. (1995). Developmental transformations in appraisals for pride, shame, and guilt. In J. P. Tangney, & K. W. Fischer (Eds.), *Self-conscious emotions: The psychology of shame, guilt, embarrassment, and pride* (pp. 61–113). New York: Guilford.

Mashuri, A., Hasanah, N., & Rahmawati, I. (2012). The effect of outgroup status and perspective-taking on empathy and outgroup helping. *International Journal of Research Studies in Psychology, 2*(2), 3–14.

Maslow, A. H. (1963). The need to know and the fear of knowing. *Journal of General Psychology, 68*(1), 111–125.

Masten, C. L., Gillen-O'Neel, C., & Brown, C. S. (2010). Children's intergroup empathic processing: The roles of novel ingroup identification, situational distress, and social anxiety. *Journal of Experimental Child Psychology, 106*(2), 115–128.

Mauss, I. B., Bunge, S. A., & Gross, J. J. (2007). Automatic emotion regulation. *Social and Personality Psychology Compass, 1*, 146–167.

Mauss, I. B., Cook, C. L., Cheng, J. Y., & Gross, J. J. (2007). Individual differences in cognitive reappraisal: Experiential and physiological responses to an anger provocation. *International Journal of Psychophysiology, 66*(2), 116–124.

Mauss, I. B., & Robinson, M. D. (2009). Measures of emotion: A review. *Cognition and emotion, 23*(2), 209–237.

Mauss, I. B., & Tamir, M. (2014). Emotion goals: How their content, structure, and operation shape emotion regulation. In J. J. Gross (Ed.), *The handbook of emotion regulation* (2nd ed., pp. 361–375). New York: Guilford.

May, R. (1958). Existence: A new dimension in psychiatry and psychology. In R. May, E. Angel, & H. F. Ellenberger (Eds.), *Existence: A new dimension in psychiatry and psychology* (pp. 24–62). New York: Basic Books.

McCarthy, J., & Zald,, M. (1977). Resource mobilization and social movements. *American Journal of Sociology, 82*, 1212–1241.

McGarty, C., Pedersen, A., Leach, C. W., Mansell, T., Waller, J., & Bliuc, A. M. (2005). Group-based guilt as a predictor of commitment to apology. *British Journal of Social Psychology, 44*(4), 659–680.

McQueen, A., & Klein, W. M. (2006). Experimental manipulations of self-affirmation: A systematic review. *Self and Identity, 5*(4), 289–354.

Mehrabian, A. (1997). Relations among personality scales of aggression, violence, and empathy: Validational evidence bearing on the risk of eruptive violence scale. *Aggressive Behavior, 23*(6), 433–445.

Mesquita, B. (2003). Emotions as dynamic cultural phemomena. In R. Davidson, H. Goldsmith, & K. R. Scherer (Eds.), *The handbook of the affective sciences* (pp. 871–890). New York: Oxford University Press.

Mesquita, B., & Albert, D. (2007). The cultural regulation of emotions. In J. J. Gross (Ed.), *Handbook of emotion regulation* (pp. 486–503). New York: Guilford.

Mesquita, B., Karasawa, M., Haire, A., Izumi, S., Hayashi, A., Idzelis, M., . . . Kashiwagi, K. (2006). *What do I feel? The role of cultural models in emotion.* Unpublished manuscript, Wake Forest University, Winston-Salem, NC.

Mesquita, B., & Leu, J. (2007). The cultural psychology of emotion. In S. Kitayama & D. Cohen (Eds.), *Handbook of cultural psychology* (pp. 734–759). New York: Guilford.

Mineka, S., & Cook, M. (1993). Mechanisms involved in the observational conditioning of fear. *Journal of Experimental Psychology: General, 122*(1), 23–38.

Mintz, A. (2004). How do leaders make decisions? A poliheuristic perspective. *Journal of Conflict Resolution, 48*(1), 3–13.

Miron, A. M., Branscombe, N. R., & Biernat, M. (2010). Motivated shifting of justice standards. *Personality and Social Psychology Bulletin, 36*, 768–779.

Mitchell, J. P. (2009). Inferences about mental states. *Philosophical Transactions of the Royal Society B: Biological Sciences, 364*(1521), 1309–1316.

Mnookin, R. H., & Ross, L. (1995). Introduction. In K. Arrow, R. Mnookin, L. Ross, A. Tversky, & R. Wilson (Eds.), *Barriers to conflict resolution* (pp. 2–25). New York: Norton.

Moeschberger, S. L., Dixon, D. N., Niens, U., & Cairns, E. (2005). Forgiveness in Northern Ireland: A model for peace in the midst of the "Troubles". *Peace and Conflict: Journal of Peace Psychology, 11*(2), 199–214.

Moisi, D. (2007). The clash of emotions: Fear, humiliation, hope, and the new world order. *Foreign Affairs, 86*(1), 8–12.

Monin, B., & Jordan, A. H. (2009). Dynamic moral identity: A social psychological perspective. In D. Narvaez, & D. Lapsley (Eds.), *Personality, identity, and character: Explorations in moral psychology* (pp. 341–354). Cambridge, UK: Cambridge University Press.

Montada, L., & Schneider, A. (1989). Justice and emotional reactions to the disadvantaged. *Social Justice Research, 3*(4), 313–344.

Montalan, B., Lelard, T., Godefroy, O., & Mouras, H. (2012). Behavioral investigation of the influence of social categorization on empathy for pain: A minimal group paradigm study. *Frontiers in Psychology, 3*, 1–5.

Moons, W. G., Leonard, D. J., Mackie, D. M., & Smith, E. R. (2009). I feel our pain: Antecedents and consequences of emotional self-stereotyping. *Journal of Experimental Social Psychology, 45*, 760–769.

Morf, C. C., & Rhodewalt, F. (2001). Unraveling the paradoxes of narcissism: A dynamic self-regulatory processing model. *Psychological Inquiry, 12*(4), 177–196.

Morrison, K. R., & Ybarra, O. (2008). The effects of realistic threat and group identification on social dominance orientation. *Journal of Experimental Social Psychology, 44*(1), 156–163.

Morsbach, H., & Tyler, W. J. (1986). A Japanese emotion: Amae. In R. Harré (Ed.), *The social construction of the emotions* (pp. 289–307). London: Oxford University Press.

Motyl, M., Pyszczynski, T., Cox, C., Siedel, A., & Maxfield, M. (2007). *One big family: The effects of mortality salience and a sense of common humanity on prejudice.* Manuscript submitted for publication.

Mowrer, O. H. (1960). *Learning theory and behavior.* New York: Wiley.

Muldoon, O. T., & Lowe, R. D. (2012). Social identity, groups, and post-traumatic stress disorder. *Political Psychology, 33*(2), 259–273.

Muldoon, O. T., & Trew, K. (2000). Children's experience and adjustment to political conflict in Northern Ireland. *Peace and Conflict: Journal of Peace Psychology, 6*(2), 157–176.

Mummendey, A., Kessler, T., Klink, A., & Mielke, R. (1999). Strategies to cope with negative social identity: Predictions by social identity theory and relative deprivation theory. *Journal of Personality and Social Psychology, 76*(2), 229–245.

Mummendey, A., Klinl, A., & Brown, R. (2001). Nationalism and patriotism: National identification and out-group rejection. *British Journal of Social Psychology, 40*(2), 149–172.

Murphy, S. T., & Zajonc, R. B. (1993). Affect, cognition, and awareness: Affective priming with optimal and suboptimal stimulus exposures. *Journal of Personality and Social Psychology, 64*(5), 723–739.

Myers, E., Hewstone, M., & Cairns, E. (2009). Impact of conflict on mental health in Northern Ireland: The mediating role of intergroup forgiveness and collective guilt. *Political Psychology, 30*(2), 269–290.

Nadler, A., & Liviatan, I. (2006). Intergroup reconciliation: Effects of adversary's expressions of empathy, responsibility, and recipients' trust. *Personality and Social Psychology Bulletin, 32*(4), 459–470.

Neale, M. A., & Bazerman, M. H. (1991). *Cognition and rationality in negotiation.* New York: Free Press.

Nesse, R. M. (1990). Evolutionary explanations of emotions. *Human Nature, 1*(3), 261–289.

Nesse, R. M. (1999). The evolution of hope and despair. *Journal of Social Issues, 66*(2), 429–469.

Nesse, R. M. (2005). Natural selection and the regulation of defenses: A signal detection analysis of the smoke detector principle. *Evolution and Human Behavior, 26*(1), 88–105.

Niedenthal, P. M., Krauth-Gruber, S., & Ric, F. (2006). *Psychology of emotion: Interpersonal, experiential, and cognitive approaches.* New York: Psychology Press.

Nietzsche, F. (1998). *Twilight of the idols.* (L. Duncan, Trans.). New York: Oxford University Press. (Original work published 1889)

Niven, K., Totterdell, P., Stride, C., & Holman, D. (2011). Emotion regulation of others and self (EROS): The development and validation of a new measure. *Current Psychology, 30*, 53–73.

Noelle-Neumann, E. (1974). The spiral of silence: A theory of public opinion. *Journal of Communication, 24*, 24–51.

Nolen-Hoeksema, S., & Davis, C. G. (2002). Positive responses to loss: Perceiving benefits and growth. In C. R. Snyder, & S. J. Lopez (Eds.), *Handbook of positive psychology* (pp. 598–607). New York: Oxford Press.

Noor, M., Brown, R., & Prentice, G. (2008). Precursors and mediators of intergroup reconciliation in Northern Ireland: A new model. *British Journal of Social Psychology, 47*(3), 481–495.

Noor, M., Shnabel, N., Halabi, S., & Nadler, A. (2012). When suffering begets suffering: The psychology of competitive victimhood between adversarial groups in violent conflicts. *Personality and Social Psychology Review, 16*(4), 351–374.

Oatley, K. (1992). *Best laid schemes: The psychology of the emotions.* Cambridge, UK: Cambridge University Press.

Oatley, K., & Jenkins, J. M. (1996). *Understanding emotions.* Cambridge, MA: Blackwell.

O'Gorman, R., Wilson, D. S., & Miller, R. R. (2005). Altruistic punishing and helping differ in sensitivity to relatedness, friendship, and future interactions. *Evolution and Human Behavior, 26*(5), 375–387.

Öhman, A. (1993). Fear and anxiety as emotional phenomena: Clinical phenomenology, evolutionary perspectives, and information processing mechanisms. In M. Lewis, & J. M. Haviland (Eds.), *Handbook of emotions* (pp. 511–536). New York: Guilford.

Opotow, S. (1990). Moral exclusion and injustice: An introduction. *Journal of Social Issues, 46*(1), 1–20.

Opotow, S., & McClelland, S. I. (2007). The intensification of hating: A theory. *Social Justice Research, 20*(1), 68–97.

Orth, U., Robins, R. W., & Soto, C. J. (2008). Tracking the trajectory of shame, guilt, and pride across the lifespan. *Journal of Personality and Social Psychology, 99*(6), 1061–1071.

Ortony, A., Clore, G. L., & Collins, A. (1988). *The cognitive structure of emotions.* New York: Cambridge University Press.

Oswald, P. A. (1996). The effects of cognitive and affective perspective taking on empathic concern and altruistic helping. *Journal of Social Psychology, 136*(5), 613–623.

Oveis, C., Horberg, E. J., & Keltner, D. (2010). Compassion, pride, and social intuitions of self-other similarity. *Journal of Personality and Social Psychology, 98*(4), 618–630.

Páez, D., Basabe, N., & González, J. L. (1997). Social processes and collective memory: A cross-cultural approach to remembering political events. In J. Pennebaker, D. Páez, & B. Rimé (Eds.), *Collective memory of political events: Social psychological perspectives* (pp. 147–174). Mahwah, NJ: Lawrence Erlbaum.

Páez, D., & Liu, J. (2011). Collective memory of conflicts. In D. Bar-Tal (Ed.), *Intergroup conflicts and their resolution: A social psychological perspective* (pp. 105–124). New York: Psychology Press.

Páez, D., & Vergara, A. I. (1995). Culture differences in emotional knowledge. In J. A. Russell, J. M. Fermandez-Dols, A. S. Manstead, & J. C. Wellenkamp (Eds.), *Everyday conceptions of emotion: An introduction to the psychology, anthropology and linguistics of emotion* (pp. 415–434). Boston: Kluwer.

Pagano, S. J., & Huo, Y. J. (2007). The role of moral emotions in predicting support for political actions in post-war Iraq. *Political Psychology, 28*(2), 227–255.

Pagliaro, S. (2012). On the relevance of morality in social psychology: An introduction to a virtual special issue. *European Journal of Social Psychology, 42*(2), 400–405.

Palestinian Center for Policy and Survey Research. (2013). *Joint Israeli-Palestinian poll, June 2013.* Retrieved from http://www.pcpsr.org/en/node/381

Paluck, E. L. (2009). Reducing intergroup prejudice and conflict using the media: A field experiment in Rwanda. *Journal of Personality and Social Psychology, 96*(3), 574–587.

Paluck, E. L. (2010). Is it better not to talk? Group polarization, extended contact, and perspective-taking in eastern Democratic Republic of Congo. *Personality and Social Psychology Bulletin, 36*, 1170–1185.

Parkinson, B., Fischer, A. H., & Manstead, A. S. (2005). *Emotion in social relations: Cultural, group and interpersonal processes.* Hove, UK: Psychology Press.

Parrott, W. (2001). Implications of dysfunctional emotions for understanding how emotions function. *Review of General Psychology, 5*, 180–186.

Parrott, W. (1993). Beyond hedonism: Motives for inhibiting good moods and for maintaining bad moods. In D. M. Wegner, & J. W. Pennebaker (Eds.), *Handbook of mental control* (pp. 278–305). Upper Saddle River, NJ: Prentice Hall.

Paulhus, D. L., Robins, R. W., Trzesniewski, K. H., & Tracy, J. L. (2004). Two replicable suppressor situations in personality research. *Multivariate Behavioral Research, 39*(2), 301–326.

Peace Index. (August, 2006). Retrieved from http://www.tau.ac.il/peace/

Pedersen, A., Beven, J., Walker, I., & Griffiths, B. (2004). Attitudes toward Indigenous-Australians: The role of empathy and guilt. *Journal of Community and Applied Social Psychology, 14*(4), 233–249.

Peetz, J., Gunn, J. R., & Wilson, A. E. (2010). Crimes of the past: Defensive temporal distancing in the face of past in-group wrongdoing. *Personality and Social Psychology Bulletin, 36*(5), 598–611.

Pennekamp, S. F., Doosje, B., Zebel, S., & Fischer, A. H. (2007). The past and the pending: The antecedents and consequences of group-based anger in historically and currently disadvantaged groups. *Group Processes & Intergroup Relations, 10*, 41–55.

Petersen, R. G. (2002). *Understanding ethnic violence: Fear, hatred, and resentment in twentieth-century Eastern Europe*. Cambridge, UK: Cambridge University Press.

Peterson, C. K., & Harmon-Jones, E. (2012). Toward an understanding of the emotion-modulated startle eyeblink reflex: The case of anger. *Psychophysiology, 49*(11), 1677–1690.

Pettigrew, T. F. (1998). Intergroup contact theory. *Annual Review of Psychology, 49*(1), 65–85.

Pettigrew, T. F. (2003). People under threat: Americans, Arabs, and Israelis. *Peace and Conflict: Journal of Peace Psychology, 9*(1), 69–90.

Pettigrew, T. F., & Tropp, L. R. (2006). A meta-analytical test of the intergroup contact theory. *Journal of Personality and Social Psychology, 90*, 751–783.

Philpot, C. R., & Hornsey, M. J. (2008). What happens when groups say sorry: The effect of intergroup apologies on their recipients. *Personality and Social Psychology Bulletin, 34*(4), 474–487.

Philpot, C. R., & Hornsey, M. J. (2011). Memory for intergroup apologies and its relationship with forgiveness. *European Journal of Social Psychology, 41*(1), 96–106.

Pierce, J. R., Kilduff, G. J., Galinsky, A. D., & Sivanathan, N. (2013). From glue to gasoline: How competition turns perspective takers unethical. *Psychological Science, 24*, 1986–1994.

Pillutla, M. M., & Murnighan, J. K. (1996). Unfairness, anger, and spite: Emotional rejections of ultimatum offers. *Organizational Behavior and Human Decision Processes, 68*(3), 208–224.

Pinel, E. C., Long, A. E., Landau, M. J., Alexander, K., & Pyszczynski, T. (2006). Seeing I to I: A pathway to interpersonal connectedness. *Journal of Personality and Social Psychology, 90*(2), 243–257.

Pitman, R., & Orr, S. (1995). Psychophysiology of emotional and memory networks in posttraumatic stress disorder. In J. L. McGaugh, N. Weinberger, & G. Lynch (Eds.), *Brain and memory: Modulation and mediation of neuroplasticity* (pp. 75–83). New York: Oxford University Press.

Pliskin, R., Bar-Tal, D., Sheppes, G., & Halperin, E. (2014). Are leftists more emotion-driven than rightists? The interactive influence of ideology and emotions on support for policies. *Personality and Social Psychology Bulletin, 40*(12), 1681–1697.

Plutchik, R. (1980). *Emotion: A psychoevolutionary synthesis*. New York: Harper & Row.

Plutchik, R. (1990). Fear and aggression in suicide and violence: A psychoevolutionary perspective. In P. F. Brain, S. Parmigiani, R. J. Blanchard, & D. Mainarcli (Eds.), *Fear and defense* (pp. 359–379). London: Harwood.

Porat, R., Halperin, E., Mannheim, I., & Tamir, M. (in press). Together we cry: Social motives and preferences for group-based sadness. *Cognition and Emotion*.

Porat, R., Halperin, E., & Tamir, M. (2015). *What we want is what we get: Group-based emotional preferences and conflict resolution.* Manuscript in preparation.

Powell, A. A., Branscombe, N. R., & Schmitt, M. T. (2005). Inequality as ingroup privilege or outgroup disadvantage: The impact of group focus on collective guilt and interracial attitudes. *Personality and Social Psychology Bulletin, 31*(4), 508–521.

Preston, S. D., & De Waal, F. (2002). Empathy: Its ultimate and proximate bases. *Behavioral and brain sciences, 25*(1), 1–20.

Pronin, E., Lin, D.Y., & Ross, L. (2002). The bias blind spot: Perceptions of bias in self versus others. *Personality and Social Psychology Bulletin, 28*(3), 369–381.

Pyszczynski, T., Abdollahi, A., Solomon, S., Greenberg, J., Cohen, F., & Weise, D. (2006). Mortality salience, martyrdom, and military might: The great Satan versus the axis of evil. *Personality and Social Psychology Bulletin, 32*(4), 525–537.

Pyszczynski, T., Motyl, M., Vail III, K. E., Hirschberger, G., Arndt, J., & Kesebir, P. (2012). Drawing attention to global climate change decreases support for war. *Peace and Conflict: Journal of Peace Psychology, 18*(4), 354–368.

Quillian, L. (1995). Prejudice as a response to perceived group threat: Population compositions and antiimmigrant and racial prejudice in Europe. *American Sociological Review, 60*, 586–611.

Rachman, S. (1978). *Fear and courage.* San Francisco: Freeman.

Radcliffe-Brown, A. R. (1993). La estructura social. In A. R. Radcliffe-Brown (Ed.), *El método de la antropología social.* Barcelona, Spain: Anagrama.

Radzik, L. (2001). Collective responsibility and duties to respond. *Social Theory and Practice, 27*, 455–471.

Ray, R. D., Wilhelm, F. H., & Gross, J. J. (2008). All in the mind's eye? Anger rumination and reappraisal. *Journal of Personality and Social Psychology, 94*(1), 133–145.

Reifen Tagar, M., Federico, C. M., & Halperin, E. (2011). The positive effect of negative emotions in protracted conflict: The case of anger. *Journal of Experimental Social Psychology, 47*(1), 157–164.

Renshon, J., & Lerner, J. (2012). The role of emotions in foreign policy decision making. In D. J. Christie, & C. Montiel (Eds.), *Encyclopedia of peace psychology* (pp. 313–317). NJ: Wiley-Blackwell.

Richards, J. M., Butler, E. A., & Gross, J. J. (2003). Emotion regulation in romantic relationships: The cognitive consequences of concealing feelings. *Journal of Social and Personal Relationships, 20*, 599–620.

Richards, J. M., & Gross, J. J. (2000). Emotion regulation and memory: The cognitive costs of keeping one's cool. *Journal of Personality and Social Psychology, 79*, 410–424.

Richardson, D. R., Hammock, G. S., Smith, S. M., Gardner, W., & Signo, M. (1994). Empathy as a cognitive inhibitor of ianterpersonal Aggression. *Aggressive Behavior, 20*(4), 275–289.

Rifkin, J. (2010). *The empathic civilization: The race to global consciousness in a world in crisis.* New York: Tarcher.

Rimé, B. (2007). The social sharing of emotions as an interface between individual and collective processes in the construction of emotional climates. *Journal of Social Issues, 63*, 307–322.

Rimé, B. (2009). Emotion elicits the social sharing of emotion: Theory and empirical review. *Emotion Review, 1*(1), 60–85.

Rimé, B., Mesquita, B., Boca, S., & Philippot, P. (1991). Beyond the emotional event: Six studies on the social sharing of emotion. *Cognition and Emotion, 5*, 435–465.

Roccas, S., Klar, Y., & Liviatan, I. (2006). The paradox of group-based guilt: Modes of national identification, conflict vehemence, and reactions to the in-group's moral violations. *Journal of Personality and Social Psychology, 91*(4), 698–711.

Roccas, S., Sagiv, L., Schwartz, S., Halevy, N., & Eidelson, R. (2008). Toward a unifying model of identification with groups: Integrating theoretical perspectives. *Personality and Social Psychology Review, 12*(3), 280–306.

Rodriguez Mosquera, P.M., Manstead, A. S., & Fisher, A. H. (2002). The role of honorconcerns in emotional reactions to offenses. *Cognition and Emotion, 16*, 143–163.

Roseman, I. J. (1984). Cognitive determinants of emotions: A structural theory. In P. Shaver (Ed.), *Review of personality and social psychology* (Vol. 5, pp. 11–36). Beverly Hills, CA: Sage.

Roseman, I. J. (1994). Emotions and emotion families in the emotion system. In N. H. Frijda (Ed.), *Proceedings of the 8th international conference on the International Society for Research on Emotions* (pp. 171–75). Storrs, CT: International Society for Research on Emotions.

Roseman, I. J. (2001). A model of appraisal in the emotion system: Integrating theory, research, and applications. In K. R. Scherer, A. Schorr, & T. Johnstone (Eds.), *Appraisal processes in emotion: Theory, methods, research* (pp. 68–91). New York: Oxford University Press.

Roseman, I. J. (2002). Dislike, anger, and contempt: Interpersonal distancing, attack, and exclusion emotions. *Emotion Researcher, 16*(3), 5–6.

Roseman, I. J., Copeland, J. A., & Fischer, A. H. (January 2003). *Contempt versus anger in interracial attitudes.* Paper presented at the fourth meeting of the Society for Personality and Social Psychology, Los Angeles, California.

Roseman, I. J., Spindel, M. S., & Jose, P. E. (1990). Appraisals of emotion eliciting events: Testing a theory of discrete emotions. *Journal of Personality and Social Psychology, 59*(5), 899–915.

Roseman, I. J., Wiest, C., & Swartz, T. S. (1994). Phenomenology, behaviors, and goals differentiate discrete emotions. *Journal of Personality and Social Psychology, 67*(2), 206–221.

Rosenberg, E. L. (1998). Levels of analysis and the organization of affect. *Review of General Psychology, 2*(3), 280–247.

Rosler, N., Bar-Tal, D., Sharvit, K., Halperin, E., & Raviv, A. (2009). Moral aspects of prolonged occupation: Implications for an occupying society. In S. Schuzzarello, K. Kinnvall, & K. Monroe (Eds.), *On behalf of others: The morality of care in a global world* (pp. 211–232). New York: Oxford University Press.

Rosler, N., Cohen-Chen, S., & Halperin, E. (in press). The distinctive effects of empathy and hope in intractable conflicts. *Journal of Conflict Resolution.*

Ross, L. (1977). The intuitive psychologist and his shortcomings: Distortions in the attribution process. *Advances in Experimental Social Ppsychology, 10*, 173–220.

Ross, L., & Ward, A. (1995). Psychological barriers to dispute resolution. In M. Zanna (Ed.), *Advances in Experimental Social Psychology* (Vol. 27, pp. 255–304). San Diego, CA: Academic Press.

Ross, L., & Ward, A. (1996). Naive realism in everyday life: Implications for social conflict and misunderstanding. In T. Brown, E. S. Reed, & E. Turiel (Eds.), *Values and knowledge. The Jean Piaget Symposium Series* (pp. 103–135). Hillsdale, NJ: Erlbaum.

Ross, M. H. (1995). Psychocultural interpretation theory and peacemaking in ethnic conflicts. *Political Psychology, 16*(3), 523–544.

Rossano, M. J. (2012). The essential role of ritual in the transmission and reinforcement of social norms. *Psychology Bulletin, 138*, 529–549.

Rothgerber, H. (1997). External intergroup threat as an antecedent to perceptions of in-group and out-group homogeneity. *Journal of Personality and Social Psychology, 73*(6), 1206–1211.

Rothschild, Z., Abdollahi, A., & Pyszczynski, T. (2009). Does peace have a prayer? The effect of mortality salience, compassionate values and religious fundamentalism on hostility toward out-groups. *Journal of Experimental Social Psychology, 45*(4), 816–827.

Royzman, E. B., McCauley, C., & Rosin, P. (2005). From Plato to Putnam: Four ways to think about hate. In R. J. Sternberg (Ed.), *The psychology of hate* (pp. 3–36). Washington, DC: American Psychological Association.

Russell, J. A. (2003). Core affect and the psychological construction of emotion. *Psychological Review, 110*(1), 145–172.

Rydell, R. J., Hugenberg, K., Ray, D., & Mackie, D. M. (2007). Implicit theories about groups and stereotyping: The role of group entitativity. *Personality and Social Psychology Bulletin, 33*, 549–558.

Rydell, R. J., Mackie, M. D., Maitner, A. T., Claypool, H. M., Ryan, M. J., & Smith, E. R. (2008). Arousal, processing, and risk-taking: The consequences of intergroup anger. *Personality and Social Psychology Bulletin, 34*(8), 1141–1152.

Sabucedo, J. M., Durán, M., Alzate, M., & Rodríguez, M. S. (2011). Emotional responses and attitudes to the peace talks with ETA. *Revista Latinoamericana de Psicología, 43*(2), 289–296.

Saguy, T., & Chernyak-Hai, L. (2012). Intergroup contact can undermine disadvantaged group members' attributions to discrimination. *Journal of Experimental Social Psychology, 48*(3), 714–720.

Saguy, T., & Halperin, E. (2014). Exposure to outgroup members criticizing their own group facilitates intergroup openness. *Personality and Social Psychology Bulletin, 40*(6), 791–802.

Saguy, T., Tausch, N., Dovidio, J., & Pratto, F. (2009). The irony of harmony: Intergroup contact can produce false expectations for equality. *Psychological Science, 20*(1), 114–121.

Sallfors, C., Fasth, A., & Hallberg, M. (2002). Oscillating between hope and despair: A qualitative study. *Child Care, Health and Development, 28*(6), 495–505.

Salomon, G. (2004). A narrative-based view of peace education. *Journal of Social Issues, 60*(2), 273–288.

Sani, F., Bowe, M., Herrera, M., Manna, C., Cossa, T., Miao, X., & Zhou, Y. (2007). Perceived collective continuity: Seeing groups as entities that move through time. *European Journal of Social Psychology, 37*(6), 1118–1134.

Savitsky, K., Van Boven, L., Epley, N., & Wight, W. (2005). The unpacking effect in responsibility allocations for group tasks. *Journal of Experimental Social Psychology, 41*(5), 447–457.

Schachter, S. (1951). Deviation, rejection and communication. *Journal of Abnormal and Social Psychology, 46*, 189–207.

Scheff, T. J. (2003). Shame in self and society. *Symbolic Interaction, 26*(2), 239–262.

Scherer, K. R. (1984). On the nature and function of emotion: A component process approach. In K. R. Scherer & P. J. Slater (Eds.), *Advances in the study of behavior* (Vol. 15, pp. 189–244). New York: Academic Press.

Scherer, K. R. (1987). Toward a dynamic theory of emotion. *Geneva Studies in Emotion and Communication, 1*, 1–98.

Scherer, K. R. (1999). Appraisal theory. In T. Dalgleish, & M. J. Power (Eds.), *Handbook of cognition and emotion* (pp. 637–663). Chichester, UK: Wiley.

Scherer, K. R. (2001). Appraisal considered as a process of multilevel sequential checking. In K. R. Scherer, A. Schorr, & T. Johnstone (Eds.), *Appraisal processes in emotion: Theory, methods, research* (pp. 92–120). New York and Oxford: Oxford University Press.

Scherer, K. R. (2004). Feelings integrate the central representation of appraisal-driven response organization in emotion. In A. S. Manstead, N. H. Frijda, & A. H. Fischer (Eds.), *Feelings and emotions: The Amsterdam symposium* (pp. 136–157). Cambridge, UK: Cambridge University Press.

Scherer, K. R., Schorr, A. E., & Johnstone, T. E. (2001). *Appraisal processes in emotion: Theory, methods, research.* New York: Oxford University Press.

Schlenker, B. R. (1997). Personal responsibility: Applications of the triangle model. In L. L. Cummings, & B. Staw (Eds.), *Research in organizational behavior* (Vol. 19, pp. 241–301). Greenwich, CT: JAI Press.

Schmader, T., & Lickel, B. (2006). The approach and avoidance function of guilt and shame emotions: Comparing reactions to self-caused and other-caused wrongdoing. *Motivation and Emotion, 30*(1), 43–56.

Schmitt, M., Behner, R., Montada, L., Muller, L., & Muller-Fohrbrodt, G. (2000). Gender, ethnicity, and education as privileges: Exploring the generalizability of the existential guilt reaction. *Social Justice Research, 13*(4), 313–337.

Schori-Eyal, N., Klar, Y., Roccas, S., & McNeill, N. (2015). *The shadows of the past: Effects of historical group trauma on current intergroup conflicts.* Manuscript under review.

Schori-Eyal, N., Reifen Tagar, M., Saguy, T., & Halperin, E. (2015). The benefits of group-based pride: Pride can motivate guilt in intergroup conflicts among high glorifiers. *Journal of Experimental Social Psychology, 61*, 79–83.

Schubert, T. W., & Koole, S. L. (2009). The embodied self: Making a fist enhances men's power-related self-conceptions. *Journal of Experimental Social Psychology, 45*(4), 828–834.

Sears, D. O., & Funk, C. L. (1991). The role of self-interest in social and political attitudes. *Advances in Experimental Social Psychology, 24*, 1–91.

Seger, C. R., Smith, E. R., & Mackie, D. M. (2009). Subtle activation of a social categorization triggers group-level emotions. *Journal of Experimental Social Psychology, 45*, 460–467.

Senor, D., & Singer, S. (2009). *Start-up nation: The story of Israel's economic miracle.* New York: Twelve, Hachette.

Sharvit, K., Halperin, E., & Rosler, N. (2008). *Forces of stability and change in prolonged occupation: Image threat, emotions, and justifying beliefs.* Unpublished manuscript, Haifa University, Israel.

Shechtman, Z., & Basheer, O. (2005). Normative beliefs supporting aggression of Arab children in an intergroup conflict. *Aggressive Behavior, 31*(4), 324.

Sheikh, S., & Janoff-Bulman, R. (2010). The "shoulds" and "should nots" of moral emotions: A self-regulatory perspective on shame and guilt. *Personality and Social Psychology Bulletin, 36*(2), 213–224.

Sheppes, G., Catran, E., & Meiran, N. (2009). Reappraisal (but not distraction) is going to make you sweat: Physiological evidence for self-control effort. *International Journal of Psychophysiology, 71*, 91–96.

Sheppes, G., & Gross, J. J. (2011). Is timing everything? Temporal considerations in emotion regulation. *Personality and Social Psychology Review, 4*(15), 319–331.

Sheppes, G., & Meiran, N. (2007). Better late than never? On the dynamics of on-line regulation of sadness using distraction and cognitive reappreappraisal. *Personality and Social Psychology Bulletin, 33*, 1518–1532.

Sheppes, G., Scheibe, S., Suri, G., & Gross, J. J. (2011). Emotion-regulation choice. *Psychological Science, 22*(11), 1391–1396.

Sheppes, G., Scheibe, S., Suri, G., Radu, P., Blechert, J., & Gross, J. J. (2014). Emotion regulation choice: A conceptual framework and supporting evidence. *Journal of Experimental Psychology (General), 143*, 163–181.

Sherif, M., Harvey, O. J., White, B. J., Hood, W. R., & Sherif, C. W. (1961). *Intergroup cooperation and competition: The Robbers Cave Experiment*. Norman, OK: University Book Exchange.

Sherman, D. K., & Cohen, G. L. (2006). The psychology of self-defense: Self-affirmation theory. *Advances in Experimental Social Psychology, 38*, 183–242.

Sherman, D. K., Kinias, Z., Major, B., Kim, H. S., & Prenovost, M. A. (2007). The group as a resource: Reducing biased attributions for group success and failure via group affirmation. *Personality and Social Psychology Bulletin, 33*(8), 1100–1112.

Shnabel, N., & Nadler, A. (2008). A needs-based model of reconciliation: Satisfying the differential emotional needs of victim and perpetrator as a key to promoting reconciliation. *Journal of Personality and Social Psychology, 94*(1), 116–132.

Sidanius, J., & Pratto, F. (1999). *Social dominance: An intergroup theory of social hierarchy and oppression*. New York: Cambridge University Press.

Sidanius, J., & Pratto, F. (2001). *Social dominance*. Cambridge, UK: Cambridge University Press.

Sinaceur, M., & Tiedens, L. Z. (2006). Get mad and get more than even: When and why anger expression is effective in negotiations. *Journal of Experimental Social Psychology, 42*(3), 314–322.

Singer, T. (2006). The neuronal basis and ontogeny of empathy and mind reading: Review of literature and implications for future research. *Neuroscience & Biobehavioral Reviews, 30*(6), 855–863.

Singhal, A., Cody, M. J., Rogers, E. M., & Sabido, M. (Eds.). (2004). *Entertainment-education and social change*. Mahwah, NJ: Erlbaum.

Skitka, L. J., Bauman, C. W., Aramovich, N. P., & Morgan, G. S. (2006). Confrontational and preventative policy responses to terrorism: Anger wants a fight and fear wants "them" to go away. *Basic and Applied Social Psychology, 28*(4), 375–384.

Skitka, L. J., Bauman, C. W., & Mullen, E. (2004). Political tolerance and coming to psychological closure following the September 11, 2001, terrorist attacks: An integrative approach. *Personality and Social Psychology Bulletin, 30*, 743–756.

Skitka, L. J., Bauman, C. W., & Mullen, E. (2008). Morality and justice: An expanded theoretical perspective and review. In K. A. Hedgvedt, & J. Clay-Warner (Eds.), *Advances in group processes* (Vol. 25, pp. 1–27). Bingley: Emerald.

Skitka, L., Bauman, C. W., & Sargis, E. G. (2005). Moral conviction: Another contributor to attitude strength or something more? *Journal of Personality and Social Psychology, 88*(6), 895–917.

Slovic, P. (2007). "If I look at the mass I will never act": Psychic numbing and genocide. *Judgment and Decision Making, 2*(2), 79–95.

Small, D. A., Lerner, J. S., & Fischhoff, B. (2006). Emotion priming and attributions for terrorism: Americans' reactions in a national field experiment. *Political Psychology, 27*(2), 289–298.

Smith, A. (1759). *The theory of moral sentiments*. London: A. Millar, in the Strand.

Smith, C. A., & Ellsworth, P. C. (1985). Patterns of cognitive appraisal in emotion. *Journal of Personality and Social Psychology, 48*(4), 813–838.

Smith, C. A., Haynes, K. N., Lazarus, R. S., & Pope, L. K. (1993). In search of the "hot" cognitions: attributions, appraisals, and their relation to emotion. *Journal of Personality and Social Psychology, 65*(5), 916–929.

Smith, E. R. (1993). Social identity and social emotions: Toward new conceptualizations of prejudice. In D. M. Mackie, & D. L. Hamilton (Eds.), *Affect, cognition, and stereotyping: Interactive processes in group perception* (pp. 297–315). San Diego, CA: Academic Press.

Smith, E. R., Seger, C., & Mackie, D. M. (2007). Can emotions be truly group-level? Evidence regarding four conceptual criteria. *Journal of Personality and Social Psychology*, *93*(3), 431–446.

Smith, R. H., Powell, C. A., Combs, D. J., & Schurtz, D. R. (2009). Exploring the when and why of schadenfreude. *Social and Personality Psychology Compass*, *3*(4), 530–546.

Smith, R. H., Webster, M., Parrott, W. G., & Eyre, H. L. (2002). The role of public exposure in moral and non moral shame and guilt. *Journal of Personality and Social Psychology*, *83*(1), 138–159.

Smith, T. W., & Kim, S. (2006). National pride in comparative perspective. *International Journal of Public Opinion Research*, *18*(1), 127–136.

Snyder, C. R. (1994). *The psychology of hope.* New York: Free Press.

Snyder, C. R. (1995). Conceptualizing, measuring, and nurturing hope. *Journal of Counseling and Development*, *73*(3), 335–360.

Snyder, C. R. (2000). The past and possible futures of hope. *Journal of Social and Clinical Psychology*, *19*(1), 11–28.

Snyder, C. R., Cheavens, J., & Michael, S. T. (1999). Hoping. In C. R. Snyder (Ed.), *Coping: The psychology of what works* (pp. 205–231). New York: Oxford University Press.

Snyder, C. R., Harris, C., Anderson, J. R., Holleran, S. A., Irving, L. M., Sigmon, S. T., . . . Harney, P. (1991). The will and the ways: Development and validation of an individual-differences measure of hope. *Journal of Personality and Social Psychology*, *60*(4), 570–585.

Snyder, C. R., Sympson, S. C., Ybasco, F. C., Borders, T. F., Babyak, M. A., & Higgins, R. (1996). Development and validation of the state Hope Scale. *Journal of Personality and Social Psychology*, *70*(2), 321–335.

Spanovic, M., Lickel, B., Denson, T. F., & Petrovic, N. (2010). Fear and anger as predictors of motivation for intergroup aggression: Evidence from Serbia and Republika Srpska. *Group Processes & Intergroup Relations*, *13*(6), 725–733.

Spencer, H. (1895). *Principles of psychology.* London,: Longman, Brown, & Green.

Staats, S. R., & Stassen, M. A. (1985). Hope: An affective cognition. *Social Indicators Research*, *17*(3), 235–242.

Statman, D. (2002). Humiliation, dignity and self-respect. In D. Kretzmer, & E. Klein (Eds.), *The concept of human dignity in human rights discourse* (pp. 209–229). The Hague, the Netherlands: Kluwer.

Staub, E. (1989). *The roots of evil: The origins of genocide and other group violence.* New York: Cambridge University Press.

Staub, E. (2003). *The psychology of good and evil: Why children, adults, and groups help and harm others.* New York: Cambridge University Press.

Staub, E. (2005). The origins and evolution of hate, with notes on prevention. In R. J. Sternberg (Ed.), *The psychology of hate* (pp. 51–66). Washington, DC: American Psychological Association.

Staub, E. (2006). Reconciliation after genocide, mass killing or intractable conflict: Understanding the roots of violence, psychological recovery and steps toward a general theory. *Political Psychology*, *27*(6), 867–895.

Staub, E. (2011). *Overcoming evil: Genocide, violent conflict and terrorism.* New York: Oxford University Press.

Steele, C. M. (1988). The psychology of self-affirmation: Sustaining the integrity of the self. *Advances in Experimental Social Psychology*, *21*, 261–302.

Steele, R. R., Parker, M. T., & Lickel, B. (2015). Bias within because of threat from outside: The effects of an external call for terrorism on anti-Muslim attitudes in the United States. *Social Psychological and Personality Science*, *6*(2), 193–200.

Steinberg, B. (1991). Shame and humiliation in the Cuban Missile Crisis: A psychoanalytic perspective. *Political Psychology, 12*, 653–690.

Steinel, W., Van Kleef, G. A., & Harinck, F. (2008). Are you talking to me? Separating the people from the problem when expressing emotions in negotiation. *Journal of Experimental Social Psychology, 44*(2), 362–369.

Stephan, W. G., & Finlay, K. (1999). The role of empathy in improving intergroup relations. *Journal of Social Issues, 55*(4), 729–743.

Stephan, W. G., & Renfro, L. (2002). The role of threat in intergroup relations. In D. Mackie, & E. Smith (Eds.), *From prejudice to intergroup emotions: Differentiated reactions to social groups* (pp. 265–283). New York: Psychology Press.

Stephan, W. G., & Stephan, C. W. (2000). An integrated threat theory of prejudice. Reducing prejudice and discrimination. In S. Oskamp (Ed.), *Reducing prejudice and discrimination* (pp. 23–45). Mahwah, NJ: Lawrence Erlbaum.

Sternberg, R. J. (2003). A duplex theory of hate: Development and application to terrorism, massacres, and genocide. *Review of General Psychology, 7*(3), 299–328.

Sternberg, R. J. (2005). The theory of successful intelligence. *Interamerican Journal of Psychology, 39*(2), 189–202.

Sternberg, R., & Sternberg, K. (2008). *The nature of hatred.* New York: Cambridge University Press.

Stewart, T. L., Latu, I. M., Branscombe, N. R., & Denney, H. T. (2010). Yes we can! Prejudice reduction through seeing (inequality) and believing (in social change). *Psychological Science, 21*, 1557–1562.

Stone, R. A. (1982). *Social change in Israel: Attitudes and events, 1967–79.* New York: Praeger.

Stotland, E. (1969). *The psychology of hope.* San Francisco: Jossey-Bass.

Stouffer, S. A. (1955). *Communism, conformity, and civil liberties.* New York: Doubleday.

Sulitzeanu-Kenan, R., & Halperin, E. (2013). Making a difference: Political efficacy and policy preferences polarization. *British Journal of Political Science, 43*(2), 295–322.

Sullivan, G. B. (2007a). A critical psychology of pride. *International Journal of Critical Psychology, 21*, 166–189.

Sullivan, G. B. (2007b). Collective pride, happiness and celebratory emotions: Aggregate, network and cultural models. In M. Salmela, & C. vin Scheve (Eds.), *Collective emotions* (pp. 266–280). Oxford, UK: Oxford University Press.

Sullivan, G. B. (2014). *Understanding collective pride and group identity: New directions in emotion theory, research and practice.* New York: Routledge.

Sullivan, J. L., Walsh, P., Shamir, M., Barnum, D. G., & Gibson, J. L. (1993). Why politicians are more tolerant: Selective recruitment and socialization among political elites in Britain, Israel, New Zealand and the United States. *British Journal of Political Science, 23*(1), 51–76.

Sully, J. (1892). *The human mind* (Vol. 2). London: Longmans, Green.

Sumner, W. G. (1906). *Folkways.* Boston: Ginn.

Suri, G., Sheppes, G., & Gross, J. J. (2013). Emotion regulation and cognition. In M. D. Robinson, E. R. Watkins, & E. Harmon-Jones (Eds.), *Handbook of cognition and emotion* (pp. 195–209). New York: Guilford.

Swim, J. K., & Miller, D. L. (1999). White guilt: Its antecedents and consequences for attitudes toward affirmative action. *Personality and Social Psychology Bulletin, 25*(4), 500–514.

Tajfel, H. (1978). Social categorization, social identity and social comparison. In H. Tajfel (Ed.), *Differentiation between social groups: Studies in the social psychology of intergroup relations* (pp. 61–76). London: Academic Press.

Tajfel, H., & Turner, J. C. (1986). The social identity theory of intergroup behavior. In W. G. Austin, & S. Worchel (Eds.), *Psychology of intergroup relations* (pp. 7–24). Chicago, IL: Nelson-Hall.

Tam, T., Hewstone, M., Cairns, E., Tausch, N., Maio, G., & Kenworthy, J. (2007). The impact of intergroup emotions on forgiveness in Northern Ireland. *Group Processes & Intergroup Relations, 10*(1), 119–135.

Tam, T., Hewstone, M., Kenworthy, J., Voci, A., Cairns, E., & Van-Dick, R. (2008). *The role of intergroup emotions and empathy in contact between Catholics and Protestants in Northern Ireland.* Manuscript in preparation.

Tamir, M. (2009). What do people want to feel and why? Pleasure and utility in emotion regulation. *Current Directions in Psychological Science, 18*(2), 101–105.

Tamir, M., Bigman, Y., Rhodes, E., Salerno, J., & Schreier, J. (2015). An expectancy-value model of emotion regulation: Implications for motivation, emotional experience, and decision-making. *Emotion, 15*, 90–103.

Tamir, M., & Ford, B. Q. (2009). Choosing to be afraid: Preferences for fear as a function of goal pursuit. *Emotion, 9*(4), 488–497.

Tamir, M., & Ford, B. Q. (2012a). Should people pursue feelings that feel good or feelings that do good? Emotional preferences and well-being. *Emotion, 12*(5), 1061–1070.

Tamir, M., & Ford, B. Q. (2012b). When feeling bad is expected to be good: Emotion regulation and outcome expectancies in social conflicts. *Emotion, 12*(4), 807–816.

Tamir, M., Mitchell, C., & Gross, J. J. (2008). Hedonic and instrumental motives in anger regulation. *Psychological Science, 19*(4), 324–328.

Tangney, J. P. (1991). Moral affect: The good, the bad, and the ugly. *Journal of Personality and Social Psychology, 61*(4), 598–607.

Tangney, J. P., & Fischer, K. W. (Eds.). (1995). *Self-conscious emotions: The psychology of shame, guilt, embarrassment, and pride.* New York: Guilford.

Tangney, J. P., Miller, R., Flicker, L., & Barlow, D. H. (1996). Are shame, guilt, and embarrassment distinct emotions? *Journal of Personality and Social Psychology, 70*(6), 1256–1269.

Tangney, J. P., Stuewig, J., & Mashek, D. (2007). Moral emotions and moral behavior. *Annual Review of Psychology, 58*, 345–372.

Tangney, J. P., Wagner, P., & Gramzow, R. (1989). *The Test of Self Conscious Affect (TOSCA).* Fairfax, VA: George Mason University.

Tarrant, M., Calitri, R., & Weston, D. (2012). Social identification structures the effects of perspective-taking. *Psychological Science, 23*(9), 973–978.

Tarrant, M., Dazeley, S., & Cottom, T. (2009). Social categorization and empathy for outgroup members. *British Journal of Social Psychology, 48*(3), 427–446.

Tausch, N., Becker, C. J., Spears, R., Christ, O., Saab, R., Singh, P., & Siddiqui, R. N. (2011). Explaining radical group behavior: Developing emotion and efficacy routes to normative and nonnormative collective action. *Journal of Personality and Social Psychology, 101*(1), 129–148.

Tavuchis, N. (1991). *Mea culpa: A sociology of apology.* Palo Alto, CA: Stanford University Press.

Tedin, K. L. (1987). Political ideology and the vote. *Research in Micropolitics, 2*, 63–94.

Tennen, H., & Affleck, G. (2002). Benefit-finding and benefit reminding. In C. R. Snyder, & S. Lopez (Eds.), *Handbook of positive psychology* (pp. 584–597). New York: Oxford University Press.

Tetlock, P. (2003). Thinking the unthinkable: Sacred values and taboo cognitions. *Trends in Cognitive Sciences, 7*(7), 320–324.

Tetlock, P. E., Visser, P. S., Singh, R., Polifroni, M., Scott, A., Elson, S. B., . . . Rescober, P. (2007). People as intuitive prosecutors: The impact of social control goals on attributions of responsibility. *Journal of Experimental Social Psychology, 43*(2), 195–209.

Thomaes, S., Stegge, H., Olthof, T., Bushman, B. J., & Nezlek, J. B. (2011). Turning shame inside-out: "Humiliated fury" in young adolescents. *Emotion, 11*(4), 786–793.

Tiedens, L. Z. (2001). Anger and advancement versus sadness and subjugation: The effect of negative emotion expressions on social status conferral. *Journal of Personality and Social Psychology, 80*(1), 86–94.

Tiedens, L. Z., & Linton, S. (2001). Judgment under emotional certainty and uncertainty: The effects of specific emotions and their associated certainty appraisals on cognitive processing. *Journal of Personality and Social Psychology, 81*(6), 973–988.

Todd, A. R., Bodenhausen, G. V., Richeson, J. A., & Galinsky, A. D. (2011). Perspective taking combats automatic expressions of racial bias. *Journal of Personality and Social Psychology, 100*(6), 1027–1042.

Tooby, J., & Cosmides, L. (1990). The past explains the present: Emotional adaptations and the structure of ancestral environments. *Ethology and Sociobiology, 11*, 375–424.

Tooby, J., & Cosmides, L. (2006). The past explains the present: Emotional adaptations and the structure of ancestral environments. *Ethology and Sociobiology, 11*, 375–424.

Torres, W. J., & Bergner, R. M. (2012). Severe public humiliation: Its nature, consequences, and clinical treatment. *Psychotherapy, 49*, 492–501.

Totterdell, P., Kellett, S., Teuchmann, K., & Briner, R. B. (1998). Evidence of mood linkage in work groups. *Journal of Personality and Social Psychology, 74*, 1504–1515.

Tracy, J. L., Cheng, J. T., Robins, R. W., & Trzesniewski, K. H. (2009). Authentic and hubristic pride: The affective core of self-esteem and narcissism. *Self and Identity, 8*(2–3), 196–213.

Tracy, J. L., & Robins, R. W. (2003). "Death of a (narcissistic) salesman": An integrative model of fragile self-esteem. *Psychological Inquiry, 14*, 57–62.

Tracy, J. L., & Robins, R. W. (2007). The psychological structure of pride: A tale of two facets. *Journal of Personality and Social Psychology, 92*, 506–525.

Tracy, J. L., & Robins, R. W. (2004). Show your pride: Evidence for a discrete emotion expression. *Psychological Science, 15*(3), 194–197.

Tracy, J. L., & Robins, R. W. (2006). Appraisal antecedents of shame and guilt: Support for a theoretical model. *Personality and Social Psychology Bulletin, 32*(10), 1339–1351.

Tracy, J. L., & Robins, R. W. (2008). The nonverbal expression of pride: Evidence for cross-cultural recognition. *Journal of Personality and Social Psychology, 94*(3), 516–530.

Tracy, J. L., Weidman, A. C., Cheng, J. T., & Martens, J. P. (2014). Pride: The fundamental emotion of success, power, and status. In M. M. Tugade, M. N. Shiota, & L. D. Kirby (Eds.), *Handbook of positive emotions* (pp. 294–310). New York: Guilford.

Tull, M. T., Barrett, H. M., McMillan, E. S., & Roemer, L. (2007). A preliminary investigation of the relationship between emotion regulation difficulties and posttraumatic stress symptoms. *Behavior Therapy, 38*(3), 303–313.

Turner, J. C., Hogg, M. A., Oakes, P. J., Reicher, S. D., & Wetherell, M. S. (1987). *Rediscovering the social group: A self-categorization theory.* New York: Basil Blackwell.

Turner, J. C., Oakes, P. J., Haslam, A., & McGarty, C. (1994). Self and collective: Cognition and social context. *Personality and Social Psychology Bulletin, 20*, 454–463.

Turner, J. C., & Reynolds, K. (2001). The social identity perspective in intergroup relations: Theories, themes and controversies. In R. Brown, & S. Gaertner (Eds.), *Blackwell handbook in social psychology: Intergroup processes* (Vol. 4, pp. 133–152). Oxford, UK: Blackwell.

Tutu, D. (1999). *No future without forgiveness.* New York: Doubleday.

Uddin, L. Q., Iacoboni, M., Lange, C., & Keenan, J. P. (2007). The self and social cognition: The role of cortical midline structures and mirror neurons. *Trends in Cognitive Sciences, 11*, 153–157.

Van Dijk, E., Van Kleef, G. A., Steinel, W., & Van Beest, I. (2008). A social functional approach to emotions in bargaining: When communicating anger pays and when it backfires. *Journal of Personality and Social Psychology, 94*(4), 600–614.

Van Doorn, E. A., Heerdink, M. W., & Van Kleef, G. (2012). Emotion and the construal of social situations: Inferences of cooperation versus competition from expressions of anger, happiness, and disappointment. *Cognition and Emotion, 26*(3), 442–461.

Van Kleef, G. A. (2009). How emotions regulate social life the emotions as social information (EASI) model. *Current Directions in Psychological Science, 18*(3), 184–188.

Van Kleef, G. A., & Côté, S. (2007). Expressing anger in conflict: When it helps and when it hurts. *Journal of Applied Psychology, 92*(6), 1557–1569.

Van Kleef, G. A., & De Dreu, C. K. (2010). Longer-term consequences of anger expression in negotiation: Retaliation or spillover? *Journal of Experimental Social Psychology, 46*(5), 753–760.

Van Kleef, G. A., De Dreu, C. K., & Manstead, A. S. (2004a). The interpersonal effects of anger and happiness in negotiations. *Journal of Personality and Social Psychology, 86*(1), 57–76.

Van Kleef, G. A., De Dreu, C. K., & Manstead, A. S. (2004b). The interpersonal effects of emotions in negotiations: A motivated information processing approach. *Journal of Personality and Social Psychology, 87*(4), 510–528.

Van Kleef, G. A., De Dreu, C. K., & Manstead, A. S. (2006). Supplication and appeasement in conflict and negotiation: The interpersonal effects of disappointment, worry, guilt, and regret. *Journal of Personality and Social Psychology, 91*(1), 124–142.

Van Kleef, G. A., De Dreu, C. K., & Manstead, A. S. (2010). An interpersonal approach to emotion in social decision making: The Emotions as Social Information model. In M. P. Zanna (Ed.), *Advances in experimental social psychology* (Vol. 42, pp. 45–96). San Diego, CA: Academic Press.

Van Kleef, G. A., De Dreu, C. K., Pietroni, D., & Manstead, A. S. (2006). Power and emotion in negotiation: Power moderates the interpersonal effects of anger and happiness on concession making. *European Journal of Social Psychology, 36*(4), 557–581.

Van-Zomeren, M., & Iyer, A. (2009). Introduction to the social and psychological dynamics of collectiveaction. *Journal of Social Issues, 65*(4), 645–660.

Van-Zomeren, M., Leach, C. W., & Spears, R. (2012). Protesters as "passionate economists": A dynamic dual pathway model of approach coping with collective disadvantage. *Personality and Social Psychology Review, 16*(2), 180–199.

Van-Zomeren, M., Postmes, T., & Spears, R. (2008). Toward an integrative Social Identity Model of Collective Action: A quantitative research synthesis of three socio-psychological perspectives. *Psychological Bulletin, 134*, 504–535.

Van-Zomeren, M., Spears, R., Fischer, A. H., & Leach, C. W. (2004). Put your money where your mouth is! Explaining collective action tendencies through group-based anger and group efficacy. *Journal of Personality and Social Psychology, 87*(5), 649–664.

Vescio, T. K., Sechrist, G. B., & Paolucci, M. P. (2003). Perspective taking and prejudice reduction: The mediational role of empathy arousal and situational attributions. *European Journal of Social Psychology, 33*(4), 455–472.

Volkan, V. (1997). *Bloodlines: From ethnic pride to ethnic terrorism.* New York: Farrar, Straus Giroux.

Vollhardt, J. R. (2012a). Collective victimization. In L. Tropp (Ed.), *Oxford handbook of intergroup conflict* (pp. 136–157). New York: Oxford University Press.

Vollhardt, J. R. (2012b). Interpreting rights and duties after mass violence. *Culture and Psychology, 18*, 133–145.

Vollhardt, J. R. (2013). "Crime against humanity" or "crime against Jews"? Acknowledgment in construals of the Holocaust and its importance for intergroup relations. *Journal of Social Issues, 69*(1), 144–161.

Vollhardt, J. R. (2014). The question of legitimacy in studying collective trauma. In I. Macek (Ed.), *Engaging violence: Trauma, memory, and representation* (pp. 74–90). New York: Routledge.

von Scheve, C., & Ismer, S. (2013). Towards a theory of collective emotions. *Emotion Review, 5*(4), 406–413.

Vorauer, J. D., & Sasaki, S. J. (2009). Helpful only in the abstract? Ironic effects of empathy in intergroup interaction. *Psychological Science, 20*(2), 191–197.

Walker, J., & Knauer, V. (2011). Humiliation, self-esteem, and violence. *The Journal of Forensic Psychiatry & Psychology, 22*(5), 724–741.

Walley, R. E., & Weiden, T. D. (1973). Lateral inhibition and cognitive masking: A neuropsychological theory of attention. *Psychological Review, 80*(4), 284–302.

Waytz, A., Zaki, J., & Mitchell, J. P. (2012). Response of dorsomedial prefrontal cortex predicts altruistic behavior. *The Journal of Neuroscience, 32*(22), 7646–7650.

Webb, T. L., Miles, E., & Sheeran, P. (2012). Dealing with feeling: A meta-analysis of the effectiveness of strategies derived from the process model of emotion regulation. *Psychological Bulletin, 138*, 775–808.

Weiner, B. (1985). An attributional theory of achievement motivation and emotion. *Psychological Review, 92*(4), 548–573.

Weiner, B. (1986). *An attributional theory of motivation and emotion.* New York: Springer.

Weiner, B. (1995). *Judgments of responsibility: A foundation for a theory of social conduct.* London: Guildford.

Wertsch, J. (2002). *Voices of collective remembering.* Cambridge, UK: Cambridge University Press.

Wertsch, J. V. (2009). Collective memory. In P. Boyer, & J. V. Wertsch (Eds.), *Memory in mind and culture.* (pp. 117–137). New York: Cambridge University Press.

Whalen, P. J., Rauch, S. L., Etcoff, N. L., McInerney, S. C., Lee, M. B., & Jenike, M. A. (1998). Masked presentations of emotional facial expressions modulate amygdala activity without explicit knowledge. *Journal of Neuroscience, 18*(1), 411–418.

White, R. K. (1968). *Nobody wanted war: Misperception in Vietnam and other wars.* Garden City, NY: Doubleday.

White, R. K. (1984). *Fearful warriors: A psychological profile of U.S.—Soviet relations.* New York: Free Press.

White, R. K. (1996). Why the Serbs fought: Motives and misperceptions. *Peace and Conflict: Journal of Peace Psychology, 2*(2), 109–128.

Wispe, L. (1986). The distinction between sympathy and empathy: To call forth a concept, a word is needed. *Journal of Personality and Social Psychology, 50*(2), 314–321.

Wohl, M. J., & Branscombe, N. R. (2005). Forgiveness and collective guilt assignment to historical perpetrator groups depend on level of social category inclusiveness. *Journal of Personality and Social Psychology, 88*, 288–303.

Wohl, M. J., & Branscombe, N. R. (2008). Remembering historical victimization: Collective guilt for current ingroup transgressions. *Journal of Personality and Social Psychology, 94*(6), 988–1006.

Wohl, M. J., & Branscombe, N. R. (2009). Group threat, collective angst and ingroup forgiveness for the war in Iraq. *Political Psychology*, *30*(2), 193–217.

Wohl, M. J., Branscombe, N. R., & Klar, Y. (2006). Collective guilt: Emotional reactions when one's group has done wrong or been wronged. *European Review of Social Psychology*, *17*(1), 1–37.

Wohl, M. J., Branscombe, N. R., & Reysen, S. (2010). Percieving your group's future to be in jeopardy: Extinction threat induces collective angst and the desire to stregnthen the ingroup. *Personality and Social Psychology Bulletin*, *36*, 898–910.

Wohl, M., Cohen-Chen, S., Halperin, E., Caouette, J., Hayes, N., & Hornsey, M. J. (2015). Belief in the malleability of groups strengthens the tenuous link between a collective apology and intergroup forgiveness. *Personality and Social Psychology Bulletin*, *41*, 714–725.

Wohl, M., Giguère, B., Branscombe, N., & McVicar, D. (2011). One day we might be no more: Collective angst and protective action from potential distinctiveness loss. *European Journal of Social Psychology*, *41*(3), 289–300.

Wohl, M. J., Hornsey, M. J., & Bennett, S. H. (2012). Why group apologies succeed and fail: Intergroup forgiveness and the role of primary and secondary emotions. *Journal of Personality and Social Psychology*, *102*(2), 306–322.

Wohl, M. J., Matheson, K., Branscombe, N. R., & Anisman, H. (2013). Victim and perpetrator groups' responses to the Canadian government's apology for the head tax on Chinese immigrants and the moderating influence of collective guilt. *Political Psychology*, *34*(5), 713–729.

Wohl, M. J., Squires, E. C., & Caouette, J. (2012). We were, we are, will we be? The social psychology of collective angst. *Social and Personality Psychology Compass*, *6*(5), 379–391.

Wolf, E. J., Miller, M. W., & McKinney, A. E. (2009). Emotional processing in PTSD: Heightened negative emotionality to unpleasant photographic stimuli. *Journal of Nervous and Mental Disease*, *197*(6), 419–426.

Wolf, K. A., & Foshee, V. A. (2003). Family violence, anger expression styles, and adolescent dating violence. *Journal of Family Violence*, *18*(6), 309–316.

Wright, L. (2006). *The looming tower.* New York: Alfred Knopf.

Wright, S. C., & Lubensky, M. E. (2009). The struggle for social equality: Collective action versus prejudice reduction. In S. Demoulin, J. P. Leyens, & J. F. Dovidio (Eds.), *Intergroup misunderstandings: Impact of divergent social realities* (pp. 291–310). Philadelphia, PA: Psychology Press.

Wright, S. C., Taylor, D. M., & Moghaddam, F. M. (1990). Responding to membership in a disadvantaged group: From acceptance to collective protest. *Journal of Personality and Social Psychology*, *58*(6), 994–1003.

Wundt, W. (1924). *An introduction to psychology.* (R. Pintner, Trans.) London: Allen Unwin. (Original work published 1912)

Wundt, W. (1998). *Outlines of psychology.* (C. H. Judd, Trans.) Bristol, UK: Thoemmes Press (Original work published 1897)

Xu, X., Zuo, X., Wang, X., & Han, S. (2009). Do you feel my pain? Racial group membership modulates empathic neural responses. *Journal of Neuroscience*, *29*(26), 8525–8529.

Yanay, N. (2002). Understanding collective hatred. *Analyses of Social Issues and Public Policy*, *2*(1), 53–60.

Yzerbyt, V., Dumont, M., Wigboldus, D., & Gordin, E. (2003). I feel for us: The impact of categorization and identification on emotions and action tendencies. *British Journal of Social Psychology*, *42*(4), 533–549.

Yzerbyt, V., & Kuppens, T. (2013). From group-based appraisals to group-based emotions. In D. Hermans, B. Rimé, & B. Mesquita (Eds.), *Changing emotions* (pp. 97–104). New York: Psychology Press.

Zagefka, H., Pehrson, S., Mole, R., & Chan, E. (2010). The effect of essentialism in settings of historic intergroup atrocities. *European Journal of Social Psychology, 40*(5), 718–732.

Zajonc, R. B. (1980). Feeling and thinking: Preferences need no inferences. *American Psychologist, 35*(2), 151–175.

Zajonc, R. B. (1998). Emotions. In D. T. Gilbert, & S. T. Fiske (Eds.), *The handbook of social psychology* (4th ed., Vol. 1, pp. 591–632). New York: McGraw-Hill.

Zaki, J. (2013). Cue integration: A common framework for physical perception and social cognition. *Perspectives on Psychological Science, 8,* 296–312.

Zaki, J. (2014). Empathy: A motivated account. *Psychological Bulletin, 140*(6), 1608–1647.

Zaki, J., & Ochsner, K. N. (2012). The neuroscience of empathy: progress, pitfalls and promise. *Nature neuroscience, 15*(5), 675–680.

Zaki, J., Schirmer, J., & Mitchell, J. (2011). Social influence modulates the neural computation of value. *Psychological Science, 22*(7), 894–900.

Zaki, J., & Williams, W. C. (2013). Interpersonal emotion regulation. *Emotion, 13,* 803–810.

Zebel, S., Doosje, B., & Spears, R. (2009). How perspectivetaking helps and hinders group-based guilt as a function of group identification. *Group Processes & Intergroup Relations, 12*(1), 61–78.

Zebel, S., Zimmermann, A., Tendayi Viki, G., & Doosje, B. (2008). Dehumanization and guilt as distinct but related predictors of support for reparation policies. *Political Psychology, 29*(2), 193–219.

Zhou, Q., Valiente, C., & Eisenberg, N. (2003). Empathy and its measurement. In S. J. Lopez (Ed.), *Positive psychological assessment: A handbook of models and measures* (pp. 269–285). Washington, DC: American Psychological Association.

Zisser, E. (2010). Towards new year: Will this be the Israeli–Palestinian year of the Iranian year? [Hebrew]. Retrieved from http://news.nana10.co.il/Article/?ArticleID=744170

INDEX

Note: Page numbers in italic indicate tables and figures.

Abuelaish, Izzeldeen 132
action: anger, targeting 52; collective action 62; generalized attribution 46
action tendencies 12; anger core appraisal themes, linkage 53; by-product 21; emotion, relationship 20; translation 105–6
acute trauma disorders, prevalence 178
affective experiences, properties 21–2
affective intelligence theory 78
affective traits, threshold-setting function 23
aggression: anger, impact (absence) 54; fear, relationship 79–80; motivation, increase 13–14, 79–80
aggressive behavior, anger (emotional determinant) 51
altruistic motivation 125–6
ambush, situation 72
anger: affective structure 55–6; anger-associated emotional goals 54–5; hatred, contrast 54; anger-inducing stimulus 64; attack emotion family 56; communication 57; constructive actions 54; constructive role 63; core appraisal themes, emotional goals/action tendencies (linkage) 53; emotional complexity/ambiguity 32–3; feeling, explanation 17; group-based anger 58–60; hatred (extreme form) 39–40; hedonic considerations 58; impact 56–7;

absence 54; implications, interpersonal level 55–8; instrumental approach 126; intergroup anger 58–65; interpersonal anger 58–60; magnitude, focus 65; motivational implications 55–6; motivational tendencies 56; nature/ story 52–5; pluripotentiality 63–4; power, social psychology conviction 51; prototypical anger, presence 18; regulation 65–6; study 54; target, concern (demonstration) 54; targeting 52; destructive implications 60–1; Utku disapproval/suppression 27
angst: collective angst 67, 75; constructive aspect, implications 81–2; defensive-aggressive aspect, implications 76–81
anxiety-inducing intergroup encounter 160
apathy, despair (impact) 98
apology-forgiveness cycle 152
appraisals 12; dominancy 41; hatred-associated appraisals 39–40; theories, integration 23
appraisal tendency framework 23–4; basis 31
approach emotion, perspective 63–4
approach-oriented steps 65
Armenians, genocide (collective memory) 69

arousal (affective experience
  component) 22
asymmetrical conflicts 112; anger
  communication, association 57;
  challenges 112–13
atmosphere 27
Atran, Scott 153
attack emotion family 56
attentional deployment 160, 175
attitudes, hatred (impact) 49
attribution errors, fear (impact) 77–8
authentic (beta) pride 142
automatic empathy, motivated empathy
  (contrast) 126–7
automatic fear experiences 72

Bar-Tal, Daniel 67
behavioral motivations, humiliation
  (association) 144–5
beta (authentic) pride 142
biased information processing 78
black-and-white thinking 8–9
Bloom, Paul 122
bonding, facilitation 169
Bosnian War, Muslims (Serbian
  treatment) 114
boundary conditions 3
burning hate 45

Chechnya, conflicts 10
chronic anxiety, experience 143
chronic hatred 44, 45
citizens, kidnapping 51
civilians, killing 51
civil religion 27, 91
Civil Rights Movement 62
cognitive appraisals, usage 19–20
cognitive-based fear experiences 72
cognitive change 160–1, 176
cognitive reappraisal 160–1
collapse of compassion 136
collective action 62
collective angst 67, 75
collective emotional orientation 27
collective emotions: evocation, context
  26–7; role 8
collective fear 67, 73–6; continuous/
  chronic feeling 67; impact 79–80;
  orientation 78–9
collective guilt, upregulation 118–19
collective hope, long-term conflicts
  (relationship) 91

collective humiliation, denominator
  149–50
collective identity, aspects (differences)
  147–8
collective immoral actions/crimes 109
collective pride: connectedness, impact
  148; group reliance 145–6; impact
  146–7; mobilization vehicle 145–6
collective responsibility 109–10
collective (perceived) threat 73–6
collective victimhood, societal beliefs 69
Colman, Peter 178
Combatants for Peace 39
compassion, collapse 136
competitive victimhood, concept 113
Component Process Model 18
compromise, opposition 153
conflict resolution 101; emotion-based
  approach 16; emotion regulation,
  impact 155; hatred, implications
  47–9; hope: impact 91–2; role 93–4;
  promotion 116
conflicts: anger, implications (interpersonal
  level) 55–8; asymmetrical conflicts
  112; conflict-related events: attitudinal/
  behavioral responses 29; framing 19;
  political reactions 167; conflict-related
  obstacles, overcoming 167; dynamics
  95–6; emotion, role (interest, increase)
  29; ethos 59, 154; humiliation, role
  139; ideology, defining 2; intergroup
  conflicts, emotions/public opinion
  (appraisal-based framework) 28–33;
  intractable conflicts: intergroup anger
  58–65; intergroup hatred 34; nature,
  change 99; peaceful resolution 182;
  post-WWII occurrences 1–2; pride,
  role 139; short-term conflict-related
  events, evaluation 47–8; situation, direct
  manipulation situation 98–9
conformity, positive valuation 169
confrontational goals, pursuit 58
context-related obstacles, overcoming 167
convicted murderers, stigma 128
coping potential, reappraisal 83
counter-empathy, expression 152

decision makers, emotions (study) 11
decision making: emotions, role 6; process,
  study 11
deescalation stage, hope (role) 93–4
demographic threat 74

despair 84; conversion 98–100; feeling
92; difficulty 88; impact 90–3; nature
86–90; orientations 87
destructive emotions, regulation 164
destructive events, impact 156–7
devalued identity, assimilation 143
dichotomous appraisal dimensions 41
discrimination, extreme events 38–9
dissipation 95

ego threats, response 142
emotional barrier (hatred) 33
emotional burden 28
emotional climate 27
emotional contagion 169–70
emotional culture 27
emotional empathy 124
emotional experiences: behavioral/political
consequences 9; interpretive aspect 20;
intractable conflict, context (impact) 9;
role 126
emotional goals 12; anger core appraisal
themes, linkage 53; by-product 21;
group-based hatred, relationship 43–4;
hatred-associated emotional goals 43;
viewpoint 105
emotional phenomena, social processes/
group processes (interlocking) 24
emotional process, cognitive appraisals
19–20
emotional reactions, ignoring 123
emotional responses 158; elicitation 120
emotional sentiments: hatred 48–9; impact
29; long-term emotional sentiments,
bias 31
emotion-based conceptual framework,
usage 16–17
emotion-eliciting events: evidence 176;
reactions 31
emotion regulation: conceptualization
157–62; context 167–78; dominant
conceptualizations 157; forward-looking
approach 159; impact 155; indirect
approach 164–5; indirect emotion
regulation *165*; instrumental emotion
regulation, occurrence 126–7;
integration 167; intractable conflicts
162–7; intrapersonal level 158; processes
65–6, 159; exposure, repetition 178–80;
process model 159; reference 157;
strategies 173–8; problems 181–2;
usage 14

Emotion Regulation Questionnaire
(ERQ) 162
emotions: action tendency, relationship
20; appraisal-based framework 28–33;
appraisal theories 19, 160–1; integration
23; change, capability 14; clarification
21–4; collective aspect 24–8; destructive
emotions, regulation 164; goals 37–42;
group-based emotions (applications)
166; group-based emotions (regulation):
emotion regulation strategies 173–8;
hedonic/instrumental motivations
168–73; hatred, comparison 44–6;
impact 9; individual-based emotions
167; individual-level emotions, criteria
24; intentionality 22; intergroup
emotion 12; moods, contrast 22;
multi-componentiality 22; nature
17–21; new approaches, implementation
(challenges) 182; operation, assumption
7; pornography, comparison 16; public
role 18–19; role 22–3; example *32*;
secondary emotions 23; self-regulation
173; social information 11
emotions as social information (EASI)
11, 96
emotions in conflicts: assumptions 7–15;
study, status 5–7; theoretical/empirical
challenges 181–2
empathic concern 123–5; pro-social
behavior, linkage 125
empathic perspective taking 129
empathy: affective aspect 124; automatic
empathy, motivated empathy (contrast)
126–7; development, underpinnings
127; empathy-focused peace education/
dialogue 121–2; feeling 120; impact
133–4; intergroup biases 129–32;
intergroup context 128–9; intergroup
empathy bias 130–1; nature 123–6;
peace catalyst 120; quantitative
upregulation 136; regulation 127, 135–8;
research 128; subcomponents 124–5;
upregulation 136; usage (intractable
conflicts) 132–5
enemy, knowledge 129
Erdogan, Recep Tayyip 139–40
ethnic groups, cessation (possibility)
75–6
ethos of conflict 59
Euskadi Ta Askatasuna (ETA), negotiation
61, 80–1

events: appraisal, factors 30–1; biased evaluations 51; emotional responses, absence 19; short-term events 87; situation modification, viability 174–5; unfairness, appraisal 63
evil/not evil appraisal dimension 41
evil, outgroup perception 42
extreme conflicts 164

fear: automatic fear experiences 72; behavioral implications 72–3; categories, automatic imposition 72; chronic feelings 68; cognitive-based fear experiences 72; collective fear 67; conscious appraisal process, impact 71–2; constructive aspect, implications 81–2; defensive-aggressive aspect, implications 76–81; emotional antecedent, impact 32; fear-aggression relationship, complexity 79–80; feelings: power 68; understanding 24; group-based fear: experience 74; role 77; impact 77–8; levels, reduction 83; long-term feelings 23; low strength/ control, appraisal 71; nature 71–3; personal fear 76; qualitative change, quantitative change (contrast) 82–3; regulation 82–3; societal level, impact 77
feelings, change 155
fight options, risk (potential) 82–3
fundamental attribution error 45

Gaza offensive, Israeli public support 132
Gaza, war 93
genocide, collective memory (Armenians) 69
Ginges, Geremy 153
glorification-based pride 148
goal-directed behavior 86
grave atrocities, commission 109
group-based actions, motivator 59
group-based anger 58–60; feelings 172
group-based emotions 17; applications 166; connections 111; elicitation 26, 174; extension 168; impact 26, 29; influences 25–6; regulation 170–1; conflicts 172–3; self-categorization, psychological basis 26
group-based emotions (regulation): emotion regulation strategies 173–8; hedonic/instrumental motivations 168–73

group-based events: direct exposure 178; modification, influence (limitation) 175
group-based fear: experience 74; role 77
group-based guilt 101, 107–14; antecedents/consequences 117; appraisal 110–12; drivers 109; elicitation 108; empirical evidence 115; feeling: dominance 31; rarity 114; identifiers, comparison 111–12; impact 115–16; implication 103, 114–16; orientation 116; upregulation 116
group-based hatred, emotional goal (relationship) 43–4
group-based humiliation 148
group-based motivations 129
group-based sadness, experience 169–70
group-based shame 109, 117
group-based similarity, process 130–1
group entitativity, perceptions 130
group members: action, psychological process 102–3; sacrifice 171
group natures, incremental/malleable view 165
guilt: antecedents, examination 108–9; appraisals 107; attributions 107; collective guilt, upregulation 118–19; costs 116; definition 104; feelings, associations 114; group-based guilt 101, 107–14; elicitation 108; empirical evidence 115; guilt-associated goals, translation 105–6; guilt-inducing manipulation 116; long-term guilt, experience 23; motivations, viewpoint 105; nature 104–7; origin 104; regulation 116–19; role 106; sense, increase 170
Gush Etzion, Israeli teenagers (murder) 101

happiness, positive feelings 141–2
harm, extreme events 38–9
haters, actions (preferences) 42–4
hating emotional attitude 45
hatred: anger-associated emotional goals, contrast 54; appraisals, targeting 44; burning hate 45; causal mechanism 45–6; chronic hatred 45; cognitive appraisals, study 54; collective emotion, transformation (ease) 46–7; destructiveness 35–6; deterministic nature 48; development, requirements 46; emotional barrier 32; emotional

sentiment 48–9; emotions: comparison
44–6; direction 41; unambiguity
37; empirical research, absence 36;
endurance 44; events 38; biased
evaluations 51; experience 44; appraisals,
uniqueness 41–2; perception 38;
hatred-associated appraisals 39–40;
hatred-associated emotional goals
43; hatred-malleability studies 166;
illegitimate social emotion, perspective
36–7; immediate hatred 45; implications
47–9; influence 48; intergroup context
46–7; intergroup emotions, importance
37; motivational/behavioral tendencies
42–4; nature/appraisal/emotional goals
37–42; outgroup hate 45; reflection
42–3; sentiment, hatred emotion
(contrast) 44–6
hedonic goals 170–1
hedonic motivations 168–73
high-power groups, humiliation
(experience) 149
hope 84; appraisals 88; behavioral
tendencies, empirical research 90;
collective hope, long-term conflicts
(relationship) 91; conceptualization
87–8; despair, conversion 98–100;
experience 89; difficulty 92; rarity 92;
impact 90–3, 96; implications 93–8;
induced hope 98–9; motivational/
behavioral role 89–90; nature 86–90;
optimism, contrast 88; orientations 87;
outgroup expressions 96; Palestinian
expression, Israeli reaction 97–8;
regulation 98–100; short-term emotion
87; upregulation 96
hopelessness: despair, impact 98; feeling 92;
difficulty 88
hostility (reduction), hope (constructive
role) 95
hubristic pride 148
human behavior: emotions: impact 5, 9;
power, assumption 9; environment,
function 7–8; pride, importance 142
human beings, nature (impact) 5–6
humiliated fury 145
humiliation: avoidance 148–9; behavioral
motivations, association 144–5;
decrease, impact 153; definition 143;
experience 149; feelings, understanding
25; formative experience 151; impact
149; intergroup context 145–50; nature

141–5; perception 140–1; post-World
War I Germany 150; regulation, usage
151–4; role 139; shame, separation 144

identification 25
ideology of conflict, defining 2
immediate hatred 44, 45
immoral actions: justification 113–14;
personal responsibility, appraisal 105
individual-based emotions 167;
impact 26
individual-level emotions, criteria 24
Indonesia, Dutch colonization 146
induced hope 98–9
inertia effect 151
ingroup: focus 116; ingroup-outgroup
dynamics, implications 59; love 45;
non-legitimate acts, relegitimizing 113;
victimization 113
instrumental emotion regulation,
occurrence 126–7
instrumental motivations 168–73
integrated threat theory 73, 74
intentional/unintentional harm 41
intergroup aggression: motivation, anger
(role) 61; restraint 122–3
intergroup anger 50, 58–65; constructive
role, process 62–5; impact,
understanding 60; phenomenon, nuance
65; political aggression, association 61;
prediction, ability 58–9; role 59
intergroup apologies 152–3
intergroup behavioral intentions
(prediction), anger (usage) 58–9
intergroup biases: amplification, fear
(impact) 77–8; empathy 129–32
intergroup conflicts: context, research
(application) 14; emotions/public
opinion, appraisal-based framework
28–33; group-based fear, role 77;
group-based guilt, implications 114–16;
hatred, influence 48; intergroup
anger, role 59; long-term intergroup
conflict, context 35–6; mass murder/
massacre, involvement (absence) 35;
outgroup, anger targeting (destructive
implications) 60–1; study, emotions
(incorporation) 6–7
intergroup context: empathy 128–9; hatred
46–7; pride/humiliation 145–50
intergroup emotion 12; integration 167;
theory 10; uniqueness 12

intergroup emotions theory (IET) 25, 111; development 59–60
intergroup empathy 121–2; bias 130–1; experience, increase 137–8; increase 122–3
intergroup hatred: experience, precondition 40; expression 43; formation, sequence 40; peace barrier 34; reduction 49
intergroup reconciliation, intergroup apologies 152–3
intergroup relations: anger, positive effects 65; research 128
internal criticism, exposure 99–100
interpersonal anger 58–60
interpersonal bargaining, guilt (role) 106
interpersonal conflicts: anger, impact 56–7; dynamic, influence 58
interventions, limitation 99
intractable conflicts: aggressive policies 151; angst: constructive aspect, implications 81–2; defensive-aggressive aspect, implications 76–81; bottom-up processes 11–12; Catch-22 139; characteristics 62, 85; chronic fear, experience 68; collective setting 8; conceptualization 68; constructive aspect 81–2; context: endurance 10–11; living 90–1; defensive-aggressive aspect 76–81; despair, impact 90–3; difficulties 1; emotion regulation 157–62; empathy: peace catalyst 120; usage 132–5; fear: constructive aspect, implications 81–2; defensive-aggressive aspect, implications 76–81; group-based guilt: impact 115–16; implications 103, 106–7, 114–16; hope: experience, rarity 92; impact 90–3; implications 93–8; indirect emotion regulation 165; intergroup anger 50; constructive role, process 62–5; impact 58–60; intergroup hatred, peace barrier 34; moral emotions 101; positive effects, empathy (impact) 133–4; pro-peace collective actions, involvement 62; psychological context 8; public opinion/behavior 4; resolution, promotion 81; stressful context 86; threat, embedding 80
intra-societal Israeli context, usage 163
Iranian atomic bomb, impact 74–5
Iraq: American military actions, support 80; American military response, support 21

Israel: deterrence capabilities, restoration 133; existence (threat), Iranian atomic bomb (impact) 74–5; government, Operation Cast Lead 139–40; intra-societal Israeli context, usage 163
Israeli-Arab conflict, collective fear (relationship) 78–9
Israeli Defense Forces (IDF), Palestinian deaths 101
Israeli-Palestinian conflict 24–5; context 64, 121; continuation, blame 59–60; future: description 99; hope, impact 98–9; solutions 25
Israeli-Palestinian negotiations 64
Israeli-Palestinian peace negotiations 80–1
Israeli-Palestinian peace process, promotion 78

Jewish Israelis 166; hope 94
Jewish state, destruction (Iranian leader call) 76
Jews, morale (decrease) 27–8
joy, positive feelings 141–2
justice, universal principles 104
just/unjust event 41

Kashmir, conflicts 10
Kerry, John 85
Kibush Naor 146
Kosovar Albanian woman, hatred experience 44

large-scale conflicts 175
Leach, Colin 116
leaders, emotions (study) 11
left-wing ideology 172
long-term conflicts 131–2; collective hope, relationship 91; context, moral emotions (impact) 103; emotions, role 22–3; escalation 35–6; examination 2–3; maintenance 35–6; negative emotions 156
long-term despair, feeling 23
long-term emotional sentiments, bias 31
long-term friendships 31
long-term guilt, experience 23
long-term intergroup conflict, context 35–6
long-term oppression, context 110
lowering 143
low/high coping potential 41

low-power groups, humiliation (impact) 149
low-power negotiators, impact 57

Mackie, Diane 58
Margalit, Avishai 151
mass atrocities, commission 109
Meatim Mul Rabim 146
media channels, ideas (embedding) 182
Memorial Day (Israel) 174
mentalizing 123
Middle East, conflicts 10
military actions support (increase), intergroup anger (impact) 60
military forces, offensive maneuvers 51
mind reading 123
Mohamad, Mahathir 140
moods: clarification 21–4; emotions, contrast 22
morale, decrease 27–8
moral emotions 101; impact 103
moral entitlement 114
moral exclusion theory 40–1
morality, subjectively oriented view 104
moral progress, involvement 128
moral values, endorsement 172
motivated empathy, automatic empathy (contrast) 126–7
motivational obstacles, overcoming 167
Muslims, Serbian treatment 114

naïve realism, concept 6
nationalistic pride 148
Nazi Germany, White Rose (story) 102
negative affective responses, response (predisposition) 23
negative emotions 106–7; appraisal theme 3–4; destructive effects, identification 5
negative information, impact 156–7
negative self-sanctions, avoidance 113–14
negotiations: anger: impact 56–7; implications 55–8; context, problem-solving tendencies (increase) 95; dynamic, anger (impact) 58; Israeli-Palestinian negotiations 64
Netanyahu, Benjamin 139–40
Netanya, Park Hotel (suicide bombing) 50
911 terror attacks 50, 60–1; anger (presence) 21; victimization 113
Noor, Massi 113
no partner belief 93
normative approach, cessation 151–2

Northern Ireland, postconflict context 61
null associations 135

Obama, Barack 84
Operation Cast Lead 139–40
optimism, hope (contrast) 88
optimistic overconfidence 4
orientation 27
other-oriented cognitive response, elicitation 120
outgroup: aggression, avoidance 173; anger targeting, destructive implications 60–1; appraisal, attribution 41; cohesive entity, viewpoint 40–1; evil, perception 42; fear, aggression motivation (increase) 79–80; focus 116; hate 45; individuals, political rights (problem) 48; ingroup, dynamics (implications) 59; internal criticism, exposure 99–100; open-mindedness, perception 94; perceived status, impact 128–9; perception 42; targeting, long-term emotional sentiments (impact) 9
outgroup/circumstances appraisal dimension 41

pain, shared neural circuit 131
Palestinian Authority, negotiations 82
Palestinian citizens of Israel (PCIs) 166; negative emotions 163
Palestinians: failed talks, responsibility (belief) 32–3; hope, expressions 97–8; humanitarian aid 162; Jewish Israeli anger 24; peace negotiations, renewal (proposal) 30; physical/violent actions 55; political/social rights, denial 55
Parents Circle–Families Forum 39
Park Hotel, suicide bombing 50
peace: barriers 34, 67; catalysts 67; empathy, usage 120; compromise, opposition 47; empathy-focused peace education/ dialogue 121–2; making: barriers 3; necessity 154; negotiations, Palestinian proposal 30; opposition structure/ narrative 4; option, availability 84; pride/ humiliation, regulation (usage) 151–4; process 84; framing/emotions/ideology/ public opinion, theoretical model *29*; pride/humiliation, role 139; promotion: feelings, promotion 155; importance, reasons 85–6; rival societies, impact 77;

support: public opinion, mobilization 86; shaping, emotions (role) *32*
Pearl Harbor attack, victimization 113
perceived collective continuity (PCC) 83
perceived threat 73–4
perceived (collective) threat 73–6
perpetual ingroup victimhood orientation (PIVO) 69
personal fear 76; continuous/chronic feeling 67
personality factors 30–1
person, lowering 143
perspective taking 123, 128–9; empathic perspective taking 128; skills 137
political aggression, intergroup anger (association) 61
political attitudes, emotions (impact) 12
political behaviors: emotions, impact 12; hatred, impact 49
political conflicts, emotion/emotion upregulation (study) 156–7
political ideology 171–2; classification 172
political leaders, threatening speeches 51
political processes, change 14
positive emotions, experience 58
positive group identification, challenge 150
positive risk taking, definitions 64
positive self-image, protection 113–14
possible stalking situation 72
posttraumatic stress disorder (PTSD) 10, 178, 180; clinical symptoms 69; prevalence 10–11; symptoms: simulation 39; stimulation 39
pride: authentic (beta) pride 142; collective pride, group reliance 145–6; definition 140; group member experience 145; implications/consequences 143; importance 142; intergroup context 145–50; nature 141–5; pride-preserving non-humiliating agreement 153; rank-related emotion 147; regulation, usage 151–4; role 139; source, preservation 141
pro-peace collective actions: involvement 62; motivation 95–6
pro-social behavior 142; empathic concerns (linkage) 125
prosocial concern 124
pro-social moral commitments 82
prototypical anger, presence 18
public devaluation, implication 144
public, emotions (role) 18–19
public opinion, appraisal-based framework 28–33

rage, experience 50
reappraisal: causal role 162–3; effect 163–4; linkage 162
recategorization 176–7
reconciliation 101; needs-based model 59
religious leaders, threatening speeches 51
reparative policies, support 15
response modulation 161; strategies, psychopathology (relationship) 161
responsibility, reference 109
Rifkin, James 128
right-wing ideology 172
risk-seeking behavior 52; inducement 13–14
risk taking 85–6
rumination 95
Rwanda, conflicts 10

satisfaction, positive feelings 141–2
schadenfreude 130
scripts 86
secondary emotions 23
Second Lebanon War, morale (decrease) 27–8
self-affirmation: group, reparations 118; studies 153; techniques, usage 166
self-affirmation theory 117
self-categorization 25, 167–8, 176; change 177; relationship 25–6
self-concept, extension 147
self-conscious emotions 106–7
self, devaluation 143
self-esteem 137; deep-rooted sense 142; derivation 139
self-image 137; derivation 139; protection 113–14
self-protection/self-defense, preparation 79
self, public devaluation (implication) 144
self-reflection 140
self-worth, feelings (increase) 150
sentiments, clarification 21–4
shame: humiliation, separation 144; nature/implications 107; shame-invoking situations 117
shared neural circuit (pain) 131
short-term actions 110
short-term conflict-related events, evaluation 47–8
short-term events 87
siege mentality 69
situation modification 160; viability 174–5
situations, appraised responsibility 110
situation-specific emotional support 125
Six-Day War, Israeli victory (1967) 146

Smith, Adam 120
Smith, Eliot 58
social change, support 96
social creativity 175, 176
social groups, cessation (possibility)
    75–6
social identity theory 139, 176
social processes, group processes
    (interlocking) 24
societies: members, collective pride
    (impact) 146–7; threats 67
sociopsychological infrastructure,
    development 89
soldiers, kidnapping 51
Sri Lanka, conflicts 10
stalking, situation 72
State of Israel, existential threat 68
Staub, Ervin 47
structured dialogue groups 31
subjugation, process 143
suffering, exposure 136
Sullivan, Gavin 145
sympathy-inducing manipulation,
    effects 116
synchrony 169
Szymborska, Wislawa 34

Tam, Tania 61
terror management-theory (TMT) 75, 80;
    studies 82
theory of mind 123

threat: collective (perceived) threat
    73–6; demographic threat 74; ego
    threats, response 142; embedding 80;
    extreme events 38–9; integrated threat
    theory 73, 74; perceived threat 73–4;
    societies 67
trauma-related psychological disorders
    179, 180
two-state solution 81

United Nations, Palestinian bid 163–4

valence (affective experience
    component) 22
victim: effect 136; identity, damage 143–4
violence: cause, collective fear (impact)
    79–80; exposure, repetition 178–80
violent conflicts 164

wartime, no-war/routine periods
    (contrast) 48
West Bank Palestinians 166
White, Ralph 121
White Rose (story) 102
World Trade Center, terrorist attacks
    (9/11) 50
World War I, Germany (humiliation) 150
worst-case scenario, preparation 70
Wundt, Wilhelm 17

zero-sum game, perceptions 97